SHOP SAVVY

Tips, Techniques & Jigs for Woodworkers & Metalworkers

Roy Moungovan

Sterling Publishing Co., Inc. New York

Library of Congress Cataloging-in-Publication Data

Moungovan, Roy, 1921–
    Shop savvy : tips & techniques for woodworkers & metalworkers / by
Roy Moungovan.
        p.   cm.
    Includes index.
    ISBN 0-8069-5800-6
    1. Workshops—Equipment and supplies.   2. Woodwork.   3. Metal
-work.   4. Automobiles—Maintenance and repair.   I. Title.
TT153.M683   1989   89-11386
684′.08—dc20   CIP

1 3 5 7 9 10 8 6 4 2

Published in 1989 by Sterling Publishing Co., Inc.
387 Park Avenue South, New York, N.Y. 10016
Distributed in Canada by Sterling Publishing
First published in hardcover by Grolier
Book Clubs, Inc., Copyright © 1988 by Roy Moungovan
% Canadian Manda Group, P.O. Box 920, Station U
Toronto, Ontario, Canada M8Z 5P9
Distributed in Great Britain and Europe by Cassell PLC
Artillery House, Artillery Row, London SW1P 1RT, England
Distributed in Australia by Capricorn Ltd.
P.O. Box 665, Lane Cove, NSW 2066
Manufactured in the United States of America
All rights reserved
Sterling ISBN 0-8069-5800-6 Paper

TO MY WIFE HELEN, who once slipped silently out of bed during the small hours of a Christmas morning to wheel a complete oxy-acetylene welding rig from its hiding place to a position alongside the Christmas tree.

METRIC SYSTEM

UNIT	ABBREVIATION		APPROXIMATE U.S. EQUIVALENT		
Length					
		Number of Metres			
myriametre	mym	10,000	—————— 6.2 miles		
kilometre	km	1000	0.62 mile		
hectometre	hm	100	109.36 yards		
dekametre	dam	10	32.81 feet		
metre	m	1	39.37 inches		
decimetre	dm	0.1	3.94 inches		
centimetre	cm	0.01	0.39 inch		
millimetre	mm	0.001	0.04 inch		
Area					
		Number of Square Metres			
square kilometre	sq km *or* km²	1,000,000	0.3861 square miles		
hectare	ha	10,000	2.47 acres		
are	a	100	119.60 square yards		
centare	ca	1	10.76 square feet		
square centimetre	sq cm *or* cm²	0.0001	0.155 square inch		
Volume					
		Number of Cubic Metres			
dekastere	das	10	13.10 cubic yards		
stere	s	1	1.31 cubic yards		
decistere	ds	0.10	3.53 cubic feet		
cubic centimetre	cu cm *or* cm³ *also* cc	0.000001	0.061 cubic inch		
Capacity					
		Number of Litres	*Cubic*	*Dry*	*Liquid*
kilolitre	kl	1000	1.31 cubic yards		
hectolitre	hl	100	3.53 cubic feet	2.84 bushels	
dekalitre	dal	10	0.35 cubic foot	1.14 pecks	2.64 gallons
litre	l	1	61.02 cubic inches	0.908 quart	1.057 quarts
decilitre	dl	0.10	6.1 cubic inches	0.18 pint	0.21 pint
centilitre	cl	0.01	0.6 cubic inch		0.338 fluidounce
millilitre	ml	0.001	0.06 cubic inch		0.27 fluidram
Mass and Weight					
		Number of Grams			
metric ton	MT *or* t	1,000,000	1.1 tons		
quintal	q	100,000	220.46 pounds		
kilogram	kg	1,000	2.2046 pounds		
hectogram	hg	100	3.527 ounces		
dekagram	dag	10	0.353 ounce		
gram	g *or* gm	1	0.035 ounce		
decigram	dg	0.10	1.543 grains		
centigram	cg	0.01	0.154 grain		
milligram	mg	0.001	0.015 grain		

CONTENTS

INTRODUCTION

The purpose of this book is to pass on to you many of the time- and money-saving tips and techniques I've discovered during the fifty-odd years I've been a home workshopper. Some of these ideas are mine; others I learned from friends and colleagues. All have been tested for practicality and have proved useful for various projects.

Shop Savvy is the result of a lifetime of tinkering with tools and making things with them. I've always enjoyed working with my hands, but to do it successfully requires a bit of head work, too. I get great satisfaction from solving workshop problems, and this book is full of solutions that I—and others—have come up with over many years.

I've always felt that almost anyone can do anything if he takes the time and effort to study the subject thoroughly. As an example, some thirty-five years ago, although I barely knew a rafter from a stud, I bought a little lot, designed a small house, and proceeded to build it. I did all the concrete work, the framing, the roof, the rough and finished plumbing, the electrical work, and the interior finishing.

This entire project was accomplished by studying each step in a book and observing other houses under construction. The house turned out very well. That's why I believe in thinking through workshop problems until you find better ways of doing things.

This book is intended for both the weekend workshopper and the professional craftsman. It covers unusual tools and techniques for woodworking, metalworking, and auto maintenance. Whatever kind of shopwork you do, I'm sure you'll find many useful ideas here.

Acknowledgments

Special thanks to my editor, Henry Gross, without whose help and encouragement this book would not have been written.

I also wish to thank the following people, some now gone, who have helped, either directly or indirectly, in my preparation for this book. Most of them have at some time during the past several decades instructed me in workshop methods. Many of their ideas are incorporated in this book, as well as those of others whose names I have forgotten with the passing years:

Dan Alvarez, Jim Cavanagh, Wes Claes, Lee Drew, Fred Espositi, Harold Gibson, Ed Girard, Normand Girard, Art Grant, Jim Grant, Bill Hussman.

Also, Dudley Mackey, M.C. (Mart) Martinsen, Mimi Moungovan, Tom and Barbara Moungovan, T.O. (Thomas) Moungovan, J.D. (Mac) McKellar, Enos Nutt, Vincent (Bim) Sanini, Don Sauer, Bob Shrader, E.E. (Stan) Stanley.

Also, Harold Halvorsen, Edward Jewett, Jack Jones—Sebastopol Hardware, W.A. (Al) Kinney, Jess Tallman Sr., Unruh's Photography Shop staff, C.J. (Cap) Weir, Roy Welch.

SAFETY NOTE

When I took the photos for this book, I removed the table-saw guide and raised the guard and upper blade guide on the band saw much higher than normal. This was done solely to provide maximum clarity.

When you are using a table saw, be sure the guard remains in place if possible. Also, keep the band-saw guard and upper blade guides as close to the top of the work as is practical. At all times, follow the safety rules that come with your equipment, keeping in mind that a saw cannot tell the difference between a hand and a workpiece.

1
SOME OF MY FAVORITE TOOLS

Hardware stores carry hundreds of tools, and hardly a day goes by without some new tool or gadget being advertised. The mail brings you catalogs from businesses that you have never heard of, while newspapers, magazines, and even television carry ads for tools that "everybody needs." If you buy one from an ad, you may find the tool is anywhere from totally useless to really good, with the vast majority falling somewhere in between. Here is a rundown on some that you may not have tried which, in my opinion, do an excellent job and really are time and money savers.

SANDPAPER CLEANERS

A few years ago, while nosing around in an industrial tool supply house, I ran across a stack of odd-looking crepe rubber blocks. Each was some 2″ x 2″ square and 12″ long and came with a flyer claiming they were excellent for cleaning used sandpaper, especially on power sanders (belt, disc, and orbital pad), and for prolonging its life several times over. I was reading all

this puffery rather dubiously when a salesman happened by and immediately waxed enthusiastic over the things. He insisted that they really worked and that everyone who had tried

Dramatic cleanup of this rotating sanding disc with a crepe rubber block. Another two seconds will finish the job, and the disc will be nearly as good as new. Crepe rubber is equally effective on belts.

one swore by (and not at) it. At $8 then, it was expensive for a little chunk of rubber, but I took one home. *That thing is terrific!*

If you work with wood at all, you know that it only takes a few minutes of operation with a sanding disc or belt for the grit to get pretty well clogged up with sanding dust. When that happens, the paper loses a good part of its effectiveness, and it's normally time for some expensive new sandpaper.

With the crepe rubber all you have to do is to move it across the belt or disc while the sander is running. It takes only a second or two to clean up the paper and make it almost as good as new. That gadget has saved me several times its cost in sanding discs and belts, and it is still almost 9″ long.

Crepe rubber also rejuvenates hand-held sheet sandpaper, although the results are not so dramatic and it is a little awkward to scrub it across a stationary sheet of paper. It also works on metal-cutting belts or discs, but not quite as effectively as on woodworking paper.

RECHARGEABLE SCREWDRIVERS

Old friend Bill Hussman got one of these for Christmas a year or so ago and told me how great it was. Not being in a tool buying phase at the time, I did nothing about it. He wisely reminded me of it in each of his letters (we live in different states) until I finally put in a "want" for one for Father's Day. Another truly worthwhile tool.

You probably have tried driving or removing screws with your reversible ⅜″ variable speed drill and found it does not work that well. Your drill cannot compare with a power screwdriver. This thing looks much like an ordinary electric drill, with a different chuck; it has a slip-in collet-type chuck that accepts ¼″ hex screwdriver bits only. Because of lower reduction gearing, the screwdriver has much greater torque at a very low speed, which makes for easier control.

You well know what a chore it is to drive a few large woodscrews with a hand screwdriver, particularly if you are working over your head or in some other awkward spot. After driving just a couple, your arm is ready to drop off, and

Rechargeable power screwdrivers really do the job because they are geared much lower than drill-screwdriver combinations.

Use a power screwdriver on an overhead job such as installing a doorbell against a shop ceiling, and you'll appreciate its convenience.

you've still got several more to go. With this little gem, you just squeeze the trigger, hang on, and in goes the screw. Slowly, yes, but still much faster and many times easier than by hand.

Be sure to get a unit that is strictly a screwdriver and not one that is sold as a combination drill and screwdriver. (These turn too fast and have too little torque to really do the job.) Mine

All it takes is a simple shopmade adapter to make this cordless screwdriver into a power driver for ⅜"-drive sockets. It also turns ½"-drive sockets with an ordinary ⅜" to ½" adapter.

came with a regular and Phillips bit included but can be used with any ¼" hex bit.

A new, smaller, and even less expensive model of the rechargeable screwdriver is now on the market. This one has a shape closer to an overweight normal screwdriver than an electric drill. It sells for less than $20 and is about 9" long and 1¾" in diameter at the motor. Although it does not have as much torque for driving big screws as the older, larger model does, it will get into tighter spots and is stored right in its charger. Thus, it is always ready to go; no need to plug in an external cord.

With the addition of a simple homemade adapter, either of these tools can also become a very useful power driver for a ⅜" socket wrench set. This is similar to the electric drill adapter described in Chapter 8 but has the added advantage of higher torque. This setup is also cordless.

To make the adapter, cut off the socket end of a ⅜"-drive socket extension bar to a total length of about 1¾". (Keep the adapter as short as possible to facilitate getting the power driver into tight spots. If more reach is needed, an extension or extensions can always be added.) Drill the cut-off end 1" deep with a ¹⁷⁄₆₄" bit. This is best done on a lathe; the second choice is to carefully center it vertically in a drill press vise. But it can even be done satisfactorily with a hand-held electric drill if care is used to accu-

rately center the drill and keep it parallel to the sides of the extension bar. (The low speed of the power screwdriver excuses a small amount of eccentricity in operation.)

Next, cut 2" from the long leg of a ¼" Allen wrench and chamfer one end slightly to facilitate starting it into the drilled hole. Press the Allen wrench segment into the hole until it bottoms. This can be done in a hydraulic press, an arbor press, a large drill press, or even in a heavy vise by carefully lining up the parts and squeezing them between the jaws. Even if your drill press is not large enough to do the whole job, it may be helpful to get the job started straight with it; then switch to one of the other methods to complete the press.

Put the Allen wrench in the drill chuck, center the extension bar stub below it in your drill vise, and then move the spindle extension lever down to start the two parts together squarely. If you are able to do so without using excessive pressure, complete the job; otherwise, remove

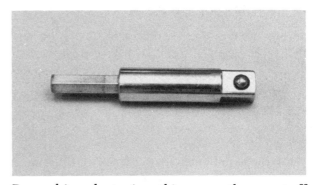

Power drive adapter is nothing more than a cut-off ⅜"-socket extension with a ¹⁷⁄₆₄" hole drilled in it and a short length of ¼" Allen wrench pressed in.

the adapter from the drill press and finish up by one of the other means.

Once you've got the adapter, you have a power socket-wrench driver that will save you no end of time. It's great for jobs with a number of nuts to be removed and/or replaced that are a little too tight to be turned with your fingers or that are in an awkward position. Adapters can, of course, be used to operate either ¼"- or ½"-drive sockets as well.

CORDLESS DRILLS

Once you've tried the cordless screwdriver and enjoyed not having to drag out an extension cord for every job, you will surely want to get a cordless rechargeable drill, if you do not already have one. There are a number available in a wide range of prices. After shopping around, I settled on a two-speed (0-250 and 0-750 rpm), trigger speed control, reversing, quick-charging drill. A second battery unit is available as an extra so that the drill can be used while one battery is recharging. Since this only takes an hour, I did not buy the extra battery for my home shop, but anyone using the tool commercially should find one or more extras worthwhile.

Cordless drill makes work up on a ladder or in other remote places easy. A tin can C-clamped to the rail of the ladder holds the drill. Another smaller can with its bottom cut out keeps a hammer handy.

When you're finished with a cordless drill, just put it back in the recharging stand. This drill shifts gears to provide two trigger-controlled speed ranges, both forward and reverse.

This particular model was rather expensive because it provides two speed ranges (operated by a sliding shift knob) for the normal trigger-speed control. But it is very convenient if you do much drilling any distance from an electrical receptacle. The same maker and several others also sell cheaper but still quite good models. Get one, and in addition to drilling with it in remote areas, you'll soon find yourself picking it up in the shop instead of plugging your regular drill into an extension cord.

POP RIVETER

Pop riveters have been around for many years, but it's surprising how many people who could make good use of them don't have one. Even though you may not consider yourself a "metalworker," a Pop riveter is just generally handy around the shop or the home. It helps with dozens of repair jobs and solves many otherwise difficult problems in the construction of various small projects.

The "magic" thing about Pop riveters is that they do blind riveting; that is, the back side of the item to be riveted to does not have to be accessible. Repairing or reenforcing tubular lawn furniture is one common job. Fastening objects to auto bodies and pickup truck sidewalls are simple jobs with Pop rivets. Once you have a Pop riveter in the shop and realize what you can do with it, you will find endless uses for it.

Blind riveting was originally developed for aircraft work and the tools and rivets are expensive. Pop rivets need only less expensive, mass-produced tools and rivets, making them practical for the home shop.

Pop rivets have two parts. One part is the rivet itself, which is hollow. The other is a mandrel, which resembles an ordinary nail except that it's head is spherical and its shank is necked down just below the head. The mandrel runs through the rivet; its pointed and extends out an inch or so from the rivet's head, while the round head of the mandrel seats against the other end of the rivet, which has been rolled down into the mandrel's necked-down area to hold the two parts together.

The pointed end of the mandrel is inserted into a riveting tool, and the ball end is pushed into the hole in the work until the rivet is fully inserted; its preformed head is then flat against the surface. Squeezing the handles of the riveting tool draws the mandrel into the tool, thus pulling the opposite end of the hollow rivet against the back—"blind"—side of the work. This enlarges the rivet, forming a head. As the spherical end of the mandrel pulls the enlarged end of the hollow rivet tighter against the rear

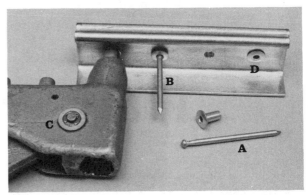

Two pieces of a Pop rivet (*A*) have been taken apart to show the necked-down area just under its ball head. The ball normally fits against the small end of the rivet with the pointed end of the shank extending from the head. A Pop rivet (*B*) is just slipped into a predrilled hole with its pointed mandrel extending. The Pop riveter (*C*) grips the pointed mandrel and pulls it into the hollow end of the rivet. This will form a head at the back of the work, pulling the two pieces tightly together. The rivet in the fourth hole (*D*) has been completely pulled (driven) and its shank discarded after breaking off at the neck.

of the work, tension builds. Finally, the mandrel "pops" at the necked point. The ball end remains in the rivet and the rest of the mandrel pulls out and is discarded.

Some of the simplest Pop-rivet tools handle only one size of rivet (1/8"), but a more expensive type, which takes 1/8", 5/32", or 3/16" rivets, is well worth getting. Rivets normally come in three lengths to handle various thicknesses of material, and are usually made of steel or aluminum. Copper rivets are also available, as are special closed-end rivets that seal out air and water.

Note: Depending on the brand of rivets you have, a given size of rivet may not want to fit into a hole of the corresponding size without being forced. Any grandmother can tell you the reason for this (at least any grandmother who worked as a "Rosie the Riveter" on aircraft construction during World War II. It is that slightly larger drills than the nominal size should be used for rivet holes. The correct drill for a 1/8" rivet is a #30, for 5/32" a #20, and for 3/16" a #10. The following are not normal Pop-rivet sizes but may come in handy if you use other types of

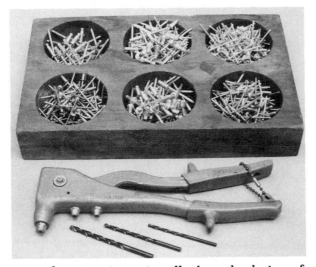

Heavy-duty Pop riveter installs three shank sizes of Pop rivets in three different lengths and of steel, aluminum, or copper. The #10, #20, and #30 drills provide the proper size holes while an old shoemaker's nail tray stores rivets of different sizes.

Thirty ⅛" steel Pop rivets have supported this 85-pound spare tire for many years and miles of off-road driving. Because the back side of the double wall truck body is inaccessible, it makes any fastener other than blind rivets quite impractical.

KerfKeepers, two shown here, make long ripping jobs easier when done by one person. They are especially helpful when cutting plywood panels.

rivets, such as aircraft rivets: #50 drill for ¹⁄₁₆" rivets, #40 for ³⁄₃₂", and a letter F drill for ¼" rivets.

With Pop rivets you can usually get away with the nominal drill size if you don't have a drill of the appropriate number, although you have to be careful that forcing the rivet in does not separate parts to be joined. If it does, the rivet may swell in the gap between the parts when tightened, instead of pulling them together; this makes a weak and sloppy joint. All in all, the correct size drill is easier to work with and produces better results. Even if you have a set of number drills, you can make life simpler for yourself by getting an extra one for each size of Pop rivets. Store these bits with the appropriate rivets.

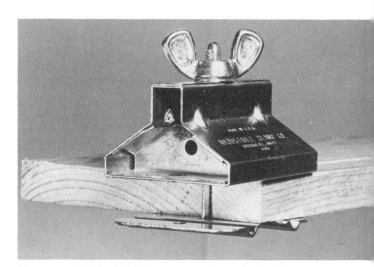

Close-up of this KerfKeeper, partly extended from the end of a board, shows its simple but effective construction.

KERFKEEPERS

If you have ever ripped a long board or tried to cut a full sheet of plywood on a table saw without a helper, you know what a headache it can be. One or two KerfKeepers can be a great help in keeping things under control.

Put one of these gadgets on a saw cut after it is well started and is clear of the saw table. A tongue slips into the kerf and a wingnut on the top part draws the top and bottom sections together and holds the wood on both sides of the kerf in alignment as the cut is continued. For a very long cut, a second KerfKeeper can be put on the end of the cut; the first one is slipped farther along the kerf and resecured so that the cut can be completed. KerfKeepers are also very helpful when making long cuts with a portable circular saw or handsaw.

SANDER-GRINDER

This is another machine that is not new, but its capabilities are often overlooked. Several manufacturers market these tools with 1" x 42" belts, while another makes a smaller one with a 1" x 30" belt. At first glance this thing appears to be an expensive toy, but the amount of work it does may surprise you. Sander-grinders got pretty pricey a while back, some models going for well over $200, but a flood of imported imitations brought prices down on domestic models.

They are excellent for sanding small wood parts and for internal cuts (like a jigsaw blade, the belt can easily be removed from the machine, inserted through the cutout, and replaced on the machine to sand or grind the internal cut). In addition, these belts can grind metal and will rapidly remove a surprising amount of stock. Belts can also be quickly cut to a narrower width to get into small grooves or corners. A number of belts are available, ranging from quite coarse for rapid stock removal to very fine, which can be used for sharpening such cutting tools as knives or chisels.

Although I have seen articles illustrating a method for sharpening chisels and plane irons by tilting the table to obtain the proper sharpening angle, I personally do not recommend trying it in this manner for safety reasons. That is because the cutting edge faces into the down-traveling belt, and I have had the blade edge dig into a belt, which almost pulled the tool out of

A 1" belt sander/grinder does a man-sized job on wood, plastic, or metal. It took less than a minute to square up the sides and round off the corners of the small steel fitting shown on the table.

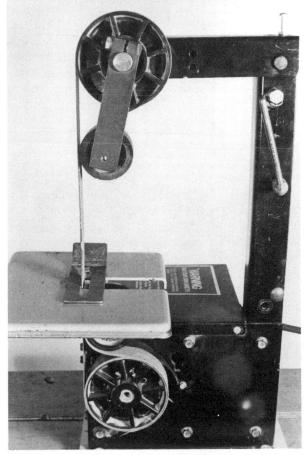

It takes only a couple of minutes to realign the pulleys and insert the belt for inside grinding, as was done here to finish this internal slot in a steel fitting.

my hand. (My instruction manual does *not* show it being used in this manner, incidentally.)

For sharpening, I hold the tool with the cutting edge facing down, so that it has no tendency to cut into the belt. If your motor is reversible and you wire it to a reversing switch, you could make the belt run in the opposite direction. Then you could safely use the table to set a precise sharpening angle.

Accessories for these machines include cleaning belts for rust removal and polishing belts for brightening up plated metal, silverware, plastics, and many other items. All in all, this is a handy tool to have around.

4½″ ANGLE GRINDER

This tool, a smaller version of the bigger industrial grinder for grinding down welds and cleaning up various steel products, has recently come down in price to a point where it is practical for the home shop. Turning some 12,000 rpm it makes short work of grinding jobs that are awkward or impossible on a bench

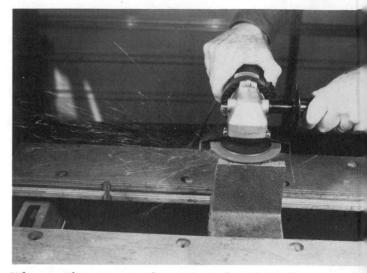

When touching up a torch-cut piece of steel, this little grinder really makes the sparks fly. It is excellent for grinding down and cleaning up welds.

grinder. Some models also have a sanding disc conversion and accessory cup-type wire wheels that are great for rust removal and other cleanup jobs. If you want one of these tools, by all means consider getting one that has these features available, especially the wire brush.

With both the 4½″ grinder and the 1″ belt grinder mentioned earlier, as with any other grinding tool, *be sure* to wear the proper safety goggles! Be sure also that you have no readily inflammable materials nearby. The little angle grinder, particularly, throws quite a stream of sparks.

OXYACETYLENE TORCH

There are several larger and much more expensive tools in my shop that I originally found hard to justify, but once I acquired them, they proved absolutely indispensable. One is an oxyacetylene welding and cutting torch outfit.

The torch is invaluable, not only to build things but to repair the otherwise unfixable as well. While an arc welder is better for heavier welding, the gas torch is more versatile for light to medium work and has the added advantage of the cutting attachment. Buy a good small

The 4½″ angle grinder is another tool that does a surprising job. In addition to the grinding wheels shown on the tool and at the right, accessories include a flexible sanding disc and a heavy-duty cup-shaped wire wheel that quickly cleans off rust. The short cutoff wrench end for mounting the wire wheel has been lengthened with a bent-up piece of ³⁄₁₆″ welding rod.

torch (mine welds up to ⅜″-thick steel and cuts up to 2″ thick) and get a good checkout on it, particularly the safety items.

A welding torch is not inherently dangerous, but there are a few basic rules that must be scrupulously followed or you could end up with your name in the paper! Practice a little; learning to weld is not hard and can be mostly self-taught once you've got the basics.

METAL LATHE

Much of the same reasoning applies to the metal lathe. Before I obtained mine (used and now approaching 60 years old, but nearly as good as new), I had visions of all the projects I would build with it. A model steam engine, perhaps a little gas engine, a locomotive model, and so on. To date, I've built none of these things, but hardly a day goes by in my shop that I do not work on the lathe for at least a few minutes. Together with the torch, I can repair many items, such as car parts or accessories, that have only a small part broken or missing but which are sold only as expensive complete units.

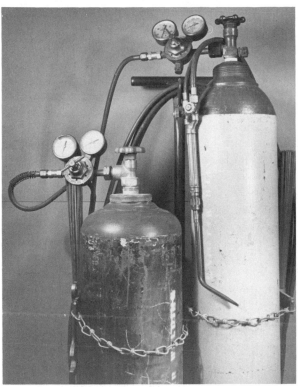

Oxyacetylene welding outfit with a wheeled cart, tanks, torch, and accessory cutting attachment is a "winner" in any small shop.

Small metal-turning lathe is another shop tool that, once acquired, will soon have you wondering how you ever managed without it.

I have saved countless trips to the hardware store by modifying items on hand to fit the requirements of a job. An odd washer can be resized in the lathe, for instance, in even less time than it takes me to get my car out of the garage.

A lathe and a welding torch used together can also repair, modify, and build many other tools and accessories as required around the shop. Some examples are: a milling attachment, indexing attachments for both the metal and the wood lathe, adapters to fit chucks from one machine onto another. The benefits are endless.

POWER HACKSAW

Another machine that is extremely useful, but which rates a second place only because many of its jobs can be done, albeit more laboriously, by hand or with portable power tools, is the horizontal power hacksaw with a band-saw blade. This tool is a tremendous improvement over the old-fashioned reciprocating hacksaw; it fairly zips through steel. Once, this tool was quite expensive, but cheaper foreign imports have almost completely taken over the market. Because it is a fairly simple tool, most models

Bandsaw-type power hacksaw saves hours of hand sawing. It cuts fairly fast and does not have to be attended. Once the cut is started, you can busy yourself with something else while it does the "dirty work." Here it is marching through a heavy section of 2″ angle iron.

seem to be pretty well made and priced reasonably.

Due to the fact stock must clear the returning side of the blade, all models have limited capacities. But even the smaller ones cut stock up to about 3″ high and 6″ wide. Short pieces can be cut from somewhat larger stock by a "back door" approach. Also, some models swing from the horizontal to the vertical position and serve as a freehand metal-cutting band saw, which is very useful for cutting parts out of sheet stock or plate.

There is one thing about this tool to keep in mind. It is possible to hit a localized hard spot in a piece of steel that may dull one side of the blade by removing part of its set. When this happens, the machine no longer saws straight down; instead it cuts a curve toward the side that still has the proper set. If you do not recognize what is happening, you can spend a good deal of fruitless effort trying to adjust the blade guide rollers to force it back to a square cut. If you spot problems of this sort, take a good look at the teeth on both sides of the blade, preferably with a magnifying glass. If you detect any difference in appearance between the two sides, you have solved your problem. The cure is to discard the blade and install a new one. Then make the cut in a new place or try another piece of metal to avoid ruining a new blade.

If your saw does not have an automatic shut-off switch, it is easy to mount a surface-type switch on it, together with an actuating arm fastened to the movable part of the saw. Adjust the arm so that it shuts off just after the saw blade clears the cut. That way you can work on something else while the saw completes the cut.

THE VERSATILE WORKMATE

Bench space is at a premium in just about every workshop. What do you do about those tools that need a fixed mounting, but that are used only infrequently? The Workmate provides an excellent answer to this problem. Each tool can be mounted on a plywood base; the base has one or two lug strips glued and screwed to the bottom to give the Workmate's jaws something

Router/sabre-saw table has a large base, so here the vise jaws are expanded against lugs on the outside edges of a shopmade plywood table base.

to grip. For smaller items, a single lug down the middle works fine; for a larger tool, a pair of lugs can be glued and screwed to the outside edges of the base. Extend the vise jaws into them, rather than closing down on them. A double lug also has the advantage of providing a stable base for storage. The tools may be stored under your workbench, on shelves, in storage rooms, closets, or wherever. It takes only a moment to haul them out and fasten them to the Workmate.

Tools I have mounted this way include: a small all-angle vise; a 4″ belt sander with a table attachment, a small arbor press, a small round anvil for light work; a combination router and sabre-saw table, a 42″ belt sander-grinder tool; and an infeed or outfeed roller for handling large pieces of stock on a table saw (the Workmate has the advantage of providing a heavier and more stable platform than the usual tripod-type stand).

Many other tools can be mounted this way;

Built-up plywood base and boss on this little all-angle vise allow it to be mounted in the Workmate in a jiffy, stored when not in use.

Modelmaker's-sized anvil made from pipe fittings can be quickly and firmly secured by the Workmate's vise jaws.

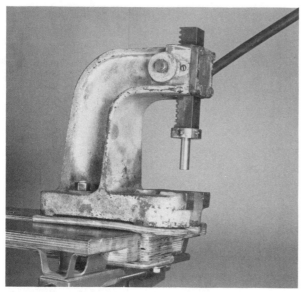

Workmate makes a dandy base for the occasional job with a little arbor press.

consider how often you use each tool. For instance, I work with my heavy-duty electric grinder almost constantly; so it has its own stand. But you probably have some tools that stand idle most of the time. Take a good look around your shop, and you'll probably find several that could be adapted to this type of mount. You may even regain a few square feet of much needed bench space.

For large jobs, such as cutting with a sabre saw or routing a big piece of plywood, you can provide a more stable platform by fully extending the jaws, turning the Workmate over, and placing the top on the floor. That way you take advantage of the wider spread of the four feet to support the work. If more stability is needed, put something heavy on top of the underside of the jaws. A sack of concrete mix, water softener salt, garden fertilizer, or anything of that sort works great.

There is a large open space behind the Workmate's lower platform, or baseboard. Filling it in with a piece of ¼" plywood makes a handy storage shelf, as well as providing a place to put extra weight when more stability is needed in the upright position. Construction of the Workmate prohibits fitting a one-piece base into place, at least in the model I have, but two half sections can be slipped in easily. After fitting

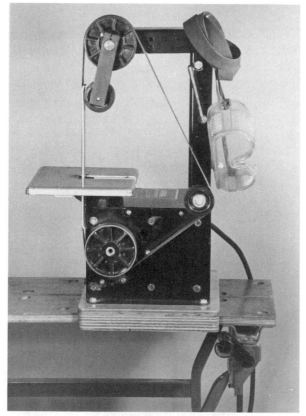

Small 1" belt sander/grinder also mounts in the Workmate. Like the router table, it fits over the outside of the jaws.

Infeed/outfeed roller secured in the Workmate can be adjusted to match the varying height of a Shopsmith saw table.

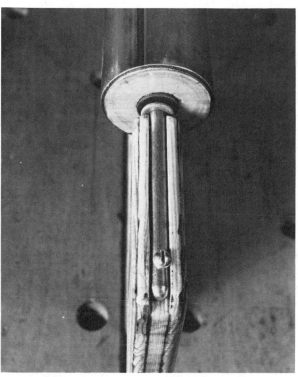

Bearings for pipe or tubing rollers take many forms. This one is simply a plywood slug from a hole saw, sanded to a press fit in the tube. The slug in turn has a plastic bushing pressed into it. The axle is a length of ¼" welding rod and rides in a dado in the plywood base. It is kept in place by a small woodscrew through each end.

Upside-down Workmate is better for holding a large piece of plywood for marking or cutting because the spread of its legs is much larger than the top. A sack of salt or any other weight helps stabilize it.

Fitted with a couple of pieces of angle iron, a hammer, and a strip of wood to spread the blows, the Workmate substitutes for a sheet-metal brake. Here the bend is about two-thirds formed.

Completing the bends makes a tool cabinet drawer divider. (The differing heights of the sides were intentionally designed that way.)

them, but prior to installation, make a cleat to fit along the joint on the bottom side. Drill both pieces of the plywood and the cleat for a few flathead screws and countersink them in the plywood. Put the pieces in place and secure the screws. Do not glue the assembly; you may want to temporarily remove the platform sometime.

The Workmate can also be used as a substitute for a sheet-metal brake to bend metal. Just slip in two pieces of straight, clean angle iron as supplemental jaws. The angle iron does not have to be cut off. Just let the excess length extend beyond the jaws. Clamp the piece of sheet metal to be bent between the angle irons at the desired bend point. Hold a strip of wood against the sheet metal and on top of the angle iron. Give the wood strip a few healthy blows with a heavy hammer, and you should get a smooth, even bend with a nice square corner.

The 5″ plastic caliper reads fractionally by 64ths or decimally by 100ths on the dial and metrically by millimeters along the beam and to tenths of a millimeter on its vernier scale. The 6″ stainless-steel caliper measures by tenths of an inch along the beam and to thousandths on the dial. With a 1″ micrometer test button between the jaws it checks at 1000 thousandths, dead on.

DIAL CALIPER VS. MICROMETER

While the micrometer has long been the standard for fine measuring, it does have drawbacks, especially in the small shop. Micrometers are expensive, they are awkward to read, and they only cover a range of one inch so that more than one is required to do any range of work. Wide-range micrometers are available with interchangeable anvils for each separate one-inch range. But this system is slow and leaves the possibility of error if each change is not made and checked with care. In addition, the normal micrometer reads only outside diameters and requires separate equipment for reading inside measurements.

By comparison, dial-type calipers have been greatly improved in recent years, are simple to read, are easily readjusted if required, and have come down in price. One 6″ instrument reads both inside and outside measurements from 0 to 6″ in one-thousandths of an inch with no changes or adjustments necessary.

Although you may have heard about machine work that is done to a ten-thousandth of an

inch, very little is actually done to these tolerances; for most work a good dial caliper reading to a thousandth of an inch is more than adequate. Try one out, and you'll find that if you already have a set of micrometers, they will soon start gathering dust. If you don't already have the "mikes," the dial caliper is, in my opinion, the only way to go, for the average workshopper. Even if you are strictly a woodworker, you will find many uses for a dial caliper. For example, you could use it to check screw sizes and pick a drill for a close-fitting clearance hole.

AUTOMATIC CENTER PUNCH

The automatic center punch is another fine tool that is not as well known as it should be. Accurate layout of parts is a key to getting a good fit and professional-looking results for any project. Center punching to locate drilled holes is a critical part of that layout work.

Accurate work with a normal center punch or with the sharper prick punch is difficult. Even if the work can be held in a vise, which is not always possible, you still have to locate the

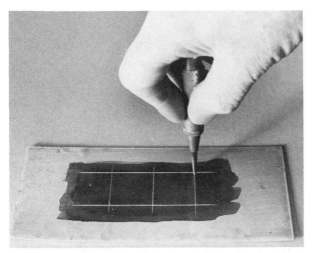

Automatic center punch, operated with one hand without a hammer, marks the work accurately.

point of the punch accurately to the scribed lines, hold it in that position with one hand, and wallop it with a hammer with your other hand. Since you cannot stay close to the work during this operation, you probably will move the punch point off the line a half smidgeon, and the result is less than perfect. You can, of course, correct this to some degree by holding the punch at an angle and restriking to move the mark over toward the correct spot, but this is not always totally satisfactory.

An automatic center punch helps solve this problem. The tool comes in several sizes, being about 4″ to 5″ long and varying from less than ½″ to nearly ¾″ in diameter. The larger ones give the heaviest blow. Operation is simple. You put the point on your mark and press down on the handle against spring tension. After the handle moves about ½″, an internal mechanism trips, giving the effect of a hammer blow to the point. The force of the blow can be adjusted by twisting a knurled ring on the end of the handle.

The big advantage is that you only need one hand to operate the tool; no hammer blow is necessary. The other hand can be used to hold small work. Also, you can watch closely to see that the point is precisely located, right up until the instant the actual punch mark is made. In addition, all marks made at a given adjustment will be uniform in size.

INEXPENSIVE NEW AIR TOOLS

An air compressor is fast becoming a "must have" in the shop, now that so many air tools are becoming available at such reasonable prices. If you don't already have one, a 2 hp motor and a 20-gallon tank provide an adequate air supply for the small shop. Thirty gallons and a larger pump is of course even better. Two hp or more normally requires 220 volts however; if you don't have it, you may be stuck with 1 hp or possibly 1½. If you've been considering adding a 220-volt circuit to the shop, now might be a good time to do it. If you do, consider running two circuits with an outlet on each side of the shop, preferably near doors where they'll be available for outside jobs as well. Consider making them 50-amp lines (60 is even better) to take care of that arc welder you'd like to get some day.

Air tools once were very expensive and were pretty much limited to professional work, where the time saved paid for their high cost. In the last few years, however, the Japanese have come onto the scene, producing some very good air tools at a fraction of the former cost. Now the Taiwanese are getting into the act and are bringing down prices still more. I haven't tried any of theirs but have been quite pleased with my air tools from Japan.

Air Hammer

An air hammer is great when you have any rivet busting or other cold chisel work to do. Choose a long barrel model over a short barrel; they hit harder and make the job easier.

You can cut odd-shaped parts out of metal that is too heavy to cut with a pair of snips by using an air hammer with chisel tip installed. There is a little trick to working with an air hammer. If you just hold it against the work, it pounds away rather ineffectively. Press hard with your weight against it though, and it starts to walk right through the metal.

Air Wrenches

There are several air wrenches available. My first choice would be the ⅜″ air ratchet wrench,

With new and inexpensive air tools continually appearing, an air compressor is invaluable. The air duster on the end of the recoil hose is unbeatable for cleaning up the shop. A venturi tube surrounding the air duster nozzle whips up a mini tornado.

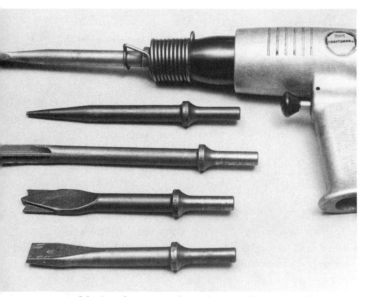

Cold chisel mounted in this air hammer shears ⅛″ mild steel sheet quite nicely. Other tools include a pin punch, a muffler splitter, a panel cutter and a rivet buster. With a little practice and a sturdy vise, you can cut straight or curved parts from surprisingly heavy steel.

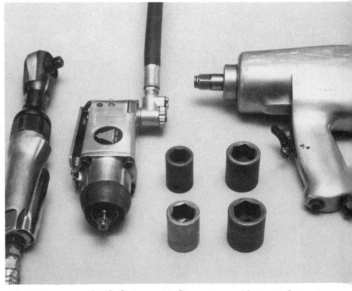

Air ratchet on the left is great for auto work in tight places. The butterfly wrench, named for its trigger shape, is also good for auto work, but is not as handy as the ratchet. The impact wrench on the right is a dandy for cross switching tires.

primarily for automotive work. See the write-up on this in the automotive chapter. Second is the ½"-drive impact wrench, a real time saver when rotating tires. Another is the palm grip butterfly wrench, so named because of its winged control trigger. It's not as useful as the other two, but hard to pass up at recent sale prices.

Die Grinder

The little air-powered die grinder is an amazing tool. Only about 1⅜" in diameter and less than 5" long, it turns some 22,000 rpm and is rated at ½ hp. It has a collet-type chuck that accepts all ¼"-shank tools (be sure they are rated for this speed). Coupled with a carbide burr tip, the die grinder carves into hardened steel that an ordinary file would skate across without leaving a mark!

The die grinders sell for around $30 at this writing, and although the carbide burrs are somewhat expensive, one catalog shows a set of five for about $40. The die grinder and one or more carbide burrs make a combination that will solve many otherwise "impossible" jobs.

Panel Cutter

A Panel cutter, another tiny palm-held high-speed air tool with a 3" diameter cutting wheel, is great for such jobs as cutting away a rusty muffler or tailpipe, simplifying an otherwise thoroughly disagreeable job.

Nibbler

New on the scene is an air nibbler for sheet-metal cutting. Being able to cut square corners and sharp curves, a nibbler speeds up many otherwise difficult internal cuts in thin metal that is within its capacity.

Sandblaster

A sandblaster is a great time-saver when it comes to cleaning up rusty metal items and gets into spots impossible to reach with a wire brush. In addition, the sandblasted finish provides a "toothed" surface for a subsequent coat of paint. Sandblaster models vary from the type that have a gun with a 1 qt canister attached, much like a paint spray gun, to those having a hopper that holds from 50 to 100 pounds or more of sand. The hopper types usually require a minimum of a 1 hp compressor; with the canister type you can get by with ½ hp.

While most air tools operate well at about

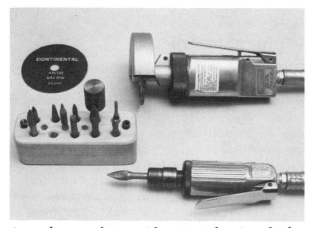

A panel cutter, shown with a spare abrasive wheel to the left, is great for cutting away rusted mufflers and for other auto sheet metal cutting. The die grinder, when fitted with one of the carbide burrs shown, eats right into hardened steel.

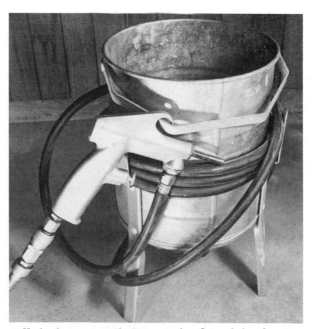

Fill the hopper with 50 pounds of sand, hook up an air hose, and you can sandblast clean badly rusted metal surfaces clean in a hurry.

90 psi, the sandblaster seems to do a much faster and better job at higher pressures. Try 125 psi if your compressor and tank are rated that high. Sandblasters throw a lot of sand around and can make a real mess; so unless you go all the way and buy or build a sandblast cabinet with a window and armholes, do your sandblasting outdoors. Properly fitting goggles, a disposable dust mask, and a pair of gloves are about the minimum safety equipment required. A hood with a plastic window keeps sand out of your ears and hair. Better yet, you can jury-rig a simple cabinet from a couple of cardboard boxes and a small sheet of transparent plastic.

I get my sand at a nearby ocean beach where sand dunes intrude on the parking lot and park authorities are happy to have it hauled away. I carry it in heavy-duty woven plastic sacks from a feed store. I strain it through an ordinary kitchen colander when pouring it into the hopper to get rid of any small twigs or other foreign material.

If you don't have an ocean handy, most building material suppliers sell sand. For more exotic sandblasting mediums, such as ground walnut shells or glass beads, check the yellow pages under "Sandblasting Equipment and Supplies."

Air Duster

An air duster, if you can find one (they're not too common), is great for cleaning up the workshop. It consists of a normal air blow gun with a venturi tube built around it to increase the air discharge and create a much greater air blast. This attachment is great for dusting off tools, benches, shelves, supplies, and the like. Open the shop door, blast away, wait a few minutes for the dust to settle, and sweep up. You'll be amazed at the results of the quick cleanup.

If you can't find the air duster, some of the new OSHA approved blow guns with holes near the tip to deaden the outlet pressure do nearly as good a job and throw a lot more air than the old fashioned straight blow gun.

Quick Connectors

If you buy any air tools, get quick connectors for the air-supply hose and for each air tool.

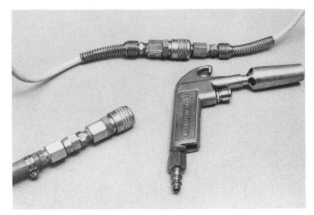

Quick couplings save time when you have more than one air tool. Just pull the knurled sleeve back, slide the tool into the coupling, and release the sleeve.

That way they can be quickly interchanged without wrenches. Quick connectors on extra hoses permit you to add length as needed.

A system of air pipes in your shop with outlets at various handy spots is nice. But if you are like me and don't want to go this far, consider one or more 25′ lengths of flex-coiled air hose. One of these will pull out to the full 25′ length and then recoil to a length of about 3′, saving the nuisance of recoiling an ordinary air hose each time. A ⅜″ hose, rather than a ¼″ one, supplies a lot more air and is more satisfactory for operating tools that use large amounts of air.

Automatic Oiler

For best operation and for longer life, many air tools need internal oiling. You can do this by inserting a few drops of air tool (light machine) oil directly into the air inlet prior to each use and occasionally during extended jobs. This is a nuisance and is apt to be forgotten though.

An in-line oil fog lubricator is a worthwhile investment. Mount it on a simple stand with a convenient length of hose permanently attached to the outlet. It only takes a moment to plug the air supply line into the lubricator inlet and the tool into the outlet. A pressure-operated drip regulator provides constant lubrication, and a transparent cup shows the amount of oil remaining. Unplug the unit and you once

Automatic oiler feeds a little oil into air tool intake continuously to keep it lubricated. Coupled to the end of your normal air hose, it is used only with tools that specifically require oil.

again have oil-free air for spray painting, pressurizing tires, air dusting, or whatnot.

ELECTRONIC STUD FINDER

Finding a stud in a finished wall in order to fasten a heavy item to it has always been something of a hit or miss business. You can tap the wall lightly with a hammer, listening for the more solid sound when you tap over a stud. Then there are the little stud finders with a magnet that wiggles when you pass it over one of the nails securing Sheetrock to the stud. Since studs are normally 16″ apart and nails some 6″ or so apart vertically on the stud, it often takes a good deal of searching to find a magnetic indication of a nail head. Even then you do not know if the nail is near the center of the stud or well off to one side.

The electronic stud finder "detects the stud position by finding variations in dielectric constant as it is moved over the wall surface." It is powered by a 9-volt transistor-type battery and has a vertical row of five LED lights.

All you do is move the finder horizontally across the wall. The lights start to glow sequentially from the bottom up as you approach a stud. The top one lights up at about the actual edge of the stud and stays on until you reach the other side of the stud.

With a little practice, you can find the center of a stud to within about an eighth of an inch! The finder works best over either Sheetrock or plywood walls, but also works on wood-lathed plaster walls. The accuracy here depends on how much plaster has been extruded between the lath. The finder also locates fire blocking in walls and joists in the ceiling.

Electronic stud finder electronically "feels" the presence of the stud behind the wallboard, instead of responding magnetically to nails in the wall. As it is moved horizontally, the lights illuminate alternately from the bottom up as a stud is approached. The top one illuminates as the edge of the stud is reached, remains on while the stud is crossed, and goes out when the far side is passed. Then the other lights go on and off in order until the bottom one goes out about ¼″ after leaving the stud. Amazing!

NUMBER AND LETTER DRILLS

Everybody has a set of fractional drills from ¹⁄₁₆″ to ¼″ and most have a set going up to ½″. But when you want to drill a pilot hole for a woodscrew in a piece of hardwood, or make a clearance hole for the axle on a child's toy, or for any of a hundred other such drilling jobs, you all too often find one size drill just a smidgen too small and the next size just a bit too big.

The answer to this is to get a set of number drills. This set usually consists of 60 drills numbered, reasonably enough, from 1 to 60. The #1 drill, sized at .228″, is between ⁷⁄₃₂″ and ¹⁵⁄₆₄″ (a little less than ¼″). The #60 drill has a diameter of .040″, about midway between ¹⁄₃₂″ and ³⁄₆₄″ or considerably smaller than your smallest fractional drill (¹⁄₁₆″). As an example of the wide choice of sizes, there are five different number drills that fall between a ¹⁄₁₆″ and a ⁵⁄₆₄″ drill, the next fractional size! Get a set of these and you'll soon wonder how you ever got along without them.

Number drills are also often needed when drilling holes to be tapped for threads. The usual tap and die set for cutting threads up to ½″ in diameter calls for eight different number drills in addition to several fractional sizes.

If you do modelmaking or other very small work, you will want a set of #61 to #80 drills. The #80 is a tiny .0135″ in diameter, a bit smaller than ¹⁄₆₄″.

If you need a wider choice in larger drills, a set of 26 letter drills (A to Z) starts just slightly larger than the #1. The A has a diameter of .234″ and the Z .413″ (a little less than ⁷⁄₁₆″). Letter drills increase in size from A to Z while number drills decrease in size from 1 to 80. There must be a reason for that, but it escapes me!

While on the subject of drills: If you have a drill press, you can save time by keeping a set of drills, preferably up to ½″ in diameter at the machine. Provide another set to ¼″ or ³⁄₈″, as appropriate, to keep with your electric drill for roving use. This gives you the advantage of having spares; if a drill breaks, you are not out of business.

You can further simplify things by getting a card or poster containing a table of the decimal equivalents of number, letter, and fractional drills. These are often available free from a number of sources. Hang it up on the shop wall near the drill press.

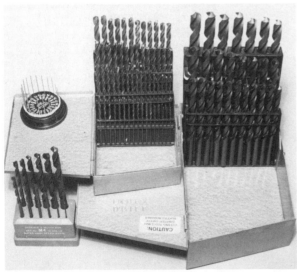

Most every shop has the ordinary twenty-nine-piece drill set from ¹⁄₁₆″ to ½″ by 64ths. But the drills shown here can be very useful. The set of tiny #61 to #80 drills (upper left corner) is needed for modelmaking, jewelry, and other fine work. The sixty-piece number drill set, #1 to #60, gives all sorts of in-between sizes not available with fractional drills. The twenty-six-piece A to Z alphabet set continues on with larger sizes than the number set. The metric drills (at lower left) are becoming increasingly useful in any shop.

SMALL DRILLS IN BIG CHUCKS

Many drill press chucks do not close down enough to hold small drills. For example, the Craftsman ½″ chuck only closes to ⁵⁄₆₄″. To mount small drills in a chuck of this type, get yourself a pin chuck, especially made to hold small drills. Be sure to get the kind with a straight shank, not the one with a swivel-end finger pad designed to be hand-held. The correct type may be difficult to find locally. Try a hobby shop that caters to model train or model airplane enthusiasts, an industrial tool supply company, or a catalog tool supplier.

small drill presses do not turn slowly enough at even the lowest speed to do a good job with oversize drills. (See Chapter 9 for a couple of ways to get slower speeds on your drill press.) The lowest speed available may still tend to overheat large drills, and the machine may not have enough power to take a normal cut with them.

Larger holes can be drilled with some success on a normal press by drilling in increments of 1/16", or even 1/32" for the larger sizes, until the desired size is reached. Be sure to use the slowest speed available, plenty of cutting oil, and as heavy a pressure as the machine will take without stalling. With lighter pressure the drill

Pin chuck enables the drill press to hold drills smaller than its chuck can grip directly.

BIG DRILLS IN SMALL CHUCKS

Most home-shop drill presses have a 1/2"-capacity chuck. This normally limits the owner to drilling a maximum of a 1/2" diameter hole in metal. For drilling larger holes with these chucks, there are larger drills available with a reduced shank of 1/2" diameter. Known as Silver and Deming drills after the original manufacturer, these drills can be very expensive, but some industrial tool-supply houses offer specials on imported sets that should be adequate for the occasional user.

As usual, however, there is no free lunch. Using Silver and Deming drills to make oversize holes does present some problems. Most

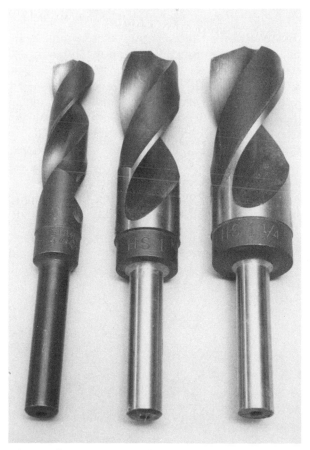

These Silver & Deming drills have cut-down shanks that can be held in a normal 1/2" drill press chuck. The 5/8" drill works well in most drill presses, but lower than normal speeds are needed for 1" and 1¼" drills. Even then the hole may have to be enlarged in increments of 1/16" or so.

tends to turn in the hole without cutting and rapidly builds up heat from friction.

Silver and Deming drills are available up to 1½″ in diameter, but without a speed reducer, 1″ is probably a practical maximum. With lower than normal speeds and by drilling in increments of ¹⁄₁₆″, I have drilled holes to 1¼″ (my maximum size drill) with a ½″ drill press.

If you have a heavy-duty, slow-speed ½″ electric drill, you can use the smaller Silver and Deming drills to drill oversize holes in items too big or too unwieldy for a drill press.

AIRCRAFT CABLE SWAGING TOOL

Aircraft control cable, now often available in local hardware stores, can be put to many uses in shop projects. It is very strong for its size (the breaking strength of ¹⁄₁₆″ cable is 480 pounds and for ⅛″ cable is 2,000 pounds). The cable is also extremely flexible, being made of seven strands, with nineteen wires each (a less flexible 7 x 7 cable comes in some of the smallest sizes).

Aircraft cable splices for end fittings were originally made by hand splicing them around thimbles or bushings, a laborious and difficult

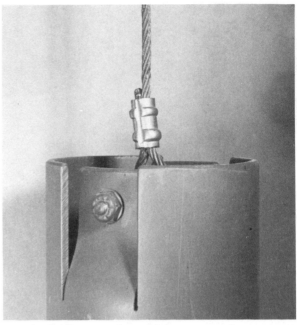

Finished splice on a ⅛″ cable supports a heavy counterweight filled with lead.

process that, when you consider the small sizes of cable involved, was more of an art than a skill. Then a tool known as a Nicopress splicer was developed. It squeezes special Nicopress copper sleeves onto the cable ends after they have been passed around the thimble or bushing and compresses them into a swaged-end fitting that is stronger than the old-time splice. It takes a fraction of the time and very little skill to produce.

The Nicopress splicer is rather expensive for the average workshop. With the spread of home-built aircraft, however, an economical swaging tool has been developed. A small hand tool, it develops swaging pressure by tightening two bolts and works on ¹⁄₁₆″, ³⁄₃₂″, or ⅛″ cable. A larger version handles ⅛″ to ¼″ cable. With either, you need the usual bushings or thimbles and Nicopress copper sleeves.

Keep this in mind as you develop future projects. Aircraft control cable can be used to simplify and improve many shop projects. If you have an airport nearby, you may be able to get this little tool locally, otherwise see the appendix of this book for a supply store. Either place can also be a source for the Nicopress sleeves, end fittings, and even pulleys to change cable direction in your particular project.

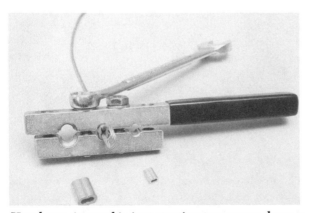

Hand swaging tool is just starting to squeeze down a copper sleeve on the ³⁄₃₂″ cable eye. A ⅛″ and a ¹⁄₁₆″ cable sleeve are in front of their respective swaging die slots.

HEAT GUNS

Heat guns soften paint and various adhesives for removal, speed up drying of small paint and glue jobs, and heat-shrink special plastic tubing to make neat wire bundles work on electronic equipment or on wiring in your car or truck. Until recently, a gun that provided high enough temperatures to shrink tubing was quite expensive, but prices have recently tumbled. Heat-shrink tubing can be obtained in various sizes at most electronic supply stores.

If you do not need the higher heat-shrink or paint-softening temperature, an old electric hair dryer often comes in handy to hasten the drying of a small paint or glue job, to heat a bit of plastic for bending, or for any other little job where a localized heat source is needed. If you don't already have an old hair dryer around the house, check the flea market or garage sales.

You find the center of any piece of work in a hurry with this rule. Just move it around until the reading on both sides of the center mark looks the same. No need to count off 32nds of an inch with this rule.

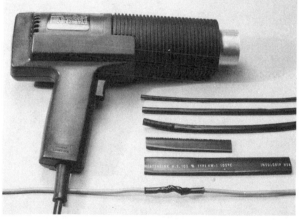

Heat gun poses here with several sizes of heat-shrink tubing, plus a sample that has been shrunk over an electrical connection between two wires.

CENTER-FINDING RULE

How often have you tried to locate the center of a piece of material that measured $1^{25}\!/_{32}$" wide, or $3^{7}\!/_{16}$", or whatever? Unless you are a little swifter with fractions than most of us, it takes a while to figure out that the answers are $^{57}\!/_{64}$" and $1^{23}\!/_{32}$". Of course, there is the old trick of laying a rule across the part at an angle to make the measurement come out even and then taking half of this to find the center. Unfortunately this does not always work; sometimes the object is irregular, the sides are not parallel, or it is too short.

The simple answer to this problem is a center-finding rule. These come in either 12" or 18" lengths. One edge is calibrated as a standard rule, but the other has the zero mark in the center and then measures out from it in both directions. In practice, you do not even have to count out the exact fractions on each side of center. You just juggle the rule back and forth until the "picture" is the same at both edges and then mark the center at the zero line. Some woodworking catalogs show this tool, but you can often get it quicker and cheaper at a local art shop, especially one that carries graphic art supplies.

METER STICK

As mentioned above, having to add, subtract, multiply, or divide fractional measurements of inches can be very frustrating. Currently on the market are some slightly longer than normal "yardsticks," meter sticks actually, that are calibrated in inches and fractions on one edge and

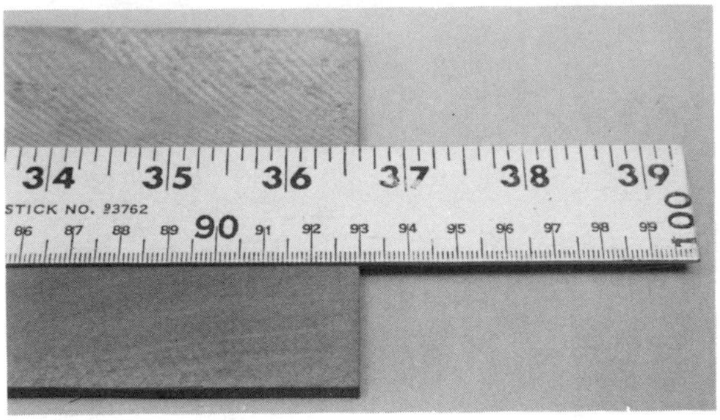

Odd measurements are easier to handle in millimeters. If you need to divide this board into five equal parts, you could call it 36⅝″ long and fiddle around with fractions until you come up with the right answer. The quick way is to call it 930mm long, divide by five, and mark out the five sections at 186mm each. The job still comes out the same size; it just gets done a lot faster with a metric scale.

in centimeters and millimeters on the other. The meter stick is 100 centimeters long, and each centimeter is graduated into 10 millimeters. The whole thing is 39 and a fraction inches long, but that is not important.

The only difficulty with metric measurement is when you convert to inches and feet. So, forget the conversion and work only with the metric side of the rule; it simplifies all your calculations. For instance, suppose you are going to make something out of a 1″ x 6″ surfaced board. It is, of course, not 6″ wide. Depending on what mill cut it, what wood it is, and how it was dried, it may be any of a half-dozen or so different widths. One that I just measured is 5⁵⁄₁₆″. Start working with divisions or multiples of that and you end up with more calculations than you have fingers and toes to count on.

Suppose you need to mark the board at ⅙ of its width. An inexpensive hand-held calculator (one should be in every shop) is of little help when you have to deal with fractions of inches; the calculator is unable to handle them directly. To use it with 5⁵⁄₁₆″, you have to multiply the 5 times 16 (80), and then add 5, to get 85 sixteenths of an inch. Then, you divide this number by 6, which gives you 14.166 sixteenths of an inch, or ⅞″ plus a tiny ⅙ of ⅟OF *⁄16″.

Instead of doing all this, try the other edge of the meter stick. When you measure the same nominal 1 x 6 with it, you get 135 millimeters. Enter 135 into the calculator, divide by 6, and the answer is 22.5 millimeters, which you can measure directly onto the board. It doesn't matter whether you call it ⅞″ plus a hair or 22.5 millimeters, the dimension is the same except that it was much more easily arrived at with the meter stick. Steel tape measures also come with one edge in metric and one in inches.

MACHINERY'S HANDBOOK

This book, which has been around in different editions since 1914, has more answers than you'll ever have questions. It is a thick book, and my twentieth edition contains nearly 2,500 pages; the current twenty-second edition is even thicker. Just a quick rundown on the contents would take pages to describe. If you do any work at all with metal or machinery, you will find this book invaluable.

This fat little book is expensive but has a lot of valuable information for workshoppers who do any mechanical work.

Check a copy in your library to see how much of it you would need. Note the many tables containing information that is difficult or nearly impossible to dig up elsewhere. Much of this pertains to all types of workshops. There are several other handbooks of this type that have been published, Audel's and American to name a couple. They are worthwhile if you can get a bargain price, but Machinery's appears to be the most comprehensive. The current edition is discounted in some industrial tool catalogs.

DEBURRING TOOL

Deburring drilled holes or cut edges of sheets in either metal or plastic can be an annoying chore. Countersinks often chatter, leaving an undesirable edge on a hole. Using a larger drill on the edge of holes is sometimes awkward and unsatisfactory. Filing the cut edge of a sheet is slow and difficult.

In recent years, a deburring tool has come on the market. It consists of a handle in which a small offset blade is allowed to swivel. Take one of these in hand, slip the tip into a freshly drilled hole (as small as ³⁄₃₂″), give your wrist a twist, and the job is done—quickly and neatly!

These things work. I've been using my little throwaway model for a couple of years of intermittent work. When it eventually does wear out, I'll get a set with several blades for different materials and jobs.

HEMOSTATS

Hemostats, also sometimes known as Kelly forceps, are normally a surgeon's "tool," but they have many uses in the workshop. Similar in appearance to a pair of scissors, they end in the form of tweezers rather than cutting blades. Hemostats come in different sizes and with either straight or curved ends. At the base of the handles, there is a ratchet-type locking device that holds them closed with two, three, or four different pressures depending on the model. They serve as a third hand to hold on to all sorts of small things while the items are maneuvered into position, cut, tied, soldered, welded, or glued. In electronic work, they also serve as a small heat sink. One or more hemostats have a place in your shop.

Another useful item is a dentist's pick. These are available with many different tip shapes and sizes, and they are made from a very tough steel, which stands up to a surprising amount of digging and prying. One or two of them can

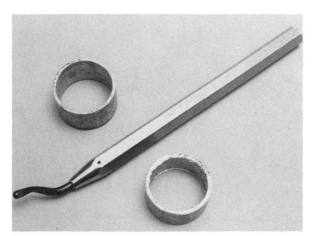

Swivel-tip deburring tool does the job in a hurry. The bottom ring from a piece of ¾″ copper pipe shows the burrs left after hacksawing. The upper ring has been cleaned up with a two-second twist of the deburrer.

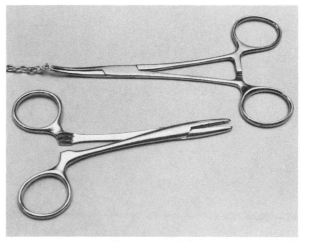

Hemostats are handy in the shop to hold all sorts of small items. The upper one is clamped onto a jump ring in the end of a length of jewelry chain. The lower one is open to show its ratchet-type lock.

come in handy for cleaning out narrow cracks and such. Both dentist's picks and hemostats are sold in some tool catalogs, in modelmakers catalogs, and also occasionally show up at flea markets.

SUPER STRAIGHTEDGE

In the past few years, some extra-long straight-edges have appeared on the market. The one I have, purchased through a magazine ad, is sold as a "universal cutting guide." But as a long straightedge, it does many other jobs around the shop and the house.

It consists of two identical 51″ lengths of extruded aluminum, each 3½″ wide and having one edge turned up 5⁄16″ to provide a guide for a portable circular saw or other power tool. The flat opposite edge is a little more than 1⁄16″ thick; this is a clamping edge for fastening the straightedge to the work to be cut. You can also use this edge with a carpenter's pencil or other marker to lay out long straight lines.

For marking or cutting anything up to 4′ long (across a sheet of plywood or hardboard, for instance), either one of the two lengths is fine. For longer work, such as cutting the full length of a sheet of plywood, you fasten the two sections together with an 18″ splice plate, also of extruded aluminum. This clamps to a raised center channel on each piece so that both edges

are unobstructed for its entire length. A quick tightening of four small screws positively holds and aligns the two parts so that you now have an accurate straightedge that is 8′ 6″ long! Clamp the tool to the plywood, letting most of the extra 6″ extend on the starting end of the cut. Now you even have a guide to get your saw lined up before it starts cutting the stock.

With the universal guide, a good portable saw, and a plywood cutting blade, you can do a better job than cutting a full sheet on a table saw. It certainly takes all the grief out of struggling to get a full sheet of plywood through your table saw, unless you have a saw with a really big table.

Other jobs for this straightedge around the house and shop are many and varied. I was recently called upon to cut several inches off the side of a long length of vinyl fabric for a pad under a table cloth. This gadget made the job a snap; the vinyl was accurately measured and marked for cutting in no time.

ELECTRIC GLUE GUN

Within its limitations, an electric glue gun is a handy tool. Since the glue sets up very rapidly, especially if it is spread out into a thin film, the gun is not for gluing large wood surfaces, such

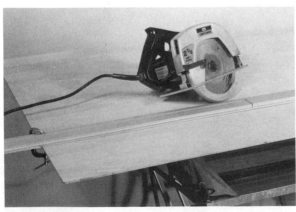

Two-piece straightedge assembled to its full 8½′ length is ideal for cutting plywood sheet.

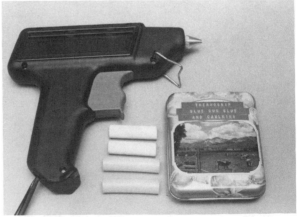

Electric glue gun is handy for quickly fastening small items together or for minor caulking jobs. White sticks are caulking, the darker ones are glue. The little candy tin holds up to twenty-four sticks.

as in furniture making. It is, however, very good at quickly gluing up small items made of wood, fabric, paper, cardboard, ceramics, foam, and plastic, especially if the parts are poorly mated or if they have voids.

The glue being an electric insulator, it can be used on or to seal electronic components. White caulking sticks are available for repairing leaks and for various other weatherproofing situations.

IMPACT SCREWDRIVER

The tool is actually misnamed. These things are almost never used to drive screws; they remove them—specifically those screws that are rusted, corroded, or driven in so tightly they won't come out by any other means. Have you ever had a badly rusted big machine screw that you couldn't budge? Even if you put a wrench on the shank of the screwdriver, the bit just slipped out of the slot and possibly damaged the screw a little more in the bargain. You probably ended up drilling out the screw and had to redrill and tap the hole for a larger screw.

It's a good bet an impact driver could have gotten that screw out. All you do is insert the driver's blade into the screw slot or socket, twist the handle in the direction you want the screw to turn (counterclockwise to remove), hold the driver in position, and deliver a couple of good whops to the end of the tool with a heavy hammer. Since the blade is driven into the slot by the blow, the tip does not jump out of the slot. The cam action of the tool turns it as it is hit, and the full force of the twisting action is applied to the head of the screw. On some models, the screwdriver chuck pulls off to reveal a square drive for use with your socket set to remove frozen nuts.

RATCHET BALL SCREWDRIVER

With its fat 2⅜"-diameter ball-type handle, this screwdriver system can make driving and removing large wood screws a much easier job. A standard driver has a handle that seldom exceeds 1⅜" in diameter. That makes a big difference when it comes to applying torque. Although you do not get the brute force of an impact screwdriver, the ratchet ball driver can remove (and drive) a number of stubborn screws that would be difficult or impossible to handle with an ordinary screwdriver.

Sold with a heavy square-shank slot-type blade and a few ¼" hex-drive bits, this screw-

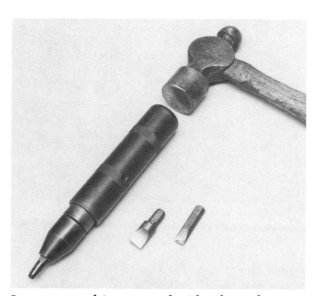

Impact screwdriver, teamed with a heavy hammer, does a great job loosening large, rusty screws.

Oversize handle of a ratchet ball screwdriver eases screwdriving work. You can get a variety of hex bits and different length shanks. Note also the ¼"- and ⅜"-drive socket adapters and the universal joint.

driver also accepts many other hex-drive bits available. Thus, you can add or exchange any other hex bits you happen to have. Adapters are available to drive both ¼"- and ⅜"-drive socket wrenches, adding another convenient ratchet-type driver to your socket set.

SPECIALTY LOCKING PLIERS

Locking pliers have been around for many years; almost everybody who has more than a half dozen tools has at least one. New and specialized versions continue to be introduced though; if you haven't been paying much atten-tion, check the display next time you go to the hardware store. Variations include: wide-jawed models for bending sheet metal; chain "strap" wrenches for large diameter pipe or other round objects, such as stubborn oil filter cartridges; horseshoe-jawed welding clamps; various sizes of locking C-clamps, some with an incredible reach; and special asymmetric-jawed pliers to clamp a length of pipe to a piece of angle iron or other material for drilling or welding. Chain breakers for disassembling and reriveting saw chains are also built around the versatile locking plier.

Check them over; you are apt to find at least one answer to a problem that sometimes "bugs" you. Some brands even have an automatic feature and do not require prior size adjustment to fit the job at hand.

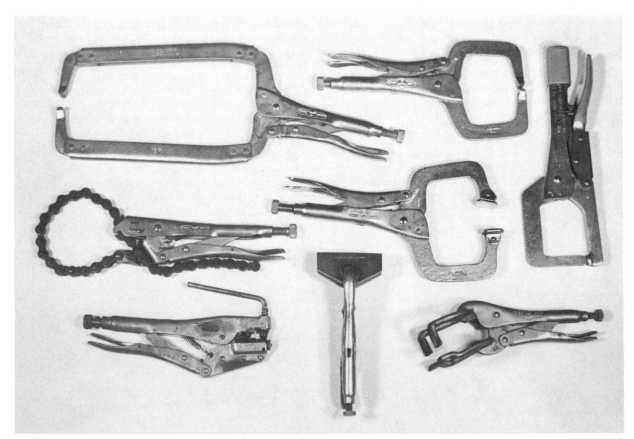

Special types of locking pliers available include (clockwise from top left): a locking C-clamp with a 10″ reach; a 3″ reach C-clamp; a one-hand, self-adjusting C-clamp for attaching items to the side of a piece of pipe; a welding clamp; a sheet-metal bending pliers; a chain breaker for chain saw repair; a chain-type "strap" wrench for round objects; and another C-clamp with swivel pads.

UNSQUARE SQUARES AND UNLEVEL LEVELS

Up until a few years ago, if you purchased a square or level from a reputable manufacturer, you could be reasonably sure that it was accurate. This is no longer true, unfortunately.

Recently, at a major retailer, I checked several name brand try-squares against one another. Out of half a dozen, no two agreed! When I told this to the hardware department manager; he just shrugged. Had this happened at this same store twenty years ago, heads would have rolled! Also, I recently purchased a torpedo level (from a well-known tool manufacturer) that was "far out" and had to return it for a more accurate, if still not quite perfect, one.

Fortunately, it is easy to test either of these tools for accuracy. To check a square, find a flat

CHECKING A SQUARE

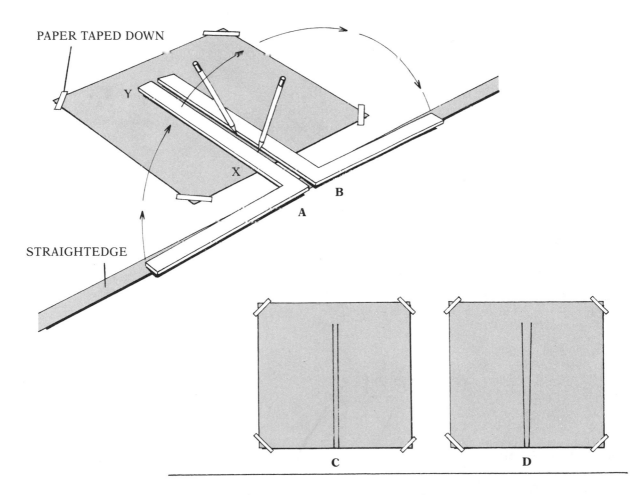

To check a square for accuracy: (**A**) **Hold it firmly against a straightedge and draw a line from x to y.** (**B**) **Flop the square over, again hold it against the straightedge and draw a second line superimposed over the first one.** (**C**) **Remove the square and exam-** ine the lines. If they appear as one or, if separated, they are perfectly parallel, the square is accurate. (**D**) **If the two lines diverge, the square is inaccurate. Check the lines drawn in each position to see whether the square is "square."**

CHECKING A LEVEL

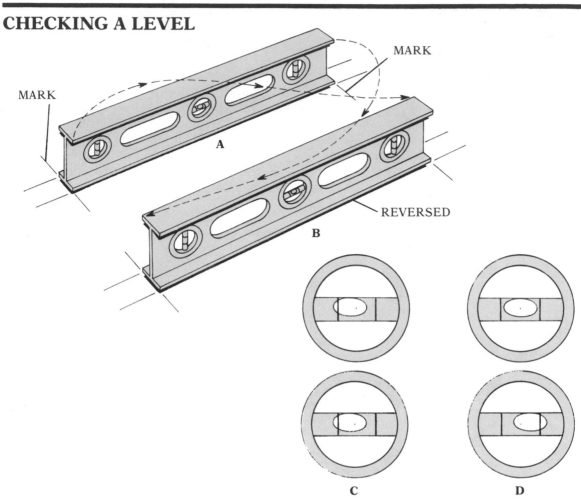

To check a level for accuracy: (*A*) Set the level on a smooth, reasonably level surface and mark the position of its ends on the surface. Note the exact position of the bubble. (*B*) Turn the level end for end and reset it to the markings. Check the bubble position. (*C*) If the bubble locations in *A* and *B* were exactly the same, the level is good. An identical reading that is off-center only shows that the test surface is not level. (*D*) If the bubble position varies visibly between steps *A* and *B*, the level is inaccurate.

surface with an absolutely straight and smooth edge. Hold one arm of the square against the front of this edge and draw a fine line across the surface along the other arm of the square. Then flop the square over so that the front arm extends along the same edge but in the opposite direction. Draw another line over the first one. If they diverge at all at either end, the square isn't square. If you do not want to mark the surface, tape down a sheet of paper first; then draw your proving lines on it.

If the square is only slightly off and is not a new one that you can return or exchange, you may be able to correct it with some judicious tapping or light hammering with the ball end of a ball-peen hammer. Lay the square flat on an improvised anvil of some sort. Tap near the inside angle of the square if its angle needs opening up slightly; tap near the outside corner if the angle needs closing down. Turn the square over and tap approximately the same number of times on this side. Test the square as previously described after every few blows; it is sometimes surprising how much the angle can be changed with just a few blows.

To check a level, find a smooth, flat, reasonably level surface. (It does not have to be exactly level.) Lay the level on it and precisely mark the position of both ends. Note the *exact* position of the bubble. It may or may not be dead center, depending on the surface. Lift the level and reverse it, placing the opposite ends in the exact positions previously marked. Check the bubble again. If it reads precisely the same as it did before, the level is accurate. *Any* discrepancy at all and the level is lying to you. If the level is adjustable (most are not), make a small correction and test again, repeating until you get it dead on.

ELECTRIC DRILL ACCESSORIES

Some years back when an electric drill in every home shop was new, a number of accessories for them appeared on the market. There were little stands to convert them into stationary grinding wheels, table saws, and lathes. Other gadgets changed them into portable saws, power hacksaws, and similar items. Nearly all of these were impractical, some downright dangerous, and most have disappeared. One notable exception is the small drill stand which can provide a

Electric-drill accessories include wire brushes of many shapes, sizes, and textures. Plastic cleaning wheels and rubberized, grit-embedded wheels are great. A drum rasp and shaft-mounted shaped rasps remove wood rapidly. Mounted stones and carbide burrs carve hardened steel.

good substitute for a drill press, at least for small jobs.

Many accessories for an electric drill on the market today are worth having though. Most are tools that insert directly into the chuck and are used freehand.

Rotary wire brushes, which mount directly into the chuck, are among the most common of these. Wire brushes come in different shapes and sizes and vary from coarse to fine texture. They remove rust or corrosion, clean up metal after welding, remove scale, and do other rough polishing jobs.

Small grinding wheels, permanently bonded to a ¼" shaft that fits the drill chuck, are available in many shapes, sizes, and grits. They are ideal for most of the little grinding jobs that cannot be done on a bench grinder and can save a lot of hand filing.

Rotary rasps make fast work of various rough wood carving jobs. Small rotary files and burrs are also sold for metal work; the more expensive ones are made of solid carbide. While these bits are most effective at very high speeds, they will work with an electric drill, although the job gets done more slowly. Carbide bits can cut hardened steel.

Rotary drum rasps of the "cheese grater" style are also made. The one I have is 2" in diameter and has a 1" face. It cuts very fast for rough wood carving and shaping, especially on the softer woods.

One of the best electric drill accessories that I have come across is a 4"-diameter cleaning wheel. About ½" thick and very light in weight, it appears to be made of loosely woven, fine plastic twine impregnated with an abrasive material. You buy the first one with a mandrel; replacement wheels are then available. Cleaning wheels are somewhat expensive and wear rather rapidly. But they really outperform rotary wire brushes for removing paint, rust or scale, and for deburring jobs. They work on wood, plastic, and metal and can even clean up grout and mortar joints. You have to see one work to believe how fast it does the job.

Also available are some 3" diameter wheels that appear to be made out of a solid rubbery plastic permeated throughout with a fine grit. These not only rapidly remove rust, they also polish out the pits in the metal surface that a wire brush cannot touch. These little wheels are excellent for all sorts of sharpening jobs, being made with much finer grit than the usual grinding wheel, and they also do not tend to overheat the cutting edge as much as a normal grinding wheel does.

ODDBALL TOOLS

If you keep your eyes open, you may find some unusual old tools that are of special interest to you. Antique shops, which usually charge ridiculously high prices for old wooden planes, often have some outstanding bargains on lesser known tools that happen to be unfamiliar to them.

For example, it is not at all uncommon to find old heavy-duty hacksaw frames up to as much as an unbelievable 10″ deep, invaluable for long cuts, at giveaway prices. While wrenches, including pipe wrenches, are usually no bargain, such items as a pipe cutter or a pipe-threading set may be offered at a tiny fraction of its current price, especially if it needs cleaning up. (Steel pipe and fittings, although widely replaced by copper and/or plastic for water-carrying purposes, still can be used in a number of ways around the workshop. Tools for cutting and threading it are worth having.) Other items, such as bar clamps and hand vises, are commonly sold in antique shops at reasonable prices.

Sometimes it can be fun to pick up a bargain

When gently advised that the pipe cutter was worth many times her asking price, the lady said, "If it's in the 50¢ box, the price is 50¢. Take it or leave it!" The interesting little lag screwdriver also came from an antique shop. (Look into those dark corners while your wife is searching for house plunder.) The sheet-metal shear was a flea market bargain.

priced tool that looks interesting but that is a complete mystery. Take it home and puzzle it out later. After buying one such gadget for 75¢, I later figured out that it was used to drive squarehead lag screws with a carpenter's brace. Since driving lag screws with a wrench is a slow and tiring proposition, it has come in handy several times in fence and gate construction.

If you find an item that you are unable to identify, hang it on the shop wall and one of your shop visitors, probably an old-timer, will eventually supply the name and use of it. I've been able to identify several odd tools this way, although I must admit that I'm still waiting for an answer on a couple of them.

Flea markets, swap meets, garage and yard sales may also have interesting buys. Look for sellers who really are just getting rid of unneeded items and who may offer real bargains.

A while back, I paid just $15 for a heavy-duty industrial-type electric metal shear, which cuts up to 14-gage (over 1/16″ thick) sheet steel. When purchased, it had a broken brush holder. A letter to the manufacturer produced a new brush holder, spare brushes, a spare set of cutting jaws, and an owner's manual. For a total investment of less than $35, I got a like-new version of a tool worth hundreds of dollars. Watch for

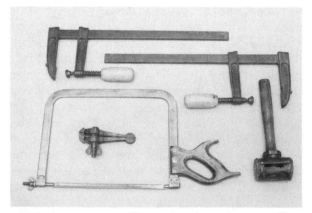

Old-fashioned but still very handy tools were all acquired in antique shops for less than $15. The 18″ bar clamps needed new wooden handles and the "persuader" needed new lead faces.

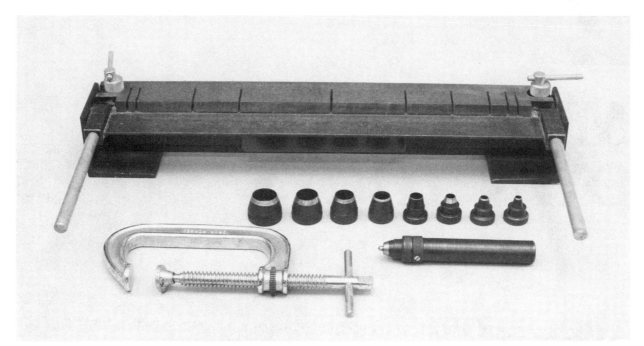

When traveling overseas, include a hardware store or two along with the museums. Japanese finds include the unusual C-clamp and the sheet-metal brake. The nine-hole punch set is English. The spring-loaded point permits the center to be relocated to make concentric washers.

good used tools that *you* can't justify the expense of buying new.

Foreign hardware and tool stores can also be fun to browse, if you have some extra time on a trip overseas. You will find some unusual tools that do not show up in stores here. For example, Japanese hardware stores have clever C-clamps.

Normal C-clamps, as you probably know, really need three hands to operate them. One hand is needed to hold the parts to be joined in the proper position, a second hand to hold the C-clamp itself, and a third to tighten the screw. Not having three hands, you have to compromise and attempt to hold the parts in position, and the clamp on them, with one hand while you tighten the clamp with the other.

Japanese clamps have a special feature that allows you to hold the clamp and do the preliminary tightening all with one hand. It is just a thick washer with a knurled outside edge to provide finger traction. The washer has an internal boss that rides in a keyway running the length of the jackscrew. You hold the clamp in one hand and turn the washer with your thumb and forefinger to tighten the clamp. You hold the parts in position with your other hand. Once the clamp is secured, you use the handle on the end of the jackscrew to cinch it down. These clamps are *great*. Why they have not been imported or produced in this country is another of life's little mysteries.

2
MAKE YOUR OWN TOOLS

TOOLS FOR YOUR TOOLS

Many tools, especially power tools, require other tools (wrenches mostly) to adjust and adapt them for attachments. You probably know how time consuming and annoying it is to have to cross the shop to hunt up a wrench and then find that it may be the wrong one. You then have to go all the way back and dig out the right one.

One solution to this problem is to have extras of the specific tools needed mounted on or near the power tool. Since the wrenches are only for snugging up adjustments, they do not have to be high quality. Less expensive brands or even carefully selected flea market bargains will do.

These tools can be bent (with heat), welded, or otherwise modified as required. For instance, suppose that a given power tool requires a 7/16" open-end wrench for one adjustment and a 9/16" box wrench for another. Instead of having two wrenches with four ends to confuse you, cut the wrenches in two and weld together the 7/16" open-end and the 9/16" box-end pieces. Save the other two parts (usually a 3/8" open-end and a 1/2" box) for future use on another tool or for modifying into a special wrench for a bolt that is difficult to get at on a car, truck, outboard motor, washing machine, or whatever.

When you need a screwdriver (to make adjustments or to remove a cover plate) and a wrench, grind down the handle end of a cutoff wrench to fit the particular screw. Or weld on a Phillips screwdriver tip, if that is required.

In some cases, it is better to weld a box wrench directly onto the nut to be adjusted (cut off the other end of the wrench and round off and smooth the cut end with a grinding wheel). One excellent example is the clamp bolt that tightens the table to the column of a drill press. The bolt head is often located in a hexagon-shaped recession, and a single wrench tightens or loosens the nut. Welding a box wrench onto the nut saves all that picking up and putting down of the wrench, to say nothing of the time spent searching for it when it has "walked away" from wherever it was supposed to be. When you do this, first put the wrench on the nut while it is still on the drill press. Position it so that it will be at a convenient angle when tightening it. Mark both the wrench and nut, and after taking off the nut, be sure to assemble it and the wrench for welding with the two marks aligned.

If you have a welding torch, welding up your own special wrenches will be no problem. If you don't look around for a small welding shop or a service station with a torch (and someone who knows how to use it). Try to find a place that will do the job for you at a reasonable price. Many big shops don't bother with small

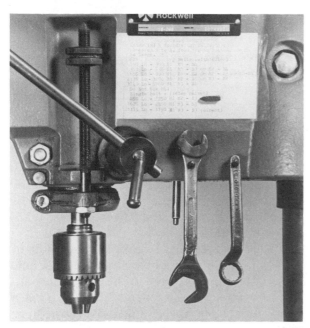

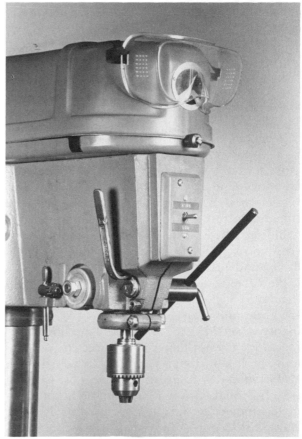

Several timesaving modifications show on this drill press head. Two wrenches, one welded up to get the desired openings, serve to secure the drill press vise and fixtures. They hang from short rods, outer ends of which are bent up slightly, while inner ends are threaded and screwed into holes tapped in the head. Locknuts keep them from working loose. A bolt securing the handle has been replaced by a longer bolt, its head turned down and bent to provide more leverage. A fabric-cored rubber washer between the two depth-stop nuts keeps them from vibrating loose but allows adjustment without a wrench. Lastly, a placard gives the available spindle speeds; the pointed magnet shows the one in use.

Safety glasses are always at hand when hung from a bolt fastened atop the housing. Labels show two speeds available from the switch. A box wrench welded to its nut tightens the quill lock. Since much of the handle was used in bends to clear the housing, a bit of bar stock was added to give leverage.

Box wrench welded to the table tightening nut saves time spent hunting for an ordinary wrench.

The bracket for this pump oiler is screwed to a pair of tapped holes in the table housing.

jobs, or if they do, their overhead is such that it is expensive. Expect to pay a fair amount at a small shop or even if you get a friend to do it; the cost of acetylene and oxygen is astronomical these days. Wherever you have it done, you can save the welder a lot of time and yourself some money by having the items prepared and jigged up in position to weld.

When you first try to cut a wrench handle in two, you will probably discover that it is difficult if not impossible with an ordinary hacksaw. One answer is to get a carbide-grit blade. Another, easier way is to cut a vee in the top and bottom of the handle with the edge of a grinding wheel. This also leaves chamfers on the end of pieces to be welded, making for an easier and better weld.

Plan ahead and make up as many newly modified tools as you can at one time. A good part of the time and effort spent on any welding job involves setting up and shutting down the torch. It may not take much longer to weld up four small jobs than it would to do a single one.

One good way to jig up the pieces for welding is to lay them out on a strip of angle iron. Fasten each piece to the angle iron with a small C-clamp, shimming up either end with small scraps of metal or tin can stock as necessary. You want the joint to be welded lined up properly with the pieces butted together. The welder can then put the angle iron in a vise and the parts will be neatly laid out, all in a line, for him to weld. After one side of each part has been welded, you simply remove the C-clamps, turn the parts over (with a pair of pliers, they'll be hot), and finish the other side. No further clamping is needed.

Find a way to keep your new tools close to the machine for which they are intended. (The drill-press clamp-nut wrench, of course, takes care of itself.) Often the body of a machine can be drilled and tapped to take a small bolt or screw for hanging up a box-end wrench. A hole for hanging can be drilled in the end of the handle of most open-end wrenches, if needed. Use a sharp drill, slow speed, and heavy pressure; most wrench steel is fairly hard. If hanging is not practical, use a small box, a drawer next to the tool, a hook on the wall, or whatever, but keep them handy!

You may find it a good idea to keep a collection of extra wrenches and screwdrivers on hand for making additional adjusting tools. Start with the cutoff wrench ends left over

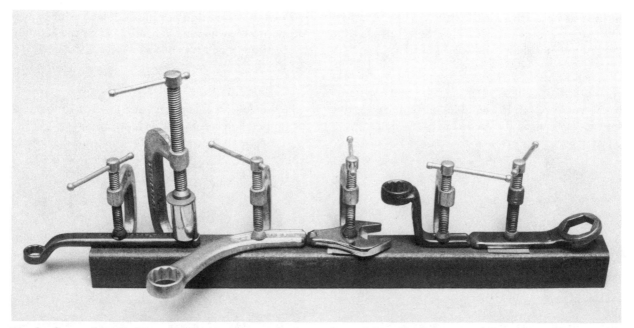

Ready for welding: Six wrench pieces, cut ends chamfered, are clamped to a length of angle iron. Note sheet-metal shims to adjust for different handle thicknesses.

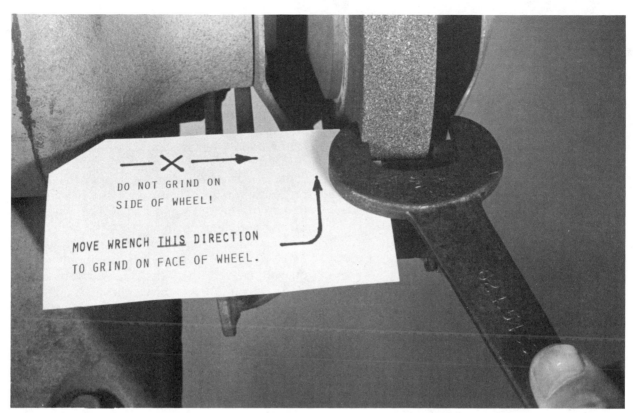

Open-end wrenches can be ground larger when used for light work such as securing tool adjustments. Be sure to grind in from the face of the wheel rather than exerting pressure on the side.

from the first modified tools and add to them any time that you find a real bargain at a local flea market or garage sale.

Keep in mind that here in the United States the ⅜" bolt is by far the most popular size for holding our mechanical world together, and that a ⁹⁄₁₆" wrench fits ⅜" bolts and nuts. You'll most likely find more uses for this size than any other. Next most common is probably either a ½" wrench, which fits a ⁵⁄₁₆" bolt and nut, or a ⁷⁄₁₆" wrench to fit ¼" diameter bolts/nuts. A ⅜" wrench fits either a ³⁄₁₆" bolt/nut, another common size, or the nut for a #10 machine screw. In the larger sizes, one of the most often used wrenches is a ¾", which fits a ½" bolt or nut. Metric sizes, too, are becoming common as more and more foreign built power tools are sold here.

Box wrenches are best, but open-end wrenches are sometimes necessary when the end of the bolt or shaft is not available to slip the closed box-end over; the motor side of a saw

Nine wrenches are all modified in some way. Four of them have been welded up from different open-end, box, and socket wrenches. Two have an end ground to form a screwdriver, one is bevel ground to fit a tapered saw arbor nut, while another's hex opening has been filed larger. The Allen wrench has a T-handle to speed adjustment of a small lathe chuck. All were reworked for specific uses and are kept with the tool they adjust.

arbor, for instance. Saw arbors usually take bigger wrenches, from ⅞" up to 1½" or even larger. Big open-end wrenches can sometimes be made a size or two larger by carefully grinding them on a coarse grinding wheel. Do not grind on the side of the wheel, but cut straight in from the front of the wheel.

Start looking at your power tools as you use them and consider what adjusting tools would be helpful to have. Once you have made a modified wrench for one, you'll find it so helpful that you'll soon have them all around your shop. I have dozens of them.

TOOLS FROM SCREWDRIVERS

Old screwdrivers with worn tips, extra screwdrivers, or flea market bargains can be made into many useful tools.

One that is especially handy is a screw starter and small hole borer for wood, plastic, or fiberglass. How often have you been faced with the job of putting a pilot hole into a wall or whatever for starting a screw? Not wanting to break out a drill and extension cord, you make do with a small nail, icepick, or awl, even though they do a less than satisfactory job. Spend a few minutes with an old screwdriver—one with a hexagon handle—and you can come

up with a dandy triangular pointed tool that, with a few back and forth twists of the wrist, makes a nice tapered hole to receive most any small screw. It can also bore, or enlarge, small holes for many other purposes.

All that you need is a small bench grinder with a fine-grit wheel (100-grit is great) and a simple wooden stand or tool rest to lay the side of the handle on. It should be high enough to bring the blade of the screwdriver up to the centerline height of the wheel. Then having cut or ground off the old tip, rest the screwdriver handle flat on the stand and work it back and forth a couple of inches across the face of the wheel at a very slight angle. Make a number of passes (a dozen, say) and dip the blade in the quench tray. Return the screwdriver to the stand, turning it two of the six sides, or facets, of the handle. Continue: grind, cool, turn two facets; grind, cool, turn. You will soon start to develop a long-tapered triangular point. To avoid overheating as the end gets smaller, cut down on the number of strokes between cooling to eight, then six, and finally four as a sharp point nears. Depending on the diameter of the original blade, the whole process takes 15 to 20 minutes and provides you with a valuable little tool. When finished, impale a cork on the end, for safety.

Keep a few old hex-handled screwdrivers in a drawer, and whenever you have a few spare minutes, grind one out. Give them to your val-

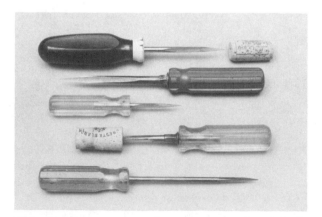

Old screwdrivers are easily converted to hand drills for making screw pilot holes and for drilling or enlarging all sorts of holes in wood, plastic, and other soft materials.

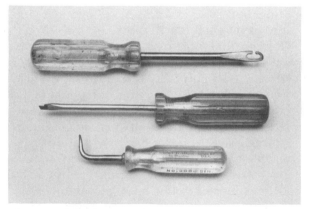

Three tools made from old screwdrivers: an installer/remover for small springs that are difficult to get at; a tiny chisel, ground for a specific application; and a cotter-key puller.

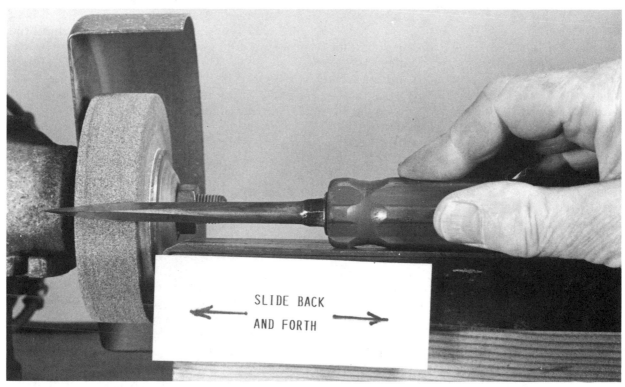

A fine-grit wheel, a stand to position the tool to its center height, and a few old screwdrivers with six-faceted handles are all you need to turn screwdrivers into hand drills.

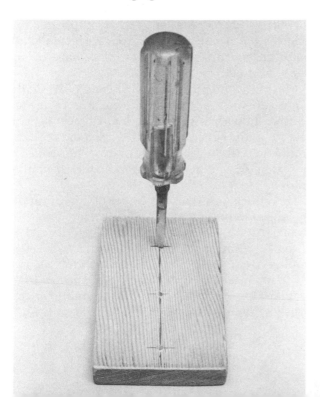

A few twists of the wrist make screw pilot holes in fairly hard wood. Thin bladed screwdrivers make good screw starter drills; fat-bladed ones make better reamers for enlarging small holes.

ued friends, and after they've had a chance to use them, you'll be amazed at the number of compliments you receive.

Screwdrivers also make many other tools. The tips can be ground to most any size or shape to make special small wood chisels to cut grooves, pockets, or other cuts and can be reshaped as needed. They can be taper ground and bent to make cotter-pin pullers. Another gadget easily made from a screwdriver is a handy little tool for installing or removing small springs that are difficult to get at. Drill and file, or grind, the screwdriver to the configuration shown. Anneal it first if it is too hard to be drilled.

If it is necessary to heat the blade of a screwdriver with a torch in order to anneal it or to bend it, soak a rag in cold water and wrap it around the blade next to the handle before starting. Keep it in place until the blade cools. This wet-rag heat sink keeps the heat from loosening the handle. A fresh raw potato cut to an appropriate length and stuck over the shank also makes a good heat sink.

EXTRA HANDS

Often you're faced with the problem of holding a couple of small pieces in a particular position and at a given angle in order to fasten them together. An excellent tool for this work can be made from an old pair of pickup truck side mirrors and two small locking pliers. Mirrors with broken or discolored glass can be gotten cheaply enough at an auto wrecker. Try to get an identical pair. Mine are about 5″ x 7″ and have a ball and socket arrangement on the back with a single screw to adjust tension. The ball and socket are the key to the operation; be sure to get this kind rather than the larger mirrors that have a separate adjustable mount at top and bottom. You will not need the arm that goes from the door to the mirror, just the mirror body and the ball and socket. If the mirrors still have any glass in them, remove it. Check the threads on the end of the ball joint shaft (mine are ¼″ x 28) and get eight hex nuts to fit this thread. Provide two pair of locking pliers. The 7″ size works out nicely with the 5″ x 7″ mirror frames.

Open the pliers fully and remove the springs so that they will not lose their temper from the brazing heat. Braze four nuts on each pair of pliers, two on the side of the frame behind the fixed jaw, and two on the top side of the frame. This allows you to set the jaws of the pliers either parallel or perpendicular to the base. The two nuts for each position are set about 2½″ apart so that the pliers can be mounted on the swivel in different places, depending on the size and weight of the parts to be held. Replace the springs after the pliers have cooled. The nuts are brazed and not welded to avoid burning the nut threads.

An open-end wrench to fit the flats on the swivel, with the other end cut off and ground to a screwdriver blade, is clipped to one mirror body. The wrench holds the swivel while the pliers are screwed on to it; the screwdriver end adjusts the ball joint tension.

With the ball joints, parts to be joined can be held at the exact position and angle required. You can even mount one of the pliers with its jaws in the horizontal position and the other in the vertical. Until you have used this setup, you cannot imagine how much time and effort it saves you. And it often produces better results as well.

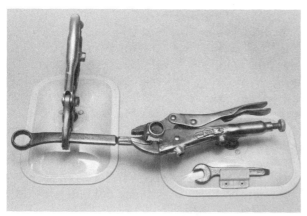

"Extra hands" take advantage of the swivel ball joints on a pair of discarded pickup-truck side mirrors (glassless). Mounted on the swivels are locking pliers, each of which has four brazed-on nuts to fit it to the mounting stud in any of four positions. Separate bases allow varied spacing, a plus over some purchased units where two adjustable grabbers are connected to a single base. The required wrench-screwdriver adjusting tool clips to one of the bases.

SOME DRILL CHUCK USES

Old electric drills, especially the cheaper plain-bearing models, eventually wear out or get so sloppy that they are discarded. The chucks however, go on forever, unless they have been badly abused.

I recently bought a popular brand of ½″ drill (inoperative) at a garage sale for $2. An inexpensive model, its switch and wiring were shot and its plain bearings badly worn. The chuck, complete with key, was still in excellent condition though and was the reason for the purchase.

This chuck now does a number of jobs around the shop, some of them quite unrelated to its former use. Its ½″ x 20 threads screw directly onto the right-hand end of a small grinding/buffing head. There it holds such things as an arbor-mounted "green" wheel for sharpening carbide-tipped masonry drills, small wire brushes, and grit-impregnated plastic and rub-

The ½″–20 threads of this ½″ drill chuck fit the shafts of most small grinders with no adapter needed. It can be used with several different wheels. Here it mounts a small "green" wheel for sharpening masonry bits and other carbide-tipped tools.

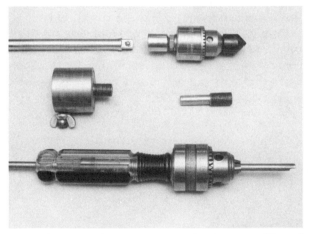

A ⅜″-drive socket extension (top), cut off and threaded ⅜″–24, allows this drill chuck to be used with a long socket extension and a speeder handle to countersink an existing hole in an assembly where an electric drill would not fit. The large adapter (center) mounts a ½″ chuck to the shaft of a hydraulic press. The smaller adapter allows the same chuck to be turned by a ⅜″ drill so that larger bits can be used (judiciously) in the smaller drill. At bottom, the ½″ chuck is mounted, via a threaded adapter, onto the handle of a discarded screwdriver. A hole has been drilled through the back of the chuck, the adapter, and the handle so that long items, such as this piece of ¼″ welding rod, are easier to hold while work is done on them.

ber cleaning wheels mentioned in Chapter 1. This arrangement is better for working on small items than a drill.

I made an adapter by cutting off the head of a ½″ bolt with the same 20 threads/inch and inserting it into a plastic handle from a large old screwdriver. Most plastic handles soften somewhat if soaked for a few minutes in very hot water (near boiling) and can then be driven off the old shank. Heated again later, it can be driven back onto a new shaft for which it has been drilled slightly undersized. The chuck is then screwed onto the handle.

This setup, with a countersink in the chuck, deburrs drilled holes. In sheet metal, it is quicker and often does a better job than a powered countersink. If you have access to a lathe, you can drill a hole through the back of the chuck, the bolt, and the plastic handle. Mine is drilled to $2\frac{1}{64}$″ and thus holds anything from a long piece of small music wire, up through several sizes of welding rod, to and including a ⁵⁄₁₆″ shaft or piece of drill rod. It gives much greater control when shaping the ends of such items on a wheel grinder.

The same chuck and handle combination also works as a better handle for the tiny, round-handled Swiss pattern files that do not lend themselves to being held in most file handles.

A second ½″ x 20 bolt has its shank turned down to ⅜″ and, provided with three equilateral flats for a nonslip grip, is a "cheater" adapter. It holds up to ½″ drills and other large shafted accessories in a ⅜″ capacity hand drill or drill press and is good for light work. Bigger holes can be drilled with a ⅜″ drill if they are enlarged above ⅜″ in small increments to avoid overloading the drill motor. Even if you have a husky ½″ drill, you may want the higher speed of a ⅜″ drill plus the ½″ chuck capacity. The ½″ drill is normally quite slow, around 600 rpm. Drilling holes in wood is one example where a higher speed is often desirable.

A third lathe-turned adapter mounts this chuck on the ram of a small hydraulic press where it holds various punches for pressing small parts together.

Don't pass up an opportunity to pick up a chuck when you see one at a reasonable price. You'll find plenty of jobs for it. Of course, if your drill press has a threaded ½″ chuck, you can always "borrow it." Most drill presses however,

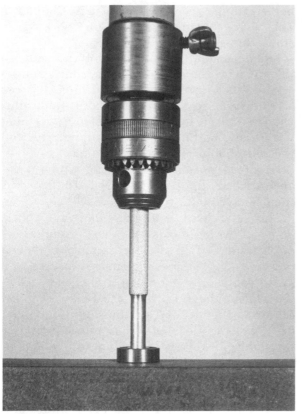

Drill chuck mounted on a hydraulic press by its adapter holds a pin punch for controlled pressing of the shaft from a small ball bearing.

most common workbenches. Mount a woodworking-type vise on one end. Since my small one (7″-wide jaws) did not have a retractable dog, I fastened two wooden faces (desirable in any case) to the steel jaws. Wood on the fixed jaw is ¼″ thick, but the face on the movable jaw is ¾″ thick and is drilled with three ⅜″ holes. Make two dogs. Start with short pieces of ⅜″ dowel; they are glued into concentric holes drilled into ¹¹/₁₆″ lengths of ¾″ dowels. Keep the top, exposed part of the dog to this length so that it will not interfere with any work being done on a piece of ¾″ stock.

Although there are three holes in the jaw insert, only one or two dogs are needed. A dog in the center hole and one outside hole holds small radius curved pieces, while the wider spacing of the two outer holes securely holds large items. The smaller dowels on the dogs were sanded to an easy fit in the ⅜″ holes. A small block mounted alongside the vise holds the two dogs when not in use. The holes were drilled at a slight downward angle, so that there is no tendency for them to fall out.

I did not want to drill rows of dog holes in this workbench. Instead, I have two 1 x 6 boards (surfaced thickness about ¹¹/₁₆″) which normally hang out of the way on the back of the

have a taper fastened chuck which does not lend itself to such uses.

SUBSTITUTE WOODWORKER'S VISE

Have you ever admired the fancy Scandinavian-type woodworking benches? They have two or three wood vises and long rows of holes into which dogs can be inserted; large stock can be clamped between them and a dog in the movable jaw of one of the vises. If you do not make furniture or do other large-scale woodworking, it is difficult to justify giving the space to such a bench, to say nothing of the expense.

But you can improvise a similar setup on

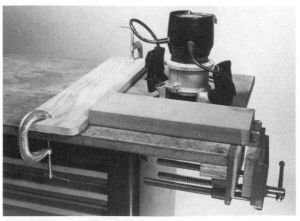

Board clamped to the bench top takes the place of bench-top dogs without requiring holes in the bench. The added wooden jaw on the small woodworker's vise has three holes to take one or two dogs, as needed. Here it holds a short piece of 2 x 6 clear heart redwood in preparation for some freehand router work.

A second board with two different sized V-notches holds odd-shaped items such as this old aluminum cam-type trailer jack.

SOFT JAWS

An easy-to-make pair of auxiliary "soft" jaws slipped into a machinist's vise makes it possible to hold wood, plastic, and delicate metal parts without marring. The two jaws can be cut out of plywood or solid hardwood. If a particularly smooth surface is desired, make them from a plastic laminate sink cutout.

As shown in the accompanying illustration, each jaw has a U-shaped cutout in the bottom to fit the slide. Make these cutouts first and get a nice fit to the slide, position the jaws in the vise, and then mark them for the final cuts. They should not be any narrower or lower than the regular jaws and you may want to make them about ⅛" higher and ⅛" wider on each side. When not in use, they can be stored in a drawer or hung up.

Soft jaws for holding easily damaged items, such as threaded bolts, screws, and other ma-

bench. I just clamp one in position on the bench. It holds one end of the item to be worked on; one or both dogs in the movable vise jaw hold the other. One board has straight sides and holds pieces such as the square end of a board being worked upon. The second board has three different sized angles cut into it, any one of which works for curved or angled pieces. Of course, additional cutouts can be made for a particular job. If the clamp at the end of the board which lines up with the vise interferes with work to be done, as when routing a ¾" board, I put it in back of the board. That way it acts only as a stop and does not protrude above the board. The other clamp is quite adequate to hold the 1 x 6 down.

Mounts for the end boards are simple enough. Two #10 roundhead machine screws are each locked to the metal back of the bench between two nuts, allowing the heads to protrude out about an inch. I drilled two ½" holes, one in each end of the boards so that they can be slipped over the screw heads. That way, no matter which way I happen to pick up a board, I just slip it onto the supporting screw. As my old dormitory roommate used to say, "I'm not lazy, I'm just conservative."

Although this vise setup was originally developed to hold an occasional large or awkward woodworking part, I find that I use it more and more. It is great for all sorts of projects that do not fit in a vise and would otherwise slide around on the bench while being worked on.

A pair of woodworking jaws for a machinist's vise are easily cut from a scrap of ¾" plywood.

chine parts, can be fashioned from soft aluminum, copper, lead, or plastic sheets. Heavy paperboard, fiberboard, leather, and even discarded firehose also works. The metal soft jaws are shaped and bent at the top and ends so that they will hang in place on the vise jaws. Other materials can be secured with double-stick tape, or just held against the work until the vise is tightened.

A SIMPLE VISE IMPROVEMENT

Trying to hold a thin piece of metal, such as a round washer, horizontally in a vise can be difficult, particularly in a drill press vise where it must be held squarely, as well as securely. But it's possible to modify your vise to solve this problem. The idea is to insert holding pins in the top of the vise jaws. That way the part is held firmly. Since it rests flat on the top of the jaws, it is also perpendicular to the drill press spindle.

Pins cut from ³⁄₁₆″ gas welding rod are a good size, although if your vise is large, you may want to use ¼″ pins. Drill rod or the shanks of small bolts (with the head and threads cut off) also work well. Drill at least two holes in each jaw. If you provide three or more holes in each

Hold small items firmly in a drill press vise by drilling a few holes in the top of the jaws. Insert short holding pins cut from ³⁄₁₆″ welding rod into the holes as needed. Odd-shaped items can often be held in place with just three pins.

jaw, space them differently. The two closest pair will hold a small washer or other item, the wider spaced pair, a larger item, and the two outside pairs an even bigger part. Regardless of how many pairs of holes you make, you only need four pins to hold almost anything securely.

WOOD LATHE TOOLS FROM OLD FILES

Before throwing away worn-out files, consider converting them into tools for your wood lathe. Flat tiles, triangular files, half rounds, rat-tails, and other shapes make high-quality tools; you can create a complete set or augment the one you already have.

In their original condition, files are too hard and brittle to use with a wood lathe and could even be dangerous if they were to snap after accidentally digging into the work. Anneal them before grinding by heating them to a red heat and allowing them to cool as slowly as possible.

Heat the files in a forge, with a welding torch, a Mapp gas torch, or for small- to medium-sized files, with a propane torch (its heat output is marginal for large files). Heating can also be done over barbecue charcoal or even in the embers of a wood fire. In this case, just leave the files in the ashes overnight to cool slowly.

After annealing, grind the files to the desired shapes on a bench grinder following the usual patterns (if necessary, refresh your memory by looking at a friend's set or at a set in a store or tool catalog).

Skews and square end chisels can be made from flat files, round-end chisels from half-round files, triangular points from triangular files, and small round-end tools from rat-tail files (grind off the top half for an inch or so back from the tip before shaping the end). Flat files can also be ground to make side-cutting bowl chisels for easier turning of the interior of bowls. Not included in a normal set of tools, these are usually sold separately and can be quite expensive. They are sharpened on the end and on the left side. Two sizes of rounded ends and one straight sided one for making straight-sided interiors and flat bottoms are usually sufficient.

To make any of the chisels, start by grinding off the teeth of the file for a couple of inches back from the end on the top side. For a skew, clean off the teeth on both sides, because either may be used as the "top," depending on the direction of the cut. Then carefully grind the end to the desired shape and to a sharp edge. After grinding, hone the cutting edge with a sharpening stone.

Reharden the tool by heating about an inch or so of the end to a light cherry-red color (as seen in a semidark room). To prevent overheating and burning of the tip, do not direct the heat onto the very end of the tool. Apply it back a bit and let it run out to the tip. In the case of a side-cutting bowl chisel, be sure to include the entire cutting edge. Immediately quench the tool endwise in a container of cold water, moving it around and up and down until it cools. This end is now quite hard again, much as it was before annealing, and must now be tempered to an intermediate hardness.

Start the tempering process by polishing the end of the tool with an oilstone, a fine belt on a sander grinder, or whatever you normally use for sharpening. If you have a buffing wheel and

Apple-shaped bowl was turned from a short piece of Douglas fir 4 x 4 (not the world's greatest turning material) with file-made tools.

compound, use it; the nearer to a mirror finish you have on the tool the easier it will be to see the tempering colors. Heat the tool again, this time very slowly. Apply heat well back from the tip. Watch closely and you will see the tempering colors (oxidation) start to move out from the heat toward the tip. The colors start with a very light yellow, then change to a light straw, followed by a darker straw and next a bronze. When the bronze color reaches the cutting edge of the tool, immediately plunge it into cold water. This should give about the right hardness for a wood chisel. Had you continued to heat the tool, the colors would have advanced through purple, dark blue and light blue, with the edge getting progressively softer. Quenching earlier in the light to dark straw range would have produced a harder edge for a metal-cutting tool such as a cold chisel.

This is, of course, only a quick overview of the subject of hardening and tempering of steel. You can find out much more about this fascinating subject by visiting your local library.

Give the chisel a final sharpening, secure a sturdy handle to the tang, and it is ready for use.

Be sure to provide a handle! When working on a

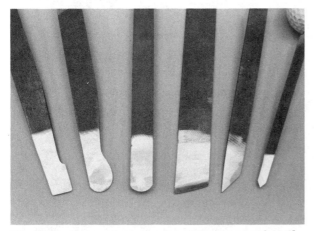

Tired files, properly ground and heat-treated, make good wood lathe tools, either for special jobs or for an inexpensive full set. From left to right are: two side-cutting bowl hollowing chisels, a round nose tool, a skew, a parting tool, and a small spear point.

lathe, it is quite possible that your chisel may at some point dig into the rotating stock and kick back at you. If you *are holding it* by the bare tang, this could result in a serious injury.

FILE HANDLES FROM GOLF BALLS

Having handles on all your files makes good sense for safety reasons, as well as for comfortable and efficient use. But a visit to the hardware store may dampen your enthusiasm for getting those handles. Some now sell for over $5! There is a simple and inexpensive solution though: golfballs. Try them! They work great! Although the shape is unorthodox, they work well on small and large files. Used golf balls that are in good shape are sold at garage sales, flea markets, or golf driving ranges, sometimes for as little as six for a dollar.

If you have a drill press with a center hole in the table, align the hole directly below the spindle and rest the ball in it for drilling. With an electric hand drill, you must be careful to keep the hole as axially centered as possible. For a tang that has very little taper, as on a small triangular file, drill a hole the diameter of the small end of the tang about three-quarters of the way through the ball. For files with a greater taper, such as large flat files, drill a small hole, as above. Then drill a larger hole proportional to the size of the taper about one-third of the way through the ball.

When drilling, wear goggles. If the ball happens to have a pressurized liquid center, as some do, the liquid can spray into your eyes when the center is penetrated. Avoid balls with "steel center" stamped on their cover. The metal center is apparently quite thin and tends to either divert the drill to one side or to catch on it.

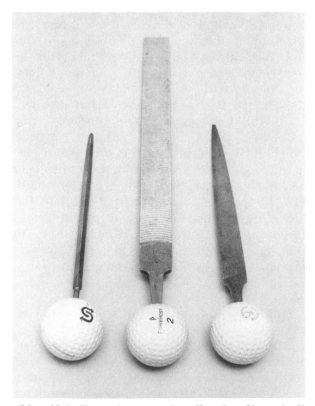

Old golf balls make great handles for files of all shapes and sizes (lathe tools too).

The table hole in many drill presses provides a ready-made drilling fixture for golf ball handles.

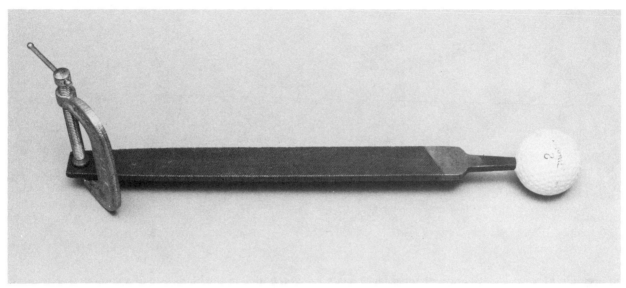

A 2″ C-clamp doubles as a second handle for heavy work with a large file.

With the hole drilled, drive the ball onto the file tang. If the hole is of a reasonable size, you will find that it holds quite well with no tendency to loosen. I was rather skeptical when these handles were first suggested to me many years ago, but I tried them, became an instant fan, and now have over a dozen on files of various sizes.

When a job requires heavy filing, a C-clamp of convenient size secured to the far end of the file provides a useful second handle.

PITCH ATTACHMENT FOR A LEVEL

An adjustable tip of wood or metal attached to one end of a carpenter's level makes a perfect tool to accurately pitch sewer or drain lines, to lay out patio floors so that they shed rain, or for any other job where a constant pitch is needed. With the usual 2-foot-long level, set the offset at twice the desired pitch per foot. Make an appropriate correction for a longer or shorter level.

For a onetime job, such as laying a drain line with a pitch of ¼″ per foot, the attachment need

Wood block taped to the end of a level lays out any of four different pitch angles from ⅛″ to ⅜″ per foot. Here, it's set for a slope of ³⁄₁₆″ per foot.

not be adjustable. A small piece of scrap wood notched so that it has a ½″ protrusion on one end can be taped to one end of a 2-foot level with a bit of electrician's tape. If you do this type of work regularly, up to four different lugs for different pitches may be cut into a scrap of wood, preferably hardwood. Just tape the wood

Shopmade aluminum attachment for a level has a spring dog, allowing quick change to any of several different pitch angles from ¹⁄₁₆″ to ¾″ per foot.

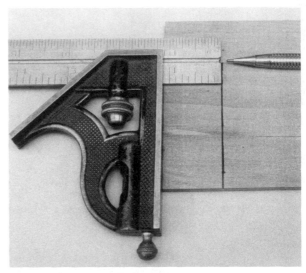

Notch filed in the blade end of a combination square keeps the pencil "in step" when marking a line and centers the line on the end of the scale.

with the appropriate notch in position as required. An even more easily adjusted pitch attachment can be made from a couple of small pieces of aluminum. It is fastened to the end of the level with small screws.

COMBINATION SQUARE IMPROVEMENT

Many of us mark measurements on stock by holding a pencil at the end of the blade on a combination square. Filing a tiny triangular notch at each end (at the groove) solves two problems. It keeps the pencil traveling evenly with the square as it is moved along the work and, if cut to one-half the diameter of the pencil lead normally used, eliminates the need to "fudge" the measurement to allow for the pencil line being beyond the end of the scale. If you use your square for marking metal rather than wood, notch it just deep enough to make the tip of the scriber mark even with the end of the scale.

Before you start hunting for your 3-corner file, check the scale on your square. Some of the newer ones already have this notch built in!

SHOPMADE LONG DRILLS

Longer than normal drills are often handy, either to drill an extra deep hole or to get into an awkward corner or pocket where there is just not enough room for the drill chuck or the drill body. Although extra long twist drills are available, they are quite expensive and are often difficult to find in any but the largest hardware stores, and then only in a few of the most common sizes.

Homemade drills for occasional work are easy to make. They do a good job of getting into difficult places. They also solve the problem of boring deep holes in wood, although they work slowly. That is because they lack flutes for chip channels; the drill must be backed out after about every ½″ of travel and the chips blown out or pulled out with a hooked wire.

To make a long drill, obtain a straight piece of wire or rod slightly smaller in diameter than the desired hole. Gas welding rod is great for this purpose as it comes in several sizes and is quite straight. Most any heavy wire works, including coat hanger wire and music (piano) wire, which is used in model making and is available at a hobby shop.

The first step in making your drill is to flatten the end of the wire with a hammer and an anvil of some sort (any heavy flat piece of steel). To do this, heat an inch or so of the wire to a cherry red. Any heat source will do, including a gas burner on a kitchen range. Soft, small diameter wire can be flattened without heat, but the larger sizes require it. With hard wire such as music wire and no heat, you will probably dent the anvil rather than flattening the wire! Flatten it carefully, hammering first on one side and then on the other so that it remains straight and the extra width extends equally from each side of the original thickness of the wire.

Next, with a fine-grit wheel, grind each side carefully to the exact width of the hole required. Grind a point on it as shown, providing two sharp edges of equal length and angled to cut in the direction of rotation. The drill is now ready for making holes in wood or plastic.

For drilling metal, you must harden the drill. If you made it from music wire, you can re-harden and temper it by the method described earlier for making lathe tools from old files. Since the drill will cut metal rather than wood, just heat it to a light straw color when tempering it.

If you made the drill from mild steel such as

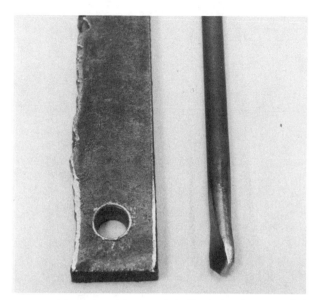

Even mild steel welding rod drills through ¼″ steel if the bit is case-hardened after grinding to shape.

welding rod or coat hanger wire, it cannot be hardened with heat alone. But it can be case hardened (after sharpening) by heating it to a red heat, dipping it in a hardening powder (Ka-senit is one brand), reheating, and quenching in cold water. When properly done, this will harden it enough for drilling soft metal, such as aluminum, copper, brass, and even mild steel. If you resharpen the drill, you will no doubt grind through the very thin hard shell; so you have to case harden it again. This takes only a minute or two if a torch or other heat source is available.

One of these drills is certainly no match for a commercial high-speed steel drill, especially when drilling in steel, but if the proper drill is not available it often can do the job for you. Turn it much more slowly than you would a commercial drill and use heavy pressure.

A one-pound can of case-hardening powder comes in handy if you sometimes make tools or other items from mild steel; the hardening helps hold an edge or prevent wear. (Light touch-up with an oilstone can usually be done on an edge without requiring rehardening.) Case-hardening powder is not commonly stocked, but your hardware store should be able to order it for you. Also, you can get it through some industrial tool catalogs.

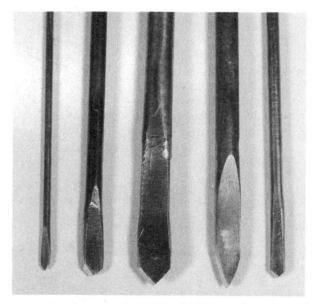

These five homemade drills of different lengths and diameters were all made to drill holes in otherwise inaccessible spots.

GRINDING A LONG DRILL

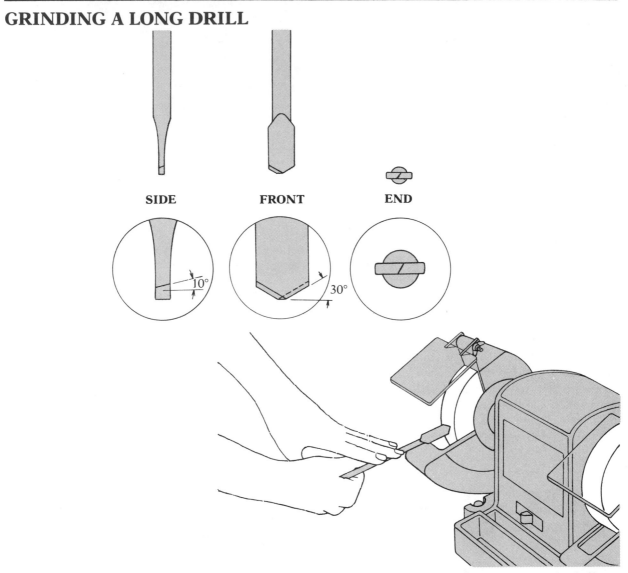

SIDE   FRONT   END

Points of homemade drills are ground to the approx-imate angles shown. Hold the shank of the drill at a 30-degree angle to the left of the wheel and about 10 degrees down. Grind one lip; then rotate the drill 180 degrees and grind the second lip with the shank held in the same relative position.

MODIFYING TAPER SHANK DRILLS

Sometimes you may find large drill bits with a Morse taper shank for sale. They mount in the tailstock of a lathe or directly in the spindle of a heavy-duty drill press, rather than in a chuck.

Since few people have a tool that accepts them, they often sell very reasonably, even in larger sizes.

If you have a small lathe, you may be able to use them. Of course, if they happen to fit the tailstock taper of your lathe, you're home free. Most often though, their taper is different. Since the tapered shank is usually soft, the drill can be chucked in the lathe and its shank easily turned down to a size that fits your tailstock or drill press chuck, a la Silver & Deming drills.

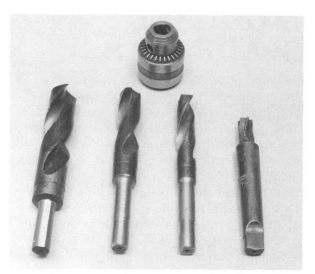

Look carefully at the shank; if it is not marked H.S., the drill is probably an old carbon steel "blacksmith" drill and must be turned very slowly, but using heavy pressure when drilling, to avoid burning the edge and losing its hardness.

Three large drills, turned down in a lathe to fit the ½″ chuck shown, previously had Morse taper shanks similar to the milling cutter at the right.

PIPE DRILL

When it is necessary to mount a large diameter pipe in a post or other wooden item, finding a drill to make the hole can be a real problem. One solution, which worked very well for a hole to fit a 2″ pipe, was to use a short section of the pipe itself for a drill. A half dozen or so large teeth were marked out on one end and cut out with a cutting torch. Each one was then filed to

HOMEMADE PIPE DRILL

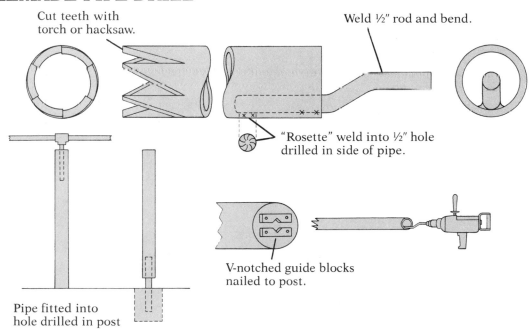

Cut teeth with torch or hacksaw.

Weld ½″ rod and bend.

"Rosette" weld into ½″ hole drilled in side of pipe.

V-notched guide blocks nailed to post.

Pipe fitted into hole drilled in post

Keeping a pole or post above ground level prevents decay. One way to do this is to mount it on a metal pipe, which is either driven into the ground or set in concrete. Pipe can also be used in the top of a post to mount a pipe arbor, trellis, or clothesline. Connecting the wood and pipe is a problem though. Expansion bits do not cut well on end-grain and other bits are often not available in large enough sizes.

a sharp edge, the points alternating to the inside and the outside much the way teeth do on a handsaw. Each tooth was given a bit of "set" with a hammer, again alternately in and out. A short length of ½"-diameter, round steel rod was given an offset bend equal to half the diameter of the pipe. One end of this was welded into the outer end of the pipe and the other end then chucked in a heavy-duty, slow-speed ½" drill. Since the pipe had no point or other pilot, a V-shaped notch was cut in each of two scraps of wood and these were tacked to the work to guide the drill while starting. The hole was continued some 10" deep and provided a nicely fitting socket for the pipe. Note that this type of drill does not make a full hole, but rather a deep circular groove with a round plug of wood in the center. It cannot be used where a full open hole is needed.

MODIFIED SPADE BITS

You can modify extra spade wood bits for different needs. The edges can be ground or filed down for drilling tapered holes (for candlesticks), stepped holes, or holes with a rounded bottom. If you need to bore a flat-bottomed hole nearly through a workpiece without the pilot breaking through, grind down the pilot to a fraction of its original width and length. This is great for boring holes on the underside of a wooden base that are to be poured full of lead for stability.

You can also make large spade bits by grinding the proper shape on a short strip of steel and riveting or welding it securely onto a shank to fit your drill chuck. The blade fits in a slot cut into the end of the shank.

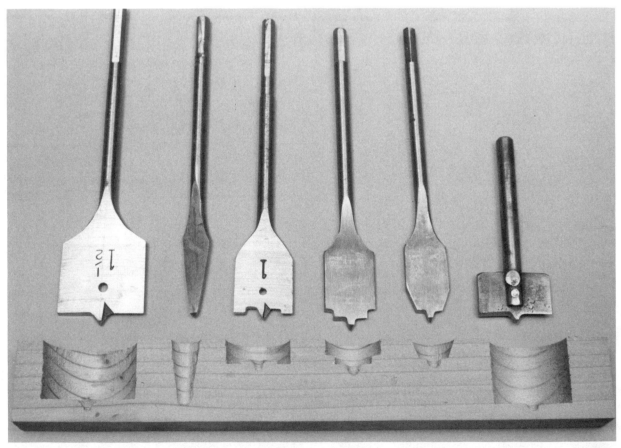

Spade bits modified with a grinder can cut various shaped holes as shown in the half section below the bits. The one at the far right was shopmade when no large bit was available.

MODIFYING AUGER BITS FOR POWER

The shank of an auger bit can be turned or carefully freehand ground, so that the end part of the taper is rounded off to fit in a drill chuck. Leave a bit of the squared portion, so that the bit can still be used in a brace. Of course, if you do not have a brace, you can go ahead and round off the entire tapered portion of the shank. You may also want to grind off part of the threads on the tip of the bit, so that they do not dig the bit into the wood too aggressively under power.

With this modification you can use a power drill and long electrician's or ship's augers to bore deep holes more easily than by hand.

TEMPORARY CHUCK KEY

An oft-reported old kink, this one is handy if you have lost your drill chuck key and need the drill before you have gotten a replacement. Put the shank end of a suitably sized drill into one of the key's pilot holes in the side of the chuck. It serves as a fulcrum for a screwdriver with a tip that just fits between the teeth on the chuck gear. Use the screwdriver as a lever to engage and turn the chuck gear.

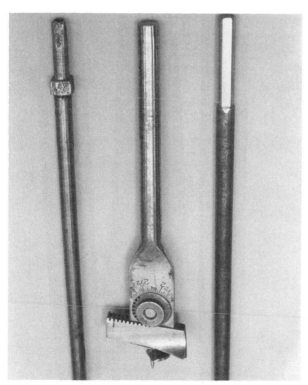

The auger bit shank at left has been cut down so that it can be turned either manually by a brace or by an electric drill. The other two are modified for full-time power drilling. To prevent grabbing, the threads on the pilot of the expansion bit are ground off to a three-cornered point.

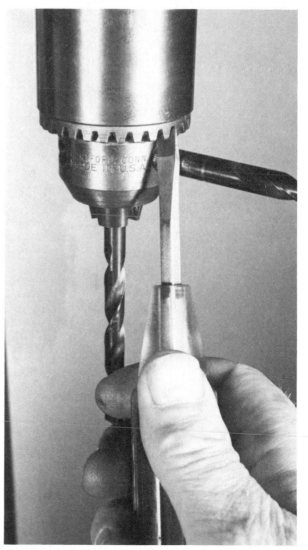

Shank of a drill bit provides a fulcrum for the screwdriver being used to loosen the chuck.

DRILL DEPTH-MARKER FLAG

When you put masking, or electrical, tape, on a drill bit as a depth gage, don't roll the end tight to the drill, but leave a half inch or so free. When the loose end starts to wipe away chips from the surface of the work, you know you are getting close to the desired depth.

Sighting with any small cube such as this child's block helps keep a hand-held drill square to the surface. This trick comes in handy when you are working away from the shop where other guides are normally available.

Flag end of the masking tape marker sweeps away chips as it approaches the desired depth.

SMALL BENCH ANVIL

A floor flange, a short pipe nipple, and a pipe cap can be screwed together to form a handy small bench anvil. File down the top of the cap in order to make a smooth surface; better yet, face it in a lathe if one is available. Caution: the

SIMPLE DRILL GUIDE

A small wood or plastic cube, or even a toy block from a child's play set, makes a good "Poor Man's Drill Guide" for drilling holes perpendicular to a surface without a drill press. Place the block on the surface so that a corner is next to the desired hole. Sight it to line up the drill bit with the vertical corner in both directions.

Three common pipe fittings combine to make a small bench anvil which can be of any size pipe. These two are made from ¾″ and 1¼″ fittings. Height is determined by the length of the nipple.

top of a pipe cap is fairly thin; remove as little metal as possible so that you still have enough material to stand up to hammering.

This arrangement is fairly stable in itself. For even more stability, you can screw the floor flange to your bench. Better yet, attach it to a small square of plywood with a lug on the bottom and mount it in the Workmate.

SURFACE GAGE SUBSTITUTE

A combination square, small C-clamp, and a marking instrument used as shown make a simple version of a machinist's surface gage. Set the height with the scale (end set flush with head) and then check at the point with another scale. For less critical work, the workbench surface makes an adequate base; for more accuracy use a ground surface such as a circular saw, drill press table, or a small square of heavy plate glass.

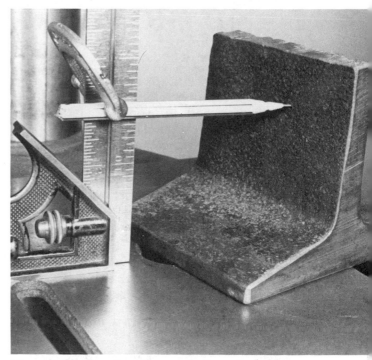

The makeshift surface gage easily lays out measurements on odd-shaped items.

Common shop items combine to make a substitute for a surface gage and surface plate.

HAND GRINDER MOUNT

Combine a corner brace and a pair of geared automotive-type hose clamps to mount a hand-held electric grinder in your vise, and you can keep both hands free to hold the work. Cut off part of one leg of the brace and position the clamps to avoid covering the cooling vents on the motor. The one shown has had additional strips welded onto one leg of the corner brace; it also serves as a toolpost grinder for light work in a metal lathe.

Bench grinder and an electric drill team up to "turn" a knob from the head of a small bolt.

Right-angle bracket plus a couple of geared hose clamps makes a mount to secure the little grinder in a vise.

SIMPLE LATHE SUBSTITUTE

In the absence of a lathe, use an electric drill and a grinding wheel to "turn" simple small parts. In the example shown, the hex head of a small bolt is being ground to a round knob. Turn the work in the opposite direction of the wheel rotation. If, as shown, it is easier to approach the wheel from the right side, work with a reversible drill and operate it in reverse.

FLEXIBLE SHAFTS

Flexible shafts are usually connected to a fractional hp motor and turn bits for freehand carving, grinding wheels, or other tools for shaping an item held in a clamp or vise.

They can also make one machine power an accessory on another; for example, a simple horizontal milling attachment for a metal lathe. The work is mounted in the lathe, which serves as a work holder, aided by the use of an indexing attachment. The flexible shaft is turned by the headstock of a Shopsmith, which has been moved into position for the job.

Conversely, for woodworking, the Shopsmith becomes the work-holding-and-locating jig, and it also has an indexing attachment. The flex shaft is driven by a chuck attached to the outboard end of the lathe spindle and operates a drill or router bit at the Shopsmith. In either case, a number of speeds are available. (Construction and use of the milling attachment and indexing attachments are covered in Chapters 10 and 14.)

Other combinations are possible, of course. One that comes to mind is to drive the flex shaft with a drill press chuck and use it with a wood lathe. Many wood lathes have a built-in indexing attachment. A two-piece wood jig with a V-groove sliding joint, fastened in place of the

Flexible shaft permits the woodworking tool to drive an end mill in an attachment on the metal lathe.

toolrest, would hold the flex shaft handpiece so that the bit can be advanced into the work for radial drilling. Details will have to be worked out to fit your lathe.

Take a good look around your shop and you will probably find some tools that you can occasionally team up with a flexible shaft.

WORK HOLDER FOR A FLAME-CUTTING GUIDE

A cutting torch provides an easy way to cut steel that is heavier than sheet-metal thickness. Done freehand, it can be pretty ragged. Even if you lay a bar along the cut as a guide, you will find it difficult or impossible to move the torch at an exactly even pace, and once again will wind up with a rough-edged cut.

The cutting guide pictured here solves this problem. In addition to providing a rolling guide for moving the torch in an absolutely straight line, a clockwork governor advances it along the cut at an even speed regardless of the pulling pressure exerted. The resulting cut is so smooth and straight that it looks as though it had been made with a saw rather than a torch.

Since the cutting guide is held to the work by two magnets, adjustable to several positions along the guide in increments of about 4", a problem can arise when making short cuts. For example, when crosscutting a piece of stock less than about 4" wide, only one magnet fits on the work and does not have enough strength to hold the guide solidly against the pull necessary to actuate the clockwork governor. If the work has any curvature to it and does not lie flat it can also create a problem with the magnetic mounts.

Friend Bill Hussman bought one of these machines after hearing my approving comments

Welded-up work holder for use with a flame-cutting guide securely holds small workpieces that cannot be held firmly by the cutting guide's magnet.

Before getting the geared cutting guide, friend Bill welded up this little guide to use with a two-wheel cutting-torch roller. A big help if your work doesn't justify the expensive geared guide.

on its work and shortly came up with a work holder that effectively solves these two problems. The magnets are fastened to his platform rather than directly to the work, and the work is clamped to the platform.

The work holder platform consists of two 18" long pieces of 1½" x ¾" x ⅛" channel stock welded to a half dozen, 24" lengths, of ¾" x ¾" x ⅛" angle. The angles are separated by different widths, as shown, so that most any sized piece can be conveniently clamped to them (clamping is not necessary with larger and heavier, pieces). The dimension between the channels is determined by the widest spread available to the magnets on the machine. With our small model, which will make cuts up to just over 2' long, the magnets at their widest are 22½" apart, so that a 24" overall width will center them on the channels.

The work holder can of course be made any desired length. Bill made his 18", a convenient size. I just happened to have a 38" length of 1½" channel, so mine ended up about 19" long. If you work with long pieces of stock and have space to store a bigger holder, you can make it as long as you want.

A couple of notes: The two outside angles are welded to the channel as shown, rather than turned around so that their sides are flush with the end of the channel, which might look a bit neater. Put together this way, they are easier to

fasten C-clamps to than if they were turned around. One convenient method of storing the work holder is to hang it on a couple of brackets welded to an end, or side, of your welding table. In use, the platform can be placed atop four fire bricks on your welding table. If this is not convenient, add legs. Never do any cutting, with or without a platform, or any other work with a cutting torch directly on a concrete floor. The intense heat turns any moisture in the concrete, which may appear to be bone dry, into steam and actually explodes small pieces out of the surface of the concrete!

PIPE VISE SUBSTITUTE

An ordinary vise without built-in pipe jaws is almost useless for holding pipe for cutting, threading, or for assembling fittings. For just occasional needs however, a pipe vise is expensive and also takes up valuable bench or floor space.

A good-sized pipe wrench, secured as shown to the end of a bench, makes a fair substitute. The bracket must allow the wrench to be inserted with the jaws facing either up or down to cover both tightening and loosening of fittings. When mounted at the right hand end of the

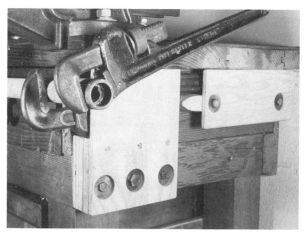

A large pipe wrench set in a pocket at the end of your bench provides a substitute for a pipe vise. Set up here to tighten a fitting, its handle rests above the tongue in the rear bracket.

To loosen a fitting, the wrench is turned jaws down and its handle goes below the rear tongue.

bench, the jaws must face up to install fittings on pipe, and will face down when removing them.

Make the bracket of such size as to hold your biggest pipe wrench in this way. When working with a long piece of pipe, clamp or otherwise fasten a small strip of wood to the far end of the bench as a support. Make it level with the improvised vise.

HOSE CLAMP PLIERS

The hose clamps shown are made out of a circle of spring steel wire and are simple, effective, and inexpensive. Made in various sizes the clamps are used in washing machines, other household appliances, and elsewhere. Attempting to put them on or take them off with an ordinary pair of pliers can be discouraging though. They tend to fly out of the jaws of the pliers while being maneuvered into place, and holding the necessary steady pressure on them with the pliers while attempting to maneuver the hose and clamp onto the pump inlet, a drain, or whatever can be difficult.

An extra pair of pliers, modified as shown, is a great help in using these clamps. Two grooves to fit the clamps are cut in the plier jaws, one lengthwise in the ends, and the other crossways just behind the jaws. Having two positions 90 degrees apart will come in handy to assemble work in awkward places.

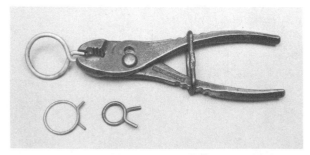

Old pair of pliers, slightly modified, eases work with spring hose clamps. Cut a groove in the end of the jaws, along with a cross groove where the first pair of teeth were. Add a few notches in the handles and a ring to hold the clamp expanded while it is slipped onto the hose.

If the jaws are not too hard, the grooves can be drilled or cut with a small round file. If they can't be cut with a file, there are several other solutions. The grooves can be cut with a small stone, such as a chain saw sharpening stone, in a high-speed grinder. Or a small, straight-sided carbide burr will do the job. If neither of these is available, anneal the pliers by heating them red hot, followed by slow cooling, as previously mentioned. After the grooves are cut they can be rehardened and tempered, although it is probably not necessary for this work. Several grooves should also be filed in each handle, and an appropriately sized rectangular ring welded up out of heavy wire. I made this one from 5/32" welding rod.

To use the pliers, you squeeze down on the clamp to open it enough to slip on the hose, then slide the ring down over the handles to a pair of grooves that hold them securely in position. This makes it much easier to maneuver the hose and hose clamp simultaneously into place, without also having to maintain a constant pressure on the handles.

¼"-DRIVE SPEEDER HANDLE

If you don't already have a speeder handle for your ¼"-drive socket set (they're not as common as the larger sizes, but just as handy), you can easily make one by bending up a handle of ¼"-diameter gas welding rod. It is strong enough for this work, although it would probably not take the torque of driving larger sockets. The one shown swings in a 6½" circle and rapidly spins small nuts onto studs or cap screws into tapped holes, as when attaching an oil pan to the bottom of a crankcase.

Start with a short ¼"-drive socket extension with the female end cut off. End drill it for about an inch, insert the end of the shaft, and braze the joint. If the extension itself is too small in diameter to drill a ¼" hole in, make a simple jig to line it up with the shaft and butt weld it. (Either way, be sure to use a wet rag on the end as a heat sink to protect its temper and the temper of the little spring behind the lock-

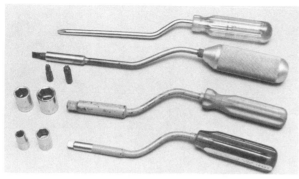

Quartet of wrist twist speed handles. A factory-made Phillips screwdriver (top) is followed by three home-made models: a replaceable hex bit screwdriver, a ⅜" socket-wrench speeder, and a ¼" socket speeder. All three have shanks of ¼" welding rod brazed into cut-off extensions with an appropriate end. One handle is turned and knurled aluminum; the other two are old screwdriver handles modified to spin.

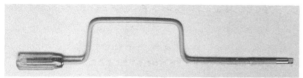

This ¼"-drive socket speeder is made from the omnipresent ¼" welding rod that has been welded to a cutoff socket extension at one end and fitted with a spinning handle at the other.

ing ball.) Install a free-spinning handle on the other end.

To prevent it from rusting in years to come, you may want to get out your spray can of tool gray paint (or even a can of gray automotive primer). Mask off both the working end and the handle, give it a couple of quick swooshes with the spray can, and you've finished another great little shop-made tool.

LEAD FACES FOR SOFT HAMMER

Old hammers of the type shown have soft faces on each end. The hammer head consists of two

metal parts that clamp down on plug-shaped chunks of soft material, such as rolled up rawhide, copper, lead, or plastic. The hammers are sometimes found in secondhand stores, flea markets, garage sales, or perhaps in your own shop; often the faces have deteriorated to the point where the hammer is useless and no replacements are available.

You can make replacements, though. Measure the head to determine the diameter of the replacement required and then drill several holes of this size in a scrap of ¾" board or plywood. If you want the faces a little heavier, tack together a couple of ½" pieces of plywood, ½" and ¾", or even two ¾" pieces. For the hammer shown, an adjustable hole saw provided the necessary 1⅞" hole. Other size holes can be made with fixed hole saws, large spade bits (including shop-made ones), fly cutters, adjustable auger bits, or even by carefully cutting them out with a sabre saw or jig saw.

A couple of freshly "baked" lead biscuits are ready to provide new faces for this old persuader. Loosening the eight-sided nut at the base of the handle will separate the halves of the hammer head. This allows the old faces to be removed and new ones inserted, after which the nut is retightened. The battered old faces go into a scrap lead bin for later reincarnation.

Tack your mold onto a plywood base, melt some lead, and proceed to pour some biscuits. Let them cool, tip over the mold, drop the faces out, and you've not only got a pair of new faces for your hammer, you've got some spares.

Lead melts at a low enough temperature that while it may scorch your wooden mold slightly, it normally will not set it afire. Just to be safe however, be sure to do your pouring outside in a place where there are no combustible materials, or on a non-combustible floor such as concrete. If you have the means to melt other materials such as copper or aluminum, you'll need a more fire-resistant mold, such as holes drilled in a steel block.

ANVIL OR GRINDER STAND

An old automobile or truck rim, which you can get cheaply at an auto wrecking yard, tire shop, yard sale, or perhaps even from your own garage, can become a sturdy base of an anvil or grinder.

For the stand shown, a 15″ length of 3″ (3½″ OD) pipe from a scrap metal yard serves as an upright. Vary it's length according to the size of your rim, anvil, and desired working height. The bottom is welded to the center of the rim and the top to a piece of ¼″ plate, flame-cut to the shape of the base of the anvil. The plate is fastened to the anvil with four bolts seated in holes drilled and tapped in the bottom of the anvil.

A piece of ½″ plywood cut to the same shape as the plate and placed between the base of the anvil and the plate provides a certain amount of "give" to the assembly. The rim itself also provides some resiliency. Many old-time blacksmiths insist on mounting their anvils on a large wooden block rather than on a rigid steel mounting, but this one seems to work out quite well.

An excellent grinder stand can be built in the same fashion. The one shown is made from a length of 2″ pipe and has three short pieces of 1¼″ angle for its base. Large round washers are welded to the ends of the feet and some rubber circles cut from thick rubber are glued to them to dampen vibration.

Old auto wheel welded to a piece of pipe makes a great stand for an anvil or a bench grinder.

An old auto rim would have worked every bit as well. Made either way, this stand is every bit as sturdy as a commercially made stand. Even if you have to pay for the welding, you can probably save half the purchase price of an expensive stand if you scrounge up the materials and cut them to size.

CUT-OFF SQUARE FOR AN ELECTRIC SAW

A portable electric saw is great for cutting large sheets of plywood down to manageable size or for crosscutting long boards that would be difficult to handle on a table saw. For the later work however, cutting them off square presents some problems. You can hold a square against the edge of the board as a guide, but you must allow for the distance from the desired cut to the side of the saw's base, which is what rides

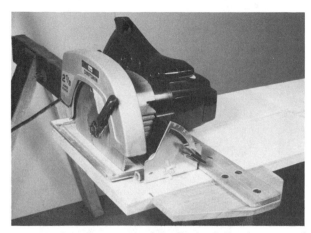

Shopmade square, one end of which has been sized by the saw itself, lets you align the square directly on your mark on the board. The square then guides the saw with no need to allow for guide setback.

against the end of the square. While on some saws this distance is an easy-to-remember number, such as an even 4 inches, all too often it turns out to be something like 4²¹⁄₃₂″, which requires either a pencil and paper or some mental gymnastics to figure out where to mark the board and place the square.

A custom-made wooden square solves this problem and speeds up sawing jobs. The square shown is made out of two pieces of hardwood. The shank is long enough to cover most any desired crosscut (here it is about 22″ long, which gives a working length of 18″). It is 2″ wide and must be thin enough to clear the motor housing when the edge of the saw base is placed against it.

Make the right side of the head of the square a little longer than the distance from the left edge of the saw's base to the blade. Align the head and the shank of the square very carefully with a square of known accuracy. Clamp the two parts together and drill pilot and clearance holes for three short, large diameter, flathead woodscrews. Countersink the holes. Glue and screw the head and shank together, double-checking their squareness against your square and making any necessary small correction before the glue sets.

After the glue has thoroughly hardened, use your left hand to hold the head of your square against the edge of a board near the end (on your right). Place the left side of the saw base against the right side of the square's shank and cut off the board, continuing the cut on through the right side of the head of the square. This permanently adapts your square to the size of your saw base.

Now, to cut a board square measure off and mark the correct length on the far side of the board as shown, align the right end of the square exactly on the mark, hold the square in position, and zip off the board.

Note that the mark is always measured from your left as you face the board. If you want to measure from the right-hand end of the board, you have to add in the width of the saw kerf before making your mark. Determine this by cutting part way through a scrap of wood and measuring the kerf. It will usually be about ³⁄₃₂″ to ¹⁄₈″ wide, possibly a tiny bit more for a carbide-tipped blade. Since a portable saw is most often used for rough carpentry rather than finish work, you can usually just eyeball the amount to allow for the kerf. That will be close enough for all practical purposes.

ADAPTER INCREASES DRILL UTILITY

Accessories intended for one tool often work with another if you make a simple adapter. The accessories shown are made in various models

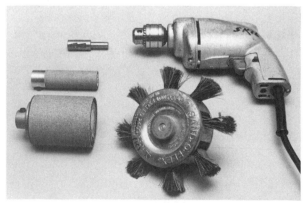

Simple adapter allows you to chuck all these tools, which were made to fasten on a ⅝″ shaft, in an electric drill.

to fit different power tools. They are a flap-wheel sander and two sanding drums that use economical strips cut from standard-sized sheets, rather than expensive ready-made sleeves. These have ⅝″ bores, to fit the spindle of a Shopsmith. The adapter shown is a short piece of ⅝″ shafting with one end turned down to fit in a ⅜″ drill chuck. Flats are milled or filed on the ⅝″ diameter to accept the setscrews provided to secure these items to the Shopsmith's spindle, and three flats are made on the cut-down shank to prevent slipping in the drill chuck.

With the adapter, you can use these sanders freehand in an electric drill. This is an item worth having specially made up by a small machine shop even if you do not have a lathe.

TWO SIMPLE TAMPERS

These two tampers are useful for compacting jobs from setting a post to patching a driveway.

Outside jobs sometimes involve tamping down loose or freshly dug earth. Tamping usually falls in one of two categories: tamping in a confined area, as around a post being set in the ground for a fence of mailbox; or tamping larger areas to compact loose dirt as a base for a walk, patio slab, or driveway.

Here are a couple of tampers you can make from readily available materials. The first tamper is for confined areas. Find a convenient length of steel pipe with one threaded end, and simply screw on a pipe cap. The tamper shown is made of 1½″ pipe, although 1¼″ or even 1″ works nearly as well. (If you put a cap on 2″ pipe it becomes a little large for most post-hole tamping.) Here the available piece of pipe was too short; so a wooden handle was rough

rounded to a drive fit and then taped for a smoother grip.

The large area tamper is made from a cut-off scrap from a large timber. This one is a piece of 4 x 8, 12″ long. (Other sizes, such as two or three pieces of 2 x 8 or four pieces of 2 x 4 could be fastened together to do the job.) Screw two 1 x 3 handles, cut to a convenient length, to the sides.

For compacting soft dirt use it "barefoot," but rock or gravel soon deforms the end and leaves an uneven finish on the compacted surface. A scrap of sheet steel (16-gage here), cut to fit and fastened by screws in lugs bent up on the narrow sides, solves this problem nicely.

3
WORKSHOP PLANNING AND STORAGE

The best time to provide for shop storage is when you are planning a new shop or are about to remodel your old one. Most of the projects contained in this chapter can be added to an existing shop, but some of them will be easier to build and will work out better if given consideration during the planning stage.

If you are planning a new or remodeled shop, keep them in mind as you read this chapter and consider integrating any of these ideas that will fit your situation.

EXTRA GARAGE DOOR

If your shop is separate from the garage, you may want to put in a single-car overhead garage door. You will need a driveway leading up to it, but there are several advantages to having a large doorway to your shop. For one, you can pull a car or truck into the shop for tune-up or repair work, eliminating the need to run back and forth between the shop and the garage for different tools. A big door provides for easy delivery of lumber, steel, or other items directly into the shop. Also, you can open up your shop for large projects, allowing some of the work or assembly to be done outside. This keeps the shop area from being overwhelmed by a large project and allows more room for working without continually stepping on, over, or around the project. Then at the end of the day the project can be moved back into the shop.

If your shop is in the garage, you could add a single garage door in the back side of the garage. (Build it with the correct size header and comply with all local building codes.) While this may sound a bit unusual, it can work out very well. With it, you can work on projects in the backyard instead of in the driveway. It provides for direct access to the backyard for storage of lumber and supplies that you do not want in the driveway and that would otherwise be difficult to transport through or around the garage.

Single overhead garage door in one wall of the shop lets you pull in a car or truck for servicing. The door is also a great help when you bring in such large items as full sheets of plywood or heavy power tools.

This big door between Bill Hussman's garage and workshop can be kept closed in the winter to avoid heating both rooms when he is working in just one.

Opening the overhead door allows easy flow of materials or work between the two rooms. Bill got the old engine hoist at a bargain price.

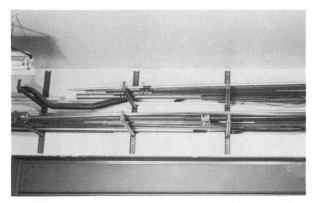

Space over the shop side of the garage door provides storage for pipe, tubing, and other long items. The brackets were welded up from 16″ lengths of ¾″ pipe and 2′ lengths of 1½″ channel iron, each held to the wall with three ⅜″ lag screws into the header. A 2″ riser of ³⁄₁₆″ x ¾″ flat stock was welded to the end of each pipe section to keep the stuff in place.

The same friend who originated this last idea was so pleased with it that he put one in the back of his new garage when he moved to a new home.

Some years later he added a large shop directly behind the garage, so that the back wall of the garage became an interior wall. In doing so, he left the garage door in place. While the arrangement is unusual, my friend can open up the entire area of the garage and shop when advantageous and can easily move large power tools or a bulky roller tool cabinet between the two rooms. In winter, he can close the large door and heat only one space anytime his work is pretty much confined to a single area.

As always, there is a trade-off to be considered. If you install a garage door in your shop, you lose valuable wall space that would otherwise support shelves, a pegboard, or cabinets.

This corner of the shop is the metal-working area; beginning at left with the drill press, next the bandsaw-hacksaw, then the 8″ metal lathe.

Behind the ¾ hp grinder a pegboard holds a mixture of tools, some antiques, others modern. The old tools have been derusted, repaired, and sharpened so that they are all quite useable. The island bench has space behind it for access to the grinder and an air compressor. To the right is the beginning of the main workbench and handwork area.

Many of the old tools mixed in with new on this panel are occasionally put to use, such as the deep-framed hacksaw at left, the 24″ pair of dividers, or the old wood plane, which pulls a beautiful shaving. Other less common tools serve as great "guess what" items for shop visitors.

At the end of the workbench there's a husky vise, behind is a pegboard panel holding the most used hand tools. At right, another mixture of old and modern tools hang above a work/storage area for automotive service. The anvil and the Workmate are easily moved to allow the nose of a vehicle to enter.

At left, the arc welder, hydraulic press, oxyacetylene welder, welding table, and a floor jack. All have wheels and are easily moved as needed. A dumb-waiter-type firewood hoist (see Chapter 13) is in the corner just to the right of the hall; at right, the Shop-smith stored under a storage cabinet.

ELECTRICAL UPGRADE

During any shop remodeling, be sure to include the electrical supply in your planning. This is the ideal time to add a higher amperage supply line, a larger junction box, and to add circuits to provide more outlets. Plan for as many duplex receptacles that you think you will ever need, add about 50% more, and within a few years you will probably wish you had doubled them.

While you are working with the electrical supply, think about your shop lighting. If you don't already have them, fluorescent overhead lights are hard to beat for general lighting. Put in plenty of tubes, but don't put them all on one switch. Depending on your shop layout, break it down to two, three, or more areas, each on a separate switch and gang mounted at the entrance door. This way, if you are working at the bench, you can have only that area well lit; if you are occupied at the woodworking machinery, metal lathe, or drill press, you can turn on the lights for them. If a project has you perambulating all over the shop, you can turn them all on.

If you have a second entrance to the shop, put a central segment of the lights on a 3-way switch to this door as well. These options provide you with good lighting throughout the shop without wasting electricity during the times that you are working steadily in just one area.

Now could also be a good time to add those useful 220-volt circuits mentioned in Chapter 1.

HANGING WALL CABINETS

Hanging wall cabinets provide storage areas above large tools pushed up against a wall. Since the cabinets project out over the machine stored below, the contents are easier to get at than if they were hung on a pegboard. In my shop I have two such cabinets, one just above the Shopsmith storage spot and the other above my welding table and arc welder.

The open-face cabinets are made from ¾" Douglas Fir A-C plywood with ¼" plywood for the back. Plan carefully, considering the wall space available and the size of the items that you will be storing against the 4' x 8' dimensions of the plywood sheet; you want to use the sheet to the greatest advantage.

A single sheet, for example, can be cut into two 8' strips, each 12⅛" wide, to be used for top and bottom pieces, as well as sides if the cabinet is to be of moderate size. (My larger cabinet required two sheets.) The rest of the sheet can be cut into two strips each 11¹¹⁄₁₆" wide for shelves. This allows for the wastage of three kerfs each ⅛" wide, and allows for a ⁷⁄₁₆" rabbet in the back of the top, bottom, and sides. After fitting in the ¼" back, ³⁄₁₆" is left for trimming the edges to any irregularity in the wall surface. Check your wall surface with a straightedge during your planning session; you may have to allow more.

Since I planned my smaller cabinet primarily to hold workshop books, I cut the plywood into five strips: three 9¹¹⁄₁₆" wide for the externals; and two 9⁷⁄₃₂" wide for the shelves. Allowing for the four ⅛" kerfs and for the back, this left ⁷⁄₃₂" for trimming to fit the wall. Since a 9" depth handles all but the most outsized books, this works out quite nicely. You may need deeper or shallower cabinets that

will cause some wastage. Careful planning will minimize it however.

At this point, you may be wondering if a back is necessary. After all, you are going to hang it on the wall, and you've got a nice sheetrock surface there. Why do you need a back? The back is there for one primary reason: to provide support for the shelves, to which it will be nailed and glued. (The back also helps to hold the cabinet square.) Tools, books, and all of the other shop paraphernalia that most of us load into any available storage space, are heavy. Shelves need all the help they can get to keep from sagging, even though we keep them short. That brings up the next consideration.

Keep your shelves short. If your cabinet is wide, use one, two, or more interior uprights to divide the shelves into shorter lengths. This also gives you an opportunity to vary the height of the shelves to accommodate items of different heights more efficiently. Note that any internal uprights are the same depth as the shelves and not the depth of the externals. That is because the back butts against the upright and is not rabbeted into it.

Shelves may be supported by either horizontal dadoes cut into the uprights, on adjustable clips fitted into metal strips nailed into dadoes cut vertically in the uprights, or by a combination of both. Note that when the metal strips

Wall-hung cabinet stores a lot of workshop supplies while leaving space to push the Shopsmith all the way back against the wall when it is not in use. Accessories are hung on a plywood panel on the wall under the cabinet.

Another simple wall cabinet stores workshop books in the space above an arc welder and welding table.

cut it into the shape of large washers and insert them between the blades.

In the side pieces, the dadoes can be cut from ¼″ to ⅜″ deep. In an internal upright where the shelf continues on at the same height, don't cut the dado more than ¼″ deep on each side. Do not cut the upright and continue the shelf through it; fitting the shelves into a continuous upright makes a stronger cabinet.

Measure carefully for all of your dadoes before cutting them. There is nothing more discouraging than starting to assemble a project of this sort only to find that there is one wild dado, cut so that the next shelf will go in on a bias! The easiest way to avoid this is to temporarily clamp the uprights together and mark out the location of all dados on the edge of all the boards at the same time.

In order to get the dado cuts made square to the uprights, you can clamp a guide to them to ride against the side of the table saw, rather than using the miter gage. The guide also works if you are routing the cuts.

A double-sided jig of ¾″ plywood can be

are used to provide adjustable shelves, the back cannot be nailed and glued to these particular shelves, and they must be kept short.

Once you are ready to go, you will probably find that it takes less time to build your cabinet than it did to plan it! Cut your plywood into the necessary strips and saw them to length for top, bottom, and sides. Cut any interior uprights out of the shelf width strips, but do not cut the shelves to length just yet.

Cut the required dadoes into the uprights, either horizontally to support the shelves directly, vertically for the slotted metal strips (available in several brands at hardware stores), or a combination of both. The dadoes can be cut with a set of dado blades, an adjustable wobble type dado, or with a router. Try the dado on a scrap first and adjust the width to a nice fit, not sloppily loose, but not so tight that the shelves refuse to slide in easily. If you use a multi-blade dado, make shims for fine adjustments to the correct width. Paper, thin cardboard, or metal from an aluminum can works well for shims;

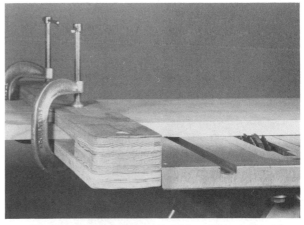

Jig glued up from ¾″ plywood (the other end is identical) simplifies cutting dadoes in long boards or plywood strips. On interior uprights where a shelf is to continue at the same level, dado one side and then flip the board and jig over as a unit and run it through the saw again without moving the jig. Before gluing the parts, clamp them together to be sure that they will slip over your stock. If they're too tight, cut out and glue in one or two paper shims in each end. Hole in top is for hanging jig.

made as shown. (This one accepts boards up to 16" wide.) Give all edges a final trim after gluing and nailing together. Clamp it to the work with two C-clamps. The jig is especially valuable for dadoing the interior uprights, where it is clamped to the board, one side is dadoed, the board and the attached jig are flipped over as a unit, and the other side is dadoed. This produces cuts of perfectly matched height for the continuation of the shelf.

Clamp the cabinet together temporarily; measure for the shelf lengths and cut them to fit. Cut the back to size, leaving a little clearance to allow for minor adjustments, and you are ready to put the cabinet together using finishing nails and either white or yellow glue, as you prefer. Square it up with a carpenter's square and fasten the back, being sure to glue and nail it to the back edge of all the nonadjustable shelves.

After the glue dries, you can nail or screw in the metal strips if you have any adjustable shelves. Cut these shelves just a tad short so they are easy to move when desired.

Leave the front of the cabinet with the raw plywood edges showing or trim them with strips of molding. I prefer ½" x 1" trim, glued and nailed flush with the outside surface of the plywood and with the bottom edges of the interior shelves. The ¼" overhang helps to prevent things from jiggling off the shelf. I just drive the finishing nails in until the heads are flush; after all, this is a workshop cabinet and not a piece of fine furniture. But you can sink the heads and fill them with wood filler if you desire.

By all means, do give the cabinet a finish of some sort before hanging it. That will keep it from absorbing dirt, oil, grease, and other stains over the years. I put on a couple of coats of polyurethane varnish, but an enamel finish is fine.

To hang the cabinet, find the studs, mark off a horizontal at the height of the cabinet base, and screw one leg of a good-sized angle brace to every stud. It's easy to load several hundred pounds into one of these cabinets without half trying; so don't skimp on support (I used 4" braces and 1¾" #10 screws on my cabinets).

Hold the cabinet in place while you mark the positions for angle braces across the top at the stud locations. These braces do not have to be quite as large, because they just hold the cabi-

net against the wall to prevent it from tipping forward into the room when loaded. Fasten the upper braces to the wall and both the upper and lower braces to the cabinet itself; take a moment to survey and enjoy your handiwork, and then proceed to fill the cabinet with all those things for which you've needed storage space.

SIMPLE WORKSHOP DRAWERS

Who among us hasn't looked at a space under a workbench or power tool and thought how handy it would be to have a set of drawers there to store tools and materials. Making drawers by normal methods takes a lot of time, effort, and precise woodworking. Here is a much simpler way of making a set of drawers which, while not up to fine furniture standards, are sturdy, smooth operating, and quite adequate for all but the showplace workshop.

The first step is to design a plywood box to fit the available space and to plan the size and spacing of the drawers before cutting it out and assembling it. Slides for the drawers are the

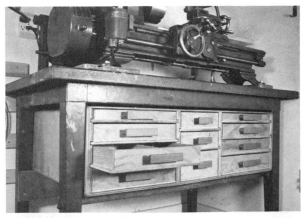

Eleven-drawer cabinet is sized to fit under the table. The partly open drawer shows its simple construction. Note how the extended drawer bottom and the dadoes in the uprights combine to provide an easy-sliding drawer.

drawer bottoms themselves, which are of ⅜"
plywood and slide in ½" wide dadoes cut into
the ¾" plywood sides of the box. The dadoes are
cut ⅜" deep, and the drawer bottoms are made
to the width of the inside opening of the box
plus about 9/16", which gives the drawers adequate support and allows enough clearance for
easy operation.

If you want only one vertical row of drawers,
they can be any height. If you make two or
more rows, the drawers in adjacent rows must
be of different heights so that the dado cuts in
the interior uprights are offset. For two rows,
the drawers must be of different heights. With
three rows, the two outside rows can have
drawers of the same height with perhaps a
smaller number of narrower, but higher ones in
the center row.

Once the dadoes are cut in the ¾" uprights,
the exterior box, using ⅜" plywood for the bottom and either ⅜" or ¼" for the top, can be
glued and nailed together. Be sure that the uprights are all square with the top and bottom
and are parallel with each other from front to
back so that the drawers will operate smoothly.
The drawer bottoms of ⅜" plywood (and dimensioned as mentioned above) are then cut and
checked for an easy sliding fit in the dadoes.
The sides, front, and rear of each drawer are
then cut out, allowing for about ⅛" clearance

Another cabinet fills the space under a workbench.
The upended lower drawer shows how these drawers
slide on four large-headed thumbtacks. Two are
mounted in the front of the cabinet bottom and two
in the rear of the drawer bottom. The dark lines
show where tack heads slide in wax tracks.

Adjacent drawers must be of different heights so
that the deep dadoes are staggered in the uprights.
Note also that the bottoms of the lower drawers are
cut flush and slide on the bottom of the cabinet instead of in dadoes.

on each side and 3/16" vertically. These parts are
also of ⅜" plywood. Each drawer is constructed
by gluing and nailing the sides and ends together first and then to the bottom of the
drawer. Drive small finishing nails from the underside of the drawer bottom up into the edges
of the sides, front, and back.

A plywood or hardboard back helps hold the
box square and keeps the drawers working
easily. But you should cut large air-release
holes in it, centered behind each drawer. Use a
1" or larger spade bit, hole saw, or expansion
bit. These holes allow air to escape during
drawer operation, rather than being momen-
tarily compressed. They make a noticeable difference.

Add pulls to the drawer fronts, rub some stick
wax on the slides, insert the drawers in the box,
and you're in business. Since the bottom row of
drawers rides on the inside bottom of the box,
rather than in dadoes, a simple way to reduce
friction here is to use four large-headed (⅝")
thumbtacks for each drawer; one in each front

corner of the bottom of the box, and one in each rear corner of the underside of the drawer bottom itself. Rub a little stick wax along the tracks where the thumbtack heads will run, and these drawers will slide as easily as the dadoed ones.

As with the previously described wall cabi-nets, you should put a couple of coats of paint or gloss polyurethane varnish onto the drawer faces and their insides to keep them looking clean. (If you prefer a satin finish, use gloss for the first coat and then finish with a satin coat. This will make a finish that resists dirt, oil, and grease better than all satin.)

CABINET WITH DRAWERS

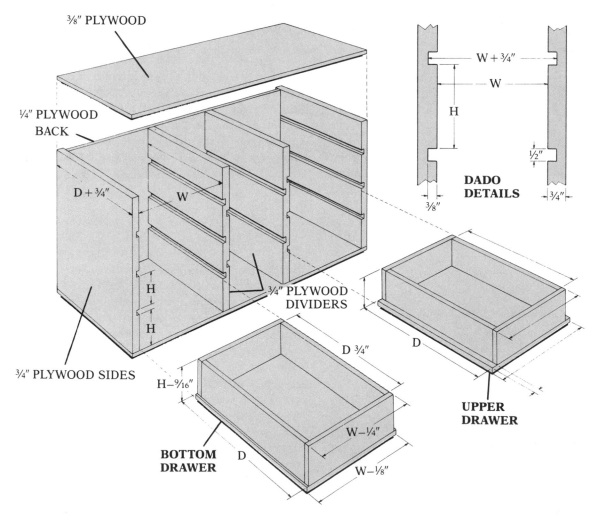

Note dimension differences for bottom drawers.

The drawing shows that once the width, height, and depth of the drawer spaces in the cabinet are known, **the drawers can be dimensioned in relationship to them. All drawer parts are ⅜″ plywood.**

DRAWER DIVIDER TRAYS

While we are on the subject of drawers—have you seen the drawer organizers sold for household use? They are plastic trays that come in several modular sizes, all 2″ in height, and that have one lipped edge so that they can be hooked together in a drawer to conveniently contain and separate different tools, gadgets, and supplies. The various sizes include 3″ x 9″, 6″ x 9″, 3″ x 15″, and 6″ x 15″. They can be put together in almost limitless combinations to suit your needs.

Think about using them when you plan your drawer cabinet. If you want them, make the inside of the drawers a minimum of 2¼″ high to give adequate clearance for the connecting lips. Also make your drawers about ¼″ wider than the total width of the trays. Since all but the last lip fits into an adjoining tray, you only have to add the ¼″ once, no matter how many of the trays you gang together in the drawer.

Get a few of these in different sizes, try them out, and you are apt to go back and get more. Many more! Most of the large discount stores usually have a good selection at a reasonable price.

CUT-OFF PLASTIC BOTTLES

Nowadays, all sorts of household items come in plastic containers. Take a thoughtful look at some of these before they get thrown out, and you are apt to find a few that can be cut down to make handy storage containers. Some of the liquid antacids, commonly kept in the medicine cabinet, come in rectangular bottles that are about 2″ x 3″ in cross section. Cut one off so as to keep the bottom couple of inches, and you have a dandy little container for holding all sorts of small items that would otherwise clutter up even the smallest of the drawer organizers mentioned above. Having several of

Drawer divider trays fill most of this bench drawer even though the drawer was not made to fit them. The different modular sizes—one 3″ x 9″, two 6″ x 9″, one 3″ x 12″, and one 3″ x 15″—all combine to make a rectangle. Trays 6″ x 15″ are also available.

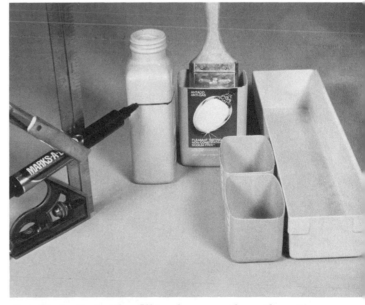

Cutoff plastic bottles fill in drawers where there is not quite enough room for another row of trays. Cut off higher, they soak a wide brush without wasting thinner. The setup shown here makes marking easier than trying to use a square on the rounded contours.

them in different drawers helps keep small things findable.

The thin plastic can be cut with shears or even with a sturdy pair of scissors. I cut them with a fine-tooth saw and then remove any roughness by deburring with a sharp knife.

OVER-HOOD GARAGE STORAGE LOFT

Depending on how your garage is laid out, the space over the hood of your car(s) can be converted to storage space by building a loft there. If you do, be sure to consider the hood height of any future cars you might get. A 4-wheel-drive rig, a pickup truck, or one of the outsize station wagons, all require more height under a loft than the ordinary car.

The loft in the accompanying photo was built to provide clearance over the hood of a 4 x 4 Blazer; it has a 54″ clearance to the bottom of the 4 x 8 support beam. This brings the top surface about 62″ from the floor, an easy reach to

An overhood loft provides convenient storage. The shopmade ladder can be used anywhere along the full length of the loft. Note the supporting posts and horizontal ladder storage on back wall.

deposit a box without having to wrestle it up the ladder. Also, there is still 56″ of "stoop over" space below the joists behind the beam for getting at such items as a weed mower, which can be stored in front of a smaller car.

The loft is 6′ deep, which allows use of an even 1½ widths of four foot wide ¾″ plywood for flooring.

Just over 20 feet long, the front beam is supported on each end by a 4 x 4 as well as by a horizontal piece tied into a couple of studs. Another 4 x 4 post under the center of the beam provides additional support without interfering with the parking space of either car.

When you measure between the walls before cutting the beam, you may find that it is hard, even with a helper, to get an exact measurement due to the sag in 20′ or so of tape. (Measuring at floor level is no answer, as there probably will be some variation at the height of the beam; no two walls are ever exactly plumb and parallel.) A simple way to get an exact dimension for cutting the beam is to find two sticks (1 x 2s, 1 x 3s, 1 x 4s, 2 x 4s; whatever is available), that are each a little longer than one half the length to be measured. Put them into position, overlap them on top of the center post, be sure that the ends are lightly butted against the walls, and clamp them together with a couple of C-clamps. Carefully lower them as a unit and put them on top of your uncut beam. Mark the ends of the beam, square off the marks all around the beam, saw it carefully, and your beam should just swish into position without the slightest gap or binding. Toenail the beam to the end and center supports.

The rear of the loft is held up by a 2 x 6 ledger fastened to the studs with lag screws and large nails. The Sheetrock is cut away so that the ledger can be fastened directly to the studs.

The 2 x 6 joists, 16″ on centers, are fastened to both the beam and ledger board with preformed metal joist hangers, especially useful here because of the large loads to be imposed on them.

A length of 2 x 4 that runs along the top front of the forward beam has a ½″ wide by ¾″ deep rabbet cut in one edge to form a groove between it and the surface of the loft flooring. I made a ladder from straight-grained 1 x 4 material; it has two hooks fashioned from ⅛″ x ¾″ steel and fastened to the top of each side rail.

Two steel hooks, screwed to the ladder rails, drop into a rabbet cut into the upper rear edge of the 2 x 4 top rail. This rail is planted on the front of the 4 x 8 beam and extends above it to match the height of the plywood decking.

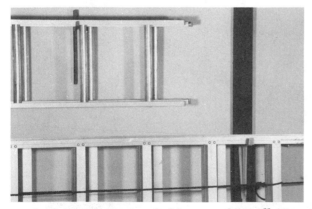

Brackets hold extension ladders on the wall. One pair was welded up from ¾" angle iron, and the other was made from modified shelf brackets.

These fit over the 2 x 4 and down into the groove, providing for secure positioning of the ladder anywhere along the length of the beam when the garage is free of cars. Even with both cars in the garage, the ladder is usable in any of three positions; next to either side wall or in the center between the cars.

If an over-hood loft is not practical for your garage, how about a loft above the garage doors? If you happen to have two sliding doors rather than a single overhead one, you have an ideal setup for a loft over the entrance.

If the beam over the door that supports the rails does not have a center post, add one to support the extra weight of the loft and contents. Fasten a ledger to the beam just above the rails.

Measure carefully before locating the position for the beam that will cross the garage itself. Its positioning and thus the depth of the loft is determined by clearance needed for the center supporting post; you must be able to open the car door on that side when the car is in the garage. If you have a four-door sedan, you might accept not opening one of the rear doors in the garage in order to get more loft space.

Except for its greater height, and consequently lesser storage height above, this loft is constructed in much the same way as the over-hood loft. One I built in a previous house gave us lots of storage space. With this one, I did not build a custom ladder and used an ordinary 8' stepladder.

If you have an overhead door in your garage, take a good look at the space available above its travel. Although it will be restricted, you can often provide for some light storage without any extra bracing. In our present house, in addition to the over-hood loft, I have placed two full sheets of ⅜" plywood atop the 2 x 8 beams that run lengthwise of the garage above the overhead door. I put light bulky items up there.

Check your particular construction carefully. You can probably find some storage area above an overhead door, especially if you do not have an electric opener; its actuating mechanism usually cuts into the space needed for installing a cross beam.

Although your shop may not be part of your garage, any storage space you can add to the garage could take care of some items that would otherwise take up space in the shop.

STORAGE BOXES

Once you get that nice new loft built, you have to figure out how to store things neatly. Some larger items can just be placed there and perhaps covered with a sheet of plastic to keep the dust off, but for most small things the most practical way to store them is in cardboard boxes.

There was a time when every grocery store had dozens of empty boxes that they were happy to have someone take off their hands. No more! Now almost all large markets have their own baling machine and as soon as the boxes are emptied, into the baler they go to be crushed, bundled, and sent off for recycling. Most smaller stores, also make other recycling arrangements. As a result, it has become much harder to find suitable boxes for storage, especially if one wants to get a number of the same size and shape for orderly layout and stacking.

Bill Hussman, who has one of the neatest shops of anyone I know, has an answer for this. He buys standard sized boxes at the Post Office. They are available in four sizes: 20″ x 14″ x 10″ high,   15″ x 12″ x 10″,   12″ x 12″ x 12″,   and 8″ x 8″ x 8″. Bill finds that he uses the 15″ x 12″ x 10″s the most. These boxes are somewhat expensive, but their ready availability in matching size, plus the fact that they are always new, clean, and undamaged is a redeeming factor.

Inside the boxes, Bill keeps most of the small stuff clean, dry, separated, and easily found by packaging it in clear plastic locking (Ziploc) bags. These same boxes can be used in the storage area of the workshop for orderly storage and protection of various items that are not used regularly.

Bill also makes good use of small toolboxes, especially the little ones that are about 4″ x 6″ x 12″. Formerly stamped out of sheet steel, these are now usually available only in

Neatly labeled boxes bought from the Post Office hold Bill Hussman's auto service equipment.

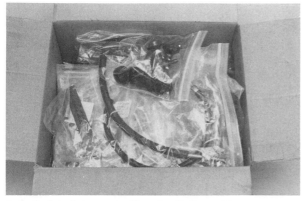

Labeled and separated in plastic bags, items are easy to locate in the boxes.

Large, heavy-duty plastic garbage bags keep Bill's oxyacetylene and arc welders clean while in storage.

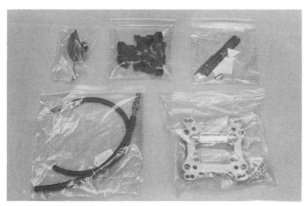

Ziploc bags keep appropriate parts together and free of dirt and corrosion.

The fifteen trays in each of these six cabinets are bigger (2¾" wide) than those in most small plastic chests, and this makes them worth seeking out. The oversize trays hold larger items.

Small toolboxes make it easy for Bill to grab just the equipment he needs for a particular job.

plastic. Store tools for specific jobs in them so that when a particular job comes up, you can quickly pick out a single, plainly marked toolbox containing all the special tools you need.

SELF-ADHESIVE LABELS

Once you get your storage boxes filled, you'll want to mark them to help you find things when you need them. One easy answer is a felt-tip marking pen. Bill lays out the ¾" lettering on the box with a pencil and plastic lettering guide before going over it with the marking pen.

This looks neat and orderly if the contents of your boxes are fairly well fixed. If you rearrange things often, though, it presents a problem and can degrade the appearance of your nice new boxes.

Most stationery stores carry boxes of self-adhesive removable labels. These come in a number of sizes, and each box contains anywhere from 100 to 500 of the labels depending on their size. Describe your contents with a bold pen and stick the labels on your boxes. When you want to change a label, you can usually lift it off by working a knife blade under one corner. If it doesn't want to come off, just stick the new label directly over it.

GARDEN TOOL STORAGE

While we are still in the garage, let's talk about garden tool storage. A lot of this stuff is pretty hard to store on pegboard or to hang directly on a Sheetrock wall. Two or three horizontal lengths of 2 x 4 spaced vertically along a wall can easily solve this problem. On the garage floor, lay out all the tools you will want to hang and allow space for the extras you are bound to acquire. Figure out the number of 2 x 4s required and the height from the floor.

Find the studs in the wall and fasten the 2 x 4s in place with nails of an appropriate length. (A garage wall on a side that is connected to the rest of the house may be thicker than the usual ½" Sheetrock panel, depending on the local fire code.) If your wall is open to the studs, just nail the 2 x 4s directly to them.

For hanging the tools, cut the heads off some 8 penny (2½") nails; grind or file the cutoff end round, and nail them into the lateral 2 x 4s at a slight downward angle. Don't drive them in too far, there's no need and as time goes on you'll need to pull and relocate some of them.

When you do need to remove one, try getting a grip on the shank of the nail with your claw hammer. If that doesn't work, tightly clamp a pair of locking pliers to the nail and then pull it out by inserting the hammer's claws under the

Three horizontal 2 x 4s nailed to the garage side wall keep these garden tools off the floor and in reasonable order. Most are hung on a single headless nail. Others, such as the broom, rake, and shovels, are upended and hung on two nails.

jaws of the pliers—a handy stunt to remember any time you pull the head off a nail while trying to remove it.

Drill holes through the wooden handles of the tools at the same angle that you drove the nails, countersink each end of the holes slightly, and hang the tools up. Some tools such as rakes, shovels, and brooms may be hung from their head end to economize on space. In this case, use two nails; no need to remove the heads on these.

STORAGE RACK

If you have an open stud wall in a workshop or nearby storage area, you can store a lot of stuff in it, especially if it has 6-inch studs.

The wall shown combines several practical storage modifications. Starting from the bottom, these include bins formed between the studs by nailing a 1 x 6 along the studs and the sill just above the foundation. This provides a series of 4"-deep pockets between the studs that are not so deep that things get buried and lost, but hold a good many small items such as plumbing fittings and scrap metal.

A shelf just above limits some of these bins to about 9" high, which is adequate. Farther along the wall, the shelves are higher to accommodate various short lengths of wood and plywood scraps, dowels, and such, stored vertically in the bins below. The tallest of these scrap bins are about 40" high.

Shelves between the studs hold more materials and supplies. A 1 x 2 nailed to the front provides a small lip to keep things in place. Some of the shelves have been widened with an extra board. A 1 x 2 provides just a bit more room to allow a double row of jars that hold a variety of nails. (I know many frown on glass jars, and rightly so, but the ability to see what is in them is a plus. If one is reasonably careful and does not have small children around, they can be quite practical.) A couple of 1 x 8 shelves

add on another 7½" to the depth between the studs for storing wider items.

The upper part of the wall is taken up with brackets cantilevered out from the wall; they can hold odd pieces of wood up to nearly 20' in length. The three lower rows project out about 12" and the two upper ones, which can hold wider plywood and hardboard cutoffs, project out 16". All of them are tilted up slightly to encourage the contents to remain in place.

Another stud wall, just beyond my storeroom and under the garage, has the same type of cantilevered brackets installed for holding odd lengths of steel, aluminum, and copper stock. Here the brackets are only extended out about 6" from the studs due to the weight of the material to be supported. Other short pieces of metal are stored vertically between the studs behind the horizontal storage.

Making shelving for an open stud wall is easy. You must plan it first of course. A session with your table saw or radial-arm saw will mass-produce many of the parts needed fairly quickly though. A piece of 1 x 6 can be ripped into three pieces to provide the (almost) 1 x 2s for supports under the shelves between the

An open 6" stud wall along a storage area holds lumber, usable wood and plywood cutoffs, and many other supplies. This low-angle shot shows shelves of varying heights holding wood scraps of different lengths. To the right, a couple of shelves extend out in front of the studs to hold bigger items. (The highest shelf is about shoulder height.)

A 1 x 6 nailed along the bottom of the studs just above the footing provides eighteen handy bins for storing scrap aluminum, copper, brass, lead, pipe fittings, and other small items.

studs. If you have 2 x 6 studs, make the supports about 5⅜″ long, for 2 x 4 studs, make them 3⅜″.

If you plan to add on wider shelves, cut supports for them long enough to support the total width. Make them of wider material to hold the cantilevered shelf and its contents. (I used 1 x 4s.) Since I had a horizontal line of 2 x 6 fire blocking (or what would have been fire blocking had the wall been closed in) about halfway up the wall, I lined up one of my wider shelves with it. In this case, the 1 x 4 supports had to be notched to allow for the difference between the 1½″ fire blocking that made up the back half of the shelf and the ¾″ 1 x 8 add-on shelf.

Predrilling for the two nails in each support and preinserting the nails will make for quicker, and more accurate installation. Chalk lines snapped along the studs help keep the supports and the resulting shelves in line, as well as giving you a preview of how the planned shelves will work out when installed. It's easier to rub out a chalk line and redo it than it is to pull out a line of shelves.

Precut your shelves to fit between the studs. For the usual 1½″ thick studs set 16″ on center, cutting the shelves 14⅜″ long should work out about right. This allows for a little clearance at each end to take care of any studs that are twisted or out of position. Check how accurately your studs are positioned first though, before you do any cutting. Of course, if your studs are the older ones, made when a 2 x 4, or 2 x 6, was 1⅝″ thick, you'll have to make the shelves ⅛″ shorter. Your house might even have the rough cut 2 x 4s (or 2 x 6s) that actually measure 2″ thick!

If you plan one or more rows of the cantilevered brackets, cut them out in pairs. I made mine from ½″ plywood scrap. For long brackets, the strips were cut about 4¾″ wide. For short ones, strips were 4″ wide.

Set the miter gage to a 2½-degree angle and cut the strips into parallelograms, the long ones 21½″ long and the short ones 17½″ (for a 6″ stud). Then set up a taper attachment or make a wooden jig to run the parallelograms through the saw. Cut each parallelogram into two tapered pieces with the smaller end about ¾″ wide on the short ones, and 1″ wide on the long ones. Round off the bottom corner of the narrow end on a disc sander and sand the edges to

Five rows of cantilever brackets store longer boards and plywood on the upper part of the wall. The top two rows, being above head height, extend farther out and hold wider pieces of plywood and hardboard. A short stepladder provides quick access to the higher shelves.

Here the brackets have been unloaded to show how they are fastened to the sides of the 6″ studs.

a rounded chamfer. This is a help if one of these things jumps out and strikes you on the head when you are climbing a ladder to get at a piece of stock up there.

Again, predrill and preinstall the nails. I used three in each bracket. Push the slightly tapered end flat against the wall, check that the front edge is at the chalk line level, and nail it up. Fasten the two end brackets first, then a center one. Use a long straightedge along the tips while nailing up the rest in order to keep them all in a nice even line.

OVERHEAD STORAGE FOR PLYWOOD

Plywood projects seldom use up a full sheet or sheets. Partial sheets are usually quite a bit more expensive per square foot, and it makes sense to buy a full sheet if you anticipate using it for another project soon and if you have the space to store it.

If you happen to have a section of the shop or storeroom with a pair of open stud walls a reasonable distance apart, you can easily build in some overhead storage for plywood, particleboard, hardboard, Sheetrock, and other panels. Just place a few horizontal 2 x 4s across the area a reasonable distance below the ceiling and tie them into the studs at both ends. My setup crosses a space about 6½' wide and has worked out very well over the years to store various partial panels.

Panels add up fast in weight; so be sure to fasten each end of the 2 x 4 sub-joists securely to the studs. In addition to being nailed directly to the studs, my overhead storage rack has a

Five 2 x 4s across the far end of the storeroom about a foot below the ceiling joists provide storage for full or partial plywood sheets, which are slipped in endwise. Inverted skids protect the light when a panel is being lifted into place.

1 x 3 strip nailed to the face of the studs for additional support. If your span is much longer than mine, it would be wise to use either 2 x 6s instead of 2 x 4s, or to tie the center of the span to the joists above for greater strength. In any case, be very careful not to overload the structure with more material than it can handle with a good margin of safety.

The partial panels are loaded by lifting one end into the open end of the area and then sliding them lengthwise into position. Since this particular space has a fluorescent light just above it, a pair of 1" skids, about 4¼" wide and with the ends rounded off, are fastened to the 2 x 4s with steel corner braces. The skids protect the light from the panel as it is raised and pushed into the storage space.

A small piece of plywood is screwed to the underside of the end 2 x 4; I store several small strips of plywood of various thicknesses on it. I use the strips as shims to support ends of long plywood strips that happen to be stored atop shorter ones. This keeps the long top piece supported in a straight line and avoids the tendency for an unsupported end to sag and develop a warp.

ROLLER CABINET AND CHEST

If you've been collecting tools for any length of time, storage is always a problem. So, when one of the big stores offers a bargain on a combination roller cabinet and chest, it is tempting even if you do not do professional automotive work.

Buy one, as I did, for a small shop, and you may find that you don't really roll it about all that much and that it takes up a good deal of room in the shop. But with a little planning you may be able to integrate it with your workbench. That way you get more bench space plus all the handy storage drawers.

The roller cabinet shown, which had a lip around the top to hold a chest, has a piece of plastic-laminate-surfaced particleboard (a "sink cutout" I obtained from a large building supply store) cut to fit it. Its heavy-duty casters

Roller cabinet with casters removed sits on blocks to match adjacent workbench. Plastic laminate sink cutout, cut to fit, provides a durable work surface.

were removed (and of course saved). The cabinet was then placed on four blocks cut to raise it to match the exact height of the workbench.

At the other end of the workbench, I built a plywood cabinet to the same height. In addition to having storage shelves at convenient levels, it includes a drop section that just fits the large chest that came with the roller cabinet. I set the dimensions so that the top of the chest is level with the cabinet as well as with the top of the bench.

The ¼"-plywood cabinet back continues behind the chest, although the top is dropped down about 2½" and has a plywood block fastened to it to hold the chest forward a couple of inches to provide the space necessary for the top to open up and back against the wall. The plywood blocking fills the gap behind the chest completely, to aid in retrieving fallen items that would otherwise drop down behind the chest.

Since this area of the shop is next to the big garage door where a car or truck can be nosed

Chest segment of the roller-cabinet set can be built into a plywood cabinet. Chest is mounted away from the wall, allowing the top to open without striking the tools hung behind it.

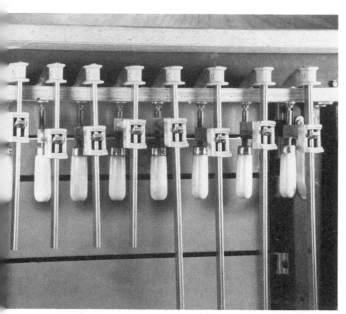

Small board fastened across the back of an island workbench and just below the top provides out-of-the-way storage for a number of bar clamps.

in for service, the chest becomes an excellent place to store socket sets and other tools for automotive work. The cabinet shelves store automotive supplies as well as other items.

This setup made the purchase of a roller cabinet well worthwhile for me. Take a close look at your shop for the possibility of building in a roller cabinet and/or chest. Purchased on sale, it might provide a great deal of relatively inexpensive tool storage, as well as giving you a "free" set of heavy-duty casters for another project.

ANOTHER STORAGE POSSIBILITY

If you are lucky enough to have a small bathroom next to your workshop, you may want to use the space over the toilet tank for extra storage shelves. To be sure, the extra humidity inherent in most any bathroom may lead to rusting or corrosion of metal items, but many other things could be safely stored there.

Be sure to make the bottom shelf high enough above the toilet tank top so that you can remove the top and get down into the tank for repairs. Of course, if you are really pressed for shelf space, you can install a removable shelf just above the tank top. In this case, fill it with just a few large items that can be quickly removed when necessary.

POP RIVET STORAGE

Pop riveters are great gadgets, but storing the rivets can be a problem. Rivets usually come in three lengths, in two or three different diameters, and in aluminum, copper, or steel. Multiply all these variables and it is easy to have a dozen or so different sizes and materials. That involves a lot of separate containers.

Check your nearby antique shops and keep an eye open for old shoemaker's nail trays. These are made of wood, with a number of good sized round and deep depressions cut into them. They are great for storing pop rivets.

Although they are interesting old artifacts, they often sell quite reasonably. I've got two different trays. One holds ten different kinds of rivets and the smaller one holds six.

Old coin trays from cash registers also work for this purpose and are relatively common and inexpensive. Another good rivet container, if you can't find a nail tray or a cash tray, is an ordinary muffin baking tin.

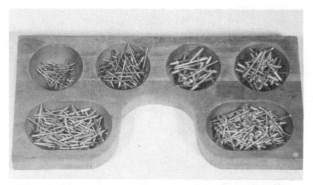

Old wooden coin tray from a cash drawer holds a goodly amount of Pop rivets in different sizes.

BREAD PANS

Bread pans, if you don't get the fancy nonstick coated type, are still fairly inexpensive and are great for storing large numbers of small items such as bolts, nuts, washers, and screws. Then the next question arises: where do I store the bread pans?

This problem can be solved by providing some closely spaced shelves in one of your open-face wall-hung cabinets. A 4-inch opening between shelves is more than adequate. The usual bread pan is about 2¾" high; so you can heap up the contents a bit and still slide the drawer in and out easily. A couple of shelves for bread pans stores a tremendous amount of assorted articles in quite a small space.

Wooden separators, glued and nailed onto each shelf, let each pan slide in or out easily without interfering with the others. The separators shown were ripped from ¾" stock, angled to match the sides of the pans and cut to be about 1¼" wide at the base. They were then crosscut to about 8½" long and the front ends rounded on a disc sander to aid in guiding the pans into position, somewhat similar to the way an old-fashioned ferry boat was eased into a slip. A few of the spacers were ripped into two halves and the half pieces were mounted against the upright at the end of each row of pans.

Since this particular cabinet was a little deep for the pans, a spacer strip was fastened along

A dozen small loaf pans hold many smaller items in this plywood case. Pan rims slide in grooves in the ¾" uprights.

the back of the shelf and the between-pan spacers were butted up to it. This holds the pans forward.

Small bread pans for an individual loaf are fine for containing smaller parts such as wood screws, sheet-metal screws, bolts, and nuts. The open-face box shown holds a dozen of these miniature pans and takes up very little space. The uprights are made of ¾" plywood; the top, bottom, and back are of ¼" plywood. The pans are hung by their rims, which slide in dadoes cut into the uprights. Since the rims of the pans are fairly narrow, some careful measuring is required. You want to space the uprights so that the pans slide in and out without binding, and yet have enough support that they don't fall out of the dadoes.

If new bread pans are a little too expensive for you, try buying them secondhand at a garage sale, local flea market, or swap meet. They are pretty much of a standard size and do the job just as well as the new ones. I've got a mixture of both.

Shelves spaced 4" apart will hold a number of bread pans in a small space. Spacers keep the pans separated for easy entry and exit.

LABEL MAKERS

One of these little gizmos is very useful around the shop, especially in the storage department. With the bread pans just mentioned, for instance, it is a lot easier to scan along a neat row of labels than it is to pull out and peer into each of the pans until you finally find the thing you want—in the very last pan, naturally!

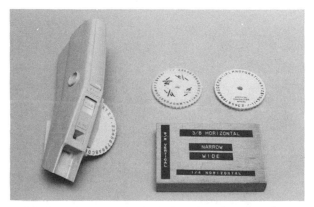

A label maker is a great help when storing things. This one uses ¼″ or ⅜″ tape, spaces narrow or wide, and prints vertically as well as horizontally.

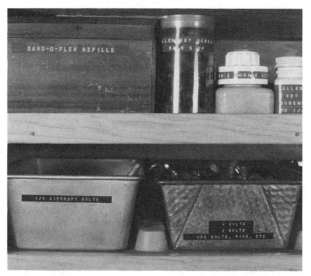

These labels stick tightly to most any clean surface, either flat or curved, and remain stuck and legible for decades.

If you don't happen to be familiar with these little machines, they form raised letters on a special self-sticking plastic tape; the tape is available in a number of colors and is usually either ¼″ or ⅜″ wide. The ⅜″ width is a bit more readable and seems to hold onto the surface a little better. But the ¼″-size allows the same amount of lettering to be fastened in a smaller space. Some models can handle both sizes in one unit—an advantage.

The message to be spelled out is selected letter by letter on a rotating wheel and a squeeze of the two-piece handle creates a raised letter in the plastic tape. Stretching the plastic fades the color out, thus providing contrasting white lettering against the tape's background color.

A built-in cutter snips off the label when the message is finished, the protective backing peels off, and the self-sticking label presses into place. With the ¼″ size, running the end of your fingernail along the tape both above and below the letters helps stick the label down securely. Once pressed down firmly onto the surface, labels stick tenaciously to almost any smooth non-oily or non-greasy surface. I've got a number of them that must have been in place for twenty years or more.

If necessary, you can peel the labels off. Just slip a sharp knife under one corner and raise enough of the tape to get a grip on it. They come off most metal or hard plastic surfaces quite cleanly, but on a painted surface they may bring some of the paint with them. Adhesive remaining on the surface may be rubbed off or dissolved with lacquer thinner or acetone. Lacquer thinner seems to work best but may raise the paint or other finish on the surface.

BETTER FILE STORAGE

Files are a necessity for most any shop, and you never seem to have too many of them. Storing them does present a problem though. You have probably heard the old admonition, don't throw files together in a drawer because they soon dull each other. But proper storage can take up a lot of space, because of the size of the handles in comparison to the thickness of the file.

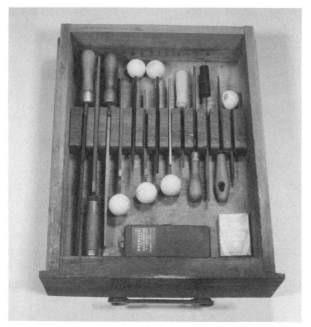

A grooved piece of 2 x 4 keeps thirteen files, some quite large and all equipped with handles, safely separated in a relatively small drawer.

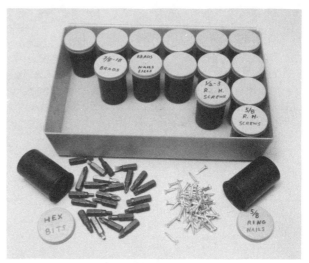

Containers for 35mm film keep many tiny items separated and available. This 6″ x 9″ plastic drawer divider tray holds two dozen of them.

I've got an easy solution for this one. Cut a length of 2 x 4 to fit across the width of your file drawer and then saw or dado slots in it to match the thickness of your files. Lay the 2 x 4 flat across the center of your drawer. You can then alternate the files end for end, so that at each end of the drawer you have a handle, then an end, then a handle, and so forth. This way you can accommodate a larger number of files in a given space, while still preventing them from being dulled by rubbing against one another. You will have to remove half of them by picking them up by the end rather than the handle, but it's still much easier than trying to pick the proper one out of a jumbled drawer.

35MM FILM CONTAINERS

If you are not a photography fan, you may not be familiar with the handy little 35mm film containers. Round plastic cylinders with a snap-on lid, they are about 1¼″ in diameter and

2″ high, an ideal size for holding all sorts of little odds and ends.

Small screws, brads, nails, lills, and any number of other little things that would otherwise end up in a confused pile can all be kept separate in these little containers. Usually black in color, many of them have light colored tops that can be written on with a marking pen to indicate the contents.

They are also great for keeping small tools together. For example, one of these little "cans" stores a dozen or so of the tips for our hex-blade screwdrivers (Phillips, slotted, Allen, Torx, Robertson, Frearson, etc.).

These containers are usually discarded when film is sent in for processing. You can obtain them from most any large photography store— often for free.

HOSE AND BLADE RACKS

Air hoses, band saw blades, and other similar items often pose a storage problem. They are bulky in size and if hung on the wall you may have difficulty finding a nail long enough to do the job. In addition, a nail supplies support

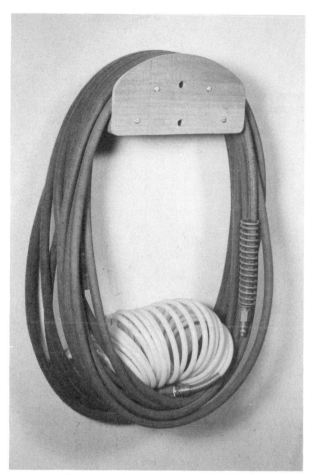

Curved racks, bandsawed from a stub of 2 x 4 and fitted with a raised lip, are great for holding hoses, band-saw blades, or rope coils. Deep counterbores allow the use of normal length screws for fastening to a wall stud.

Empty rack shows its construction. For a 1″ lip, just draw a curve with a radius 1″ greater than the body of the rack.

over a very limited area, which may lead to kinking or other damage, such as dulling the teeth of a blade.

Band saw blades can be folded into three smaller coils, but this way they gain in "thickness" as they lose in diameter, and can still pose a storage problem.

One answer is to make up simple curved wooden racks as shown. Coil the item you want to hang to a practical size and measure its approximate inner diameter. Use one-half this measurement for a radius to draw a curve on a short block of wood that will be thick enough to hold the bulk of the coil. A short end block that has been cut off a 4 x 4 is often just right.

Saw it to size with a band saw or one of those long 6″ blades in a sabre saw. If this is not practical, you can always laminate the block from two pieces of 2 x 4 material, or even more laminations of 1″ stock. You may want to smooth off the curve with a power sander, particularly if you have sawed it out in two or more laminations.

Next, get a scrap of ¼″ plywood and cut a piece to form a front lip for the rack. Decide on the depth of the lip needed to adequately hold the coil and make the radius of its curve equal to your previous radius plus the height of the lip. Fasten this lip to the rack body with wood screws or glue and nails.

Since the rack would require extremely long screws to secure it to the wall, you can counterbore it to a depth that allows normal length woodscrews to be used. For example; if you allow for 1″ into a stud, ½″ for the Sheetrock, and 1″ in the rack itself, 2½″ screws will do the job. Choose a counterbore bit big enough to clear the head of the screw(s) chosen and drill to a depth that leaves the back 1″ of the rack undrilled. Continue on through the rack with a clearance bit for the screw; go on into the wall to the thickness of the Sheetrock. Finish up with a pilot hole into the stud itself and fasten the rack in place.

A single screw is adequate for a small rack to hold a few band saw blades; for a heavy coil of air hose, two are better.

You can build garden hose racks of this type. Use 4 x 4 fence post stock (redwood, cedar, or other wood that holds up well outdoors) and finish it off with a lip of the same material. The finished product is sturdy and long lasting.

4
WOODWORKING TIPS

Hardly a month goes by without a woodworking magazine describing the construction of one or more jigs for performing various operations, most of them pertaining to the table saw. In addition there are several books available that give heavy coverage to woodworking jigs. There are also a number of manufactured jigs available to make certain cuts easier, more exact, or both.

Most of these jigs are great for a specific job. There is only one problem. If you were to build or buy all of the jigs that are around these days, you would need a barn, a large barn, to store them all!

Consider them carefully; if you will be doing much picture framing, for example, one of the many excellent miter jigs can really help you. If you are about to build some furniture, you will probably need a good tenoning jig. If you will be doing neither of these jobs, the jigs may not be worth the space that they take up in your shop. Having said all this, I'm going to describe a couple of handy jigs.

AN ANGLE-CUTTING JIG

A table saw's miter gage enables you to crosscut a board at any angle between 45 and 90 degrees, and a taper attachment guides you in ripping a board at an angle from 0 to about 15 degrees.

If you need to saw an angle between 15 and 45 degrees to point some garden stakes or to cut an odd angle for a project, there is no guide available and you may end up angling the stock across the saw freehand, a dangerous operation that also leads to a rough cut.

This jig borrows from machine shop practice to provide a safe hold-down for the stock at any angle. It consists of a base with a bottom slider, which rides in either miter-gage slot to position it relative to the saw blade. This base has eleven evenly spaced tee nuts which, together with a pair of threaded rods and hold-down fixtures, secure the stock for sawing. Few dimensions are given here as they will vary with the size of your saw table and the placement of its miter slots.

Make the base first from a solid piece of ½" plywood that lies flat on your saw table with no bends or warps and no voids in the laminations. It must be at least as wide as the distance between the two miter-gage guide grooves. Make it as long as possible but not so long it tends to fall off the table when placed with its front at the leading edge of the saw blade.

Cut a hardwood strip to a smooth sliding fit in your miter-gage grooves. This is usually about ⅜" x ¾" but varies between saw models.

Be sure that the strip is thin enough that it rides free of the bottom of the groove. For a small saw table you can make the strip somewhat longer than the base to aid directional stability.

Lay out the location for the slider strip on the bottom of the base so that when it is placed in either miter groove, one side of the base will overhang the line of cut of the saw. Drill the strip and the base with pilot, clearance, and countersunk holes for three or four flathead screws, being sure that the heads will drive flush to, or just below, the surface.

Screw the parts together (do *not* glue), lower the saw blade below the table surface, and check the unit in both grooves. Make any corrections necessary for smooth operation. Raise the saw blade and make two cuts, one with the slider in each groove, to trim the sides of the base to size.

Procure a supply of ¼" tee nuts and a length of ¼" threaded rod to fit them. Try to find the tee nuts that are only ⅜" long. The longer ones (½") will have to be ground or filed shorter to keep from protruding above the base after its bottom has been counterbored for their heads.

Put your jig in place on the saw table and, using stock of different widths, visualize where the tee nuts should be placed to be as close as possible to the edge of the stock and well short of the outer end of the hold-down strip (See the accompanying photos). I use two outer rows of four each with a center row of three (under the miter slider strip).

Unscrew the slider strip and lay out the location of tee-nut holes on the bottom side of the base. Use a spade bit to counterbore the holes just enough (about ³⁄₃₂") to bury the base of the tee nuts. After counterboring, drill the holes on through with a clearance drill for the shank of

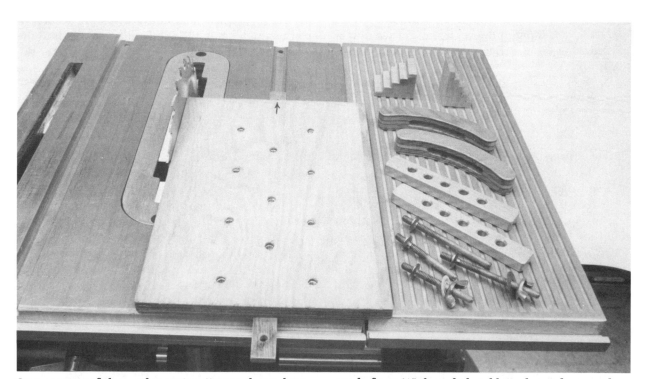

Components of the angle-cutting jig are shown here. The hardwood slider under the jig's base can be placed in the miter-gage slot on either side of the saw blade, as needed. The eleven holes have tee nuts installed from the bottom. At the right, four studs made from ¼" threaded rod have brazed-on washers to prevent them from being screwed in too far and dragging on the saw table. Two washers plus wing nuts provide the clamping pressure. Shown above the rods are the wooden hold-downs.

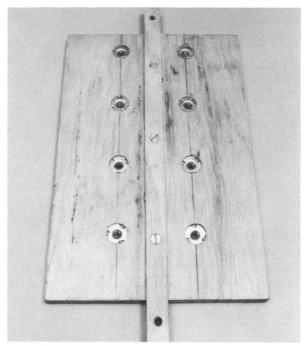

Inverting angle jig shows how the tee nuts and the screws fastening the miter-slot slider are recessed so they do not drag on the saw table. The slider is not glued to the base. This permits it to be removed for replacing or adding to the center row of tee nuts if needed. Holes in the ends of the slider are for hanging it up.

Angle of the cut to be made has been lined up with an edge of the base. The two short studs have been screwed into the two most conveniently located tee nuts. The wooden hold-down strips are locked in place by tightening the wing nuts. Outer ends of the hold downs are supported by scraps of wood of the same thickness as the workpiece.

the tee nuts. A ¾″ spade bit and a ⁵⁄₁₆″ drill should do it.

If you had to accept the longer nuts, grind or file them to ⅜″ long. Before grinding, run two hex nuts onto the threaded rod and lock them together ¼″ from one end. Using this as a stop, screw a tee nut up against it. The rod becomes a handle for grinding the tee nut to ⅜″ long. Use a ⅜″ wide slot, cut in a piece of cardboard or tin, as a gage. After shortening, remove any burrs with a file and a countersink so that the rod will thread in smoothly.

Drive in the tee nuts, using a small socket, or a hex nut, between them and the hammer in order to bury them below the surface of the base. Replace the miter slot slider strip.

Cut the threaded rod to make four hold-down studs. Two long ones will do any job, but shorter ones are handier when working with thin stock. I cut a 12″ rod into 3½″ and 2½″ lengths.

The studs need a stop ⁷⁄₁₆″ from the bottom end to keep them from turning on through the tee nuts and dragging on the saw table. I brazed a washer on each one, using a steel-block jig with a ¼″-hole drilled ⁷⁄₁₆″ deep, to position them for brazing. Without a torch, epoxy the washers to the rods, or use pairs of nuts, locking them together at the ⁷⁄₁₆″ position.

The final parts are the hold-downs themselves. Three variations are shown, the more complex ones are easier to adapt to different stock thicknesses.

The simplest setup consists of two hardwood strips with five ⁵⁄₁₆″ holes drilled through them. My strips are ½″ x ¾″ x 5¼″. The holes are ¾″ apart, but the end holes are ⅜″ closer to one end than to the other. By turning them end for end, I

ANGLE-CUTTING JIG (CROSS SECTION)

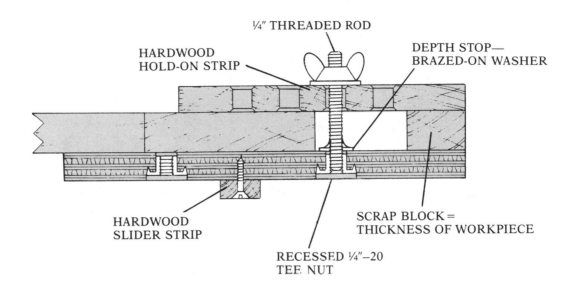

¼″ THREADED ROD

HARDWOOD
HOLD-ON STRIP

DEPTH STOP—
BRAZED-ON WASHER

HARDWOOD
SLIDER STRIP

SCRAP BLOCK =
THICKNESS OF WORKPIECE

RECESSED ¼″–20
TEE NUT

Here outer ends of the hold-down strips are supported on step blocks instead of scraps. Note that the step blocks can be used in two positions, each of which makes slightly different heights available.

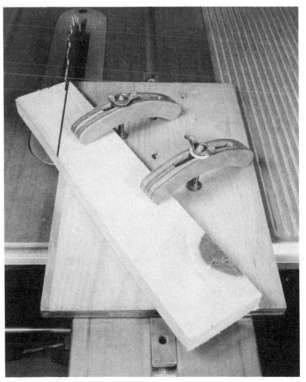

Rocker hold-downs, shown here, are a little more work to make but are easiest to use. They require no blocking except on very thick stock.

have the same number of adjustments as if the holes were ⅜″ apart instead of ¾″.

To use this setup, you need two small scraps of wood of the same thickness as the work. The stock is placed in position to be cut at the desired angle, the studs are screwed into a pair of appropriately located tee nuts, and the hold-down strips are placed on the studs to bridge the work and the scraps. Tightening the wing nuts over large washers on the hold-downs locks the work in position for the taper cut.

Making step blocks to use with the same hold-down strips eliminates the need for scrap blocks that are the same thickness as the workpiece. Mine are 1¼″ x 1½″ x 1¾″ and are shown in the illustration set in two different positions, making any of nine different heights available. With two added pairs of small blocks cut from ⅜″ and ⅝″ plywood, they provide ⅛″ steps from ¼″ to 2¾″, enough to secure stock about as thick as a 10″ table saw can cut.

Rocker hold-downs require more effort to construct but do not need blocking. I cut the ones shown here from ¾″ plywood with a band saw but a jigsaw or sabre saw would do as well. The rockers are 5″ long with an outside radius of 4½″ and a 3¾″ radius inside.

The 3″ slots were made in a drill press with a ¼″ router bit. First, I clamped two strips of wood to the drill table to provide a close sliding fit on the rocker. Then I put the rocker in this guide, concave side up. The router bit was drilled through at one end of the cut. Then I locked the spindle and pushed the rocker endways against the bit, rocking it as it went to keep the bit perpendicular to the curve.

These rockers secure stock up to about 1¾″ thick. Adding a ¾″ block increases their capacity to as thick as the saw can cut.

When using the jig, locate the studs as close to the edge of the workpiece as possible. This gives better leverage and a tighter grip.

The edge of the jig's base always represents the line of cut. For rough work, such as making stakes, just eyeball the desired angle, lay it along the edge of the jig, and clamp it down. Run it through the saw, loosen the wing nuts, flip the stock over, and repeat.

For more accurate work, draw your angle on the top of the stock and use a square to extend the ends of the line down the sides (or a side and end) of the work. Line these marks up with the edge of your jig and secure the hold-downs.

When both edges of a piece are to be sawed at an angle, it is easiest to flip the stock over after the first cut. When this is not practical, move the jig to the opposite table slot and move the hold-downs to line up the cut on this side of the jig.

A SIMPLE END-SAWING JIG

If you do much furniture making, a good tenoning jig is a necessity; otherwise it is an expensive luxury. Nevertheless, every so often you need to saw an end cut in a piece of work. If the stock is of a small size, it is difficult to move it squarely and accurately across the saw blade. If it is short as well, the operation can become downright terrifying. Here is an easy-to-make, inexpensive jig that helps make this kind of occasional sawing job much safer and more accurate as well.

The jig is nothing more than two scraps of ½″ plywood, glued together to make a piece 1″ thick. (1⅛″ plywood subflooring also works

This end-sawing jig consists of nothing more than two scraps of ½″ plywood glued up to 1″ thickness and cut to the shape shown. The 45-degree lines are for lining up mitered corners when slotting them for a spline. A couple of C-clamps and some hardboard pads are the only accessories required to complete the setup.

here, if you happen to have a scrap available.)

After gluing up the plywood, cut the piece to the shape shown; the base of this one is 8″ long and the height 7″. These dimensions are not engraved in stone though; you can make the jig larger or smaller to suit your saw and the type of work you do. Be sure, though, that you have a true right angle between the base and the lead-

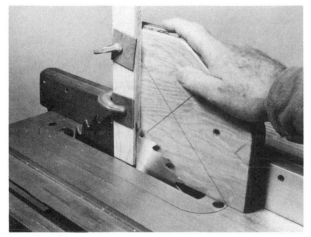

Slotting the end of a plywood strip is both simple and safe with this jig.

ing edge of the jig. The 45-degree angle cut, about 4½″ long, serves as a hand grip.

Round off the top and the trailing edge of the jig, I did that with a corner-rounding router bit. If no router is handy, you can chamfer the edges with the table saw and then round them with a Surform tool or with coarse sandpaper.

To use the jig, line up the stock to be end cut with the leading edge and base of the jig. Clamp the stock in position alongside the jig using two C-clamps. Put the lower clamp on the jig as close to the bottom as possible, allowing just enough room to clear the fence. Then put the second clamp as high up on the jig as the length of the stock allows.

Even pieces of stock too short to clamp above the fence can be cut with the jig. Put a scrap of the same material against the jig as a spacer and then clamp a "bridge" between the two. Be sure your bridge is heavy enough that the clamp will not bend it and that it does not just hold the stock by the edge. Set your saw blade height for the desired depth of cut, secure the fence at the proper position, and make your cut.

The saw blade (or table) can be tilted to cut a bevel on the end of a piece or to cut a dovetail. A groove to receive a spline can be cut in the end of a mitered joint such as a picture frame. In

Cutting a rabbet on this tiny plywood square is another potentially dangerous job that can be done safely and easily with end-sawing jig.

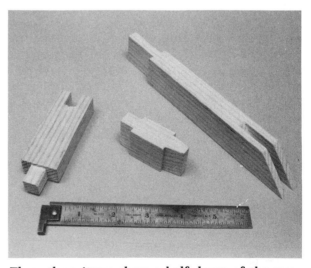

These three items show a half dozen of the many cuts that can be safely made with an end-sawing jig. The rule shows the size of the parts. Just the thought of trying to run the two smaller pieces across a saw without the help of a jig terrifies me.

this case, you may get a more accurate cut if you align the stock with one of a pair of 45-degree lines marked from the lower and upper corners of the jig. This is more reliable than just trying to keep the short face of the angle flush on the table surface.

Another feature of this jig is that the stock mounts against the side of it rather than directly in front of the leading edge, as is done with some other homemade jigs. Thus the saw blade does not chew up the front of the jig at the end of a cut.

As with any wooden item, a couple of quick coats of gloss polyurethane varnish will protect the jig for many years. In fact, you should do the same for the angle-cutting jig too.

SAFER AND MORE EXACT CROSSCUTTING

Lining up a pencil mark on a piece of stock to be crosscut with the exact edge of the teeth on the saw always tends to be an "iffy" proposition. For safer and more accurate cuts, try this simple accessory.

Most miter gages have holes or slots for attaching a wooden extension fence with recessed carriage bolts or something similar. Using the setup proved with your miter gage, make an extension fence, preferably of hardwood, that is just deep enough to reach nearly as high as the blade when the saw is set for its greatest depth of cut. Make the fence a little longer than the distance between the two miter-gage slots in the table. Fasten it securely to the miter gage and then saw it to length, first with one miter-gage slot, then the other.

You now have a miter-gage fence with each end exactly aligned with the cutting edge of the saw blade. Mark your stock, pull the miter gage well back from the saw blade, and line up the mark with the end of the fence, being sure that the piece to be saved is resting against the fence. Double-check your mark to see that it is aligned with the end of the fence, hold the stock in this position, and make your cut—safely and accurately.

Lining up a mark with the end of a special fence on the miter gage is easier than trying to line it up with the teeth of the saw blade. Getting the fence itself cut to the correct dimension is no problem. Make the extension fence a little long, attach it to the miter gage, and then let the saw cut it to length with the miter gage riding in the slots. Each end then provides an exact indication of the saw cutting line when the gage rides in the respective slot.

MITER JIG

If you cut many 45-degree miters, as in picture framing, you will find this simple miter jig helpful. Shifting a miter gage back and forth from 90 degrees to 45 degrees left, then to 45 degrees right, and finally back to 90 degrees again is a nuisance and leaves open the possibility of errors in setting angles. It only takes one to spoil the joint.

This jig is a simple triangle of ¾" plywood with one 90-degree angle and two 45-degree angles. With it, you set your miter gage to the 90-degree setting and leave it there. To cut a 45-degree miter, just lay the jig on the saw table with its hypotenuse against the miter-gage face and hold it in position with the miter-gage hold-down clamp. Hold the work against the angled face of the jig and run it through the saw. Now move the miter gage and the jig to the miter-gage groove on the other side of the saw blade and make your second cut.

Make your jig so that its hypotenuse is somewhat longer than the distance between your

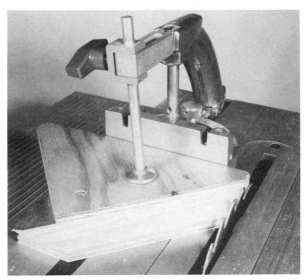

Simple triangle made from ¾" plywood lets you cut 45-degree angles to both left and right without ever having to change the miter gage itself from its normal 90-degree setting. If your miter gage does not have a hold-down clamp, glue a strip of fine sandpaper along the hypotenuse of the jig to help prevent it from slipping sideways while in use.

miter gage grooves. I used an 11½" hypotenuse for a 7" distance between grooves. Double-check the miter-gage settings to get an accurate 90-degree angle at the apex of the jig and two exact 45-degree angles at the base. Return the miter gage to an accurate 90-degree setting, and you won't have to fiddle with it again until you need to make an odd-angled cut other than 90 degrees or 45 degrees.

Cut ¾" off each end of the 45-degree points, so that when you make a cut, the work is backed solidly instead of by the very tip of the triangle.

COVE CUTTING ON A TABLE SAW

You may need to cut coves for various projects, such as making two pieces to be clamped around a drill press column to support a tool tray. Since this involves considerable stock removal and there is no tool specifically made for the job, it can be difficult and time-consuming.

You can make this cut with a table saw by passing the work across the table at an angle to the saw blade rather than straight across it. The trick is to lower the blade until it barely protrudes above the table. Only the very tips of the teeth do the cutting. By means of repeated passes, raising the blade about ⅟₁₆" between cuts, the cove is done much quicker and more accurately than trying to plow it out by hand with a gouge.

Set up by raising the saw blade to the total depth of cut. Provide a temporary wooden fence, to be fastened to the table with a C-clamp at each end. Set this fence at such an angle that the difference of the measurements between the saw blade and the fence, taken at

Two coves are shown at left. The wide shallow one was sawn by pushing the work across the saw blade at 90 degrees to the normal direction. The deep one was cut by angling the work across the saw against a wooden fence C-clamped to the saw table. To set this fence, the saw was raised to the depth of cut desired. The parallelogram was adjusted to have a distance between its strips equal to the desired cove width, as indicated by the scale. The parallelogram was then placed over the saw blade and angled until a tooth of the saw, at table level, just touched each of the parallel strips. The fence was then set to this angle and at the desired distance from the blade. Next the saw blade was retracted until it barely extended above the table. The work was passed along the angled fence and across the blade a number of times, raising the blade ⅟₁₆" or so between each pass.

the back of the blade and again at the front of the blade, are equal to the cove's width.

With the fence located and clamped, lower the blade to where it protrudes above the table only about ¹⁄₁₆″. Using a feather board, hold the stock against the fence and run it across the blade. Make repetitive cuts, raising the blade about ¹⁄₁₆″ between each one. (Slightly deeper cuts may be made in soft stock.) Proceed until the desired depth and width of the cove has been reached.

A parallelogram made from wood strips, as shown in the photo, can speed up fence setting. You just tighten screws on it to hold the desired cove width. Then you can move it around the blade to determine the angle of the fence.

CARBIDE-TIPPED BLADES

Carbide-tipped blades for table saws and radial saws are popular today and deservedly so; they cut fast and clean, often making cuts so smooth that a jointer is unnecessary. But one thing the ads don't tell you is that these blades are aggressive!

My first inkling of this came at a large woodworking show a couple of years ago. A salesman was demonstrating a well-advertised carbide-tipped blade when a man from the next booth came over. He asked the salesman to rip a piece of hardwood needed for his display. The salesman started the cut normally but about halfway through began feeding it faster to demonstrate the blade's cutting speed. All of a sudden the saw groaned, there was a thunk, and the piece of hardwood kicked back against the salesman's stomach. The hardwood was ruined—a large, curved gash was torn out of it.

The salesman was taken aback, and the owner of the once beautiful piece of wood was dismayed. At the time I thought the fiasco was entirely due to the salesman's grandstanding. Later, I bought a 10″ carbide-tipped blade for my own saw and found out otherwise.

I have worked with power saws of one sort or another for some fifty years, including a couple of summers in a large lumber mill. I consider myself a fairly careful operator, still having a full complement of arms, hands, and fingers. In

What can happen to stock with a carbide-tipped saw blade, if the stock is not held very carefully against the fence until the cut is completed and the stock has cleared the rear of the blade. These short samples are taken from the ends of what were longer pieces when the cuts were made.

the last year or so, however, in spite of my attempts to be careful, I've had more pieces of wood thrown violently across the shop than I have had in all the rest of my experience.

The problem lies with the cemented-on carbide tooth tips. On most of these blades, they stick out to either side of the blade itself quite a bit farther than the normal set of the teeth. When cutting wood with one of these blades, you must hold the stock tightly against the fence until the stock has completely passed by the back end of the blade. Otherwise, the tips of the uprising teeth on the back of the blade may dig into the work and throw it violently up and backward, tearing a large curved gash in the wood in the process.

These blades are good, they are fast, they make an excellent cut, but they are aggressive. The watchword is caution; much more so than with an ordinary blade. Plan and execute your cut so that there is no possibility of the work being allowed to deviate the slightest amount away from the fence, especially after the cut itself is finished but before the work has cleared the back of the blade.

Safety goggles should always be worn when doing any power sawing. But with a carbide-tipped blade, I consider a full face shield a necessity. Until you've seen a slip-up with one of these blades, you won't believe the force it can exert.

FALSE SAW-TABLE TOP

When cutting small, thin pieces on a table saw, the gaps around the blade on a normal saw table insert can draw work into the blade and damage it.

A false table top solves this problem. Tempered hardboard with its smooth side up is excellent for this purpose, but a piece of thin plywood (best side up) also works. Raise the table to clear the saw blade and clamp the false top in position with a C-clamp at the front and rear of the table. Be careful to allow space for the fence to be installed at the required position and place the clamps so that they will not interfere with the work.

C-clamps may be impractical if small strips are being cut off a large piece. In this case, hold the false top in place with countersunk flathead screws tightened into holes drilled and tapped into the table itself.

Once the false top is secured to the table, start the saw. Slowly and carefully lower the table until the blade has cut up through and is extended sufficiently above the false table to cut your thin stock.

HEIGHT GAGE FOR TABLE SAW

When the saw is used to make a kerf in the workpiece which is less than full depth, it is difficult to measure accurately the height of the blade. If you make many of these cuts, a height gage can help.

Plywood ⅛" thick is the best material for making this gage, if you have a scrap available. Hardboard would also seem to be a good material, but much of it is way off in thickness; many ⅛" pieces are actually closer to ⁵⁄₃₂". Stack a few of these together and the errors add up fast. If you have no ⅛" plywood available, ¼" does a fair job, but you get fewer exact dimensions. However, eighths and even sixteenths can be estimated fairly accurately alongside ¼" steps.

A false top, made from a piece of tempered hardboard clamped or screwed to the saw table, makes a safer and easier job of cutting short, thin pieces. To cut its slot, the false top is fastened in position and the saw table lowered down over the rotating blade.

Nine strips of ⅛" plywood cut to appropriate lengths and glued together make up this handy height gage. Two sets of labels allow it to be easily read when positioned on either side of the blade.

Check the plywood closely to be sure it is the advertised thickness. I recently checked a scrap of ¼″ plywood with a dial caliper and found it correct to within a thousandth of an inch! Other pieces were also quite close, but some were significantly off.

If you don't have a way of measuring accurately, cut enough small pieces to add up to 1″ in thickness, remove any rough edges, press them together and measure them. If they add up to an inch within, say, ¹⁄₆₄″ that should be quite adequate accuracy, especially if it is on the short side. (Each glue line on the finished gage builds it up a couple of thousandths.)

Stock that is a little thick can be sanded a little to bring it down to the proper measurement. If you don't have any material of an acceptable thickness, rip some out of solid stock. Try to get it just a hair under the desired dimension to allow for the glue line.

Once you have the proper material, cut it into strips. The gage shown is 2″ wide to give adequate room for four rows of label tape. Make the first piece about 3″ long, and then add about ⅜″ in length to each succeeding piece until you have enough pieces to measure up to 1″ in height of the blade. This will take nine ⅛″ pieces, or five ¼″ pieces. Glue them together so that one end of the built-up block is straight and the other end is stairstepped.

There is no need to go beyond 1″. Any variance in thickness would continue to build and compound the error. It is easier and more accurate to cut out a block to exactly 1″ x 2″ in size and use it in conjunction with the stairstepped block to set the saw height from 1″ to 2″ or from 2″ to 3″, as required. If your saw cuts to depths beyond 3″, you can saw off your 1 x 2 block to an exact 3″ in length; then you can measure blade heights up to 4″.

Mark the top of the gage to indicate the various heights with ⅜″ label tape. In order to match the tape markings to the steps, I used two tapes, and alternated the dimensions. I put a separate pair of tapes on both edges of the gage so that I can take a measurement on either side of the saw blade and still have a set of readings that are right side up. Note that one set of readings must be printed out so as to increase from left to right; the other decreases from left to right.

To use the gage, set your blade to an approxi-mate height and then move the gage over it. Adjust blade height until the highest tooth just touches the bottom surface of the step that indicates the correct height. You should also find it easy to estimate in-between heights to the nearest ¹⁄₃₂″ if your gage is made from ⅛″ strips, or to ¹⁄₁₆″ if you have ¼″ steps.

PUSH STICKS AND FEATHER BOARDS

Every table saw should have an assortment of push sticks and feather boards. Some of these can be purchased, others are shopmade. One can never have enough push sticks to cover all situations, and it is easy to take a few moments to cut one out of scrapwood to fit a special situation. Some cuts will be easier if the push stick itself is cut into while in use. It is better to spend a little time to make a helper that will self-destruct than to take a chance on chewing up a finger.

Several different push sticks are shown here. The one with the handle is made from the same

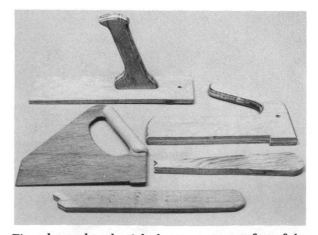

Five plywood push sticks here represent a few of the many configurations that can be used. The upper one is for work on a jointer, especially with thin stock, and has a small crossbar glued into a slot on the bottom near the right end. The crossbar protrudes ³⁄₁₆″ to catch on the end of the stock to push it along.

Thin push stick allows very narrow strips to be safely pushed on past the rear of the saw blade.

⅛" plywood stock that was used for the steps on the saw-height gage. Notice that its handle brings the hand up well away from the saw, while still allowing very thin and narrow strips to be cut.

The dimensions are optional; make it to suit your saw's fence height, the size of its table, and the size of your hand. Set the handle at a comfortable angle, depending on your height versus the height of the saw table.

Make the handle from a dowel, an old broomstick, closet pole stock, or whatever is available and provides a comfortable grip for your hand. If you make the push stick out of ⅛" material and have a saw blade that cuts a ⅛" kerf, cut a slot about three-quarters of the way through the handle and then just glue it onto the push stick. If you can't match the kerf to the material's thickness, rip the round stock into two pieces and glue one on each side. Either

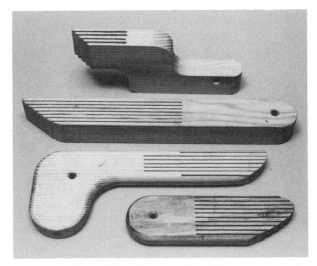

An assortment of feather boards. The top one is designed for resawing boards on the band saw. The short one at the bottom is for mounting on either the band saw or drill press table.

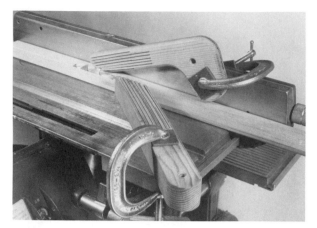

Feather board holding the stock against the fence is kept ahead of the saw blade so that it does not pinch the kerf against the blade. A vertical feather board is secured farther along to check any tendency of the rising rear teeth to lift the stock. The "pistol grip" on the vertical board allows it to be fastened to the small fence at a sufficient angle to provide an adequate hold-down force. Hardboard pads, kept available in the C-clamp drawer, prevent the feather boards from being chewed up by the clamps.

way, you will find it easier and safer to make the short rip cut into the end of the full length of round stock first. Then cut off the short handle.

When you lay out the push stick for cutting, do so in such a manner that the best (smoothest) side of the plywood will be the side that rides the fence.

Feather boards, or spring boards, can also be purchased or shopmade, simple or elaborate. You should have at least a couple available to hold the stock closely against the fence and eliminate a wavering cut.

The simplest ones consist of just a strip of wood with a series of saw cuts in one end. The end can be cut at a taper so that all the segments bear equally against the work, or it can be left square.

In either case the spring action is varied by how much of the feather board overlaps the end of the work when it is clamped in position.

A vertically mounted feather board on the rip fence becomes a valuable hold-down when making a groove or dado rather than a through cut. The feather board insures that the depth of the slot will be uniform. An elongation on the

clamp end of the feather board allows it to be fastened to the relatively low fence and still be at enough of an angle to do the job.

Feather boards placed against the side of the work should be completely ahead of the saw blade so that they will not pinch the cut against it. When they are clamped on a fence to hold down the work, they can be mounted alongside the blade. They may work best if applied near the rear of the blade where they directly counteract the tendency for the work to be lifted by the uprising teeth.

CARRYING 4' x 8' SHEETS

Carrying full sheets of plywood, particleboard, or hardboard from station wagon or pickup truck to the shop is an awkward job, especially in the case of the heavier sheets. Where obstructions such as stairs must be negotiated it is that much more difficult. Here are a couple of practical answers to the problem.

The simplest solution is to take a length of light rope, tie it into a loop, and fasten it about

A short length of light rope with its ends tied together makes a simple aid for carrying a full sheet of plywood. This one has its ends spliced together, and the splice is wrapped with duct tape to make a convenient handle. It also keeps the two loops positioned so that they can be quickly thrown over the corners of the sheet.

the two lower corners of the panel as shown. Grab the two parts of the rope where they meet, tuck the panel under your arm, and walk away with it.

If the distance from your armpit to the ground does not provide adequate clearance to carry the 4'-wide sheet, arrange the rope so that the handle is on the inside rather than the outside; lean the top of the sheet against your shoulder as you lift it. Then hold the top of the panel with your free hand.

The rope can be any size from ¼" to ½" or even a little larger if that happens to be the only thing available. Depending on your reach, it should take a bit more than 20 feet by the time

you make a knot in it; 25 feet should be more than enough.

If you wish to make a permanent carrying sling, you can cut and splice it to the correct length and tape the two parts together at the handhold position.

The advantages of this carrier are that it is quickly and simply made and it presents no storage problem; just roll it up into a coil or a ball and stow it. The disadvantage is that it takes a little arranging to get the rope into position on the panel and then a little juggling to hang on to the rope while you get the panel into position under your arm.

Another carrier that is easier to use can be made from a few scraps of wood and plywood. This holder is cut out with either a band saw or sabre saw from a ⅜" to ⅝"-thick plywood scrap. Make it of a length appropriate to your height and arm length.

The carrier may be made in one of two types. The simplest one has a single handle for carrying the sheet under your arm or against your shoulder with the top steadied by your other hand. A 1" strip of wood at the bottom separates a ¼"-plywood lug to keep the sheet from slipping off the lifting strip and allows a panel up to ¾" thick to be easily carried. Glue and screw or glue and nail the three pieces together.

The other plywood lifter operates exactly the same when the upper handle is used. But it also

Plywood sheet carrier is made of ⅜" plywood and is 6½" wide and 29" long. Size yours to suit your height and reach. The carrier has two handles for carrying the sheet at different heights. This one has a rabbet in the bottom crossbar to hold the sheet, but the crossbar could have been made in two parts, one a little wider to create a plywood lip.

On fairly level terrain, put the carrier on the outside of the sheet and grip the upper handle. Your other hand steadies any rocking tendency.

On stairs put the carrier on the inside of the sheet and hold onto the lower handle. This raises the panel another 12″. The upper part of the panel rests against the outside of your arm and shoulder. Hold the sheet in this position with your other hand.

has a lower handle to lift the sheet to a higher position for maneuvering it up or down stairs or over obstructions. Used this way, it must be carried on the outside of the arm, and the upper edge of the sheet may be so high as to be hard to reach and hold. After the obstruction is passed, you will probably find it easier to stop and transfer your grip to the upper handle.

With either model, if you make the inside cuts with a sabre saw, start the saw with the usual drilled hole. If you use a band saw, just cut straight through the middle of the handle section. Later you can cover the kerf(s) by gluing a curved strip on each side of the handle; the strips also serve to round out the handle for an easier grip.

Rounding off the edges of the plywood with a router prevents splintering and makes for easier handling and a better appearance. I recommend putting on a couple of coats of polyurethane varnish.

If you don't have plywood handy, the carrier can be made out of other materials; for example, some ½″ or ¾″ copper pipe and a few fittings left over from a plumbing job. Solder a tee to the top and bottom of a suitable length of pipe. The top tee, which may have very short lengths of pipe and caps added if you desire, serves as the handle. To the bottom tee add a

couple of short lengths of pipe with a 90-degree elbow turned horizontally at each end. To each of these solder vertically either a street elbow or the very minimum length of pipe and a regular elbow.

The same type of carrier could be made from plastic pipe and fittings, provided you have the heavy type of pipe. The light-gage plastic might be a little too weak to carry heavier sheets. Old-fashioned steel pipe and fittings also work, but they get pretty heavy, especially if you use anything larger than ⅜″ or ½″ pipe. Carry a panel of ¾″ particle board, and you will not appreciate any extra weight!

A broomstick, large dowel, or scrap of closet pole stock also makes a solid upright. Cross drill a hole near the top for a dowel T-handle and build up a wooden carrier at the bottom similar to the one on the plywood carrier described above.

One of these carriers can also be used to swing up one side of a panel and lay it gently down on a pair of sawhorses without scratching or otherwise damaging it.

EASIER, BETTER EDGE ROUTING

When a router is used to round-over, chamfer, or rabbet the edge of a piece of stock held atop the bench, it is off balance and its base must be held flat against the top of the work. Any inattention to this requirement can result in a less than satisfactory result.

To avoid this problem, use a small scrap of wood of the same thickness as the work. Screw it to the bottom of the base of the router on the opposite side to where the work is being done. Depending on the size of the scrap, one or two flathead machine screws can be countersunk into the scrap and screwed up into the router base (most router bases have holes for fastening on accessories or securing the router to a router table). If no threaded hole is available, one or two wood screws can be put down into the leveling block from the top. Drill a hole or holes through the base if needed.

This simple addition requires only a few minutes to set up and makes for easier and safer

Edge routing is easier if you temporarily screw to the router base a small scrap of wood the same thickness as the work. This avoids the problem of having to hold the router flat against the work while balancing it on less than half its base.

To resaw, you need a fence. A simple fence can be made from two different width boards glued together at a 90-degree angle and backed up by glued-in corner braces. By making it of two widths, one side provides a backup for the widest boards your saw handles, but when re-sawing smaller boards you can use the narrow side as a fence. That way the upper blade guides and the guard can be brought down closer to the top of the cut for better guidance and safer operation. For a band saw that cuts to a 6″ depth, 5″ and 3″ fence widths should work out well.

For reasons which will become apparent shortly, make the fence 2″ longer than the table and set the corner braces back at least 3″ from each end. Cut the fence boards and the corner braces accurately and be sure that the unit is made up into an exact 90-degree angle. Securely glue and nail, or even better, glue and screw it together. Be sure to countersink either the nails or screw heads well below the surface.

The fence should be used in combination with a feather board, finger board, or spring board, whichever you prefer to call it, to hold the stock firmly against the fence for an even cut. In order to hold a wide board evenly

operation. It usually provides appreciably better results as well.

BAND SAW NOTES

Once you have a band saw, even a small bench model, you'll wonder how you ever got along without it. Here are a few suggestions to speed along your introduction to this versatile tool.

Resawing is the term for edge-ripping a wide board into thin ones of the same width. A band saw does this much more effectively than a table saw. Most small band saws cut up to 6″, and even the benchtop models usually cut to 4″. Most table saws cut to about 3″ maximum, work much more slowly, and leave a wider kerf, thus wasting more material and limiting the number of pieces that can be cut from a given board.

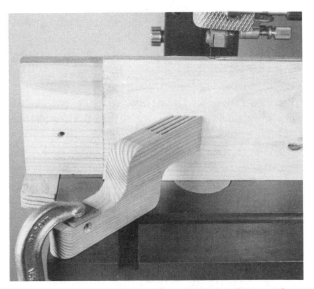

A band saw is dandy for resawing boards into thinner ones than are normally available. A deep fence, as shown here, is essential. The S-shaped feather board holds the center against the fence.

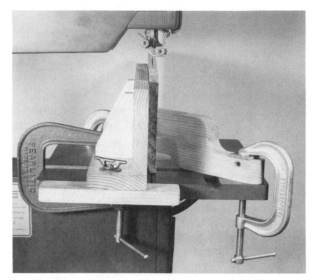

Angle braces keep the fence square to the table. If a blade has any tendency to "drift," the fence is adjusted to that angle and the crossbar locked in place with the modified wing nut. To reset the fence, just hold the crossbar against the table, move the fence to the desired distance from the blade, and then secure it with the C-clamps.

against the fence, the feather board should be raised toward the center of the board. Since you will be cutting many different widths of boards, setting it to the exact center each time is impractical, but an approximation will help. This can be done in a couple of ways. An offset cut can be made, with your band saw of course, in a short length of 2 x 4. Slot one end with a number of parallel cuts to provide the spring action up against the center of the stock, while the other end provides a tabletop platform for a C-clamp to secure it to the saw table. If you don't have the 2 x 4 handy, the same effect can be had by gluing and screwing together two smaller pieces of scrap at an angle. Be sure to install the feather board so that it does not press against the open kerf at or beyond the blade.

To resaw, you will usually find that installing the widest blade you have (½" for many small band saws) is a good idea. A skip-tooth blade is also especially good here because it removes more sawdust, which clogs up the cut.

Clamp the fence to the saw table, set up your feather board, and try a sample cut in a piece of scrap. Unless you happen to be very lucky, you will find that the saw blade tends to drift, or "lead", away from the desired line of cut at a slight angle. Common to band saw blades, this problem is corrected by angling the fence slightly in order to feed the work parallel to the lead. Reset the fence and clamp it at the new angle and you should get a nice straight cut.

This is well and good, but every time you set up the fence or reset it to cut a thicker or thinner strip, you are faced with again finding the exact angle to correct the lead. To avoid this, clamp a short piece of scrap crosswise to the front of the fence's bottom board (this is what the extra 2" in length is for) at such an angle that when it is pushed against the front of the table it aligns the fence properly to negate the saw's lead. If the cross strip is kept clamped to the fence at this angle, it will only have to be changed when the saw blade is changed or when the other board of the fence is used.

An ordinary C-clamp can be used for this purpose. Better yet, secure the two pieces with a bolt and nut, together with large diameter washers to keep the pieces from slipping.

For resawing work where accuracy is not critical, some people prefer to use a round-nose wooden guide clamped to the table alongside the blade. They hold the work against it and adjust the angle of the work by eye to correct for the lead of the blade.

Resawn boards that are less than 4" wide can be planed to a smooth surface on a 4" jointer by using a hold-down type pusher. Be sure to set the jointer for a very thin cut any time that you surface the flat side of a board, since it will be cutting over a much larger area than on the narrow side of a piece of stock.

With a band saw it is obvious that the narrower the blade, the tighter the curves it can cut. No matter how narrow a blade you have on the machine though, you always seem to need to cut a shorter curve than it will comfortably make.

One solution is to first saw a number of cuts in from the outside edge of the waste to intercept the desired cutting line at the points of sharpest curvature. Then, when you proceed to the actual cut, waste at the sharper curves falls away as the previously made cuts are reached. This allows the blade freedom to negotiate the short turns.

To cut sharp curves with a wide blade, run in a number of cuts through the waste up to the cutting line at the points of sharpest curvature. As the finish cut is made, the pieces will move aside and allow the heel of the blade more without binding.

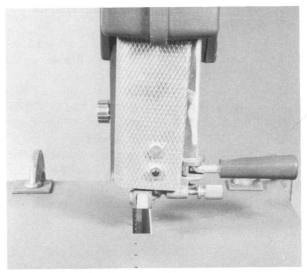

Circle-cutting jig on a band saw makes circles from 2″ to 30″ in diameter. It needs no complicated pivot slider and locking mechanism. Instead, you insert a small pointed pivot pin in one of the holes located 1″ apart. A 6″-long slot, a bit wider than your widest blade, allows the jig to be clamped to the saw table at a point that provides any fractional radius required. (To cut a circle with a 6¼″ radius, put the pivot pin in the hole 6″ from the end of the slot and then clamp the jig to the saw table with the blade located ¼″ from the end of the slot; thus you get a 6¼″ radius.) The leading edge of the blade should be aligned with the line of pivot holes.

Circles are easily cut freehand on the band saw, but if you do a lot of circle cutting, you may find that a circle-cutting jig is worthwhile for the more accurate and smoother cut that it produces.

There must be dozens of circle-cutting jigs for the band saw that have been shown in various woodworking books and magazines. But basically almost all of them consist of a plywood auxiliary table mounted on the normal saw table and bolted or clamped from below. A slide, mounted perpendicular to the blade, is recessed into the table in either a dadoed or a dovetailed slot. The slide has a means of locking it in any position and also a small, sharp pivot point, such as a cut off and sharpened nail, that protrudes through the slide directly in line with the teeth on the blade. The stock is impaled on the point and rotated around to make the cut.

The starting side of the cut must of course be at an edge of the stock. Otherwise a groove the width of the blade must be provided up to the line of the cut in order to position the blade prior to beginning the circle. If you would like to have a circle jig for your band saw but do not

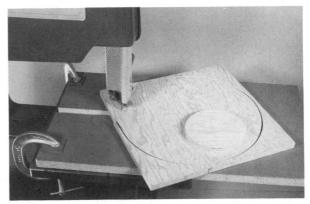

Cut was started freehand here to get the blade into the edge of the work. Then the stock was tapped down onto the pivot pin and swung around it to saw out the circle. For large circles the corners of the stock are first sawed off freehand to avoid their hitting the C-clamps during rotation.

want to go to all the trouble of building this jig, consider this simpler version.

Make your table of ¾" plywood stock and instead of grooving it for a slide, drill a series of holes 1" or 2" apart in a line perpendicular to the blade. Line up the holes with the cutting edge of the teeth. The holes should be a slip fit on your pivot point and should be ⅝" deep. Continue the hole on through the table with a smaller drill to allow the point to be pushed out from the bottom afterward. I use a ³⁄₃₂" hole for a point made of ³⁄₃₂" welding rod and have a ¹⁄₁₆" pusher hole. The pivot should be about ¹⁄₁₆" longer than the depth of its hole; grind its top ¹⁄₁₆" to a point for the work to pivot on.

Cut a slot into the opposite edge of the table for several inches to allow the jig to clear the blade. This allows the jig to adjust to any exact cutting radius desired, thus taking up any part of the 1" or 2" spacing of the pivot point holes. It also extends the auxiliary table far enough beyond the line of cut so that it can be simply clamped to the normal table with a couple of C-clamps.

With this setup, the large corners on the waste side of a large circle must be cut back before starting so that they do not interfere with the hold-down clamps.

A jig with pivot holes extending out only 12" from the blade cuts circles up to 24" in diameter. If even larger circles are to be cut, the jig can be made any length needed.

Straight, smooth groove can be hand chiseled quickly with a guide block clamped to the line of cut. Keep back of chisel flat against guide.

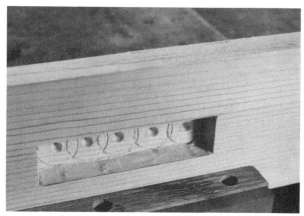

Compare this "best effort" cut, made along a pencil line, with the previous one cut against a guide block.

HAND-CHISELING STRAIGHT LINES

No matter how many power tools we have, there always seems to come a time when it becomes necessary to hand-chisel a groove, mortise, or recess of some sort. The cut needed invariably is longer than your widest chisel, which means you have to make overlapping cuts along a line. Without a guide the cut usually ends up a little ragged.

There is a better way though. Cut out as much of the waste material as possible by boring or drilling a number of holes as shown. Then use a vise, C-clamps, or a couple of nails to fasten on a small block of wood directly along the line of cut. Lay the back of the chisel flat against the wood block and work along it to cut away the material in a smooth straight line.

NO-DING NAILING

Who among us has never accidentally put a ding in a finished surface by swinging a hammer too enthusiastically when driving nails? But a guard around the nail eliminates, or greatly reduces this hazard.

Make the guard from any of several materials. For light work, such as with small finishing nails, heavy rubber from a truck inner tube works well. Or you can cut scraps from the tire flap or liner found between a truck's tube and wheel rim. If you get a liner, cut your guard out of the central part, which is usually the thickest. Used or damaged truck tubes and flaps are often obtainable, free at most large tire shops that cater to truckers. (Some of this material will always come in handy around the shop for other jobs.) Another good guard can be made from a scrap of ⅛″ plywood or a bit of ⅛″ tempered hardboard.

Drill, or in rubber punch, one or more holes in your guard. A small hole in one end for finishing nails and a larger one in the other end for regular nails works fine. (If you happened to choose a scrap of pegboard, you have the nail holes already drilled for you, although you will have to enlarge one hole to clear the head of large nails.)

The guard works this way: Carefully start your nail in the correct spot and then slip the guard over it. You can now bang away safely until the nail is about flush with the guard. Lift off the guard and, using a nail set of the correct size, finish driving the nail either flush to the surface or countersunk.

MODIFIED LATHE CENTER

When making two or more spindle turnings in a wood lathe, it is common practice to remove them from the lathe and then later re-insert

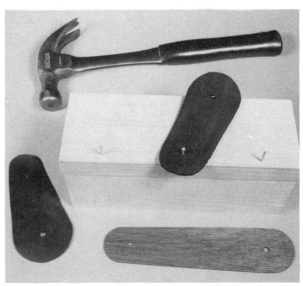

Guard shown on the finishing nail is cut from a rubber truck-tire liner which makes some of the best guards. The other two are made from a piece of old inner tube and a scrap of ⅛″ plywood. Any of these will protect finished surfaces.

Filing one or two notches in a lathe center spur will leave a distinctive mark in one notch on the end of the stock. That makes it possible to later replace the stock in the lathe in the same position and eliminates the off-center wobbling common when turned stock is put back in a lathe.

them for final sanding and finishing. More often than not, though, you find that they do not spin concentrically when replaced. This error can be eliminated or at least diminished by placing the turning back on the headstock with the drive spurs in the original position. To do this, file one or more deep notches in the sharp edge of one of the drive spurs. This spur then leaves a distinctive mark in its notch on the turning, allowing it to be easily identified and the spindle replaced in its original position.

DRIVING THREADED INSERTS

Threaded inserts, available from woodworking suppliers, are great when you need to bolt something to a wooden part because they allow the bolt to be tightened directly into the part without requiring a through hole and an external nut.

The insert is a double-threaded sleeve; an inside thread fits the bolt to be used, and a coarser outside thread turns into the hole in the wood by means of a screwdriver slot across the top of the insert. When attempting to install them in hardwood however, the edge of the screwdriver slot often strips off before the insert is buried.

Avoid this problem by using one of the bolts itself as an installation tool. Thread a nut onto the bolt until it jams against the unthreaded part of the shank. Then thread on the insert until it jams against the nut. (If your bolts are an all-thread type, screw on two nuts to an appropriate position and then jam them together using two wrenches.) Now you can screw the insert into the wood with a wrench on the head of the bolt. A socket turned by a speed handle usually does the job in a jiffy. If more torque is needed, try a ratchet on the socket or a box end wrench. When the insert is fully buried, just back out the bolt along with the jam nut.

V-TABLE

Small auxiliary work tables that clamp to a table or workbench have been around for many years. They have a V-shaped cutout to give clearance for the saw blade while supporting the work on either side of the cut. I first worked with one in connection with an elementary school project nearly sixty years ago, and it was not a new idea then.

One of these tables is still handy for work with a coping saw and sabre saw. The C-clamp always gets in the way, however, and the work

Mutilated slot on the threaded insert at left shows what often happens when attempting to drive one of these with a screwdriver, even in relatively soft wood. The second one was easily driven without any distortion by using a bolt and a jam nut. When the insert is driven flush, just loosen the jam nut and back out the bolt.

V-notched board to support coping-saw work is a very old idea. Fastening a small block to the bottom of the board makes it possible to mount the board in a vise. That leaves the top free of the C-clamp that normally secures it to the workbench.

must be juggled around into a new position or the clamp shifted to the other side of the table. This is unavoidable where the auxiliary table must be clamped to an ordinary table. But where there is a vise of some sort available, I have an easy solution. Just glue and screw a wooden lug to the bottom of the V-board. You can then secure the lug in even a small vise in a jiffy. Now you have an obstruction-free work surface.

COPING WITH A COPING SAW

Ever wonder how a coping saw got its name? It was originally designed for coping, a process for fitting molding to a corner without mitering. A close-fitting miter joint is not easy to make even when the two sides are at an exact right angle; often they are not square in the corner of a room, and then mitering a joint becomes extremely difficult.

With a coped joint, one piece of molding is measured and cut off square so as to continue flush into the corner. The end of the other piece is cut in an arc to match up with the contour of the first piece. This produces a tight fitting joint that has the appearance of a mitered joint.

I first saw this method demonstrated back in 1937 when a workman was laying a new linoleum floor in a little bathroom in my par-

ent's home. Once the linoleum was down, he brought in the quarter-round pine molding (about ¾″ on a side) that was to finish off the edges. He square-cut a piece to the length of one wall and started to nail it down. Being a smart aleck high school shop student, I asked why he didn't miter it. He simply smiled and invited me to "watch."

He sawed a piece to the length of the next segment of the wall. The molding being soft and of a small cross section, he didn't even use his coping saw. With a sharp pocketknife, he cut a curved section out of the end of this piece to match the curve of the quarter round. He held it tentatively into position to check the match, made a small correction with his knife, and nailed it into place to make a beautiful "mitered" corner.

To ensure a nice fit, the workman cut it to a little more than a 90-degree angle with the face of the material. This did two things. If the corner was at all splayed out to greater than square, the molding still fit in a tight joint. Further, if a correction cut was needed, he only had to touch up the front section of the molding; the rest was already relieved.

For a molding more involved than a simple quarter round, you can locate the cutting line by sawing the molding initially at a 45-degree angle, just as though you were making a mitered corner. Then use your coping saw to cut along the line of the cut where it meets the face of the molding. Hold your saw at a slight angle

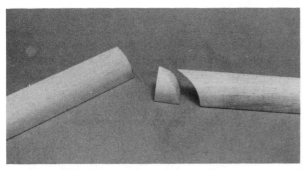

A coped joint often works out better than a mitered joint, particularly if the corner is not a true right angle. One piece of molding is cut off square and nailed into the corner. The second piece is "coped" with a coping saw, or even a pocketknife, to fit the

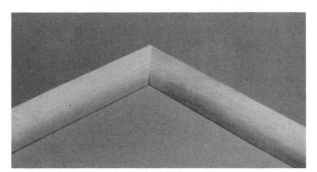

shape of the molding. If the angle is more than 90 degrees, the back of the cut is relieved as necessary for a good fit.

Joint appears to be a normal mitered corner once the coped end is pushed up against the first strip.

to make a cut of a little more than 90-degrees, and if your match isn't exact, you can easily touch up the front to a perfect fit with a couple of strokes of a sharp knife.

SHARPENING CHAIN SAWS

Out in the country, owning one or more chain saws has become common. When you buy a new saw, you usually wind up with a special round file to sharpen the teeth. This works fine the first time or two, and then mysteriously it doesn't seem to work so well anymore. Even a new file doesn't do the job. The problem is that the chain has been pounded around the driving sprocket link by link so many thousands of times that it has become work hardened to the point where a file will hardly "touch" it.

After a couple of rather futile attempts at sharpening it, you may struggle along with it for awhile until you finally give up and buy a

One of these stones, used as shown, quickly sharpens a chain that is so work hardened that a file skates across it without leaving a mark.

new chain, even though there is still a lot of potential mileage left in the old one.

There is an answer for this problem, but somehow it hasn't become as well known as it deserves to be. Little rotary stones are especially made for this purpose. Combined with a high-speed grinder, they do a great job of sharpening any chain, work hardened or not, and are to my mind a tremendous improvement over the usual file. The stones come with a ⅛" shank, are packed two or three to a card, and are available most anywhere chain saws are sold. They come in several sizes; be sure to get the ones that are appropriate for your chain. (The ⁵⁄₃₂" stones fit chains on many of the smaller saws.)

Most of the chain saw outlets also sell two high-speed tools to turn the stones; you can get one for 110v AC or one for 12v DC with a plug to fit the lighter outlet in your car or truck. The latter is a good choice for sharpening the chain if you do much cutting out where power is not available. If you do most of your wood cutting at home, you may not need to buy the motor tool. Any kind of high-speed grinder with a collet to accept a ⅛" shank, even one of the little hobby motor tools, will do an excellent job. An air-driven die grinder, if you have one with a reducer collet to take the ⅛" shaft, is also a good power source. (If you happen to have a die grinder and can't get a ¼" to ⅛" collet reducer for it, Sears part #1-621248-01 for their model 315.25841 hand grinder will do the job.)

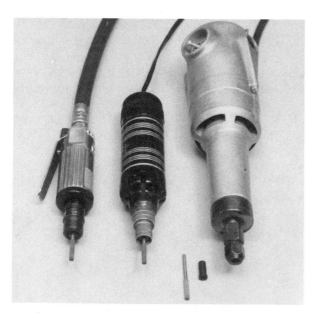

Any high-speed tool, air or electric, with a collet that accepts a ⅛"-shank rotary stone, will do a much faster job of sharpening a chain saw, especially after it has become work hardened. Twelve-volt motors that plug into a pickup's cigarette lighter are available for resharpening chains out in the woods.

A ⅜" drill usually peaks at about 1200 rpm and is just too slow to be used with these tiny stones. A ¼" drill turning to about 2500 rpm works but only marginally. At this low speed the stone sharpens quite slowly, and there is a tendency to try to speed up the operation by increasing pressure. This will wear out the stone quite rapidly and they are expensive.

If you don't already have a small hand grinder, sometimes called a rotary tool, this might be a good time to get one. The price is about the same as the single-purpose chain saw tool, but the hand grinder will do the same job and come in handy for many other jobs around the shop.

Of course, most of the chain saw tools do have special guides on them that show you how to line up the tool to a specific angle with the chain teeth, but these are not really necessary. You can just eyeball it to the existing angle on the tooth with no problem. Besides, some of the chain manufacturers differ by 5 degrees or more in the angle recommended, so that an approximation is sometimes closer to the correct angle than is the one marked on the guide.

Chain saws dull down slowly and, since the engine is doing the work, you sometimes don't really notice it until they have become quite dull. One way to tell whether the saw is sharp is by watching the chips thrown out. Notice that with a sharp chain the waste comes out as definite large chips. When the chips get smaller and take on more of the appearance of sawdust, it's time to take a break and give the chain a once-over with the little stone. You will make up the ten minutes spent doing this in the first hour of work afterward!

CLEANING A CHAIN SAW BEFORE REFUELING

In order to keep them light in weight, most chain saws have limited fuel and chain oil capacity; so they require frequent refilling. Due to the combination of flying chips and chain oil, the saw also quickly gets covered with a greasy gunk that can get into the fuel and chain oil tanks when you take off the caps.

One way to avoid this is to carry an old paintbrush as part of your chain saw kit. A 1" or 1½" brush, with about ½" of the length of bristles cut off to stiffen them, quickly cleans around both filler caps. Do this before opening and you reduce the possibility of contamination.

The same brush is also quite useful for cleaning around the bar and sprocket area after removing the guide bar cover.

Old paintbrush with its bristles shortened makes quick work of cleaning around the fuel and chain-oil caps before removing them for refill.

5
GETTING THE MOST OUT OF PLYWOOD

Plywood comes in large sheets and in varying thicknesses. It is known to almost everyone—plywood is used worldwide to make countless items from tiny toys to huge buildings. In this chapter I will cover some of the lesser-known plywoods and will mention some unusual uses for plywood, as well as for the plywood scraps that accumulate in every shop.

Actually, you may find plywood cutoffs to be so handy to have around the shop that you will want to check with your local cabinet shop or other plywood user. They often have cutoff pieces that are too small to be of any value to them. These scraps can often be had at a fraction of their original cost per square foot, and the cabinetmaker may be as happy to get rid of them as the workshopper is to get them at a bargain price.

had with either plain edges or tongue and groove. Longer sheets up to 14' or 16' can be special ordered in ¼" thickness, and up to 12' long in the thicker sheets. Some plywood is also available in 5-foot widths.

Plywood comes in both interior and exterior types and in grades from A-A (front and back face) to C-D. A is made from the best veneer and with only limited patches, while D contains large gaps, open knotholes, and other voids. Marine grade plywood meets certain specifications for waterproof glue and for higher grade interior plies.

Hardwood plywood normally comes in thicknesses from ⅛" to 1" and is made in four types and five grades; the types indicate the water resistance of the glue used, and the grades indicate appearance.

SIZES OF PLYWOOD

Softwood plywoods, of which Douglas Fir is the most common, normally come in sheets 4' x 8' in size and in thicknesses from ¼" to ¾". In addition, 1⅛" fir plywood is commonly used for subfloors in building construction. It can be

SMOOTHER SAW CUTS

Smooth, splinterless cuts on plywood can be a problem when crosscutting; the surface ply is particularly prone to this on the exit side of the saw blade (the underside when using a table saw, for example). To alleviate this, special

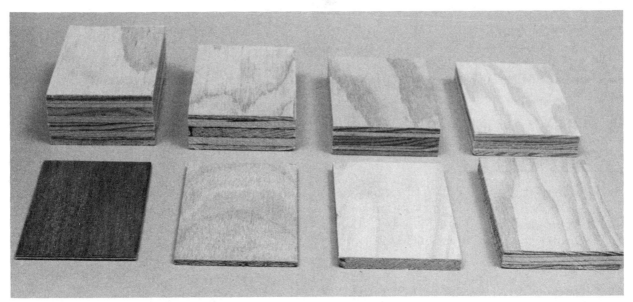

Samples of plywood in thicknesses commonly available at most lumberyards. Top row, from left: 1⅛" T. & G. subfloor, ¾", ⅝", ½". Bottom row, from left: 1/16" aircraft plywood, ⅛", ¼", ⅜".

plywood cutting blades are available, having smaller and more numerous teeth compared to an ordinary combination blade.

According to some experts, a strip of masking tape put down along the line of a projected cut also results in fewer splinters and a smoother cut. To check this out, I made some test cuts on a piece of ½" fir plywood. Eight cuts were made; four rip cuts along the grain of the surface ply, and four crosscuts. I used both an ordinary combination blade and a plywood blade with and without masking tape.

The results were much as I expected. On the rip cuts there was very little difference between the four cuts, although with a good imagination you could see a very slight improvement in the cut made with the plywood blade. There was even less difference between taped and untaped cuts.

When the cut was made across the surface ply, differences became more dramatic. The combination blade cut was quite ragged; somewhat less so with masking tape. The cut with the plywood blade was better, and the plywood blade used with the masking tape was the best of all. It was almost totally splinterless.

The top sides of the cuts were interesting. Here the combination blade made just as smooth a cut and possibly even a tiny bit better

than the plywood blade, although both were quite satisfactory.

The conclusion: If the appearance of the back side of your cut is unimportant, use whichever blade you happen to have on the saw. If the back side is important, put on a plywood blade for crosscutting. For the very best results, tape the

Rough underside of four circular saw crosscuts in ½" plywood. From left, the first is a cut with a combination blade. Next, comes a cut with the same blade but with its exit line previously covered by masking tape. The third is a cut with a plywood blade, and last, the plywood blade through masking tape. The cuts improve from quite ragged to very smooth.

line of cut with masking tape before sawing. (Once the cut is complete, take off the masking tape right away. If left for any period of time, it can be difficult to remove and may pull up some of the surface fibers with it.)

A SIMPLE SELF-EDGE

One problem with using plywood for table tops, desk tops, bench tops, and things of that sort is that the raw multi-ply edge lends a discordant, and by contrast, unattractive note to the overall appearance.

One of the easiest and most attractive ways to solve this situation is to cut off a narrow strip of the plywood itself and use it as a self-edge. Miter the cut at a 45-degree angle and glue it together for a nice smooth edge with no raw plies showing. In addition, if you cut the apron strip somewhat wider than the plywood's thickness, say 1½" or so, the top will have a heavier, more attractive appearance.

If your plywood has both sides good (A-A), a single miter cut will do the job for both the top and apron. Just reverse the apron piece end for end, and the miter will provide a square edge. If only one side is good, the cutoff piece will

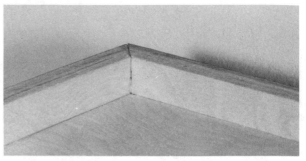

Underside view of one of the front corners of the table top. Both the bottom of the table and the top of the apron strips were mitered at 45 degrees, as were the ends of the apron strips. Even though the joints are less than perfect, sanding the outside edges and corners makes them look quite good.

Since the back of the table goes against the wall, no rear apron was fitted and the top and apron ends were left square cut. If the fourth side needs an apron, the final end miter of this piece is the only cut that needs an exact measurement to fit properly.

Self-edged aprons, glued up from 45-degree miter cuts, provide an easy solution to the "raw edge" problem in this ¾"-plywood worktable top. It sits on a pair of old oak chests of drawers separated by a knee space.

have to have the mitered edge recut so that the miter "leans" in the opposite direction. Use a plywood blade or perhaps a planer blade to get the smoothest cut possible on the miters. You want a good fit with only a hairline glue joint showing.

For the ends, you can either cut the apron strip off the end of the plywood, which gives a "waterfall" effect, or cut the strip from the length of the plywood, in which case the grain runs lengthwise across the end. If you want to use the full length of the plywood and don't need its full width (the usual case), the latter treatment will allow it. If you have birch plywood, the grain hardly shows either way. In any case, be sure to cut off your apron strips before you cut the top to final size, so that you have enough length on the apron strips to provide for the end miters.

If the back side of the table or desk is to face a wall, you can leave the back edge untrimmed. Start with the top surface upside down, its front and ends mitered. Miter the ends of the front apron strip to just fit the length of the top. Tape it temporarily in place with masking tape and then miter one end of each of the end aprons before trimming them to length. Match their end miters to the front strip. They probably won't match exactly; if the front strip is a smidgen long, the side strips won't quite come to its end; if the front is a bit short, the sides will overlap slightly. If this distance is 1/16" or less, there is no problem; just hold the end pieces in position while you mark the back ends and then cut them off.

Glue the joints starting with the front strip. A few small finishing nails will clamp it sufficiently. Glue and nail on the end strips, being sure to get a good glue joint on the end miters and along their length.

After the glue dries, bury the nail heads and fill them, along with any small gaps in your glue joints, with a matching wood-based putty. At this point, your joints may look a little ragged. Not to worry!

When the wood putty has hardened, take a piece of 100-grit sandpaper and round over all the edges to a radius of about 1/16". Sand off any overlap on the ends of the miter joints and round them to the same radius. The transformation will be surprising. Your slightly mismatched mitered ends suddenly become perfect in appearance!

If you do need to finish the back side with an apron; follow the same procedure except that the back sides of the end aprons also must be mitered. Fit, glue, and nail the front and side aprons into position before mitering the back strip to length. This is the one piece that you must cut for as exact a fit as possible. That is because it is the last piece and must fit at both ends with no juggling possible. It is best to plan to keep this last side in the position that is least exposed to critical view.

Try out this edge treatment on your next appropriate project; I think that you'll like it.

PLYWOOD SCRAPS

Rough or surfaced lumber comes in many sizes, but all too often not in the size that you need at the moment! If you want a small piece of wood that has to be 2¼" thick, for instance, you usually must cut down some 4" stock to size.

But if you do woodworking often, you probably have a supply of various odd sizes and thicknesses of plywood on hand. Since these commonly come in ⅛" increments from ¼" up to ¾" thick, it is a simple matter to glue up two or more pieces to get almost any thickness you need. Three thicknesses of ¾" gives a 2¼" piece of stock, as would three ⅝" pieces plus a ⅜" piece, or four ½" pieces plus a piece of ¼".

These manufactured sizes can solve all sorts of minor shop problems and provide stock for various small projects. When I needed a holder for a pair of small pump-type oil cans, for example, I glued together two small scraps of ¾" plywood and bored a pair of 2" holes through them. I glued on a piece of ¼" plywood to give the holes a smooth bottom. Then I sawed the exterior to size, smoothed the edges, and rounded the corners on a disc sander. Presto! No more misplaced or tipped over oil cans to fret about.

Another good use for this material is to build small odd-size boxes to hold accessories for various tools. Just glue solid scraps of plywood to the thickness of the desired internal depth of the box and then cut out the inside with a band saw, entering through one end of the box along the extended inside line of one side. After the interior is removed, glue up the entry kerf, glue on the bottom, and saw and sand the outside to final size.

If desired, the inside walls can be sanded by hand or with a 1" belt sander prior to gluing on the bottom. The box can be slipped onto the belt via the open kerf or, if you have already glued it up, you can still sand the inside by slipping the entire belt into the box and reinstalling it on the machine.

If a top is required, it can either be rabbeted

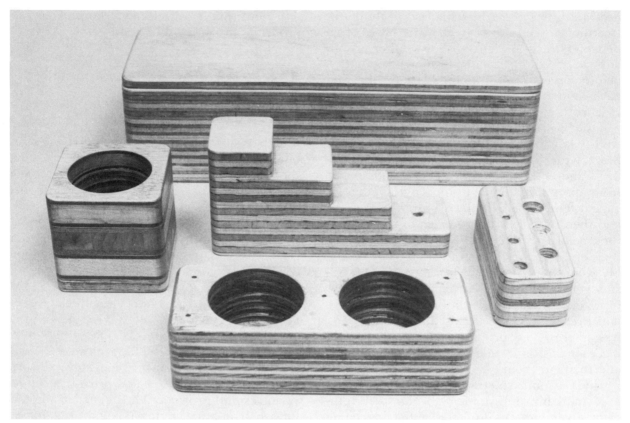

Some items made from plywood glued up to make the desired "lumber" thickness. At top is a toolbox, followed by an oilcan holder of lumber-core plywood, a nail pulling block for a claw hammer, a rack for some center drills, and at the bottom, a stand for a pair of oilcans.

on the edges to fit in place, or a piece of thin plywood or hardboard can be cut to fit the inside of the box and glued onto the underside of the top.

If a band saw is not at hand, the inside of the box would be cut out with a jigsaw or a sabre saw. If you wish, the blade can be inserted through a drilled hole, rather than coming in from the end as is necessary with the band saw. The end entry is simpler, however, and the kerf almost disappears after gluing up.

A step block for use under your hammer head simplifies pulling different length nails. You will find that it is much easier to glue one up of pieces cut from a narrow strip of scrap plywood than it is to find a suitable solid block and cut out the steps. A strip about 1½″ to 2″ wide is best.

The block shown was made from ¾″ plywood cut into four lengths; 6″, 4½″, 3″, and 1½″ long.

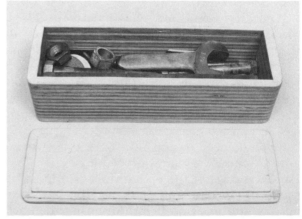

Box made from a block glued up to 2½″ thick. The interior was removed with a band saw (a sabre saw or jigsaw will do) by entering through the upper left end. The interior was sanded, the saw kerf glued closed, a ½″ bottom piece glued on, the exterior sanded, and a top rabbeted to fit.

They were glued together in a stairstep configuration, a ¼" hole was drilled in the end for hanging, and that was it. Smaller steps might be even better. Either four steps of ⅝" or five steps of ½" plywood would add up to a 2½" total height. That should be plenty unless you work with really big nails!

Plywood scraps can be glued up into blocks and made into attractive bookends. They can either be made in pairs or singly to support just one end of a group of books. I usually find more uses for a single bookend than I do for pairs.

Glue up the plywood to make appropriately sized blocks and then cut and sand to form shapes such as cubes, pyramids, leaning braces, multiple angles, curved pieces, or any others you can dream up. In all of them, the multiple laminations of end grain provide an unusual and attractive texture.

A slightly different type of bookend can be made of stepped blocks. Cut the plywood scraps into different sized pieces and sand the edges prior to gluing them up. These blocks show a combination of plain and end-grain surfaces. Many of them are reminiscent of the Art Deco, or "1930s Modern," type of architecture.

To provide the needed stability, drill a 1½" hole an inch or so deep in the bottom of the bookend with a spade bit. Then pour the hole nearly full of molten lead.

Do you have a situation where a bookshelf is almost, but not quite, filled with books? There is not room for bookends between them, but there usually is just enough space to allow the books to spread apart and lean at awkward angles.

Spacer blocks are a good solution to this problem. Make them of plywood scraps glued up to form blocks 2" or 3" thick and about 6" tall and 4" deep. They can be cut and glued so that the end grain laminations run either horizontally or vertically. For slightly larger gaps, a 4" cube makes a good spacer.

Make up a few extra spacer blocks of different sizes, store them in a nearby drawer, and you'll be able to keep your bookshelves neat and orderly as your stock of books changes with time.

Once you have any of these plywood articles glued up, work them over with a disc or belt sander to get rid of any unevenness between the glued up laminations and to provide a nice smooth surface. Fill any gaps or voids in the

Attractive bookend made from a glued up length of 3 x 3 with its ends cut off at 45 degrees. The bottom surface has a 1½" hole drilled with a spade bit and poured nearly full of melted lead. A self-stick felt pad on the bottom protects the table finish.

Spacer blocks for bookcases can be made in any size and with their plies oriented either vertically or horizontally. One block, turned on its side, shows how smaller blocks are stabilized with lead weights to keep books upright.

Bookcase spacer block keeps the books neatly standing at attention.

plywood edges with a plastic wood patching material, let it dry, and sand the patch flush.

A good finish is a big help in keeping plywood articles clean and neat looking, especially with all the exposed end grain in plywood laminated in this manner, which would otherwise speedily soak up dust, dirt, or oils. Due to this thirsty end grain, three coats of polyurethane varnish are usually needed. The first two coats should be gloss, sanded with 220-grit paper between coats; the final coat may be either gloss or satin.

Another much quicker and simpler finish can be provided by one of the newer penetrating oil finishes, sometimes referred to as plastic oil or Danish oil. These finishes brush or wipe on, and after a ten-to-fifteen-minute period to allow the liquid to soak in, another coat can be applied. Allow a few minutes for the final coat to be absorbed and then gently wipe the surface with a soft cloth. A three-coat finish can be completed in an hour! While not as good as a varnish finish, these oils are quite satisfactory for many purposes.

BUILT-UP PLANKS

Narrow strips of plywood cut to the same width, either from leftover scraps or specifically cut for the purpose, make unusual and attractive "planks" for many jobs. Made up with the normal faces of the plywood glued together, they present a continuous edge-grain appearance on the entire top and bottom of the plank. If the planks are glued up so that the face grain of each piece runs across the plank rather than lengthwise, the sides of the plank will present edge grain as well, rather than a face grain. Made this way the only plywood face surface showing is on the ends of the plank and even this can be avoided if desired.

One way is to saw off the ends to make a round or oval-ended plank, leaving no face grain showing anywhere on the plank. If you desire a square end on the plank, set your table saw to cut a 45-degree bevel cut and run the ends of the plank through the saw twice. This removes the entire face, leaving a full-width V-groove along the end of the plank. With the saw set at the same angle, cut a previously glued-up strip of plywood into a V-shaped piece that can be glued into the end of the plank. Align it with the edge grain along the end of the plank.

If the plank is a short one, it can be run through the saw to cut the V-groove after being glued up. If it is of any length however, it would be simpler and safer to glue together two or three of the plywood strips, depending on their thickness and their width, to make an end piece capable of accepting the V-cut. Then you could saw the groove in it before fastening it to the end of the plank.

Small planks make cutting boards, serving boards, cheese trays, trivets, and things of that sort. Fill any voids and sand thoroughly. Items that will be used around food can be finished by wiping on several coats of mineral oil.

An interesting trivet can be made by cutting a number of strips to an equal width, say ¾" or 1", and then dadoing several evenly spaced slots exactly halfway through each of them. Glue them together so as to provide an openwork trivet with the edge grain showing on the top, bottom, and ends of the strips. The face grain of the plywood shows on the sides.

Much larger planks can also be glued up in this manner from strips that are cut 1½" or 2" wide; a plank 2 feet wide and 4 to 5 feet long is quite practical. One of this size could be used as a top for a coffee table.

For a plank this size provide additional strength in the form of three steel rods running nearly the length of the plank. Rods up to 3′ long can be easily made from ¼″ steel gas welding rod, inexpensively obtained at any welding supply shop. A steel supply house, a welding shop, or steel fabricating shop can supply longer rods. Thread the ends of the rods and provide washers and nuts to tension the rods for clamping the strips when gluing them together. The rods end just short of the ends of the

Plywood tabletop has been glued up after being slipped over three lengths of welding rod with threaded ends. The nuts have been tightened; end strips are ready to be glued on to cover the nuts. These end strips have been miter grooved and a mitered strip has been glued in so that no face grain will show on the ends.

plank and are covered by gluing on final strips with counterbored holes large enough and deep enough to cover the nuts and washers on the ends of the rods.

If you make a simple drilling jig and use a drill press, an extra ⅟₃₂″ (a ⁹⁄₃₂″ hole for ¼″ rod) should give clearance enough to allow you to slip on the strips as you glue up the plank. If you drill with an electric drill, you may want to add as much as ⅛″ (⅜″) for possible misalignment among the numerous holes that must be drilled.

Assemble the plank on a flat surface covered with strips of newspaper to pick up the squeezed out glue. Use a slow setting glue and assemble and glue up the strips on the rods as rapidly as possible. You might consider drafting a couple of helpers to spread the glue on both sides of each strip while you assemble them. Tighten the nuts securely and then after a few minutes recheck them and tighten them again. Cover the plank with newspaper and weight it down evenly with as much weight as practical to avoid any warping.

After the glue has completely set, retighten the nuts, saw off the ends of the rods, and glue on the end strips. When these joints have cured, you can tear and scrape off as much of the newspaper as possible. Then sand the plank, starting with a belt sander and a coarse belt.

After coarse sanding, choose the best looking side to be the top surface. Fill in any minor voids in the plywood laminations, and then

Finished tabletop after the end strips have been glued on and the entire piece sanded.

Close-up of the mitered end piece. Note how it does not show any face grain in the glued-up plank.

continue sanding the top and edge surfaces with progressively finer grits before giving it the finish of your choice. Hand sand with very fine-grit paper between coats.

Legs for Your Table

If you are using your built-up plank for a tabletop, you will need some legs. The length will vary with the type of table of course. Plan on an overall height of 15" to 16" for a coffee table, 19" to 21" for an end table, and from 28" to 29" (the latter seems to be the most favored) if you go all out and build a really large plank for a dining table.

The legs can be made from any of a number of materials. For example, how about glued-up laminated legs to continue the theme of the top itself? Glue up small squares of plywood to make legs of the required height, either straight sided or sawed to a slight taper. Round legs with the same appearance can be made by gluing together cutouts from a hole saw of the appropriate size. Either of these types can be reenforced with threaded rods inside them if necessary. Depending on their height and size, the more spindly ones may need additional support.

Plain wood legs can either be made up, or purchased ready-made at a hardware or building supply store. Metal legs are also available.

Round copper legs, made from pipe available at a plumbing supply house, offer another possibility. Depending on how you finish the top, the warm appearance of the copper may go quite well with it. Pipe sizes of ½", ¾", and 1" are quite common, being regularly used for household water supply lines. In each case, the OD is about ⅛" larger than the nominal size, which is about ¹⁄₁₆" smaller than the actual ID of the pipe. Larger sizes up to 4" nominal are also available, but may have to be special ordered.

Copper is rather expensive, especially in the larger sizes, but you won't really need very much of it and can often buy a short piece left over from a job, rather than a full 10' length.

To provide a better bearing surface against the floor, put feet on the legs. Just sweat solder a copper pipe cap to the end of the pipe. Caps are press formed from the same thickness copper as the pipe itself. Neatly done, soldering leaves only a small ring of gray solder at the joint between the cap and the pipe. If you want, you could epoxy the caps on so that no solder shows.

Make table legs from copper water pipe of a diameter appropriate to the size of the table. The copper color goes well with the plywood. Pipe caps are either soldered or epoxied on to protect floor.

Legs made from two strips of plywood slotted together are one of several plywood leg possibilities.

SINK CUTOUTS

Sink cutouts, usually having a particleboard base, are not strictly plywood, but this seems a good place to talk about them. If you are unfamiliar with these items, they are leftovers, sawed out when kitchen and bathroom plastic-laminate countertops are prepared for installation.

The cutouts come in sizes up to about 20″ x 30″ or so and in various shapes, such as round, oval, or rectangular. They also have a variety of durable finishes, varying from solid colors to multicolored patterns and even textured surfaces.

Sink cutouts can usually be found at giveaway prices in various building supply stores, particularly those that offer kitchen and bathroom cabinets and remodeling services.

Either straight or curved cuts are easy to make in cutouts with most any type of wood-cutting saw. You can paint the ¾″ particleboard edge (flat black often works well). They make such items as a shelf below a portable gas barbecue, a lazy Susan for the center of a patio table, a smooth work top for a mechanic's roller cabinet, or a cutting board for a tiled kitchen counter.

Keep an eye out for cutouts and pick up a few when you see them in a color or pattern you like. No doubt you'll soon be looking for more.

Circle sawed from a sink cutout is mounted atop a built-up plywood base with a lazy Susan bearing from the hardware store.

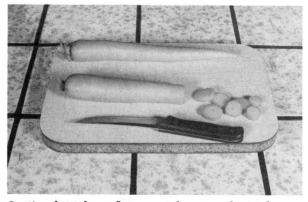

Cutting board cut from a sink cutout keeps knives off the kitchen tile. A couple of coats of varnish on the particleboard edge stops it from soaking up greasy or oily foods.

Plastic laminate sink cutout, trimmed to fit the top of this landlocked former roller cabinet, extends the workbench top. The plastic surface stands up well under use.

LAMINATING CURVED PLYWOOD

Sometimes you need a curved piece of plywood for a project, to form the backrest of a chair, for instance. While plywood of any appreciable thickness is difficult to bend, the job can be done by gluing up laminations of thin (⅛″) plywood and clamping them in a curved mold until the glue sets.

Make your mold by sawing a base and top from ¾″ plywood, cut just a little larger than your finished chair back will be. Then, also from ¾″ plywood, cut several caul blocks which will form both halves of your actual curved mold. Saw them into strips that are as long as your base and about 2″ wider than is necessary to contain the arc of your proposed curve.

Draw the curve on one of the strips. Use a radius that is just a smidgen shorter than the desired curve to allow for a bit of "relaxing" when the plywood comes out of the mold. Stack

Curved strips are evenly spaced and then glued and nailed to top and bottom bases to form a two-piece curved mold for the plywood. The bottom half is at right, while the top sits on its side at left.

the strips with the marked one on top and fasten them together for sawing. Duct tape works well for this. Run the curve through a band saw, keeping the cut as smooth and even as possible.

Without a band saw, cut the strips separately with a sabre saw or jigsaw, making them as uniform as possible. After cutting, fasten them together temporarily and sand off any irregularities.

Nail the concave halves of the strips to the mold base, spacing them evenly. Nail the convex pieces to the mold top piece, spacing them the same so that when the two parts are placed together, the curved caul blocks will sit exactly atop one another.

Depending on the thickness needed for the final product, prepare several blanks of ⅛″ plywood (the example here required four to produce ½″ thickness). Cut the blanks slightly larger than their final dimensions. Keep handy an adequate number of bar clamps, large C-clamps, or other means of supplying clamping pressure. Try a dry run without glue to be sure that the clamps are adequate to pull all the thin plywood blanks tightly together between the caul blocks to the full extent of the bend.

Cover the bottom section of the mold carefully with a single sheet of waxed paper or kitchen plastic wrap to catch any squeezed out glue.

Carefully lay out the blanks in the desired order and grain orientation and spread the glue with a wide putty knife, a roller brayer, or a wide brush. Place the blanks on the lower half

Six strips of ½″ plywood, temporarily fastened together with duct tape for simultaneous cutting, are being bandsawed to the required curve to make a caul block, or mold. It helps to form and glue up a bent plywood laminate from several thin layers.

Four blanks, cut slightly oversize from ⅛" plywood, were covered with glue and then placed on the concave half of the caul block mold. The convex upper half of the mold was then placed on top and the two halves clamped together, forcing the plywood laminations into a curve which will be permanent after the glue sets up. A total of 125 lbs. of lead weights provide the clamping pressure in this instance.

Twelve-ton hydraulic press supplies all the pressure needed to form and maintain the curve in the plywood laminations. If none of the clamping methods shown is available, you can always jack up the front of a car and then lower one wheel onto the mold. Keep the car level by inserting a jack stand in the proper position next to the other front wheel.

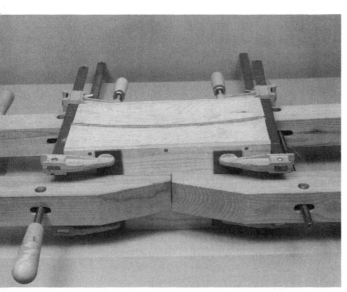

Several methods can be used to clamp the mold together until the glue sets. Here two large carpenter's wooden hand screws and four small bar clamps maintain pressure on the mold.

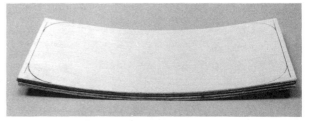

After the glue has thoroughly set, the bent plywood blank can be removed from its mold. This curved chair back has been marked and is ready for bandsawing and edge sanding to its final shape. If needed, considerably sharper bends can be formed by this laminating method.

of the mold in the proper order, cover them with a top sheet of the protective waxed paper or plastic, and then put on the top half of the mold. Align it precisely with the bottom half. Clamp the mold tightly together and allow the glue to set completely; at least overnight.

Remove your curved plywood panel from the mold and trim it to final size and shape using a fine tooth blade in your bandsaw or jigsaw.

HALF-SLOTTING

It is often desirable to construct an item so that it can be easily dismantled and reassembled later. Some things that come to mind are bookshelves and other furniture for college students or young adults who have not yet settled down into permanent quarters, some children's playthings, and even items for the shop, including extra saw horses and large assembly benches that are only used occasionally.

Half-slotting is a construction technique you can see in the interior separators inside cardboard boxes. (A case of wine with a dozen bottles each in its own little nest is an excellent example.)

While half-slotting works fine for cardboard boxes, it doesn't work very well with normal wood construction. Wood tends to split along

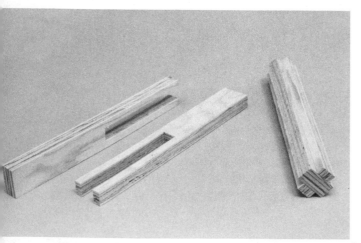

Two pairs of slotted strips; one separated and one assembled. Slotted components provide an assembly that can be dismantled for storage or glued together permanently.

the grain from the end of the slot when subjected to any twisting load. With plywood, however, the laminations have alternating grain direction, and this problem disappears. Half-slotted projects can be dismantled and reassembled any number of times.

Planning and construction for half-slotting is quite simple. The slots are made as wide as the opposite board is thick. Usually all pieces are the same thickness, but this is not necessary and is sometimes undesirable. Normally the slots are made exactly halfway through each piece, but this is a rule only when the two parts both must wind up with their edges located in the same plane. For other items, the slots must be less than half the depth. For example, when making toy-sized interlocking square timbers, the slots on each piece should be only a quarter of the depth of the piece. That way each block overlaps the next halfway, allowing continued overlapping as the building is erected.

Accurate layout and cutting of the slots is necessary to ensure that the parts fit closely enough that they do not wobble in use; on the other hand, slots must not be so tight that parts cannot be easily assembled and dismantled. You can cut the slots in various ways, depending on the size of the item and the number and depth of the slots required. For shallow slots, especially when a large number are needed (as when making a set of interlocking toy blocks) a dado setup in a table or radial saw works well. For larger items, two separate cuts with a plywood blade on either of these saws is necessary. For smaller items, saw with a band saw, jig saw, or a sabre saw.

Except for shallow slots cut with a dado blade, squaring the end of the slot is the most difficult part. With a band saw, jigsaw, or sabre saw, the blade may be backed away slightly and then turned for another cut. If the slot is fairly wide and the blade narrow, work the blade around to reach the opposite corner flush with the bottom of the slot. Then reverse the cut to clean out the remaining small angle. For narrower slots, or with wider blades, the slot can be squared off by working the saw blade back and forth a few times.

Another method is to drill a hole at the end of the slot, either before or after the cuts are made. Brad point wood bits work best, but spade bits will do. In either case, be sure to use

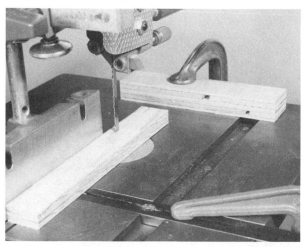

Plywood legs are slotted on the band saw. The miter gage is clamped so two cuts, each made with an edge against the gage, form a slot of the proper width. An end stop halts work at the halfway mark.

After outside cuts have been made in all the pieces, the miter gage is withdrawn. Then the waste is removed by a single curved cut, followed by several short cuts to square the end of the slot.

a backup block to prevent splintering. The remaining rounded corners can be sawed or chiseled out.

A sharp wood chisel also removes the material between parallel saw cuts and squares off the end of the slot. When using a chisel, clamp a straightedge board to both the front and back of the plywood, each exactly aligned with the required end of the slot. Use these as a guide against the back of the chisel. Cut half way through from each side to avoid splintering.

Following are some of the many articles that you might consider building with this type of construction. Keep the technique in mind; it is sure to solve some problems for you, especially where objects must be stored for long periods.

In the home, slotted construction can be used for tables, including even a dining table for occasional use in a small apartment. When disassembled, it takes up very little room and stores flat against the back of a closet. Coffee tables, end tables, and occasional tables can also be made this way. For tops on the smaller tables consider the previously mentioned sink cutouts; their plastic laminated top surfaces are impervious to most anything.

With a little planning and ingenuity you can also make extra chairs for dining or occasional use. They assemble quickly when company comes and "disappear" when not needed.

Other household articles made this way include such things as a waste basket or a completely enclosed box, which can pass as a small table but also provides storage for magazines, games, and extra pillows. For the box, give extra clearance to slots for the part that is to become the openable top so that it operates easily.

Slotted plywood makes many children's items. Small playhouses can be quickly erected and just as quickly taken apart to await the next rainy day. Open top dollhouses can be designed so that walls can be assembled in different ways to vary room layout and size. Small scraps of ¼" plywood can be cut into modular sizes and slotted on all four sides; children will use them to build forts, robots, houses, service stations, and hundreds of other things. Modular blocks can be cut out rapidly with a saw and dado set, once the sizes have been decided on.

Slotted construction can be used in toymaking to build such things as paddle wheels for a steamboat. In this case, the slots are for simplicity of design, and the pieces can be glued together permanently. The same sort of wheel can be used as a waterwheel when a brook or other source of running water is at hand.

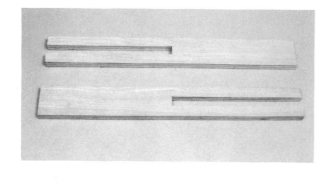

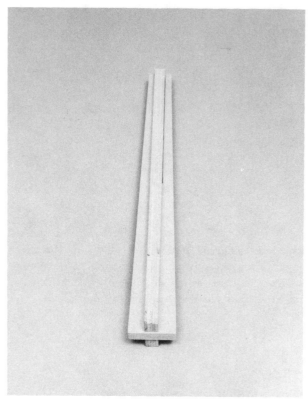

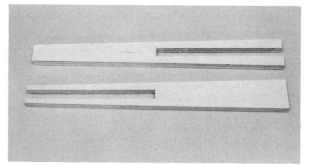

Slotted legs with a taper. After the slots are cut in the strips, saw the taper.

Assembled slotted and tapered leg exhibits twelve surfaces—four showing edge grain and eight showing face grain. The leg has an unusual appearance.

With a little planning, many different items that can be dismantled for storage can be made from slotted plywood. Shown here in small scale are bookshelves, a table platform, and a pair of sawhorse legs.

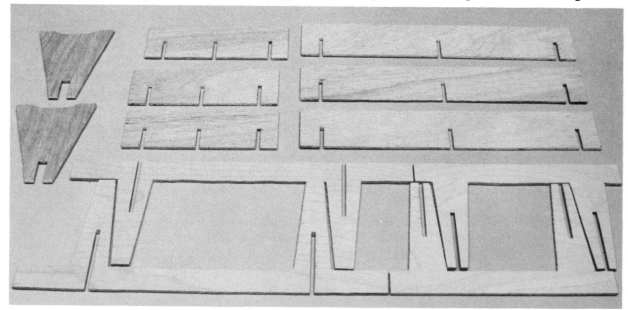

EASY BOX CONSTRUCTION

All three pieces can be quickly taken apart for storage. The cleats on the sawhorse are screwed to the crossbar to form half of the "slot."

In the workshop, you can build a low assembly bench or table, or many types of sawhorses, either all plywood or of a composite construction. Make the sawhorses with plywood legs and either 2 x 4s or 2 x 6s for the tops. Instead of slotting the 2 x 4s, just slot the plywood to fit the full depth of the top piece. Then glue/nail four small strips of wood, two on either side, near each end of the 2 x 4 to secure the slotted end of the plywood leg to the top piece. Fastening the strips at a slight angle, so that the legs are canted out slightly, helps make the sawhorse even more stable.

A pair of legs of this type, combined with three or four evenly spaced 2 x 4s, each about 6' long, makes an excellent support to hold a full sheet of plywood for sawing with an electric saw. It is much more effective than the makeshift supports usually used and, once again, it stores compactly when not needed.

Plywood is an excellent material for the construction of storage boxes of all sizes. Making them can be a bit of a chore though, if you use the normal method of building an open box and then constructing a top to match.

A much easier method for making most boxes is to cut all six sides of the box and then fasten them together into a sealed box with no opening. After this is done the box is sawed apart at the desired point, providing a top that exactly matches the body of the box.

Of course, prior planning is necessary to insure that there are no nails or screws crossing the line of the saw. You can cut open quite large boxes on a table saw using the rip fence to make all four cuts equidistant from the top. Other boxes, such as a small cabinet for 3 x 5 file cards, can be opened with a single cut on a band saw. In this case an ogee curve is often sawed to lower the open front of the box while maintaining a high back.

You make one of these boxes quickly from ¼" plywood by cutting mitered edges on all surfaces. An easy way to do this is to cut two strips; one as wide as the depth of the box from front to back and long enough to make both sides plus the top and bottom. A second strip should have a width equal to the height of the box and be long enough to make both the front and back.

Set your saw to cut a 45-degree miter and miter both edges of both strips. Then with the same miter setting, saw the six pieces to length, striving to get both sides the same length and equal to the exact width of the front and back strip. Miter the ends of the top and bottom pieces to the exact same length. Then miter the ends of the front and back pieces to match the exact length of the top and bottom pieces.

Tape the top, bottom, and both sides together with masking tape on the outside of the joints and fold the four parts into a rectangle. Tape the fourth corner. The front and back pieces should fit neatly into place.

If there is a tiny overlap on any of the joints it will disappear after you glue the box together and radius off the corners with a bit of medium-grit sandpaper.

After this plywood box was glued up and sawed into a box to corral the parts of a bending jig, the block cut from its center remained. Later it became a toy car body by "cutting away all of it that didn't look like a car," to paraphrase the sculptor.

With wheels and axles added, the waste block became a sturdy toy car. It has survived several years of play by three active children. Note the glued-up kerf along the extended hood line; that is where the band saw entered to cut out the window.

Six pieces for a small file box. They are made from two strips of ¼″ plywood sawed with a 45-degree miter and then cut to length at the same angle.

Glued up into a sealed box and "clamped" with masking tape, the mitered edges look a little rough at this point. A piece of waxed paper from the kitchen is a big help when gluing.

Cut open with a band saw, and sanded a bit, the box's appearance improves amazingly. Add a small pair of brass hinges, give it a couple of coats of varnish, and the box is finished.

This larger box was also glued up as a sealed unit, but with butt rather than miter joints. The top was then cut off with four cuts against a rip fence on the table saw. Three routed finger grips make for easy opening without protruding knobs.

Box has ample room for two chain saws, along with oil, tools, and wedges. The strip at the rear strengthens the thin plywood back under the three hinges. It was glued in when the box was built and sawn in two when the top was cut off.

Glue the joints sparingly. Be especially careful toward the inside of the seams. You don't want any heavy glue runs on the inside of the box where you can't get at them until after the glue hardens and you saw the box open. After the glue has dried, cut the box open. Make an ogee cut on a band saw if the size of the box permits, or either an angled cut or a straight cut on a circular saw, again depending on the size of the box and the capacity of your saw.

The large box shown, made to give dust- and dirt-free storage to a couple of chain saws and their accessories, was made from plywood odds and ends.

About a yard long and a foot wide, the box was made using ⅜" plywood for the bottom, ½" for the ends, and ¼" for the top. The front and back were made from what was also supposed to be ¼" material, but this particular sheet of plywood was scant, measuring only a bare 7/32" thick.

Due to this thinness, ½" thick strips of solid wood were glued to the inside of the front and back before the top panel was fastened in place. These strengthen the cut edges of the top section and provide a nailing/gluing area for attaching the top board. The back strip extends down to reenforce the hinge line and provides material to hold the hinge screws.

After the box was sawed open, another ½" strip was added to the inside front of the box itself; its top was extended and relieved slightly to form a lip that engages the top section when closed. Three finger slots were routed into the front of the top section with a V-groove bit to allow easy opening. A pair of chains hold the top in a convenient open position.

Using the above technique the box was built in much less time, and with a better fitting top, than if it had been built in two separate units.

If you want to build a large box with a drop front, make the front and back cuts on a table saw and then use a pattern to draw in identical ogee curves on either end to match up with these cuts. Then make the curved cuts with a sabre saw.

PLYWOOD STRIP BOXES

Odd scraps of plywood can be cut into narrow strips and then glued together to form square or rectangular boxes that have a striking textured appearance because of the plywood edge grain.

Set the rip fence on your saw and cut the plywood into narrow strips. Make them ½" wide for easy sawing and gluing, although you can cut narrower strips if you wish.

Next, set the stop rod on your miter gage (or use a C-clamped stop block) to cut the strips to length. Since you will glue them up with alter-

nate overlapping corners, cut them to the desired length and width of the box—minus the width of one strip. If, for example, you want a box 7" long and 5" wide made of ½" strips, cut enough pieces 6½" long and 4½" long to pile up to the box height desired. (If the inside dimensions are more important to you, work with these and add ½" for both strips.)

Glue up the first course. Assuming that your box will be rectangular, glue the end of a short piece to the side of a long piece at its end. Then glue the end of another long piece to the side of the short piece at its end. Complete the rectangle with another short piece glued against the side of one long piece and against the end of the other.

Immediately glue on a second layer in the same manner, but start with a long strip overlapping the joint between a long and short piece in the first layer. Continue around the perimeter making a solid overlap over all the joints in the first layer. For the third layer, proceed as with the first layer, so that the joints once again overlap a solid section.

Continue adding layers until you build the

Narrow strips ripped from ½" plywood scraps, and cut to two different lengths, are being piled up and glued, again on a piece of waxed paper. Note that the joints are alternated and overlapped from one row to the next.

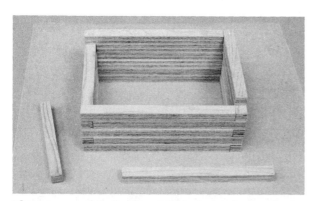

Almost completed, the sides of the box pile up quickly. The overlapped joints add to the appearance of the box, as well as strengthening it.

The belt sander, with its belt threaded inside the opening, makes quick work of smoothing the inside of the box.

With a ⅛″ hardboard bottom glued on and its sides and corners sanded, the box is almost finished.

Top is made from two pieces of ⅛″ hardboard, one cut to fit snugly inside the opening and glued to the underside of the other. Once varnished, the strip box becomes another attractive example of a raw-edged plywood piece.

box to the desired depth. Keep the corners square and the layers even as you proceed. Do not glue on either the bottom or the top of the box at this time.

After the glue dries, sand the inside of the box. This can be done by hand with coarse sandpaper and a sanding block or with a 1″ belt sander set up in the doubled belt manner, with the belt inserted through the box and then put back on the rollers of the machine.

After the inside is smoothed down, you can

glue on the bottom and sand the outside of the box. Either a disc or a belt sander works well. The top can be made by gluing on a panel and then sawing it off, along with a small section of the top of the box itself (in which case you would glue it on before sanding the outside). Hinge the top directly to the box or rabbet the edges of the top to fit the interior of the box (for a lift-off, unhinged, top).

If you do not care for the contrast between the face grain of a plywood top and the edge grain of the rest of the box, you may prefer to make a plain top from a piece of tempered hardboard, or perhaps from a scrap of plastic laminate material.

Fill gaps in the laminations with wood filler, then sand and finish as desired. The completed box will be a nice little conversation piece, made from material that you otherwise probably would have discarded.

BANDSAWED BOXES

Over the past several years, bandsawed boxes, many of them quite intricate, have become popular. There have been a number of articles and at least one book published describing the process. Basically this consists of sawing off a couple of side strips from the block at hand, cutting out a drawer and then regluing the sides back on the case. The sides of the drawer are then cut off, the interior cut out, and the sides are glued back on.

The same general process works for glued up plywood boxes, except that by cutting out the interior before the side pieces are glued on, one or more steps can be eliminated. Once again, you can design your boxes to show off the textured edge grain of the plywood.

TURNING GLUED-UP PLYWOOD

Circles and rings sawn from odd bits of plywood can be turned on a wood lathe to form

Bandsawed boxes are fun. Glued-up plywood can be cut before all the laminations are glued, thus avoiding open kerfs in the finished product. The two backs (left) were cut off before the drawers (right) were sawed out. Then the four center pieces were glued into a single block and the backs reglued.

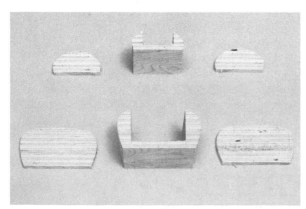

Thin front and back sections have been cut off the drawer units (right and left) and the drawer openings cut out. After the interior surfaces are sanded, the front and back pieces will be glued back on.

Pattern for the final saw cut has been drawn on the glued-up block. The drawer units await sanding.

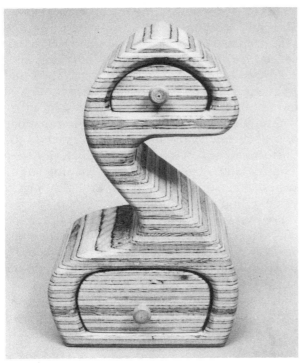

Free-form box, edges rounded, sanded, and finished, appears to be an escapee from a childhood fairy tale.

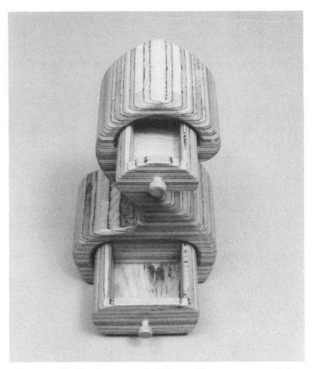

The two little drawers hold small treasures, either children's or adult's.

any number of useful and attractive articles. Salad bowls, fruit bowls, vases, small round boxes, rolling pins, desk accessories, gearshift knobs, hammer handles—the list is unlimited. Let your imagination run.

The shape of the bowl shown here was influenced by bowls and baskets made by Indians of the American Southwest. The plywood edge texture combines with the shape to give an attractive primitive effect.

To make this bowl, cut a circle from ¾" or ⅝" plywood to a diameter of about 10" or 11". Then saw out several plywood rings. The number depends on their thickness; you want enough to pile up to a total of about 4" including the base piece. Cut the rings with either a jigsaw or sabre saw. Drill a small hole to insert the blade for the center cutout.

If you have a band saw, you can cut the rings quickly by first cutting the outside of the circle and then sawing from the outside to the inside circle via about a 45-degree angle. Once you have the rings cut, glue up the kerfs, contracting the rings slightly with string or tape to

Glued-up plywood circles and rings, turned on a lathe, make interestingly textured turnings. This vase was inspired by Southwest Indian pottery.

close up the gap. This method leaves a hairline glue joint on each of the laminations, but combined with the texture of the plywood, it will be hardly noticeable. Just position the glued-up kerfs on the different rings around the diameter of the piece so that they do not all fall in one area.

You can vary both the interior and exterior diameter of the rings to conform to the approximate shape of the bowl, but be sure to supply enough material to allow for a little eccentricity in gluing them up; it's difficult to get them all exactly concentric. Rims 1″ wide provide a good dimension to start. On later projects, you may find that you are able to cut that down somewhat and still have enough material to work with.

Glue the base and rings together; clamp or weight them down. Allow the glue to set thoroughly before mounting the glued up block on your lathe faceplate. Turn the bowl by starting at a very slow speed. You will probably find that despite your best efforts, the block is not concentric and may be well out of balance.

Plywood glue is tough stuff; sharp tools and frequent resharpening are necessary. After you have both the interior and exterior concentric and roughly cut to shape, you will find that one of the "cheese grater" type of rasps, such as the Surform, does a better job on the exterior than a normal lathe tool. Do the final shaping with a very coarse sandpaper. Start with #30 grit if you can find some; otherwise use #50.

Proceed with finer grits until you have a fairly smooth surface. If your lathe is reversible, or if you can reverse the rotation of the work by moving it to the outboard end of the spindle, this quickly improves the finish.

Before the final sanding, stop and take time to fill the voids with wood putty. There will

Another project inspired by American Indian design, this fruit bowl was glued up from one ¾″ plywood circle plus several rings cut by a sabre saw. It was then turned on a lathe.

Large (16″ diameter) salad bowl had one ring of lumber-core plywood incorporated, giving it an unusual striped appearance. All the rings on this bowl were cut by a band saw. Entry kerfs were made at an angle and later glued closed. They can be seen on the finished product only by a very close look.

probably be a good many. With deep gaps, you may have to go to a second application to fill shrinkage. Put the bowl back in the lathe and sand until you have a nice smooth surface.

Finish as desired; possibilities include polyurethane varnish, plastic oil, or several coats of mineral oil if the item is to be used with food. This particular bowl was stained before varnishing; I usually prefer plywood items unstained.

While the finish is drying, consider what to do with leftover centers that were cut from the rings. They can be cut into rings to make a smaller bowl or a round plywood box; the interior of those rings being used again for an even smaller bowl or box. The process can continue until the final core piece is turned into an item

such as a one-of-a-kind gearshift knob for your "four-on-the-floor" sports car, or for the transfer case shift knob on a boondocks 4 x 4.

Small plywood circles, cut out with a large hole saw and complete with a concentric center hole made by the pilot drill, can be strung on a dowel and glued together. Add free-turning handles to the extended dowel ends and you have a striking rolling pin for the baker in your family. Be sure to fill in all the little gaps and voids in the plywood and sand it to a nice smooth surface so that the rolling pin will have no tendency to "pick up" the dough.

Although sound, well-seasoned chunks of wood large enough to make big bowls are often expensive and difficult to obtain, plywood provides stable, inexpensive, and attractive turn-

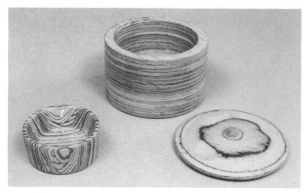

Round box was glued up and turned from the inside leftovers of rings cut for a larger box. Its interior pieces, in turn, made an even smaller item. Turned top shows contoured glue lines between the laminations. Irregular contour of one was apparently caused by a less than perfect surface between the two plywood laminations. Different patterns on the small nut bowl were created by turning it from the end grain of a glued up block.

ing material up to the size limit of your lathe. Most wood lathes will turn items up to 12″ in diameter and even much larger if they have outboard turning ability. Combination tools, such as the Shopsmith, will turn bowls over 16″ in diameter.

Do you need an outsize V-pulley for some gadget you are contemplating, such as a speed reducer to operate your band saw with a metal-cutting blade? Cut a circle from ¾″ plywood and turn a V-groove in the rim to fit the particular belt. For a hub, drill a hole to fit over the shaft. Then fasten your wood pulley against a smaller metal V-pulley that has an appropriately sized shaft hole and the necessary set screw. Just drill holes through the web of the smaller pulley, and bolt or screw them together.

If you get started turning glued up plywood circles, you may find it hard to stop! The possibilities are endless and the projects are attractive, useful, and fun to make.

6
WORKING WITH SHEET METAL

Mention sheet-metal work and the first things people usually think of are the ducting in heating and airconditioning systems, flashing around roof valleys, chimneys, and vent pipes, and gutters used to carry rain water from the eaves.

Although few if any workshoppers ever take on the large job of making up ducting for the heating system of a house, many small wood- or metal-working projects will benefit from sheet-metal parts. What about making a simple bent-up dump body for an otherwise all-wood toy truck, for instance, or some easily made drawers for a storage project?

Here are a few ideas that make it easier for you to work with sheet-metal. This chapter also shows you how to make various small sheet-metal fittings, brackets, and other parts. With a little thought, these items can improve the design, construction, and durability of many of your projects.

In conjunction with this chapter, please see the notes on using the Pop riveter in Chapter 1. It is an extremely useful tool for sheet-metal work. Also in Chapter 1, note the remarks on using the Workmate as a makeshift sheet-metal bending brake.

MATERIALS

For some of your projects, very light metal such as tin or aluminum from cans may be satisfactory. For most items however, thicker and larger pieces are required.

If you have a building construction project going on nearby, some fair sized cutoffs, which a contractor deems not worth hauling back to the shop, may sometimes be had for the asking. Otherwise, you'll have to get your supply at the nearest sheet-metal shop or heating and airconditioning contractor, where you will often find that scraps are sold at the full per-pound price. Thus it may cost less to get pieces of the size you need, rather than going for larger "scrap" pieces.

In addition to the usual galvanized steel, sheet-metal shops sometimes have copper available. Although considerably more expensive, copper is desirable for its attractive color and durability. Brass sheets, quite valuable for some uses, are usually difficult to find. They are sometimes available in small sizes at model and hobby shops.

Many hardware stores carry aluminum

sheets of the do-it-yourself type. Often available only in 24" x 30" sheets and in one thickness (approximately ⅟₃₂"), this aluminum comes in "soft" grade only. Aluminum flashing in widths of 4", 6", 8", 12", or 18" is usually sold at hardware stores—by the lineal foot or in full rolls of 50'. This too is soft aluminum.

Aluminum sheets are made in a number of alloys, hardnesses, and thicknesses for aircraft use. Small pieces of this material may be available from an aircraft maintenance shop at a nearby airport, while larger sheets can be obtained from an aircraft supply house. One that caters to home builders is more apt to have it available in partial sheets or in cut pieces. Be aware that this material, like any other item sold for aircraft use, is *expensive!*

SHEET-METAL GAGES

The first problem you will encounter if you don't work with sheet metal much is the gage—thickness—of the metal. How thick is a gage? Or 16 of them, or 22, or whatever?

Getting into sheet-metal gages opens a real can of worms! Formerly there were any number of different gages in use; not only different systems in different countries, but in our own country different manufacturers or major production areas each had their own gage system.

Even today, after much effort, the system has not been completely straightened out. Some knowledgeable sources still recommend ordering materials by the exact decimal fraction desired.

A given gage of galvanized steel is slightly thicker than uncoated steel. Aluminum, copper, and brass are normally sold by decimal fraction thickness. If sold by gage, they are measured by a different gaging system than steel. They are also slightly thinner for a given gage.

Keeping these limitations in mind, you may find helpful the following *approximations* to fractional inch measurements. Most of them are within a few thousandths for galvanized steel; ranging upward from almost no error in 30 gage to about .015" deviation in the thickest gages.

Remember this: The *higher* the gage number,

the *thinner* the material. Here is the most important one to remember: *16 gage is almost exactly ⅟₁₆" thick.* If you will remember a couple more, you can easily estimate all the others. Ten gage is about ⅛" and 22 gage is very close to ⅟₃₂".

Here is the list of gages that approximate fractions:

⅟₆₄"	= 30 gage	⁵⁄₆₄"	= 14 gage
⅟₃₂"	= 22 gage	³⁄₃₂"	= 12 gage*
³⁄₆₄"	= 18 gage	⅛"	= 10 gage*
⅟₁₆"	= 16 gage	³⁄₁₆"	= 6 gage

*13 gage and 11 gage material are slightly closer to these two dimensions, but odd-numbered gages are usually harder to find than even-numbered ones.

Beginning with a thickness of ¼", steel is no longer referred to as sheet metal, but is called plate, and its thickness is measured in fractions of an inch.

LEVER SNIPS

If you have done any amount of sheet-metal cutting you probably have a couple of pair of compound action "aviation" snips. These are a

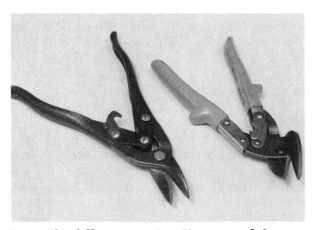

Notice the difference in the offset jaws of the new snips on the right compared to the older "aviation" snips on the left. The new ones have an open path at the rear for the cutoff piece. With the old pattern, this piece curls up over the continuation of the jaw where it blends into the handle.

great improvement on the old-fashioned tin snips, both in the amount of effort required and in their ability to cut tight circles. They still do involve a lot of undesirable bending of the metal though, especially when making long cuts.

A new development in offset head snips is an improvement in this regard, greatly simplifying such cuts. They are known as Lever snips and, as with aviation snips, are compound action. You need two pair. The black-handled pair cuts straight as well as to the right, while the orange-handled one cuts either straight or to the left. Sears also sells these tools under their own label, except that their handles are coded green and red.

The only minor drawback to these snips is that they seem to me to require slightly more pressure to cut a given thickness of material, but otherwise they are a great improvement over the older type.

INTERNAL CUTOUTS AND CORNERS

No matter how good your sheet-metal snips are, some cuts are extremely difficult or almost impossible to make with them, particularly when there are internal corners to be made in small cutouts. However, these can be made quickly and easily with a sharp cold chisel (preferably ground to a single facet "rivet buster" configuration) and a hammer.

If your cutout is a simple U-shaped one with an open side extending to an edge of the part, mark the cutout and make the two side cuts with your snips. Then place the metal in a vise and align the proposed bottom cut with the vise jaws. Holding the chisel at an angle to the work, start at one corner of the cut and proceed to the other end, shearing off the metal with the chisel and hammer.

Actually, there are two angles involved here.

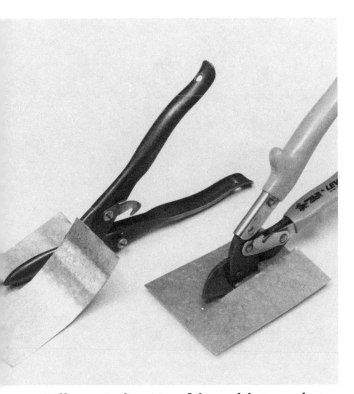

Difference in distortion of the work between the two snips is apparent. The new snips will sail right through a large sheet with little distortion while the older snips curl the metal to clear the tool.

Cold chisel on the top has a single facet, making for easy sheet-metal cutting because the flat lower side can be kept lined up with the edge of a vise jaw. The center tool is an ordinary cold chisel which cuts sheet metal quite well, but its short lower facet takes more care to keep it flat against the vise jaw. The bottom tool is a single-facet chisel, sold for cleaning up welding slag and spatter; it has a wide cutting tip and works great for shearing sheet metal.

The chisel is held at such an angle to the horizontal that the bottom facet of the cutting edge lies flat against the top of the vise jaw. (The single-facet rivet buster is thus held at a much flatter angle than is a conventional double-facet cold chisel.) Looking down vertically from above, either chisel is held at an angle of 30 degrees or so to the work so that it shears off the waste material in a bend toward the rear of the vise.

To make a completely internal cutout, mark the metal and then drill a hole next to one of the lines, or in a corner, and use this to start your chiseled cut. Especially in heavier gages of material, you may find it necessary to alternate your cut in both directions from a corner initially, in order to bend the waste metal out of the way without tearing it. Cut to a corner, turn the material in the vise to align the next side with the jaws, and proceed.

If your vise jaws are in good shape, the cut should be quite smooth. Somewhat battered jaws may produce a more ragged cut, it can be smoothed up with a file. Alternately, a better cut can be obtained by using a pair of auxiliary jaws made from short lengths of sharp-edged angle iron clamped in the vise jaws.

If the "tail" of the piece is too deep to fit in the vise and the piece is not too wide, it may be clamped between angle irons extending out to the side of the vise jaws, the extended ends being held together by a heavy C-clamp. (Put a scrap of the same material that you are cutting between the angle irons at the other end of the vise jaws to equalize the grip.)

If your work is too large to be held in a vise or the extended angle irons, a pair of square-edged angle irons held between the jaws of a Black & Decker Workmate will handle much larger work, at least in the lighter gages. Any time you use the angle iron method, be sure that both pieces are quite straight and that you align them in the vise so that both edges are at exactly the same height.

With a good husky vise, a large chisel, and a heavy hammer, this method of cutting can be used on mild steel up to ⅛" or more in thickness. I still have a small steel wrench I made that way for a beginner's machine-shop project nearly fifty years ago.

Making an interior cut with an ordinary cold chisel. Note that the lower facet is flat against the vise jaw and that the chisel is held at an angle to the work, shearing the waste out to the rear.

Finished inside cut has some slight burrs but will clean up nicely with a few strokes of a file. It was cut in a fraction of the time needed for most other methods of making this type of cut.

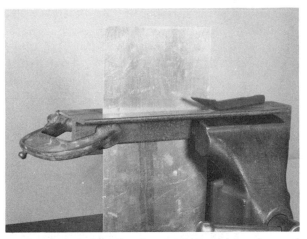

Workpiece too deep for the vise jaws can be clamped between a couple of short pieces of angle iron off to the side. Be sure to line up the tops of both angles.

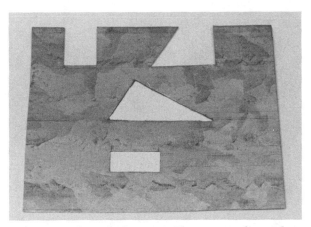

Some samples of sheet-metal cuts made with a chisel. The open-end cuts are quickly made by cutting the sides with a pair of snips and then shearing out the bottom with a chisel.

HACKSAWING THIN SHEETS

Sheet metal can be cut with a hacksaw, but thin material becomes a problem. It tends to bend, twist, tear, and jam against the blade, making

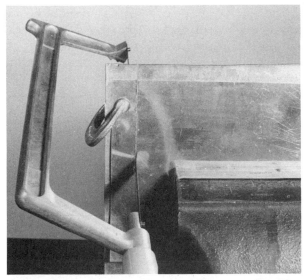

Sawing thin sheet metal with a hacksaw is often easier if a piece of heavier material is clamped behind it as a backup.

for very slow going. If you find it necessary to cut thin material with a hacksaw, use a piece of heavier backup material. Put a scrap of about 16 gage metal (1/16″, remember?) in the vise behind your thin stock and then saw through the two pieces simultaneously. If you have a long cut and your backup piece is not big enough to handle it, you can reposition it in stages along the cut in the thin piece.

FRICTION SAWINGS

Sheet metal up to 16 gage or so can be cut quite rapidly with a power saw using a smooth-edged friction-cutting blade. The one I have is labeled a "Steel Slicer." About 6½″ in diameter, it has 16 slots about 5/8″ deep equally spaced around the rim to dissipate heat and prevent warping. It actually burns its way through the steel and zips through 16-gage steel almost as fast as one could push it through a board!

Friction sawing of sheet metal can also be done on a band saw. I recently tried this using an old ½″ woodcutting blade that I had dulled cutting soapstone. Since the blade only had 4 teeth per inch, I turned it inside out so that it would run backward (teeth upside down), and the "hooks" on the tip of the teeth would not catch on the thin metal. Operated at the normal

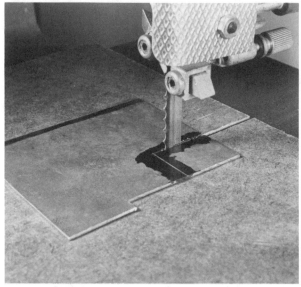

Friction-sawing 16-gage steel on a band saw. The blade was inverted to keep the teeth from catching. A backup sheet of hardboard had a slot cut in it to keep the burr formed on the bottom of the cut from dragging on the table.

Saw cut sheet steel even faster after the greatest part of the teeth was ground off because the friction area increased.

woodcutting speed, the blade sliced rapidly through several different thicknesses of material up to 16 gage. It does take a fair amount of pressure; just holding the material up to the blade will not result in a cut. A 10-gage scrap (⅛" thick) cut much more slowly and required very heavy pressure.

With any of these cuts, the burning action of the cut produces a wire edge on the bottom of the material along both edges of the cut. This is easily removed with a file later, but it does tend to catch in the edge of the saw slot and drag on the table. A scrap of thin plywood or hardboard clamped to the table with a narrow slot beyond the blade and in line with the saw kerf will alleviate this.

Thicker metal can be cut on a band saw equipped with a metal-cutting blade (similar to a hacksaw blade), but this requires a much slower operating speed than most woodworking band saws are capable of without some sort of speed reducing equipment.

VIXEN FILES

Sheet-metal files, usually referred to as Vixen files after the original manufacturer, are much faster and better for working with sheet metal than ordinary files, both for removing burrs from cut edges and for smoothing out hammered surfaces.

The teeth are formed into a shallow curve across the face of the file. They are quite coarse with only about twelve to sixteen teeth per inch; each tooth has a more forward-angled hook to it than on a normal file.

If you will be doing much sheet-metal work,

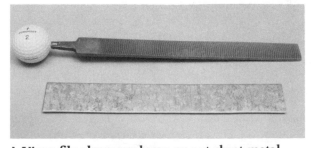

A Vixen file cleans up burrs on cut sheet metal.

one of these will be quite useful. If you don't find it at the hardware store, try an auto supply store.

BENDING PLIERS

Locking jaw pliers are available with 3" wide jaws for sheet-metal work and are used as a sort of "poor man's bending brake" to bend up small parts. A single pair makes a sharp bend in a piece of material held in a vise; two pair can be used together to make various bends in small brackets, toy parts, and suchlike.

MAKING MULTIPLE BENDS

Smooth and accurate bending of sheet metal without the proper tool, a bending brake, is always a problem. As previously mentioned, the Workmate, your vise jaws, and the special locking-jaw pliers provide some answers.

In other cases, such as making multiple bends close together, you have a problem be-

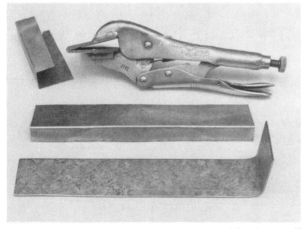

One or two pair of locking pliers quickly do small sheet-metal bending jobs. The jaws, shown here in end view, are 3" wide.

Multiple bends, not possible between the vise jaws, can be made by clamping the material between square bar stock off to one side of the vise jaws. A spring clamp at other end aided in setting up jig.

Bends made by a single pair of sheet-metal pliers with the material held in a vise. The steel is 16-, 18-, 26-, and 30-gage.

Trio of bent up samples made by the vise and bar stock method. For some bends here even a bending brake would not be practical.

cause the vise jaws often get in the way of the second bend. In this case, two pieces of steel-bar stock extending to one side of your vise jaws works to hold the metal while the second bend is made. Or the steel bars can make a first bend in a part too deep to be held directly in the vise jaws. Various widths and thicknesses of steel bar can be used as required for the particular part, and large, square key stock works for some smaller jobs.

Remember to clamp the extended ends of the steel bars with a heavy C-clamp. Use a scrap of the same thickness sheet metal between the two pieces of bar stock at the far end of the vise jaws to equalize the grip.

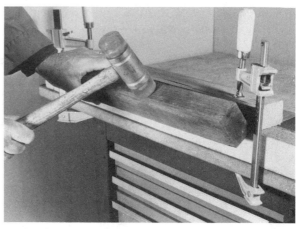

With the stock clamped in position between the scantlings, the hammer is used on a 2 x 3 to form the second bend.

ANOTHER SUBSTITUTE BRAKE

Three straight lengths of 2 x 4, a pair of large C-clamps, and a heavy hammer serve to make straight bends in a fairly large piece of sheet metal.

Clamp the sheet metal between two of the scantlings with the desired line of bend lying along one edge. Clamp the whole assembly to a workbench or sawhorse. If your bench has a heavy, straight front edge, you can eliminate

Two scraps of plywood cut to width are held in a vise to make a substitute brake for the end bends.

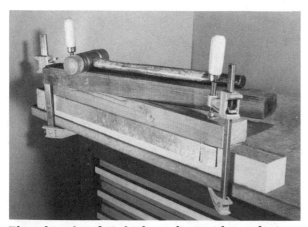

Three lengths of 2″-thick stock provide a substitute brake for sheet-metal bending. Here, a first bend has already been made.

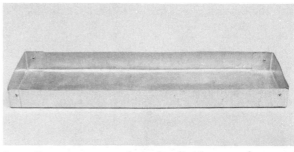

Four Pop rivets complete the divider tray for a tool cabinet drawer.

the lower strip. Clamp the work directly between the upper strip and the bench.

With one hand, hold the third 2 x 4 on top of the sheet metal and butted up against the top 2 x 4 at the point of bend. With the hammer in your other hand, strike heavy blows along the outer edge of this piece. Work your blows back and forth along the full length of the bend and keep the bend even from one end to the other. For the thinner gages of metal, especially with shorter length bends, 1 x 2s or 1 x 3s may be used instead of 2 x 4s.

With careful work and a little practice, a surprisingly good job can be done by this method. In the Orient it is not at all unusual to see sheet-metal shops turning out professional work this way.

If you do much sheet-metal bending, you may want to purchase the small brake offered in some tool catalogs. It will bend light gages of sheet metal up to 18″ in width.

LAYOUT WORK

Before any sheet-metal work such as cuts, bends, or rivet holes can be made with any accuracy, the material must be properly measured and marked, or laid out as this step is called.

This sounds simple enough, but when you try to mark it, you will find that a pencil mark, a ballpoint pen, or even a scribed mark does not show up well on the shiny surface. The answer to this is to cover the surface, at least the part where the marks are to be made, with a layout dye.

Layout dye is available in 8-ounce and larger cans, complete with a small brush. When applied to a surface it dries in five minutes to a smooth glare-free surface that makes even lightly scribed lines show up sharply. It can also be used for finding high spots on gears, bearings, and other mechanical parts and has applications in many other types of metalworking layout as well. Layout dye can be found at larger hardware stores, industrial supply houses, and some auto supply stores.

If you don't do enough layout work to justify hunting up a can, there are several ersatz materials you can substitute. A wide-tip marking pen, preferably a "permanent" one, works nic-

Steel marking dye is almost indispensable for accurate layout work. The real stuff is shown on the left along with a couple of substitutes. The shoe polish ran third but was usable. The wide-tip marking pen does a good job on small areas, but the professional material is more practical for large jobs.

cly. As with regular layout dye, it can be removed later with acetone or lacquer thinner, sometimes even with paint thinner (the "permanence" pertains to water resistance.) Another substance that works is a thin coat of liquid shoe polish. Those that I have tried did not show up the scribed lines as well as the marking pen fluid. An acquaintance reports satisfactory results using typing correction fluid, but I have not tried it.

BEND ALLOWANCE

Bend allowance is a real ball of snakes that has to be dealt with in any sheet-metal work, especially in the thicker gages.

Suppose you need to make a U-shaped yoke for some project. To keep it simple, let's say that you want it to be exactly 1″ wide on the inside of the two legs and also 1″ deep inside. Since you are going to make it out of ⅛" material, that will make your outside dimensions 1¼" wide and 1⅛" deep. So, you add up those lengths; two at 1⅛" and one at 1¼". It comes to 3½" overall, right?

You cut off a piece of the material 3½" long and go to work. Since it is fairly thick, you decide that a ¼" radius bend should be about right. Subtracting that from 1" gives you ¾" for the inside length of each leg to the start of the bend. You measure in ¾" from each end, mark it, set one mark to the top of your vise jaws and make the first bend. Put the other end in the vise and make the second bend. Assuming that you made the bends to the desired radius, the depth came out just fine; right on. But what about the width? Instead of being 1" between the two legs of the yoke it is about 1½"! Old demon Bend Allowance strikes again!

There are pages of tables to cover this situation. They evolve from the following formula which you can run out on any hand-held calculator.

Bend Allowance = (.01743R + .0078T) per degree of bend.

R = the radius of the bend, and T = the thickness of the material. Thus, for our problem, the formula works out as follows:

B.A. = (.01743 x .250 + 0078 x .125) x 90
B.A. = .0043575 + .000975 x 90
B.A. = .0053325 x 90
B.A. = .479925 or about ³¹⁄₆₄"

Now, you can lay out your yoke as follows. The first ¾" takes us from the top of one leg down to the start of the first bend. Then ³¹⁄₆₄" takes us around the bend. Next, add ½" for the distance to the start of the second bend. Allow another ³¹⁄₆₄" for this bend and a final ¾" for the straight length of the other leg. Add up all five measurements and the overall length of your blank comes to 2³¹⁄₃₂". No wonder the first attempt turned out a little long.

About now you're saying, "There's got to be an easier way." For the needs of most of us, there is. Once you have figured out your basic dimensions, take a narrow strip of the material that you want to use and cut it to a length that you know will be more than adequate. Make a note

Bend allowance must be considered even when working with fairly thin material and short radius bends. Here the desired result was a U-shaped piece with three 2" sides. In the first example, a piece of material 6" long (2" + 2" + 2") was used. Bent up with two 2" legs; the width turned out to be 2¼"! For the second example, a bend allowance calculation was made, and the stock length figured at 5¾". Bent up with the same radius of bend used for the first piece, it came out right on the desired dimensions: 2" x 2" x 2".

of the exact dimension. Then bend up the strip so that the interior dimension is the one you need. In this case, you would measure ¼" to each side from the center and bend the legs so that your width comes out right on. Measure the legs and find out how much longer they are than your desired dimension. Add the extra length for both legs together and subtract this extra amount from the overall length of your experimental sample. Measure and cut your actual stock to this corrected length and proceed to bend up your part.

Fortunately, on thin sheet metal with minumum radius bends, bend allowance is a minor problem as long as you are aware of what is going on and make corrections. If you do get involved with bending heavier gages with larger radius curves and don't want to mess with the formula, you can find bend allowance tables in the library. Look for a mechanical

CALCULATING BEND ALLOWANCE

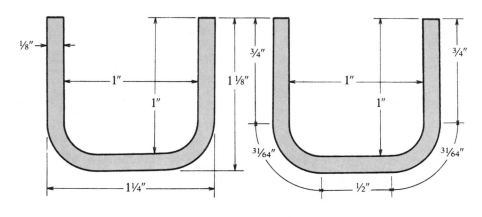

DESIRED DIMENSIONS   **BEND ALLOWANCE CALCULATED**

drawing text, a drafting room manual, or a machinist's handbook. *Machinery's Handbook*, for example, has a half-dozen pages of fine-print text and tables on bend allowance.

MAKING CORNER BENDS

While I am on the subject of bending, consider the situation where you want to bend up two flanges at right angles to make a corner. The usual first impulse is to just make two intersecting cuts and bend it up. For good work this is considered a no-no. For one thing, it is difficult to get the bend exactly aligned with the intersection of the two cuts, and for another, the sharp corner provides a natural place for cracks to form under any stress on the piece.

Three methods of corner relief are shown in the accompanying photo; they are often used in aircraft sheet-metal work. One uses a small hole, ⅛″ or so, drilled at the intersecting bend

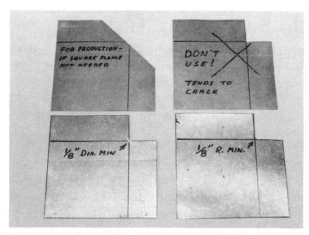

Here are three recommended ways of cutting the sheet metal for a bent-up corner, plus one that is not approved. The method not recommended involves two straight cuts into a corner; this often leads to cracking when the bend is made. A 45-degree cut across the corner just inside the bend lines is the simplest of the approved methods. If square corners are required on the flanges, either cutting to the center of a small drilled or punched hole, or to tangents on a slightly larger hole, are recommended. The latter case requires more precise cutting.

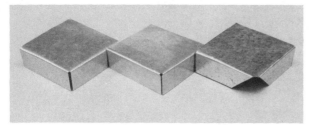

Three approved corners after bending. Left, cuts made to a tangent; center, cuts to the center of a circle; and right, the production type 45-degree cut across a corner.

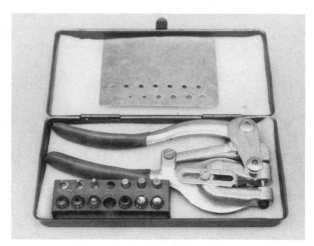

Hand punch is a great help if you make a lot of holes in sheet metal. The lower row of holes in the sample in the box shows the seven sizes that can be made. The upper row was made at an equal distance from the edge by means of the adjustable guide in the throat of the punch. Note how clean and burr-free all the holes are compared with the average hole made by a twist drill in sheet metal.

lines. The second provides a small radius (1/8″ is usually considered minimum) at the corner. Make it by drilling or punching a 1/4″ hole and then cutting the metal to intersect the hole tangentially. The third method is the easiest and is usually used in places where a square corner is not required on the flanges themselves. Simply slice off the corner at a 45-degree angle so that the cut comes just inside the intersection of the two bend lines.

HANDY PUNCH

Although in the workshop most holes are drilled in sheet metal, drilling does have some disadvantages. In thin metal, the ordinary twist drill usually makes a hole that is ragged, out of round, and has a burr on the back side that must be removed.

In production work, holes are often punched in metal with powered punch presses. This is impractical for the small workshop, but there is an inexpensive alternative in the form of a hand punch.

Often called a Whitney punch after the original manufacturer, these are now mostly imported. The one shown came from Japan. It provides seven quick-change punch and die sets, which makes holes from 3/32″ to 9/32″ by 32nds. Each punch has a small point on the end which can be indented into a center punch mark for accurately locating the round, clean, burr-free hole. It also has an adjustable guide, allowing a series of holes to be made at the same distance from the edge of a sheet.

If you get involved in a lot of sheet-metal work, you will find out just how handy a hand punch can be.

SPACING JIG

Measuring and center punching for a line of rivet holes is all very well, but it requires a good deal of effort and concentration if the holes are all going to come out exactly the same distance apart.

A jig saves a lot of grief here. Bend up a small scrap of sheet metal to slip over the edge of your stock. Drill or punch a pair of holes in it at the correct distances, and it automatically locates your holes accurately, both in edge distance and spacing.

Depending on the size of the holes you make in it, you can use your jig with a center punch to mark the holes, or directly with a drill or punch to cut the holes. The locating hole can be eyeballed over the previous hole. For more exacting work, it can be precisely located by inserting a rivet, a pin punch, or a short piece of appropriately sized rod through it while the next hole is marked.

Jig for punching (or drilling) evenly spaced holes is made from a folded-up scrap of heavy-gage sheet metal. After each hole is punched, the stock is moved till that hole lines up under a second hole in the jig. A pin is inserted into the second hole to position it. The punch is positioned in the jig's first hole and struck to make the next hole in the work. Holes are clean and burr-free, even though the end grain of a wood block is used in lieu of a die.

Drill press punch setup. The other end of the bar stock is clamped to the drill press table. The die hole was drilled in the bar stock, and a piece of gas welding rod of the same diameter was then substituted for the drill bit to make a punch. The rod's end has been ground off at a slight angle so that the punched hole is started at one side and then is sheared out across the hole. This requires less effort than with a straight-end punch.

If you make the locating holes in your jig with a hand punch, put a thin shim between the jig and a scrap of the metal that you will be using, in order that the punch will not press the jig into too tight a fit on the stock. That would make it difficult to slide from one position to the next. A shim cut from an aluminum beer can is just about the right thickness. If you have to drink the beer to get the can, that is just one of the sacrifices you occasionally have to make for your craft.

MAKESHIFT PUNCH AND DIE

If you have a drill press, you can easily provide a punch and die for light work (small holes in thin gages). My press easily punches 5/32″ holes in .040 aluminum and ¼″ holes in 26-gage steel, for example.

By actuating the spindle feed handle you can punch a series of holes quite rapidly. The compression spring acts as a stripper, holding the work against the die while the punch is withdrawn.

Use any convenient scrap piece of steel for the die. Secure it in your drill press vise and bolt the vise to the drill table. Drill a hole of the desired size completely through the die so that later the punched out "holes" will be pushed on through. Keep the vise and table locked in this position while proceeding to remove the drill from the chuck and replace it with a suitable punch of the same diameter. This can be a pin punch made from round stock, a short piece of drill rod, or a piece of steel welding rod. (The end must be ground to a slight angle to provide a shearing cut.)

Place the work on the improvised die and bring down the punch with the drill feed lever. A number of holes can be made quite rapidly with this setup. Use common sense and don't overload your spindle by trying to punch too big a hole through heavy material.

If you use a pin punch, don't forget to grind the end back square before replacing it in your set.

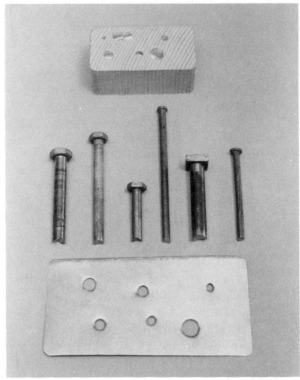

Several makeshift punches, along with an end-grain wood block used in place of a die and samples of the holes. For larger holes made without a die, a fish-mouth end on the punch often works better than a square end or an angle.

PUNCHING HOLES WITHOUT A DIE

With thin gages of sheet metal, surprisingly smooth-edged holes can often be punched without a die by placing the material on the end-grain of a wood block (preferably a close-grained hardwood) held in your vise.

Pin punches, various sized bolts with the threaded section cut off (leaving a smooth shank), or even short nails of various diameters work as punches. Whatever you use, touch up its end on a fine-grit wheel so that you have a sharp-cornered end rather than a blunt or rounded one.

Small punches may be ground straight across to a perfectly square end. Punches that are a little larger should be ground at a 5 to 10-degree angle for an easier shearing cut. For even larger punches, the end can be carefully ground to a slight U-shape on the corner of your grinding wheel. This starts a cut at two opposite sides of the hole and shears both ways toward the center.

Keep your punch short to avoid any tendency toward bending, and use a heavy enough hammer to punch the hole through with one good "whop" instead of just pecking away at it.

Depending on several factors, such as the thickness and hardness of your material, the size and sharpness of your punch, and the hardness of your backup end-grain block, you may find a slightly raised circle of material on the back of your sheet. If this is enough to cause a problem, put the work on a flat surface and flatten it out with a hammer blow. This will decrease the diameter of the hole slightly, you may need a slightly larger punch to get holes the correct size.

Experiment a bit on a scrap of the metal from your workpiece. Try various punches; they only take a minute or less to grind. You will probably stash several of them away in a drawer to use again and again.

DRILLING SMOOTHER-EDGED HOLES

As previously mentioned, normal twist drills usually do not make very good holes in sheet metal. The holes are often out of round, ragged, and have an excessive burr on the back side.

A particular grind for a twist drill bit works out quite well for cutting smoother holes in sheet metal however, although to look at it you would not believe it. To sharpen a normal twist drill to this shape, start by grinding off the end on a coarse wheel until it is absolutely square ended, as though it had been sawed off. Then, move to your fine wheel and, starting on one side, tilt the lip up a few degrees and grind the edge to a normal clearance angle, proceeding from the side toward, but just short of, the center. Do the same on the other lip and continue to grind both sides down until you have nice

sharp lips, a good clearance angle, and a short nub at the center. Then, carefully grind this nub to a point until your bit looks just like a brad-point woodcutting twist drill, except without

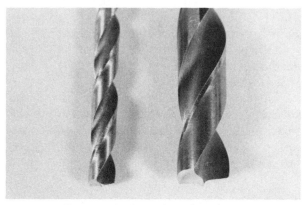

Twist drills reworked to this shape, strange as it seems, cut a rounder and cleaner hole in sheet metal than an ordinary twist drill.

REGRINDING A TWIST DRILL

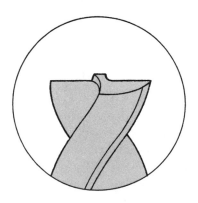

SIDE VIEW

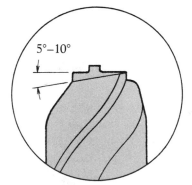

5°–10°

EDGE VIEW

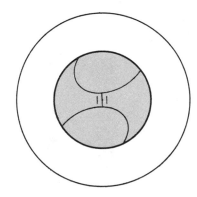

END VIEW

Grind off end of twist drill and resharpen to this shape to cut round, burr-free holes in sheet metal.

the edge lips. The center spur does not have to be as long as on a wood bit.

When you've got the bit looking as though it wouldn't safely cut a hole through a piece of cardboard, much less thin sheet metal, it's probably about right. Secure a center-punched test scrap to your drill press table and back it up with a piece of wood. Try out the drill using a fairly slow spindle speed. You will probably see it lift off a nice curled chip and quickly go right through the metal. Better still, it should leave a nice round hole with no distortion and little if any burr on the back side.

I have made several of these modified bits ranging up to ½″ in diameter, and they all work great. A friend who did radio work, which required large holes in metal chassis, told me he had good results with these bits for holes up to 1″ in diameter.

UNIBITS

Unibits come in at least three different models. All of them drill several different sized holes in sheet metal with a single drill. Due to the drill's single-lipped cutting edge, all of the holes turn out perfectly round and smooth with little if any burr on the back. Any slight burr that does result can be removed with the bit itself on all but the very largest hole. Just touch it with the start of the next larger portion of the drill. This saves the chucking of a separate countersink.

Unibits are expensive, but one model drills thirteen different holes from ⅛″ to ½″ by 32nds and is self starting, requiring no pilot hole. A second model is also self starting and drills nine holes from ¼″ to ¾″ by 16ths. A third drills eight holes from ⁹⁄₁₆″ to 1″ by 16ths. This one does require a ½″ starting hole.

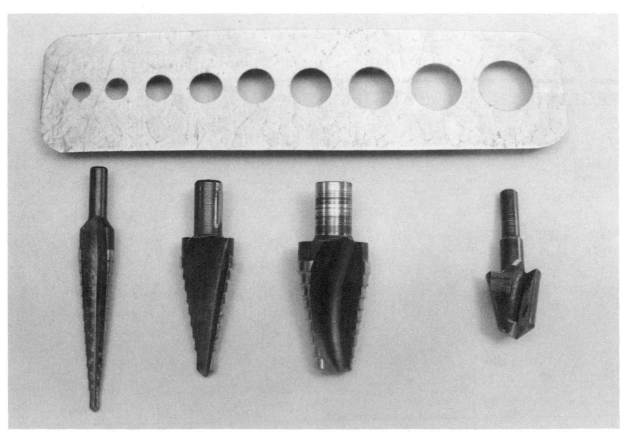

Three Unibits plus a taper-type sheet-metal bit. The nine different holes in the sample were drilled with the second bit from the left. The first bit drills thirteen different holes. The third one drills eight larger holes but both it and the taper bit (far right) require a ½″ predrilled pilot hole.

All three models drill material up to ⅛″ thick. You get a stepped hole on thicker stock. The smallest Unibit has a ¼″ shank, the mid-size one has a ⅜″ shank, and the largest has a ½″ shank. Unibits are terrific for making holes in sheet metal if you drill enough of them to justify the expense.

Taper type bits are also available at somewhat less cost. You can drill many sizes of large holes with a single bit, but they do leave the sides of the hole tapered. This may be a disadvantage depending on the gage of the metal and the use to which the part is to be put.

DRILLING BIGGER HOLES

A plumber's taper reamer, normally for deburring the inside edges of pipe ends after cutting, enlarges round holes in sheet metal. It also provides an effective substitute for expensive chassis punches for occasional radio/electronics work. They come in various sizes; I have two, both picked up at flea markets; one has a maximum diameter of 1½″ and another that goes to 2¼″.

Samples of holes enlarged with a taper reamer. The one on the right was drilled much faster, since less wood had to be removed from its thinner backup block. It also turned out smoother than the one on the left, due to the effect of the more pronounced grain in the thicker block.

Normally rotated by a carpenter's brace, the reamer's shaft can be turned or ground round to fit into a drill chuck for powered operation. The only problem with doing this is that since they were designed for hand-turned operation, little effort was made to be sure that the shank was forged concentric to the reamer itself. It may be difficult or impossible to turn the shank true to the cutting edge of the reamer. If this is the case, it will work better in a hand-held electric drill. Then the reamer can rotate smoothly while the eccentricity is taken up by the operator's hand and arm.

In either case, use a slow speed and be sure to hold the material securely; in a vise for portable drill work, or clamped to the table if you are able to use a drill press. (Check it for concentric turning first.)

Since these reamers have a blunt end, drill a pilot hole through the sheet metal and also through the wood backup block. You must clamp a backup to the back of the sheet to prevent a ragged and heavily burred hole. While enlarging the hole in the sheet metal, the reamer has to enlarge the hole in the backup block; so do not use a piece of wood any thicker than necessary.

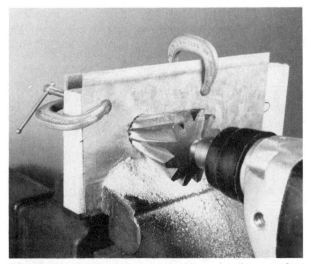

Plumber's taper reamer, its square shank turned to fit a drill chuck, can enlarge holes in sheet metal up to 2″ or more. A backup block is a necessity.

CUTTING REALLY BIG HOLES

If you need to cut even larger holes in sheet metal, a circle cutter is the answer. Various models are available and cut circles up to 8″ in diameter.

The circle cutter consists of a central shaft, which has a pilot drill at its end, usually ¼″ in diameter; the shaft also holds a swinging bar, which is adjustable as to reach. The cutting tool itself, often a ¼″-square lathe tool bit, is secured to the end of the bar. The two ends of the bit can be ground so that one end provides a straight cut at the outside of the radius while the other cuts straight on the inside. Thus, by reversing the bit, you can cut either a straight-sided hole (with an angle cut on the central blank) or a straight-sided circle blank. (Circle cutter bits can also be ground to cut a groove, to cut a specific design, and to make ornate rosettes in woodworking.)

While some manufacturers imply that you can use a circle cutter in a portable electric drill, I would be very cautious about using it in anything other than a drill press. Although it is true that circle cutters were originally turned by a carpenter's bit brace, such operation is quite slow and if the bit should grab, there is little problem. With a portable drill the speed is much greater and if the unit is not held absolutely vertical to the work, binding and grabbing is almost certain—with possibly disastrous results.

Even in a drill press, several precautions must be taken. The material must be securely fastened to the table atop a piece of plywood or other material to prevent the bit from scoring the table on breakthrough. The press must be operated at its very lowest speed, and the operator should be careful that long sleeves or any other loose clothing does not get caught in the cutter. Cleaning rags or other loose items should be removed from near the table. Keep your hands and arms well clear of the cutter and the work. Remain clear until the drill is turned off and has come to a complete stop.

To determine the diameter of a circle to be cut, measure from the center of the pilot hole to the cutting edge of the bit. A jig helps out here. Make it from a scrap of wood or metal and drill a hole the diameter of the pilot drill in one end. Obtain a short scale that is as long as the maximum radius of the circle cutter. This can be part of an inexpensive ¼″ metal scale, a piece of flex scale from a tape measure, part of a wooden or plastic foot rule, or anything of the sort.

Assuming that your pilot drill is ¼″, cut ⅛″ off the end of the zero end of the scale and mount it on the block with its cutoff end just at the edge of the pilot hole. By bringing the bit down into the hole, you can then use the scale to set an exact radius at the cutting edge of the tool bit.

For even larger holes the circle cutter is the answer. This one cuts holes up to 8″ in diameter. Used with a backup block in a drill press, it makes a smooth cut.

CLECO CLAMPS

If you do any Pop riveting or other fastening of sheet-metal pieces, a few Cleco clamps can come in handy. Now usually generically known as "sheet holders," you need the clamps plus a pair of the special pliers to insert them. They are great for keeping two or more pieces in alignment while drilling a series of holes.

Drill one hole, slip in a clamp, and drill a second hole. If you need more than two holes, use a second clamp or more, as in the case of a long seam with a large number of rivets. While the same thing can be done with machine

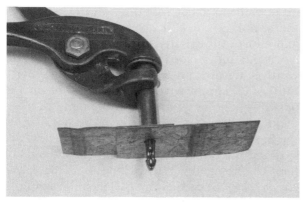

With its spring compressed by a special pair of pliers, a Cleco clamp, or sheet holder, can be slipped through the mating holes in sheet-metal work.

When the pliers are removed, the spring expands the split tongue of the clamp against the sides of the holes and also pulls the two sheets together.

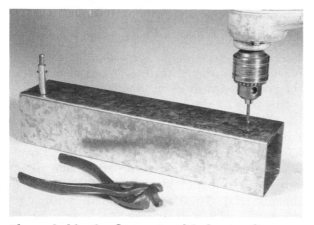

Clamp holds the first pair of holes in alignment while a second set is drilled, after which another clamp will be inserted.

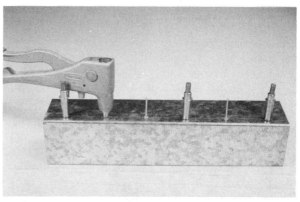

Three Cleco-type clamps kept the parts aligned while the remaining holes were drilled. Now the first pop rivet is being pulled. The clamps will be removed one at a time as the final rivets are inserted.

screws and nuts, the clamps are faster and more convenient, and also hold the sheets in more precise alignment than all but the most closely fitting screws. Cleco clamps are spring loaded to expand against the sides of holes as well as to pull the sheets tightly together. A separate set of clamps are required for each diameter of rivet.

A current aircraft supply catalog catering to home builders (see appendix) sells the clamps for about 50¢ each and the pliers for less than $10 new. On the other hand, another mail-order supply house for auto restorers advertises a

"Panel Holding System" consisting of 10 clamps and a pair of pliers for about $25. This is a good example of how you can pay double or more for an unusual tool if you do not check the prices of more than one supplier.

If a nearby airport has a branch of one of the aircraft supply houses, you might check with them before sending away for the clamps. Or one of the local mechanics may know of a nearby source. A half dozen clamps for each size rivet that you use and the special pliers take care of all but the most extensive projects. This is another inexpensive "professional" tool that is quite handy but usually does not come to the small workshopper's attention.

CUTTING BLIND SLOTS

Blind slots (both ends closed) are usually cut with a milling machine in professional work. Desirable as it may be, a milling machine is just too expensive for most small shops. The usual answer for jobs of this sort is to drill or punch a series of holes, either overlapping or as close to one another as possible. You then file out between the holes and along the sides. This is a tedious job that often falls short of the desired result unless you are both quite capable and very careful.

Here is an alternate procedure that works quite well on sheet metal or on flat bar stock that is not too thick. It saves a great deal of time and effort and usually produces better results.

Lay out and scribe the slot. Carefully drill full width holes at both ends. Then bend the metal into a "U" shape with the scribed slot on the outside of the bend and with the bend perpendicular to the long dimension of the slot. Center the bend at the middle of the desired slot. Secure the part in a vise with the bottom side of the "U" facing up. With a fine-tooth hacksaw, cut out the slot by making two parallel saw cuts just inside the scribed lines from end hole to end hole. Carefully straighten out the part to its original flat configuration and clean up the slot to final dimension with a file.

Cutting a blind slot in a piece of stock is always a problem without a milling machine. If the material is thin enough to be bent and later straightened, a hacksaw will do the job quickly and easily.

After the part has been straightened out, the edges of the slot are touched up with a file.

TIGHTER SHEET-METAL SCREWS

Sheet-metal screws are dandy gadgets, but when used with the thinner gages of material, they often tend to work loose.

One way to alleviate this is to punch or drill smaller than normal holes in the sheet which holds the threads (the attached item usually has clearance holes). Then flare the holes downward so that the screw threads make better contact than if they just went straight through the material. The flares are made with a tapered punch which in some cases can be the same punch that makes the holes. For this the punch must have a long radius fillet between the diameter of the punch and its handle section (many pin punches do).

Place the material on the end grain of a block of wood and punch the hole. After punching the hole, move the metal over a previously drilled hole that is slightly larger in diameter than the punched hole. Let the punch hang into the center of this hole and give it another careful wallop. This deforms the metal down into the hole alongside the punch, providing a considerably greater bearing surface for the thread of the sheet metal screw to engage.

Before doing this on the job at hand, experiment on some scrap stock of the same thickness. Determine the correct size of the hole to be punched and the depth of flare best suited to the screw.

7
MISCELLANEOUS METALWORKING METHODS

MULTIPLE HACKSAWS

Almost every small workshop has a hacksaw. For metalwork or auto repair, it is a necessity. Even if you are strictly a woodworker, you probably have a hacksaw and have found many uses for it. One problem constantly recurs though. No matter which blade you have in the frame, it always seems to be the wrong one for the next job that turns up.

You probably know to use a coarse-toothed blade for sawing thick material and a fine-toothed blade for cutting thin metal and for pipe and tubing. So, what happens? You come up with a little job, say cutting off a piece of thin-wall tubing, and find an 18-tooth (per inch) blade installed in the frame. Rather than take the considerable time and trouble to change the blade for such a small job, you try to make do, and either break the blade or strip some teeth off. Plus you get a ragged and inaccurate cut in the bargain. Another time, you try to cut a heavy piece of metal without changing from a fine tooth blade and either take forever to cut

off the part or end up breaking the blade because you tried to rush the job.

The solution is simple, *but not one small shop in a hundred uses it*. Get a second hacksaw frame and keep a coarse-toothed blade in one and a fine-toothed blade in the other. This way you always have the correct blade immediately available and only have to change blades when one breaks or wears out. In addition, because you are using them properly, the blades last much longer.

Hacksaw blades are normally made with either 14, 18, 24, or 32 teeth per inch, although many hardware stores stock only the 18 and the 32. These two are satisfactory for most work. If you do a lot of heavy sawing, you might want to hunt up some 14's or, for a lot of medium to thin work, the 24's may be better for you.

When purchasing blades, consider buying the more expensive alloy steel ones, especially when getting coarse toothed blades for heavy work. They last much longer and give better results than the cheaper ones.

Before you go out to buy a new hacksaw, think about this: If you already have a heavy frame, keep it for the coarse blades and get a

159

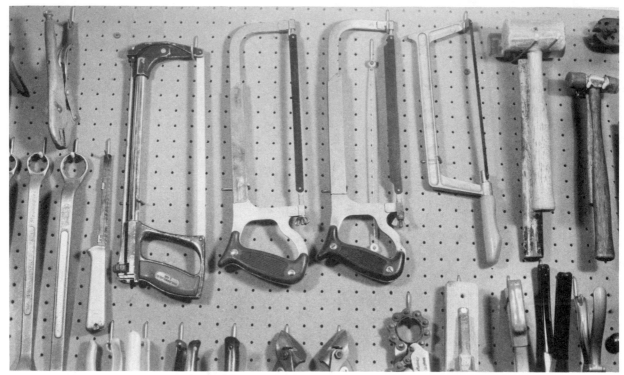

Extra hacksaw frame is so handy that having tried it you may end up with several! These frames mount, from left, an 18-teeth-per-inch blade for heavy cutting, a 32-teeth-per-inch blade for thin stock and tubing, a carbide-grit blade for hardened steel and ceramics, and a 32-teeth-per-inch blade permanently mounted at a 45-degree angle for cutting off long strips without interference from the frame.

lighter, less expensive, frame for the fine-toothed work. Conversely, if you've been doing all of your work with a light frame, this might be the time to get a good strong frame for the heavy stuff and relegate the old one to the thin material.

Good new tools are expensive. You may want to wait and look around for a suitable used hacksaw at the flea market. After all, if you've been struggling along with one hacksaw for years, you can put up with it for a few more days.

Once you've tried the multiple hacksaw idea you probably won't stop at two. I have a third with the blade permanently mounted at 45 degrees (most frames use 90 degrees) for cutting long strips. A fourth has a carbide grit blade—the kind once shown in advertisements cutting a Coke bottle in two, although I'll readily admit that I haven't found much need to cut Coke bottles. It does come in handy for cutting a number of other things, including hardened steel and ceramics. My fifth hacksaw is an old heavy one with a 10"-deep frame, very handy for cutting large pieces.

If, like the vast majority of craftsmen, you currently have only one hacksaw frame, do *not* pass up this idea! In a short time you'll wonder how—and why—you ever struggled along with a single hacksaw before.

CUTTING METAL WITH A COLD CHISEL

Cold chisels can be powered by air, as mentioned in Chapter 1, or by hand with a heavy

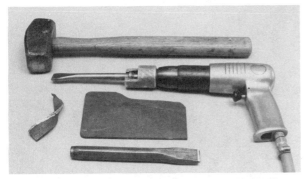

Steel as thick as this ³⁄₁₆″ sample can be cut straight or curved with the long-barrel air chisel or with the cold chisel and 4 lb, single jack. The workpiece shears along the top of vise jaws and retains its shape, but the waste is violently distorted.

This little wrench was cut to rough shape by the vise, hammer, and chisel method as a school machine-ship project some fifty years ago.

hammer. In chapter 5, I discussed how to cut sheet metal with a cold chisel. Used in either manner, with a heavy vise, they will make straight, curved, and internal cuts in mild steel up to over ⅛″ in thickness. Although this is still labeled as sheet metal, you usually do not think of it as such.

To make a curved cut with a cold chisel, proceed as discussed for cutting sheet metal, but every ⅛″ or so, reset the metal in the vise so that the cut continues along the desired line. Actually, you are cutting a series of short tangents, rather than a true curve, but it takes only a bit of filing or grinding to fair it in nicely.

USES FOR WELDING ROD

If you do not happen to have an oxyacetylene welding outfit, you may not be aware of the many nonwelding uses for gas welding rod, available from any welding supply shop. This material normally comes in 3′ lengths and in several diameters from ¹⁄₁₆″ to ¼″. While coat hanger wire is also quite useful around the shop, it usually comes in only one diameter, and the straight pieces are short. Gas rod also has a very thin copper coating which retards rust. (Electric welding rods are much shorter in length and are heavily coated with a fluxing

compound; that makes them impractical for our purposes.)

Smaller gas rods work well for various wire-sized projects while the large rods are fine for any number of sturdier things. The ¼″ rod makes brackets and hangers to store the heaviest ladder for instance, either horizontally or vertically. Shelves can be hung from overhead joists using bent up brackets of ⅛″, ³⁄₁₆″, or ¼″ rod depending on the expected load.

The ends of ³⁄₁₆″ rod can be threaded either 10–24 or 10–32, and ¼″ rod can be threaded ¼″–20, or ¼″–28. Threaded rods make all sorts of long bolts that would otherwise be difficult or impossible to find. An improvised bolt head is easily made by just threading the rod a short distance and then screwing on two nuts. Use

Ladder bracket made from ¼″ welding rod. The rod was bent to a U shape and driven into holes drilled into the horizontal plate behind the Sheetrock in this garage wall. One bracket supports the 10′ ladder on the left. The other bracket normally holds a 6′ ladder by its top.

Curved ³⁄₁₆ welding-rod brackets, again driven into the 2 x 4 plate, keep rope coiled and convenient.

Another ³⁄₁₆″ welding-rod bracket holds this string trimmer up out of the way in the garage. A second bracket fits around and supports the far end of the shaft next to the cutting head.

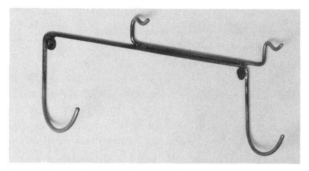

Broom closet bracket, bent up from ⁵⁄₃₂″ welding rod, is fastened to the wall by two screws through the welded-on washers. It holds a folded ironing board up off the floor. The smaller attached fitting stores a portable fixture for holding shirts on hangers.

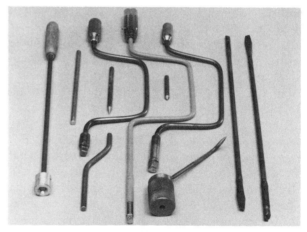

Gas welding rod (¼″) makes or modifies all sorts of tools for the workshop. The item at far left drives Morse taper centers out of the lathe's hollow headstock. The two tools on the far right are spiral screwdriver blades, cut in two and with an extension welded in to suit a specific application.

two wrenches to lock the nuts against one another.

To hang things from studs or joists, chamfer the ends of a rod slightly and then bend the rod to a sharp right angle at the appropriate distance from the end (1½″ for a joist; longer for a stud if it will go through Sheetrock as well). Then drill a hole that is ¹⁄₃₂″ or ¹⁄₆₄″ (depending on the hardness of the wood) smaller than the rod and drive it in with a hammer.

Many other uses can be found for this material. The larger sizes make good sturdy axles for wheels on wooden toys. Grind a chamfer on the

ends of the rod and press it into slightly undersize holes in the wooden wheels. Or cut just a very short set of threads on each end, drill the wheels to turn free on the axle, and secure them by locking the nut against the end of the threads. This requires careful calculation of length so that when the nuts are locked on the rod an appropriate amount of end play is available to allow wheels to turn freely without too much "slop." Castle nuts on the axles of toy trucks give a rugged look. Or press small push nuts on the ends of axles to hold wheels in place.

Make or modify tools to fit special situations with welding rod. For example, I have some hard-to-reach screws in a bunk bed that is occasionally removed or reinstalled in a Blazer. For this purpose, a spare blade from a spiral screwdriver was cut in two and a 10″ length of ¼″ rod welded in. Over the years this has saved a good deal of time. Quarter-inch rod can be bent up to make speeder handles for specific uses. In addition to the ¼″-drive socket speeder mentioned in Chapter 2, I keep a couple more at the metal lathe. One is for chuck adjustment and the other for the milling attachment. Both have working ends made to fit the specific tool. Welding rod can also be bent as required and welded to a cut off wrench end to make a special tool for a situation where no normal wrench will fit. While not overly strong, it is quite adequate as a handle for smaller wrenches.

This stuff can also be used around the house as well. We've got bookends made from it. A bookshelf in the utility room hangs from a couple of welding rod brackets and there is a bracket to hang up an ironing board in a closet.

BENDING JIGS

Although the welding rod and coat hanger or other wire can be bent to various angles with a vise (with a hammer assist for the larger diameters), one often wishes to do other things with it, such as putting an eye in one end to fit the shank of a screw or bolt, or to form it to a curve of a given radius.

There have been, over the years, several tools made for this job. One of the handiest is the Wireformer, an inexpensive tool that bends a neat angle or an eye in wire up to almost ³⁄₁₆″ in diameter. This was sold by mail for many years but does not seem to have been advertised lately. If you see one, latch onto it.

If you have one or more socket wrench sets, you can improvise a simple bending jig to make bends of as many different radii as you have socket sizes (outside diameters). To make the jig, you need a short piece of heavy steel bar

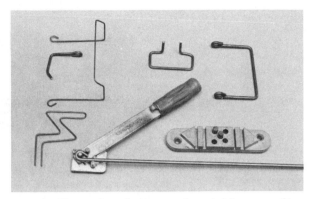

Two small wire-bending jigs, along with a sampling of bends. The jig on the left is held in a vise by its small rectangular base, and the handle is turned to form all sorts of bends between the three pins. The other jig can either be screwed to a bench or held in a vise. With it, the extended wire becomes a handle to form it around the pins or grooves.

stock. The exact size is not critical; mine is made from a piece ⅝″ x 2″ x 10″ (7″ would have been long enough). It is adequate to handle four sizes of socket sets of from ¼″ to ¾″ drive, including sockets up to about 2½″ in outside diameter.

A bolt with a diameter equal to each socket drive size is required in order to secure the sockets to the base with no play. These can be through bolts secured with a nut, or the base can be threaded and the bolts screwed into it directly. Washers of sizes as required to fit the range of sockets are used under the heads of the bolts. Adjacent to each socket-securing bolt hole, and spaced to fit the range of sizes, one or more holes is drilled and tapped to hold a ¼″ or ⅜″ bolt. These hold the end of the wire or rod while it is bent around the desired diameter socket.

To prevent the small bolt from bending when using heavy rod or bar stock, a tie bar can be used to connect the top of the socket locating bolt and the top of the small bolt.

This little unit easily bends any size welding rod into a great number of different radius bends and also bends up to ⅛″ x 1″ or ³⁄₁₆″ x ¾″ flat stock or even a little larger. With any item, keep the full length of the stock (within reason)

Shopmade bending jig is built around the bar of ⅝″ x 2″ steel in the foreground. Any one of the dozens of sockets from four different size wrench sets serves as a die to bend around. In addition to bend-

ing welding rod, it also handles small bar stock and light wrought-iron work. The bolts, nuts, washers, and braces secure the various sizes of sockets or provide a fulcrum.

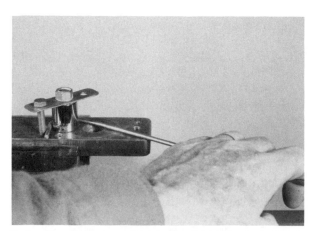

Bolted-on ⅞″ OD socket, teamed with another bolt for a fulcrum, gives a desired radius of bend to the end of this piece of ³⁄₁₆″ welding rod.

Deep socket along with a couple of bolts and a tie bar work when you want to bend a 2″ wide strip of thin stock.

Large eye has been formed in this ³⁄₁₆″ x ⅝″ bar stock by bending it around a 1⅞″ OD socket. A reverse bend is now being made to align the center of the eye to the bar itself.

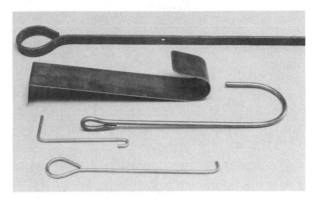

Five pieces show a small sampling of the many bends that can be made with a socket-wrench bending jig.

to use as a lever for forming the bend; cut it to length after bending.

An even simpler jig for bending flat stock or rod up to ⅛″ in thickness can be made from a steel block and a couple of bolts from ⅜″ to ½″ in diameter. Choose bolts that are long enough to have an unthreaded portion at least as long as the widest stock you will be using. Locate two holes in your block so that they provide ⅛″ plus a smidgen between the bolts; for ½″ bolts, locate the holes ⅝″ plus ¹⁄₆₄′ (⁴¹⁄₆₄″) apart. ⅜″ bolts would require a ³³⁄₆₄″ distance. Drill the holes with the tap drill required for the thread on the bolt and tap them. Since the bolt heads would interfere with one another, saw them off and then saw a slot in the end of each bolt so that they can be turned into the block with a screwdriver.

To avoid any tendency of the bolts to bend and spread at the top under a heavy load, as when bending a wide strip of ⅛″ bar, make a tie bar that can be slipped over the two bolts atop the item to be bent. Use stock at least ⅛″ thick; ³⁄₁₆″ or ¼″ is even better. Drill clearance holes for the bolts, being sure to use exactly the same separation measurement that you did on the steel base block.

During bending operations, the base is secured in a vise. Just slip the bar stock between the pins and drop the tie bar over the pins and down against the stock, thus holding the pins securely on both sides of the stock. Make your bend. If you bend the bar while maintaining one position, you end up with a tight radius

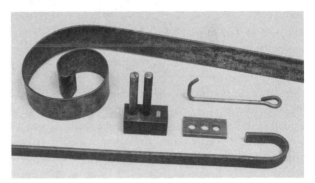

Simple bender is made from a 1″ square steel block and a couple of headless ⅜″ bolts. The three tapped holes allow two different spacings of the bolts. The block is held in a vise, the stock slipped between the bolts, and the tie bar dropped on to prevent any spreading. Large-radius bends, as in the scroll, are made up of a series of small bends with the work moved slightly between each bend.

bend, just slightly larger than the radius of the bolt pin around which it is being bent. If you bend the bar just slightly and then move it a bit, bend it a little more, move it again, and so on, you can make the radius of the bend come out to most any size desired.

Using this gadget or the previous one, you can make all sorts of bent up "wrought-iron" items—plant hangers, lamp stands, knick-knack shelves, whatever.

Two or more bent-up strips can be joined with Pop rivets to make fairly ornate assemblies, and they can be combined with wood parts to make such things as shelves, stands for potted plants, telephone stands, or a base for a clock.

By the way, the term wrought iron is pretty much a misnomer today. Originally made of an easily forged and welded form of iron, today's wrought-iron work is almost universally done with mild steel.

HEAVIER WROUGHT-IRON WORK

Wrought-iron work using heavier forms of mild steel, such as ½" square or round stock, can also be done in the small shop. One additional "tool" is required: a source of heat. This can be an old-fashioned forge if you happen to have one. An old gasoline blowtorch used by plumbers and sheet-metal workers also works, although finding white gas for one of these may be difficult. Camp stove fuel is the same thing, but is expensive. Other possibilities include a welding torch and a small propane hand torch, although again fuel can get expensive. Even a charcoal

barbecue works as a source of heat, and if a controlled source of moving air is provided, it makes an effective modern forge.

Once you have a source of heat, all you have to do is to get the steel red hot in the area to be worked. You will find that it "moves" quite easily. A heavy vise and a large ball-peen hammer do wonders in forming the stuff, especially when a round bar and a couple of pieces of square stock are provided to bend it around. By securing the hot end of a rod or bar in the vise alongside a piece of round stock, a bend can be started at the very end of the material. Once bent as far as the vise jaws permit, the work can be slipped down and around the form bar, resecured, and the bend continued. By proceeding in three or four steps, reheating as necessary, a complete circle can be formed.

Bends with a sharp angle can be formed outboard of the vise jaws over two square steel bars, such as were mentioned in the sheet-metal section, although they must be of heavier stock. Keep the job as close to the jaws of the vise as possible, secure the outer edges with your huskiest C-clamp, and use a spacer of appropriate thickness between the bars at the far end of the vise jaws.

An anvil, especially one with a long horn, helps you quickly form hot steel to an infinite

Start a bend at the very end of a piece of bar stock by holding it in a vise along with a former of the desired radius (a piece of pipe here). This procedure requires heating. After each bend, the bent end is then moved slightly on down around the pipe in a clockwise direction, regripped, reheated, and rebent. Continue the process as many times as required.

Several heating and bending sequences along, the end of the bar is approaching a full circle. Repositioning in the vise will ready it for bending in the opposite direction to align the center of the ring to the bar.

number of different radius bends. Old anvils often sell for more in dollars per pound today than they originally did in pennies per pound, but bargains occasionally show up in flea markets and yard sales. There are also some new anvils being sold today, but the ones I have seen have such woefully short horns as to be of doubtful use.

My first anvil was found at an antique shop. It weighed 120 pounds and was quite reasonable in price by current standards, but it had a fairly short horn. Later I found a dandy long-horned 85-pounder at a flea market. It would be a little light for a working blacksmith but is quite adequate for a small shop. The old one was easily

sold for what I had paid for it. Since then, I've found two more bargains at flea markets; one I bought for a cousin who had asked me to keep an eye out, and the second is currently in storage for the next friend who asks where he can find an old anvil at a reasonable price.

Once you get into wrought-iron work, you are really doing blacksmith work and perhaps the old blacksmith's adage regarding keeping the work red hot is in order here. "Never strike black iron!" It's always a temptation to give it a couple more whops as it cools off, but if you resist and reheat it first, your work will go better and the results will show it.

Hot iron can also be twisted to anything from a quarter turn to a multiple twist on either flat or square bar stock. Hold one end of the stock in a vise, heat, and twist with an adjustable wrench. Reheat continually as you proceed.

Pop rivets are too light for fastening most wrought-iron projects using this size material. Regular steel rivets are the alternative and can be found in many hardware stores. Cut them to length (the end extending through the work should be about one and one-half times its diameter in length). Place them in position, heat the end, being sure to get it red hot clear down to the piece being fastened so that it will deform to a good tight bond. With the head set firmly on a solid support (an anvil, a vise jaw, or a steel block held in the vise), proceed to upset it with the flat end of your ball-peen hammer and then round it off with the ball end.

Wrought-iron items can also be fastened to-

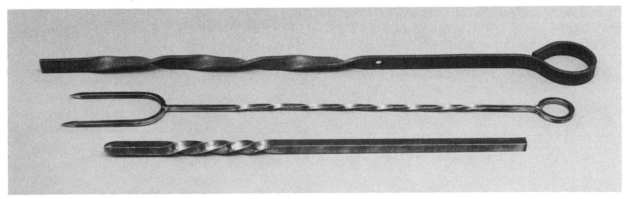

Samples of lightweight wrought-iron work done with a vise and torch. The center piece has been made into a sturdy barbecue fork.

gether with bolts or machine screws, either together with nuts, or screwed directly into tapped holes in one of the mating parts. They can also be brazed or welded together. Soldering is pretty marginal and usually will not provide a joint that will hold up satisfactorily.

While on the subject of wrought-iron work, one more thing comes to mind that is applicable to any metal bending using heat and to welding. Many years ago, my aero shop instructor "Mart" Martinsen had a favorite saying: "The hot side is the short side."

This has two applications. First, in bending metal with heat, apply the greatest heat on the side that will be on the inside, or short side, of the bend. This way, most of the bend is made by compressing the inner part of the bend. If the outside, or long side, of the bend is hotter, it is forced to expand during bending more than the inner side compresses, weakening the bend and often opening up cracks or voids on the outer side.

Selective heating of this sort is easier with a torch than with a forge. With a forge, do not make as sharp a bend (such as hammering a thick section sharply over a vise jaw), but form the bend to a more gentle radius instead.

The second application of this useful saying occurs during welding. Assume you have a length of steel tubing and are welding another tube to one side of it at a right angle. Most of the heat is applied to one side of your first tube; so, when your weld is finished, you almost always find that the first tube has bent, or warped, at the weld point to form a shallow angle, with the new piece on the inside or "short" side of the angle. This can be corrected by heating the opposite side of the first tube to a red heat and allowing it to cool and shrink. Two or more heating and shrinking cycles may be necessary to straighten the tube and sometimes a little pressure, brought to bear while the material is hot, will help.

Wrought-iron work is commonly finished with a coat of flat black paint and sometimes with off-white paint, but there is no reason you cannot paint it any other color, even hot pink or purple if it suits a contemporary decor.

OTHER USES FOR REBAR

Steel concrete reinforcing bar, more commonly known as rebar, has many other applications besides being buried in wet cement. Since it is made with a raised pattern rolled into it to give it a grip on the concrete, it is actually quite decorative and can be bent and welded to form many useful items.

Rebar comes in nominal sizes of from about ⅜" up to 2" or more in diameter. The diameter over the raised portion is slightly larger than the named dimension, while the diameter of the body of the material is slightly less than the nominal size. Most building material supply yards carry the smaller sizes in 20' lengths. Large towns often have a supplier catering to heavy construction contractors; these suppliers carry large diameters and lengths up to 60'. If you need some long or large diameter rebar and don't have a place of this sort locally, your building supplier can probably special order it for you.

Now that you know where to get the stuff, what can you do with it? I first saw it used decoratively in a hotel on Tahiti where it was used as a stair railing. Lengths of ⅞" material just had the ends bent 90 degrees and cemented into the concrete block walls so that the railing was held out a couple of inches from the walls. The railings looked great and had a good non-slip grip. Painted a medium brown, they were quite utilitarian, and probably not one person out a dozen realized that they actually were rebar.

Rebar Railings

Shortly after the trip to Tahiti, we were having our new house built; so I had the designer note in the plans that the owner would supply the stair railing down to the lower workshop level. When the builder, an outstanding contractor, heard what I planned to use, he was not enthusiastic. Rebar was to him something that one hid in concrete.

When the house was far enough along, I hauled my tanks and torch out to the job and proceeded to work up a length of 1⅛" rebar (the ⅞" material in the hotel had looked a little

Rebar (concrete reinforcing bar) makes an attractive stair rail with an excellent nonskid grip. It's great fun to work with, if you have a welding torch available. This rail is 1⅛″ nominal rebar and the support brackets are ½″ rebar. Two #12 screws in each plate go through the Sheetrock into studs, providing more than ample support.

skimpy). Since this railing would be fastened to a wood-frame Sheetrock-covered wall, I made three brackets. Each consisted of a plate 2¼″ by 4″ and about ⅛″ thick (10 gage). To the center of each of these was welded a short length of ½″ rebar, which extended out about 2¼″. The ½″ rebar was then bent at a 90-degree angle to reach up about 2″ for welding to the rail.

A chalk line was snapped on the wall at the appropriate height and angle. I located three studs, one near each end and one at the center of the run. The three plates were fastened to the studs through the Sheetrock with two long and

heavy #12 woodscrews each. Once the supports were in place, the rail was held on top of them and carefully marked. I then took the plates down, replaced them in position in a jig made up on the garage floor, and welded them onto the rail.

The two ends of the rail were rounded off slightly with the torch and a grinder. The top end of the rail was turned about 60 degrees using the torch with a "rosebud" heating tip, so that it extended in toward the wall but ended about ½″ short of it. At the bottom of the stairs, two steps extend out into the room itself; so the rail continues out into the room about 5 inches to provide a grip at an easy reach for a person about to mount the first step. The railing then curves down and back until it once again is over the wall. At this point, the lower end bends in toward the wall and ends up just short of it.

After welding and bending, the complete job was given a thorough wire brushing with a rotary wire brush turned by an electric drill. This removed not only the scale caused by welding and heating, but the original mill scale which exists on most of this material. I then gave it a coat of rust-resisting primer, followed by a couple of coats of a chocolate-brown enamel, chosen to harmonize with the stair carpet and the wall color.

Once the rail was finished and in place, the contractor quickly changed his opinion and became an admirer of it, even suggesting that I might do well to make a sideline of building them to order for other jobs. In the ensuing years there have been many times that a visitor has gotten about halfway down the stairs to the shop only to stop abruptly and exclaim, "I'll be . . . that's rebar!" This is usually followed by a short announcement about what a good grip it gives and how attractive it is.

Some time later we added outside concrete stairs at each end of the house. Even larger rebar (1¼″) was used for this, welded to 1″ rebar uprights. One of the rails required a piece 28′ long, as I recall, and the other was only slightly shorter. Getting these home was an adventure in itself but was accomplished with a small utility trailer. One end of the rebar was tied securely at the front of the truck and it was again tied at the back end of the trailer. This allowed it to slide sideways on the tailgate of the truck and the front end of the trailer around each turn. Even with this arrangement there were many feet of rear overhang, requiring the usual red flag at the end and a well-chosen route along with some cautious driving for the trip home.

These outside stair railings were given two coats of ruddy-brown rust-resisting primer only. For outdoor use this works great, since when a spot of rust does start to appear, it only requires a quick wire brushing and a touch-up with a spray can of the same stuff. If a topcoat of enamel had been used, any rusting would have required wire brushing through all the coats of paint, then priming, plus a matching coat of enamel—a much more involved job.

Rebar Racks and Other Items

Rebar can be used in other rooms of your home. In our kitchen, a U-shaped pot rack of ¾" rebar extends out over a maple topped peninsula. The ends of the U have large washers welded to them; the washers are then held against the wall of an adjacent oven cabinet with a couple of pan-head sheet metal screws. These are great for fastening thin metal objects to wood. They are threaded full length and do not have the unthreaded shank of a normal wood screw, which is designed to hold one piece of wood of substantial thickness against another.

The outer end of the U is supported by a couple of welded-on struts of ½" rebar. They reach to the ceiling and are held with screws that extend through welded-on washers and up through the Sheetrock into a ceiling joist.

A number of S-hooks were made up in three different lengths so that different sized pots and pans would all hang down to approximately the same height. These S-hooks were made from ³⁄₁₆" welding rod, using the socket wrench wire-bending jig described earlier in this chapter. A few extras of each size were made at the time and are kept handy in a kitchen drawer to cover any new pots and pans.

In addition to being decorative, the raised pattern on the rebar tends to keep the hooks in place on the rack.

On the end of the peninsula below the pot and pan rack, a couple of short strips of ⅜" rebar, with the ends bent back and small washers welded on, form a two-step dishtowel rack.

Sturdy pot and pan rack over a maple-topped peninsula in this country kitchen is made from ¾" rebar. The uprights of ½" rebar fasten to a ceiling joist. Pot hooks were bent from ³⁄₁₆" welding rod with the socket-wrench bending jig.

Two dishtowel bars of ⅜" rebar hang the towels over a conveniently located heater vent in the floor. These bars are supported by machine screws mounted through the door and into holes drilled and tapped in their ends. The round ends are large washers.

Conveniently located over a furnace outlet in the floor, they dry damp dishtowels quickly in the winter. These racks are fastened through the cabinet wall by machine screws in tapped holes in the ends of the rebar.

I tried this same method of fastening with the pot rack just mentioned, but that piece of rebar was so hard that I was unable to even drill it,

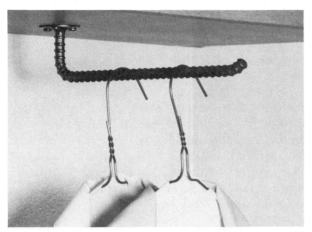

Mounted below a cabinet in the laundry room, this cantilever bracket of ⅜" rebar can hold several shirts or blouses to drip-dry over the utility sink below.

much less tap threads into it. Thus I had to settle for screws through the welded-on washers.

I used ⅜" rebar for a short rod welded to a bracket that slips over a door in the clothes ironing area. It serves to hang up freshly ironed items until they are moved to the bedroom closet. Another short piece of the same rod hangs below a cabinet over the utility room sink and serves as a holder for drip-drying shirts and blouses. On both these items, the heavy embossing on the rebar helps to keep the clothes hangers separated.

We have at least one pair of bookends that are made with rebar, and it also serves as supports for candle holders in a table centerpiece made from different sized pieces of steel water pipe.

Outside the house, I have cut several 20' lengths of ½" rebar into appropriate short lengths. I sharpened one end of each on a grinder to make pins to spike together old railroad ties for steps and retaining walls. For this job, you should drill pilot holes through the ties to the nominal size of the rebar; the raised embossing then holds the pins securely. Spike them together and/or into the ground using a sledge or, at least, a 4-pound single jack.

Working Rebar

Rebar varies greatly in hardness and resistance to bending. I have a hunch that much of it

is made from remelted scrap steel with little re-refining, thus causing the wide variance in its properties. It is often quite hard; trying to cut it with a bolt cutter may void the guarantee as well as the bolt cutter! Cut it with a hacksaw or a cutting torch. (Special rebar cutters are available but are so expensive as to be impractical.)

Rebar can be welded with either gas or arc and is easily bent when heated to a red heat. The smaller sizes can be heated with a propane torch or a large welding tip, but for the larger sizes you will need a "rosebud" heating tip.

Are you familiar with rosebud tips? Made specifically for heating larger work, they consist of a round copper bar ⅝" or more in diameter with several (usually eight) holes arranged in a circle on the end. They give multiple flames to provide more heat over a wider area than a single-flame tip. If you have a welding torch and have ever had problems heating a large item, invest in one of these.

Even with a small rosebud tip, 1⅛" or 1¼" rebar is about the limit that you can get hot enough to bend. If you want to go beyond this range, you'll need a larger torch and rosebud tip or another source of heat, such as a forge or a charcoal briquette fire with a supply of forced air.

Without welding equipment, your ability to work rebar is somewhat limited. But you can bend up items with an alternate heat source (even a hot fireplace gets smaller items hot enough to bend), and cut and fit them as required. Then take them to a welding shop for welding or brazing.

ALTERNATE METAL SOURCES

When looking for sources of metal, you first think of the hardware store for small items and then a metal supply house for larger material. For the small workshopper, both of these have drawbacks.

While the hardware store may have a number of sizes of steel rods, angles, and other bar stock, it usually provides only the smaller sizes of these materials in short lengths. In addition, the steel is often galvanized, a liability if it must be welded or brazed.

Galvanized steel leaves a rough edge where the coating is burned off, and the galvanizing material itself is quite toxic when heated. Care must be taken to do this only in a well ventilated area and to avoid breathing any of the fumes.

Going to a metal supply house can also be discouraging for the small user. There is usually a minimum charge of anywhere from $10 to $25 along with a cutting fee of $5 to $10 for any piece that is wanted in less than mill length, usually 20′.

This is no problem if you use the stuff regularly or have a major project and need several lengths of rebar, square tubing, angle iron, or other material. But for small projects where you may need just a couple of feet of this and a few feet of that, it rapidly becomes prohibitive.

One likely alternate is the junkyard, euphemistically listed in the Yellow Pages under Scrap Metals. These places have different policies, but many of them will let you wander around and pick out what you need, after which it is all weighed up and a per-pound charge assessed. They often have a gent available with a torch who will cut off the length you need from a piece of angle iron, bar stock, etc, for a very nominal fee (providing its not a long cut across a piece of plate).

Some scrap metal yards have a per-pound price for basic steel shapes that drops sharply when you purchase 100 pounds or more. Then it often pays to pick up a few more pieces of material beyond what you need for your current project to get the price break.

The metal available at a junkyard varies greatly. Some of it is truly junk, badly rusted and twisted or bent beyond practical use. Other pieces may be like new, but the vast majority falls somewhere in between. Since even "new" steel may have a light coating of rust if it has been stored for any length of time, this may not be a major drawback. Light rust can be fairly easily removed with a rotary wire brush.

Another advantage of a junkyard is that if you happen to have any electronic or other "high-tech" manufacturers nearby, and they're almost everywhere these days, you may find all sorts of valuable material. You could come across pieces of various aluminum alloys, often ¼″ or even as much as ½″ in thickness, plus all sorts of bar, rod, and tube stock in aluminum

alloy and sometimes in brass or copper as well. While all of this stuff is too small for the manufacturer to work with, it is often more than adequate for the things one makes in a small shop.

So the junkyard can be a source of supply for material that would be quite impractical for the small workshop to obtain otherwise. If you are not already familiar with it, next time you have a couple of hours to spare, put on some old clothes and check out the nearest scrap metal supplier. You should find it a pleasant surprise!

About now I can hear some of you saying,

Plywood brackets nailed to a 6″ stud wall hold lots of metal stock, both new from a supply house or used from a scrap metal yard or even a refuse disposal area. Similar to the brackets used in the wood storage area, these are shorter due to the weight of the material. Additional wide, short, or heavy pieces are stored vertically between the studs in back of the horizontal stock.

"That's all well and good for some guys, but I live way out in the country; when I need any tool more exotic than a simple hammer, wrench, or screwdriver, I have to get it by mail order. The nearest junkyard or metal supplier is probably in Podunk City some hundred-odd miles from here."

If it's not beneath your dignity, check out your local dump occasionally, especially if metal is otherwise difficult for you to obtain. I've always found it was easy to park my dignity in my back pocket for the length of time that it takes to do a bit of scavenging.

The dump, or "refuse disposal area," as they are often called today may have more or less restrictive policies. Your dump may be just an open area where you are free to roam and pick up any useful material, and there is a lot of it. Other dumps are a little more structured and may not allow scavenging, but they often separate the metals as they arrive and hold them for a junk dealer who comes around in a truck every once in a while and buys the lot. Here you can often pick out the stuff you need and get it at the scrap buyer's price. Other places, usually the ones with the "refuse disposal area" label, neither permit scavenging nor separate any metal themselves. All the stuff just goes over the edge and is compacted and covered by bull-dozers.

Your only opportunity, a slim one at facilities of this sort, is to keep your eyes open when you make a trip to drop off your own refuse. The guy parked nearby may be about to dump some metal over the edge and be more than happy to give it to you instead. Our local disposal area is of this type, but I've sometimes picked up some good usable metal this way.

One caution to scavengers. Be aware that steel angle-iron bedframes may be of little value to you. Rather than being the mild steel that most angle iron is made from, old bed frames are usually made of high carbon steel. The steel is so hard that it is difficult to saw and sometimes impossible to drill except with a carbide-tipped drill. The high carbon content also makes it difficult to weld and any welds that you do make tend to crack easily.

Stay away from this stuff unless you have a need for high carbon steel. You could probably grind a pretty good knife, chisel, or other cutting tool out of it, for example.

Useful sizes and shapes of various metals are often found at flea markets, and yard sales. Keep your eyes open; you can often add some valuable material to your "stockroom" for a very reasonable price.

TAKE ALONG A MAGNET

Any time you go for metal supplies, it is a good idea to have a small magnet in your pocket, along with the thin (¼" wide) 8' steel tape that you always carry.

Even in a hardware store, many items that appear to be solid brass aren't; they're plated steel instead. At the other places, it's anybody's guess. A magnet does have some limitations, but if an item is plated steel instead of all brass, copper, or other nonferrous metal, it will let you know. It is only attracted to ferrous metals. Checking a piece of material with a magnet can often prevent unwelcome surprises when you start to machine a bargain piece of metal.

One exception is that although stainless steel is basically a ferrous metal, many good grades of stainless are non-magnetic. If a purported item of stainless steel is magnetic, it is not one of the highest corrosion-resistant stainless steels, although it may have other valuable properties.

USES AND SOURCES FOR LEAD

Lead is handy stuff to have around the workshop. It is easily melted and usually can be poured into wooden forms without burning them, although it will scorch them a bit. Its weight can provide stability for many things from bookends to floor lamps, and lead counterweights can ease the operation of mechanical items. If you're a fisherman, you probably melt it in your shop to make sinkers. Diving weights can also be easily made at a substantial savings. I've got the stuff all over the shop and around the house in pourings that vary from

Mold bent and welded from 16-gage steel reduces untidy piles of scrap lead to pigs weighing about 7½ lbs each. When lead is needed, one pig nearly fills a small cast-iron melting pot.

only a few ounces up to a couple of counterweights that each weigh nearly 30 pounds.

If you melt your scrap and pour it into a mold to make small pigs, they can be used around the shop until needed for a project. They are great for holding things in position and for weighting down many glue jobs that would otherwise be difficult to clamp. My mold is a piece of bent up sheet steel with a couple of ends welded on to form a mold about 2" high, 2½" wide, and 4" long. Both the sides and ends are provided with a fair slope, or "draft," so that after the metal cools it can just be turned over and the pig will drop out onto the floor. This mold makes pigs that weigh about 7 pounds.

You can also make a wooden mold. Make it from heavy material and be sure to make tight joints so that the hot lead won't leak out prior to solidifying. As mentioned above, expect some scorching and pour in a safe area just in case the wood does actually start to burn.

Never pour molten lead or any other melted material into any mold that is not completely dry. The molten metal turns moisture instantly into steam which expands violently and can throw some or all of the hot lead several feet into the air. I once got a badly scorched eyelid by neglecting to heed this precaution.

Up until a few years ago, lead was widely used in the plumbing trade for caulking joints in cast iron waste lines. Every plumbing supply shop had it available in 5-pound pigs. These were usually poured in a mold that made a group of five, each connected to the next one with a small lead tie-bar. The store kept a small hatchet handy and could quickly whack off any number of pigs desired. Now, plastic waste lines are widely used and asking for lead at a plumbing shop may draw only a blank stare.

Junkyards take in scrap lead, and you may find it there. Flea markets sometimes have it in various forms: unwanted diving weights, heavy fishing sinkers, small boat anchors and lead trays that had been used to contain certain chemicals. One of the best sources for scrap lead is a large tire shop. While wheel weights are not pure lead, being alloyed to give them enough rigidity to do the job, they are still quite heavy, which suits our purpose. Also they are still relatively easy to melt.

Every time tires are replaced or rebalanced the old weights come off and are discarded. Tire shops usually have buckets of them, which they eventually sell either to scrap metal dealers or directly to users such as fisherman to make sinkers. Since they usually sell the stuff direct for a little more per pound then they get from the junk dealer, they are often happy to do so.

Another source of wheel weights, if you happen to be a walker or a jogger, is alongside the road. It is amazing how many of these things fly off, especially on hard curves. Apparently on a sharp turn, the lateral force on the tire pulls it away from the rim just enough that centrifugal force can pop off one or more of the wheel weights. Going over a bump or a dip in the road also often knocks wheel weights loose.

I followed the advice of an unrecalled poet who said, "Keep your eye upon the bluebird, and not upon the ground," until I finally awoke to the treasures waiting there in our modern civilization. After this I started carrying a small canvas bag during my walks. In the years since then, I have brought home several hundred wheel weights of many different sizes, plus any number of good nuts, bolts, washers and other miscellaneous hardware, as well as a surprising number of tools dropped alongside the road by the motoring multitudes. Sorry about that, bluebird.

Now that you've got your scrap lead, how do you go about melting it? You can melt it directly with a torch, but I find it more convenient to use a small electric hot plate. Any self-

Two poured lead "biscuits" stabilize this reading lamp stand. Before gluing, the bottom ¾" plywood piece had four holes bored in it for weights, but two proved adequate. Since the lamp stands on a floor with uneven rustic tiles, three rubber pads were used instead of four.

respecting flea market has a half dozen or so available.

Place the scrap lead in a small cast-iron pot and put it on the hot plate. To speed things up, I enclose the pot in a "stove" which is nothing more than a 6" length of leftover 6" ducting from a hot air furnace. You can easily roll up a substitute from a bit of light gage galvanized sheet metal. Secure the seam with a few Pop rivets.

My first stove was cut a couple of inches longer; I then made several vertical cuts at one end and turned the strips in to form a top to hold in more heat. Since the turned in sections did not form a complete top, I fastened a small scrap on to cover the remaining hole. A single sheet-metal screw, plus a turned-up tab, allowed the scrap to be pushed aside to peek in to see how the melt is progressing. To speed the melting even more, I now use a straight sided stove. Another small $2 hot plate is inverted and put on top. This way it melts down one of my 7-pound pigs in just a few minutes.

When I first started using wheel weights as a source of lead, I manually cut the lead away from the steel clip with a small cold chisel and hammer. This took about a half minute per weight, which adds up to a waste of time when melting a number of them. It finally entered my head that although steel is heavy it's still quite a bit lighter than lead and therefore floats in it. Since figuring that out, I now just melt the lead and skim the steel clips, along with the inevitable dross, off the top with a putty knife before pouring.

To make lead stabilizing weights in wooden items, just drill one or more large holes in the bottom of the item with a large spade bit. If the item to be weighted is fairly thin, use a modified spade bit with the pilot point ground down, as mentioned in Chapter 2, in order to allow a deeper hole without driving the point through.

V-BLOCK SUBSTITUTE

To drill a hole through the center of a piece of pipe or tubing without a drill press and a V-block, try the following. It even works on pipe that is too large in diameter to be accurately held by a V-block.

Wrap a strip of heavy paper or thin cardboard around the pipe to form a tube; make it

To drill a hole through the center of a large pipe without a drill press and V-block, start by wrapping a strip of heavy paper around the pipe snugly, but not tightly. Secure it with a bit of tape.

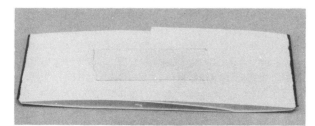

Slip the paper off the end of the pipe and fold it flat. Mark the crease of the folds with a pen and cut a tiny angle in the front part of each end.

Slide the paper back onto the pipe and center punch the pipe twice, once at the apex of each small V-notch at the end of the line.

Drill a smaller pilot hole through each side of the pipe at the center punch marks and then drill the full-size hole completely through from one side of the pipe. Although the hole appears to be slightly below center when compared with the far end of the pipe, this is due to camera angle. The actual hole is quite well centered.

snug fitting but not so tight that it cannot be slipped off the end of the pipe. Tape it together and slide it off the pipe. Fold it flat and, holding it so that each half is quite equal in length, crease the seams. Mark one end of each crease carefully with a pen or pencil.

Reform the paper into its tubular shape and slip it back onto the pipe to the position where the marked end is aligned with the location of the desired hole. Center punch the pipe at the exact ends of the marked creases on the paper tube. Then drill into the pipe at each of the center punch marks. For the best fit, drill an undersized pilot hole from each side and then drill the final hole completely through the pipe from one side.

CUTTING TABLES

When machining metal with a lathe, drill press, milling machine, or other cutting tool, it is important to use the correct cutting speed for the particular metal. There are a number of tables available with this information: in owner's manuals, machinist's handbooks, metalworking magazine articles, and textbooks. But all too often the information is buried somewhere and forgotten so that when you really need it, it is unavailable.

An easy solution to this problem is to copy the material and keep it handy to the pertinent machine. Specific tables may be xeroxed or portions of a table applicable to your particular machine may be excerpted and typed on a 3 x 5 file card.

These tables of cutting speeds are normally shown in surface feet per minute (sfpm) for the various materials. In order to use this information with the lathe, for example, it is necessary to know the rpm of the machine at its various speeds, and to correlate this with the diameter of the object being turned, in order to provide the correct cutting speed.

Once you know the various rpm's available, a few minutes with a hand-held calculator provides you with the sfpm's of the cutting tool when machining different diameters at these speeds.

Suppose one of your rpm's is 250. To find the

sfpm when turning a 1″ diameter item at this speed, proceed as follows. 1 x 3.1416 = 3.1416 (circumference in inches) x 250 = 785.4 (surface inches per minute) ÷ 12 = 65.45. Drop the .45 and you have your answer of 65 sfpm when turning a 1″ diameter shaft at 250 rpm. Halve this figure and you come out with approximately 33 sfpm when turning a ½″ diameter shaft at this speed. Double it and a 2″ shaft is traveling 130 sfpm. Double it again to get 260 sfpm for a 4″ shaft.

Make these simple computations for each speed on your lathe and you can produce a table of the cutting speeds available to your particular machine. For example: my lathe is an old flat-belt model with a three-cone pulley; so it has three normal speeds plus three backgeared speeds for a total of six. On the top part of a 3 x 5 card I have these rpm's listed; low, medium, and high for both normal and back geared. Below this, another table shows these six rpm's and for each of them gives the sfpm at this speed for ½″, 1″, 2″, and 4″ diameter turnings.

If I want to turn a brass hammer head of 1″ diameter for instance, I can look at my first file card which tells me that the desired cutting speed for finish turning on brass is 200 sfpm. (This chart gives three desired speeds, one for rough turning, one for finish turning, and one for cutting threads.) Looking at the cutting speed table, I find that 700 rpm, my highest speed, gives 183 sfpm when turning a 1″ diameter item, so this is the closest available speed to the optimum.

These cutting speeds are only a guide, of course. Even a modern lathe with more and higher rpms available does not provide an exact matching speed for all materials and diameters. In practice too, every cut you make reduces the diameter slightly and thus changes the sfpm cutting speed for the next cut. It would be quite impossible to match the optimum cutting speed at all times as you proceed with the job at hand. However, keeping as close to the desired speed as possible provides for faster and better machining.

If you don't have a table of cutting speeds available, here are the ones posted on a card alongside my lathe. Others, such as one for stainless steel, would be desirable, but I haven't run across them.

Cutting Speed—sfpm

	Rough	Finish	*Thread cutting*
Annealed tool steel	50	75	20
Cast iron	60	80	25
Bronze	90	100	25
Mild steel	90	100	35
Brass	150	200	50
Aluminum	200	300	50

DETERMINING MACHINE RPMs

Having cutting speeds handy is of little help if the owner's manual for your machine does not give the various rpm's available, or if you don't happen to have a manual for a secondhand machine. If the tool is belt powered, you can measure the diameter of the pulleys and, knowing the rpm of the motor, can easily calculate the approximate speeds available.

Suppose you've acquired an old lathe powered by a fractional hp motor with a placard giving its speed as 1725 rpm, or possibly 1750.

The way many small motors are built, they theoretically should turn 1800 rpm on 60-cycle AC current. The 1725 or 1750 is an estimate of what they turn with a normal load. I just checked the rpm of my lathe motor with a mechanical revolution counter. Running free, it turns 1780 rpm. Turning the jackshaft only, it turns 1745 rpm. Belting the lathe to the jackshaft via the medium pulleys slows the motor to 1720 and using the high-speed pulleys drops it to 1670. With a cutting load, it would be somewhat slower still. This particular motor is rated as 1725 rpm. (High-speed motors, as on bench grinders, are usually listed as turning 3450, down from a frictionless theoretical 3600.)

So pick a number. Since we are interested in actual cutting speeds under a working load, a slightly lower speed than placarded is probably more practical. Let's estimate it at 1650.

Suppose you have a 2″-diameter pulley on the motor and a 10″ pulley on the jackshaft. Divide 1650 by 10 and multiply by 2 and you get 330 rpm for the speed of the jackshaft. Assume that your jackshaft is equipped with a three-step flat-belt cone pulley of 4″, 5″, and 6″ diameter and the lathe's pulley steps are 5″, 4″, and 3″. For the slow speed, divide 330 by 5 and multiply that by 4 to get 265 rpm (taken to the closest 5). The medium speed will be 330 divided by 4, times 5, or approximately 410. High speed is 330 divided by 3, times 6, or 660.

For back-geared speeds, count the teeth on each of the four gears. Suppose the little gear on the lathe headstock has twenty-five teeth and its countershaft mate has fifty. This gives a reduction of 2 to 1. If the small countershaft gear has twenty teeth and the large headstock gear has fifty, you get another 2½ to 1 reduction. Multiply them and you come up with a total reduction of 5 to 1. Divide your three normal speeds by five and you'll have your three back-geared speeds of approximately 55, 80 and 130 rpm.

Using a Speed Indicator

There is an even simpler way to find the rpm of any machine spindle, electric motor, gas engine, or jackshaft that has an uncovered end. A speed indicator made by a precision tool manufacturer is a fairly inexpensive little hand-held tool about 5″ long. It consists of a 100-toothed gear in a case with a protruding handle held between thumb and forefinger. A worm gear meshes with the large gear and is rotated by a small shaft about 2″ long that ends in a triangular point. Two slip-on rubber tipped points

Surface-speed attachment slips onto the speed indicator. The attachment shows surface speed per minute directly after a timed run, regardless of the rpm and diameter of the work.

are provided, one conical and the other flat. The instrument has a circular scale marked from 0 to 100 in both directions. A rotating dial with a single raised marker is attached to the big gear and rotates within the fixed scale.

To measure rpm's, you set the marker to 0 and press the end of the indicator's shaft against the end of the rotating shaft. At the same time, you check the time on a sweep second hand. Hold the indicator in place and count the number of revolutions of the dial (each time the marker passes 0). At the exact end of a minute, pull the indicator away from the shaft read the remaining number of revolutions from the dial. This amount is added to the number of hundreds (full revolutions) previously counted in order to get the total number of rpms.

In practice, it is of course not necessary to hold the gadget in place for a full minute. You can read it for 30 seconds and double the number, for instance. Either of the two pointed ends can be used with a shaft that has been center drilled, while the flat tip is used against an undrilled shaft end.

A surface speed attachment is available for this tool. It will quickly give a surface-feet-per-minute reading for any rotating piece of lathe work, pulley face, band saw blade, etc. It consists of a small rubber wheel with a circumference of exactly 6″ that slips over the point of the tool's shaft. You just hold the wheel against the rotating object and take a time reading. Since the perimeter of the wheel travels one-

Where rpms are a factor in your work a speed indicator is very helpful. Used with a second hand on a watch, it consists of little more than a 100 to 1 worm-gear reduction with a dial and marker.

half foot per revolution, the number of revolutions made in a minute is divided by two to get the SFPM.

One of these little tools can be a great help in the shop if you do much metal machining or work with mechanical contrivances where shaft speeds are a factor.

TURNING METAL WITHOUT A METAL LATHE

Although they are a poor substitute for a true metal-turning lathe, some other tools such as a wood-turning lathe, a Shopsmith, or even a drill press can turn some simple small parts out of aluminum, brass, copper, or even mild steel round stock.

For a wood lathe or the Shopsmith, you can use the normal tool rest. For a drill press you need a vertical tool rest. One can be made out of a convenient length of angle iron. Cut a pie-shaped piece out of one leg of the angle and bend it 90 degrees (heat helps). Then either weld up the joint or bolt a brace across the angle. Thus made, the improvised tool rest can be clamped or bolted to the table so that the vertical leg is close to and parallel with the work.

If the workpiece is so long that it tends to bend under the force of the cutting tool, make a tail center. Do this by putting a short piece of small shafting or rod in the drill chuck and filing it to an approximate 60-degree point while it turns. This improvised center is then held in a drill press vise and located directly below the center of the drill spindle.

The center can be found in a number of ways: one of the simplest is to take a straight piece of welding rod and cut it to an appropriate length compared to the length of the stock to be turned. Place it in the drill chuck and file a

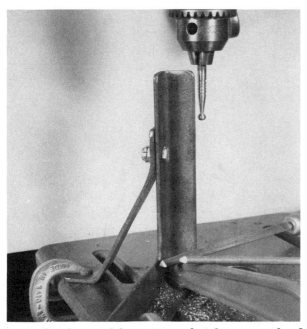

Little finial turned from ¼″ steel rod is a sample of "lathe" work that can be done without a lathe. The vertical tool rest is welded and bolted together and clamped to the drill press table. Small rat-tail and three-corner files have had their ends ground and sharpened for cutting tools.

First step in turning an adapter from a ½″ headless bolt is to center drill a hole in its end for the "tailstock." The rotating bolt will be brought down on the stationary drill, centered below the chuck.

concentric point on it as above. Then line up the "tailstock center" with the tip of it. While doing this, turn the drill spindle by hand to be sure that the rod is straight and that the end travels concentrically. If it is slightly eccentric, the tail center can be very closely located to the true center by eyeballing the offset as it rotates and lining the tail center up to the center of the offset circle.

Once the improvised tail center is locked in the vise below the chuck, remove the welding-rod telltale and replace it with the workpiece; the tail end of which has been drilled with a center drill. Put a drop of oil on the tail center, use the quill feed to bring the work down gently onto the center, and lock it in place with the spindle lock.

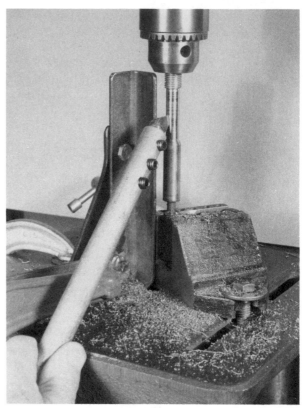

Carbide-tipped tool bit for metal lathe turns part of the bolt to ⅜" in diameter. When cut off, this adapter will hold a ½" drill chuck in the chuck of a ⅜" drill, thereby expanding the drill's capacity.

Improvised tailstock has had a 60-degree point "turned" on it with a file. It is now being centered exactly below the center of the spindle by using a pointed length of ¼" rod held in the chuck as an indicator. The center drill in the previous picture was centered to the chuck (and subsequently the work) in the same manner.

For lathe tools, carefully grind the ends of small round, square, or triangular files. For metal turning, do not anneal and reharden them as is done for woodworking; leave them in their hard state. This will require that you grind them to shape slowly, cooling them frequently in the process. Metal turning tools are ground to a much less acute angle than wood turning tools. For aluminum or steel, grind in a few degrees of front rake; for brass, keep the top of the tool flat. The files are brittle and may break if they happen to dig in. Be sure to wear safety glasses.

Use slow to moderate speeds, depending on the diameter of the stock (higher speeds for smaller diameters) and the material. A speed of 1500 rpm is enough when turning a ¼" steel rod; a little faster for brass, and more so for aluminum.

Six samples of "metal lathe" jobs that were done in the drill press; four are steel and two are brass.

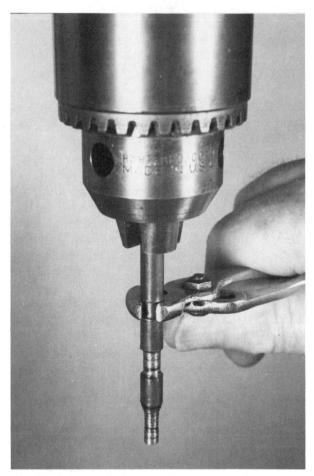

Small shafts can be roughly turned down to a smaller diameter just by squeezing the toothed jaws of a good pair of pliers around them while they are rotated. Finished up with a file and/or emery cloth, they can be "turned" to a fairly accurate fit.

The work that can be done with this setup is limited, but various small items such as a model ship's tiny cannon can be successfully made with a little care, ingenuity, and practice.

A small three or four jaw lathe chuck (3" is a good size; 4" at the very maximum)) can be provided with an adapter to fit a drill press, wood lathe, or Shopsmith. With it, you can handle somewhat larger pieces of material than the ½" limit of the usual drill press chuck. Either of these chucks provides more capacity than you can use; probably an inch in diameter is about the most you can easily turn in this way without taking forever and/or putting too much of a side load on the spindle of your machine. Depending on the relative hardness of the particular alloy, brass or aluminum can be successfully turned in larger diameters than mild steel.

There is another ridiculously simple way that small chucked shafts can be turned to a smaller diameter. Turn the work fairly slow and then encircle the part you want to reduce with a pair of ordinary slip-joint pliers. Engage the shaft with the toothed area of the pliers in back of the jaw tips themselves. Squeeze down on the handles and watch the material come off!

By working the pliers along the shaft you can "turn" an extended portion, or by choosing a narrow pair of pliers you can cut a small groove. In addition to slip joint pliers, you can use other types with parallel cross teeth, such as water pump pliers or battery terminal pliers. I wouldn't use a locking type pliers though. If you got careless and had them adjusted so that

you inadvertently let them lock on the work while it is turning, you would have a tiger by the tail that could do severe damage to you, your machine, and your work.

This plier setup works surprisingly fast and keeps the diameters quite concentric, although it does leave a fairly rough surface. However, by stopping a little short of the desired diameter and doing the finish "turning" with a file, you can end up with a surprisingly accurate, and nice appearing, job. You can even use this process with a portable electric drill. With either setup, stop and clean out the teeth of the pliers often, otherwise they'll clog up with chips.

HAND-HELD CARBIDE-TIPPED TOOL BITS

Carbide-tipped lathe tool bits, more properly known as Cemented Tungsten Carbide Bits, can be used hand-held for turning metal. They are especially good for turning metal with a makeshift lathe, as previously described.

Carbide tools usually consist of a tungsten carbide tip cemented to a square steel shaft that fits a standard lathe toolpost tool holder. They come in sizes from 1/4" square up to 3/4" square and in several patterns: right-hand turning, left-hand turning, square nose, pointed, etc.

Tool bits are available at most machine tool suppliers (look in the phone book under "Machine Tools" or "Machinery") or by mail from a number of catalog suppliers. They are priced at about a couple of dollars each in the smaller sizes.

Here the 1/4" or 5/16" size (3/8" at most) is the best. Since these bits are only about 2" to 2½" long, you need a way of providing a longer handle for them. One way to do this is to weld the back end of the steel shank to a length of square steel rod of the same size and provide this with a wooden handle. Another way is to drill a hole large enough to fit over the diagonal of the square tool in the end of a round shaft and secure the tool with a setscrew. This will require a minimum of a ½" shaft for a 1/4" lathe tool and 9/16" or 5/8" for a 5/16" tool. The round shaft, in turn, can be inserted in a wooden handle. Whichever route you take, the overall length of the tool should be about 10" to 16" long, depending on the size and type of the work you will be doing; the shorter size for tiny model work and longer for larger items.

Carbide tools can be run at considerably higher speeds than normal high-speed steel tools, thus making them more useful with wood lathes and drill presses that cannot be turned as slowly as a metal lathe. For work 1/4" in diameter, 3000 rpm is about right; for ½", 1500 rpm; for 1", 750 rpm; and for 2", 375 rpm.

These tools can be ground with a "green" wheel specifically made for sharpening carbide-tipped tools, or they can also be sharpened with one of the little diamond dust "stones" favored by wood carvers for sharpening their tools.

Cutoff socket extension has been turned down to fit a 3/8" drill chuck with a carbide-tipped lathe tool bit held in a 3/8" pipe handle. Three more carbide-tipped bits of different configurations are on the drill press table next to the handle. A 3/8" square bit will not normally fit into a 3/8" pipe, but rounding off its top corners slightly on a grinding wheel allows it to just slip in. Because the bit still has square bottom corners it can be mounted securely in a normal lathe tool holder if needed.

ENGINE-TURNED FINISH

An engine-turned finish is made up of neat little overlapping swirls; you sometimes see it on nice metalwork—the engine cowling on Lindbergh's *Spirit of St. Louis* is an unusually large example of this. You can duplicate this on items of soft brass or aluminum with a pencil eraser. Ink erasers, if you can find them, give a more pronounced cut.

All you do is chuck the pencil in a drill press. The metal can be moved freehandedly between the overlapping spots for a random effect, or can be moved in measured steps along a fence in order to provide a more formal pattern.

The eraser on an ordinary wooden pencil, turned in a drill press chuck, makes a surprisingly good engine-turned finish on small jobs.

Using erasers is only practical for very small pieces of work, as they wear quite rapidly. For more extensive work or on harder material, and for larger swirls, use a short length of dowel or a large flathead machine screw. Glue a sheet-rubber pad and circles of medium- or fine-grit metal-cutting paper onto the head. Cut from the back side of the paper with an arch punch or a similar type for best results.

FITTING PIPE OR TUBING FOR WELDING

Before two pieces of steel tubing or pipe can be welded together in a "T" joint, one of them must be shaped to fit up to the contour of the other in order to make a decent weld. This often "throws" people. At first glance, it appears that there is no way to fit the two pieces together without sawing, filing, or grinding a concave cut on one end of the vertical tube of the T. I have seen people spend a great amount of time and effort in filing out a curve to fit, attempting to grind a close-fitting concave end on the tube, or making up a jig to cut the curve with a metal-cutting sabre saw or jigsaw. This is all very frustrating and unnecessary.

Instead, realign your thinking 90 degrees and consider the side view of the T instead of the end view. Mark off two 45-degree cuts, the point of which is centered on the end of the tube. Grab a hacksaw and make these cuts. Then, looking at the end view, you will see the desired

curve is nicely cut, except that the points prevent the curve from seating on the longitudinal tube. Turn your cut tube back 90 degrees to the position where you made your saw cuts and grind, or file, off the points to a rounded curve. Check it occasionally, touch it up as required, and you will have a nice fit.

Accepted practice is to weld the joint in four alternate segments, starting each at the center of the intersection of the two tubes and working to an outside face.

If a third tube is to be welded in at a 45-degree angle, as in building up a truss of some sort, cut this tube in the same manner. Here you use an angle of approximately 22½ degrees to the line of the tube and grind off much more of the points to get a fit. With a little experience you can avoid this by starting these cuts a little distance apart on the end of the tube. In a joint of this sort, be sure that the first intersection is welded all around before fitting up the third tube and welding it. Don't leave any hidden unwelded joints.

Fifty to sixty years ago, most airplanes were made with a fabric-covered, steel tube fuselage, and this was the accepted practical method for cutting and fitting the tubing. It works just as

First step in fitting one piece of pipe or tubing up to another to make a T-joint is to cut two 45-degree angles at the end, leaving two points as shown. After the second cut is finished, the tube is transferred to a grinding wheel and the two points are rounded off, checking against the other piece of tubing until a good fit is obtained.

Grinding of the points to the proper radius now complete, the tube end snugs neatly up to the side of the other tube, ready for welding.

Square steel tubing welds easily but can be Pop riveted if a torch is not available. The 1″ tubing is fastened with angle brackets while the ½″ pieces are attached with gussets. In either case, the 45-degree cuts for the 90-degree ends are only cut through the inner three sides of the tube. The fourth side is left solid and is bent to the 90-degree angle, making a stronger joint.

well today whether you are building an engine overhaul stand or just welding up a couple of pieces of pipe for a clothesline support.

SQUARE STEEL TUBING

Now that you've been briefed on how to fit up round tubing for welding, here is an even easier way to do the job: use square steel tubing instead.

If you haven't run across this stuff, check it out. It has a lot going for it. It comes in a number of sizes; I've used it as small as ½″ square and it is available up to 6″ square. Rectangular sections of various sizes are also available.

Fitting it up for welding is a breeze compared to round tubing; just cut it off square, or at any desired angle. A band saw-type powered hacksaw is a great help, but the old "Armstrong" method does the job with a bit of effort. In addition, square tubing has a couple of other good points. It seems to be much more readily available than round tubing, at least in this area, and the price is only about half that of round tubing!

Many steel supply houses carry it in standard 20′ lengths and in a number of sizes. Most of these come in several wall thicknesses as well. I find the ¾″ size to be the handiest for projects I build with it, but have sometimes used the 1″, plus the ½″ previously mentioned.

It normally is available only in mild steel,

Rear carrier for this little trail bike was welded up from ½″ square tubing. The plywood tray is bolted to the four welded-on lugs with countersunk flathead machine screws and nuts. The slots in the tray allow bungee cord ends to be slipped through and then turned to hook on in place.

plus some sizes in stainless, and one would not want to use it for high load and fatigue-resistant assemblies, such as an airplane structure where 4130 chrome-moly round tubing is indicated. But for normal jobs, the stuff works great.

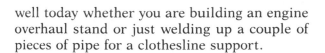

8
AUTO AND RV SERVICE

There are some people who actually enjoy working on their own cars and trucks as a hobby, while many others of us do it only because we are disgusted with the miserable work, exorbitantly priced, that has been passed off on us by so-called professionals. (There are many competent, honest, and hardworking auto repair persons out there, but at times they seem pretty few and far between.) Whichever of the two groups of "Saturday mechanics" you belong to, here are some suggestions to make the job easier, more pleasant, and less time consuming.

Many of these ideas, along with the accompanying photos, come from the shop of Bill Hussman, a long-time friend who belongs to the group that really enjoys working on automobiles; he does a first-class job of it, and his shop is centered around automotive work.

FILE CARDS

Various recurrent services on automotive equipment, coming due anywhere from every 5,000 miles to every 30,000 miles, occur infrequently enough that you can forget from one service to another just how you set up the car, the size wrenches that you needed, and so forth. Nothing is more annoying than to have to crawl out from under the car a couple of times to get a wrench that you forgot to take with you.

File cards and a file card box are available at any stationery store. You may want to make a simple plywood file box as described in Chapter 5.

The next time you do a service job, tune-up, tire rotation, or whatever make note of just how you set the car up, the tools required, and any other helpful notes or comments. Later, neatly write the notes onto one of your file cards, labeled for the car and type of service, and file them alphabetically in your file box. Abbreviate words and whole sentences as necessary to get all the info on the small card. This stuff doesn't have to be good literature; all that is required is that you can make sense of it when you next refer to it.

Include any pertinent sketches such as tire rotation sequence, cylinder numbering, firing order, spark plug wiring layout, position of wires on the distributor, and distributor rotation. Add anything else that you may have difficulty remembering next time and that takes time to look up in your shop manual.

This sample from a file card for a 4 x 4 Blazer serves as an example that you will find useful:

Oil & Filter Change—Lube—Cross Switch Tires. Rear on apron, wheels clear of door. Front on red jack stands, 1½" ext. Rear on orange stands, 4½" ext. Oil drain, ⁹⁄₁₆" box. Filter, cap wrench & 6" ext. Transfer case & rear axle, ⁹⁄₁₆" square socket. Tranny, ⁹⁄₁₆" sq. & 4½" ext. Front axle, ⁵⁄₈" sq. Grease fittings: 4 on steering, 1 on

Sturdy 10-gage steel top not only stands up to heavy automobile parts repair jobs, but can be cleaned easily with a solvent-soaked rag. The drawers keep fasteners and fittings organized.

clutch shaft, 1 each, front & rear slip joints, 1 on rear U-joint & 1 on winch (total 9). Lug nuts ¾", tighten with 60 psi static air pressure.

Another card provides tune-up data:

Plugs, Champ RJ12Y or AC Delco R44. Gap .035. Dwell 30 ± 2. Timing 6 Adv. Firing order, 1-8-4-3-6-5-7-2. Note: get points with integral condenser (easier to install).

STEEL-TOPPED WORKBENCH

Some years back Bill got tired of trying to keep a hardboard workbench top clean and covered it with a sheet of heavy 10-gage steel. He finds it especially good for working with dirty car parts since it is easily wiped off and doesn't become grimy looking. He has it secured to the bench with a few countersunk flathead woodscrews.

A lighter steel top, such as 16-gage galvanized, would also work for a workbench. It is

Close-up shows how Bill fastened the heavy steel top directly over the old ⅛" hardboard bench top. Countersunk flathead screws secure it to the tongue-and-grooved 2 x 6 subtop.

cheaper and easier to install, but it probably will dent a little easier. Bill Hussman does some pretty heavy work on his bench and appreciates being able to do some hard hammering without disturbing the heavy-gage metal.

CARPET CORRAL FOR TINY PARTS

When working with a carburetor, distributor, or other item that has a lot of small screws and other parts that, if dropped, might roll off the bench, Bill works on a small rectangle of short-nap carpet (easily obtainable from scrap at any carpet installer). Once the parts are removed, he keeps them separated in the dozen depressions of a muffin baking tin, safely located toward the back of the bench. For working with really tiny screws, he reverses the carpet. The back side has a textured rubberized plastic surface that keeps the parts from rolling without any possibility of them disappearing into the carpet nap.

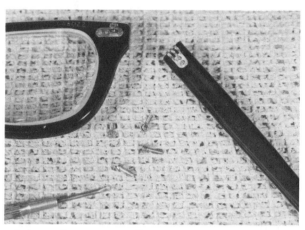

When working with really small parts, such as these tiny eyeglass screws, the carpet's back side keeps them from rolling without losing them in the pile.

SPACE-SAVING DROP-LEAF TABLE

Some time ago, Bill intercepted a household drop-leaf table that was about to be discarded. With a little modification, he finds it to be one of his most useful, and most often used, work-

Any small parts that drop from this carburetor during repair will be caught by the carpet remnant before they can roll onto the floor. Parts are put into the muffin tin to keep them separate.

Drop leaf table, its legs braced and mounted on casters, takes up very little space when stored sideways against the wall. The top has been resurfaced with ⅛" tempered hardboard.

Unfolded, the table becomes a spacious roll-around work area for bulky parts such as the Jaguar valve cover and intake manifold.

Roll of plastic-coated butcher paper hangs from strap-hinge brackets below the end of a workbench.

shop helpers. He resurfaced the top with ⅛" hardboard and fastened a small strip of wood across the bottom of each pair of legs to brace them and to act as a support for a set of casters to make the table mobile.

With the leaves down it takes up only 27" x 44" of space. With the leaves up, it provides a generous 44" x 62" surface for doing steel-plate or sheet-metal layout work, seat-cover work, rebuilding a differential, or even just dumping out a large box full of small parts to find a required item.

Strip of the coated paper provides a clean surface for work on items such as this tachometer.

DISPOSABLE COVER FOR WORK TABLE

Modern-day butcher paper is plastic coated on one side and is quite impervious to grease or oil; it is much better than old newspapers. Bill bought a 24" wide roll some years ago and covers his work table with it any time he has a dirty job to do. It is also excellent for putting down under any parts that should be kept scrupulously clean during adjustment or repair. The paper was purchased from a local butcher shop; although it is expensive, a roll lasts for many years.

SHOP BATTERY AIDS TROUBLE-SHOOTING

When troubleshooting electrical parts used in your vehicles, a source of 12v. DC power is a necessity. It is often not convenient to take the item from the bench to the vehicle for checking, not to mention the added nuisance of hooking up temporary test leads.

Bill gets around this problem by keeping a 12v. battery on the floor at one end of his workbench. It is enclosed in a plastic battery box, of the type used in motorboats and RVs. The battery is wired to a switch on the bench leg, complete with a small red light which is illuminated when the switch is on, both as a check that power is available and as a reminder to turn it off before leaving the shop. Hanging alongside are a pair of test leads terminating in alligator clips, for testing radios, windshield wiper motors, and other electrical parts.

The battery is recharged when required, about once every two or three months. For any dedicated automotive hobbyist, this is another invaluable addition to the shop.

WELDING CLAMP

At his welding table Bill uses a commercially available clamp that has two pairs of locking pliers, each mounted by a ball joint to an arm, which is in turn ball-jointed to a base attached to the table. Each pair of pliers can be rotated through 360 degrees as well as being positioned through a wide range of angles.

The clamp can hold most items that can be gripped by the pliers and position them accurately to one another for welding. It does have

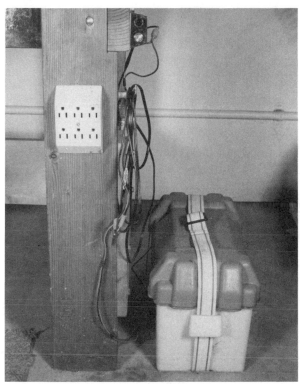

A 12v battery kept on the floor in a plastic case provides power for troubleshooting automotive electrical units. A switch on the bench leg "hots up" the test leads and turns on a telltale light.

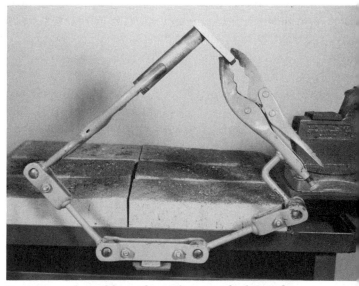

Factory-made welding clamp has two locking-plier clamps and four ball joints to solve a range of clamping problems. A clamp with an adjustable distance between the two lower ball joints would be even more versatile.

With the battery test leads clipped to its power leads, this pickup radio can be quickly checked out.

some limitations because both arms are mounted on a single base. This unit could be modified so that each arm is ball-jointed to a separate base which could be independently clamped to the table.

V-BELT INSTALLER

Installing V-belts in a restricted area can be difficult. Bill made a tool from an old screwdriver to help. About ¼" of the end is bent slightly, then back about ½" from that, another sharp bend is made at 90 degrees in the opposite direction. The belt is slipped over the tool up beyond the second bend and the hook at the end is slipped over the rim of the pulley. The tool is then swung through an arc to stretch the belt up and over the pulley's rim.

Bends like this require heating, and care must be taken that the heat does not run up the blade and soften the plastic handle. This can be done by using a big enough torch tip so that the job is done quickly. Also, soak a strip of rag in cold water and wrap it around the upper part of the shank as a heat sink while the bend is being heated.

A V-belt tensioner is indispensable for adjusting the belts in many cars. It is available in auto parts stores or from tool catalogs.

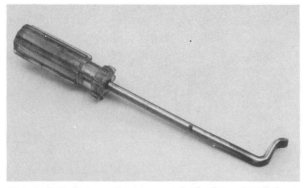

Handy V-belt installer was made by friend Bill from a screwdriver. The tool is slipped under the belt, the notch at the end is hooked over the rim of the pulley, and a pull on the handle works the belt over the rim and into the groove.

AIR RATCHET WRENCH

If you do much automotive maintenance and repair, and if you have an air compressor (almost a necessity for this work), you will find that an air ratchet wrench is one of the most useful air tools that you can acquire.

While it does not have the torque capacity of an air impact wrench, it is great for removing and replacing all those many nuts that are just a little too tight to be turned with the fingers and that are in such an awkward position that a conventional ratchet cannot be used conveniently. With a ⅜" drive air ratchet, even though it is a little more bulky than a conventional ratchet handle, you only have to get the socket on the nut, using whatever extension and/or universal is required, and then pull the trigger. You do not need any space to swing the wrench.

Another great use for the air ratchet is with hard-to-reach spark plugs. Over-torquing plugs can damage them, but in many instances it is impossible to get a torque wrench on them. With another wrench you often must apply force at such an awkward angle that it is extremely difficult to judge the torque being applied.

In this case, the air pressure can be reduced with its regulator to a setting where the wrench will stall at the required torque. Then, all that is necessary to do is to be able to get a plug socket, and the ratchet, in position on the plug and to hold down the trigger until the air motor stops turning. With my air ratchet, for example, reducing the static air pressure to 45 psi torques a spark plug to 25 foot-pounds.

There has been a great reduction in prices of these tools in the last few years, and various discount tool outlets often have them available for around $30. Until just recently they all seemed to come from Japan, but lately they have been appearing from Taiwan as well. Having heard of several problems with the air motors on the Taiwan jobs, I'd personally stay with the Japanese, at least until the others have had a chance to work out the bugs.

Both the air ratchet wrench and the air impact wrench (following) are pictured in Chapter 1, in the section on the air compressor and its tools.

AIR IMPACT WRENCH

The ½"-drive air impact wrench has limited scope compared to the air ratchet wrench, but is invaluable for changing tires. If you cross-switch your tires regularly and you have air available, you will find one of these is well worth its higher cost.

One thing to be aware of when using this tool is that it is quite possible to install lug nuts too tightly. Then it is difficult or impossible to remove nuts with your manual lug wrench if you have to change a tire alongside the road. As with the ratchet, this problem can be alleviated with an adjustment of the air pressure. Although many impact wrenches have an adjustable trigger position to vary the torque applied, I find it easier and more reliable to use a full trigger and adjust the air pressure to a known figure that will torque the nuts adequately without overtorquing. For the wheels on my Blazer, 60 psi is just right, while on the smaller Honda, 50 psi does the job.

COMPRESSED AIR PLUMBING

Having an air compressor along with air wrenches and other air tools is invaluable in a shop that does any auto work. Getting the air from compressor to tools is another problem. Ordinary air hose is awkward to handle and store and is usually underfoot. Many of us make do with the coiled flex hoses that retract at least partially when not in use.

Bill went all out and plumbed three walls of his shop with high-pressure-rated ½" plastic pipe at about waist level. On each wall he has quick-disconnect outlets spaced so that a single flex hose can be plugged in to provide a compressed air supply anywhere in the shop area. The compressor itself is quick connected and can be easily moved to another area if needed.

AIR GREASE GUN

If you do your own lube jobs, you know what a headache the conventional manual grease gun can be under certain conditions. There always seems to be a couple of fittings in such a position that it is extremely difficult to hold the tip of the gun in position on the fitting and operate the pump handle at the same time.

An air-driven grease gun, now quite reasonable in price, is a big improvement in this regard. As with the air ratchet wrench, you only

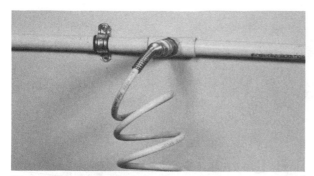

High-pressure-rated ½" plastic pipe runs around three walls of Bill's shop and has several quick-disconnect outlets, making compressed air easily available anywhere in the shop by plugging in a flex hose.

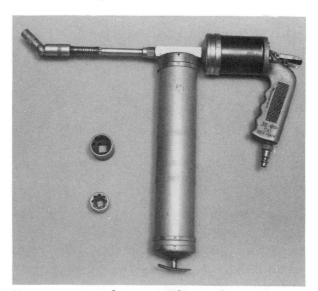

Air grease gun and square sockets to fit transmission and differential plugs save time when you have to get under your machine for a lube job. Note the handy multiangle nozzle on the grease gun.

have to get the gun solidly on the fitting and then press the trigger. Each pull on the trigger gives a single high pressure squirt, similar to each pump of the handle on a manual gun. Just continue to actuate the trigger until grease appears at the parting surface of the joint.

Loading of the gun is the same as with the manual models and can be equally messy, even when using a cartridge, but once you get the thing loaded the operational problems are greatly reduced.

SQUARE SOCKETS FOR SQUARE PLUGS

While we are on the subject of lube jobs, let's consider the various gear boxes: the transmission, differential, and with a 4 x 4, the transfer case and second differential as well.

If your machine has been serviced for some time by a "professional" using his trusty 12" adjustable wrench for most everything, you may find that the square plugs on these gear boxes for checking the oil levels have been rounded off

so much that it is difficult to remove them, even with a "real" wrench. In this case, get one or more 8-point (square) sockets along with an adequate handle; these should help you remove and replace the plugs without damaging them further. On my Blazer, two 8-point sockets (⁹⁄₁₆" and ⅝") take care of all four boxes, even the one on the rear differential. The "pro" had rounded that one off so badly that he could no longer remove it and had neglected it for several services. I happened to catch him in the act and decided I'd better do the job myself in the future.

SOCKET-DRIVE ADAPTERS

If you have a ⅜" reversible electric drill with trigger speed control, you can easily make or have made a very simple adapter to power drive your ⅜" or ½"-drive sockets.

Get a spare extension of the required drive size(s). Even a cheap Taiwan extension works here because the drill does not produce a very high torque. Place the female end of the extension in a three-jaw lathe chuck and turn down

These three adapters for ⅜", ½", and ¾"-drive socket sets allow the ⅜" and ½" drills shown to power on and off nuts ranging from ⅜" across flats to the big 2⅜" nut.

Three adapters were turned from extensions similar to the ½" one above. The smaller two fit a ⅜" drill chuck while the large one is for a ½" drill. Three flats are milled (or filed) on the shank of each to avoid slippage.

1½" of the shank (as close as possible to the male end) to ⅜" in diameter. Then mill or file three equally spaced flats along the turned-down shank to give the drill chuck a good grip. One easy way to space the flats uniformly is to position the spindle of the lathe so that one of the 3 jaws of the chuck is exactly vertical and lock the spindle in position by engaging the back gears. File the first flat holding the file horizontal. Release the spindle, rotate it until a second chuck jaw is vertical, lock it again, and file the second flat to the same width. Follow the same procedure to locate and file the third flat. If done carefully, the three flats will be quite uniformly located. Cut off the extension, keeping only the male end and about 1¼" of the turned down shank, and you're in business.

If you don't have a lathe, you may have a friend who can do it for you. This job is small enough that even a little model maker's lathe of the Unimat type can handle it. Failing this, you may find a commercial machine shop that will do a small job such as this without a prohibitive minimum charge. At any reasonable price you'll find it well worth while.

This tool is a real timesaver when you come across a series of bolts that are just tight enough that the nuts can not be run on or off with the fingers or where there is no room to swing a speeder handle, thus requiring them to

be ratcheted on or off. If you can get a socket onto them and connected to the drill with this adapter, using any needed universals and/or extensions, you can do the job in a hurry.

Another handy use is as a "poor man's impact wrench" for rotating tires. In this case, the initial job of loosening and final tightening is done with the normal lug wrench, but otherwise the nuts can be spun off and on with power; zip, zip, zip, zip.

If you use bigger sockets, such as a ¾" or even a 1" drive, you can make an adapter for it from a similar sized extension, but you'd better plan on using a ½" reversible drill, rather than ⅜". You need extra torque to turn the bigger nuts.

Over the past decade, I have made up at least three dozen of these little adapters from inexpensive extensions picked up at flea markets or garage sales and have given many of them to friends. Once they have been tried out, they have been almost universally appreciated.

One caution in using these gadgets: do *not* try to tighten a nut by slamming it home at high speed. If you do, it is possible to damage the internal gearing in the drill. You can safely approach the final setting at a slow speed until the drill stalls; just don't race it down to a sudden stop at full speed. In any case, final tightening by hand is usually required.

PSEUDO UNIVERSAL JOINT EXTENSIONS

Flexible jointed sockets and separate universal joints are a great help where there is not enough space for a straight shot from a nut to the position where a handle can be swung. They are not without their aggravations, however. Most of them swing nearly 90 degrees, and they have a habit of doing just that when you are trying to snake a socket with nut inside onto a bolt located in an otherwise inaccessible spot. Makeshift procedures such as taping the universal to hold an approximate position with a couple of turns of masking or electrician's tape sometimes do the job, but they are a nuisance.

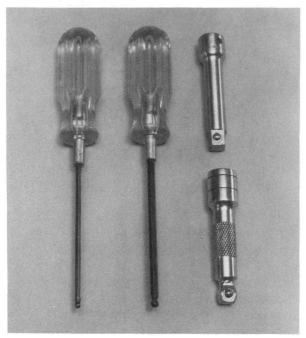

Two ball-end hex wrenches at left show the six-sided "balls" that work at an offset angle on Allen head screws in tight spots. The ⅜″ socket extension at lower right uses the same principle to give limited universal-joint action. An ordinary extension is shown for comparison.

Retired Air Force pilot Harold Gibson, who has been an automobile hobbyist for over fifty years, recently stopped by for a short visit. Before leaving, he lifted the hood of his car to make a small adjustment. During the ensuing conversation, he commented that on a previous car he had found it much easier to change the spark plugs by drilling holes in the fender wells and slipping a long extension in from the outside. He just put the extension and spark plug socket through the hole and onto the plug and then turned it from the outside of the wheel well where there was more room to swing a handle.

To locate the holes, which were made for only the most difficult plugs, he put an extension of the appropriate length on a plug socket, put it on the plug, and then extended the line of the extension to the inside of the wheel well. He marked it there and them made a punch mark to indicate the location to drill the hole from the outside.

Since these are relatively small holes and are

Fairly recently, a new type of extension has come onto the market that solves this problem in cases where only a slight offset is needed. One of these gadgets looks like an ordinary 2½″-long ⅜″-drive extension, except that all four sides of the square male end have a double taper on them, thus allowing the socket to flex up to a 15-degree angle from the extension while being turned.

SPARK-PLUG ACCESS

While the designers of many of the newer cars have tried to make items such as oil filters, distributors, and spark plugs more accessible for service, there are still millions of cars, especially the V-8s, where such things as the spark plugs can seldom be seen, much less easily reached.

Spark plugs on this Blazer, impossible to see and extremely difficult to reach from the engine compartment, are easy to change via holes cut in the wheel well. Each hole is large enough to allow a hand through to slip plug wires off and on. The rear cutout is shown with its dust cover installed.

located in the upright portion of the wheel housing, he had no problem with mud or dirt being thrown through them by the wheels. If this were the case, it would be easy to provide some sort of plug or removable cover for them.

Since replacing the spark plugs on my Blazer has always been extremely difficult, I decided to try this approach on my next service. This machine required a variation of this solution since the problem here is not only room to swing a wrench. It is difficult enough to even reach the plugs to pull the cable terminals, much less get a plug socket on them.

After much peeking around corners and through small holes, I decided that holes large enough to admit a hand would solve the problem. There was a reasonably clear space directly between the plugs and the side of the wheel wells. Accordingly, I cut four holes, two in each wheel well, and each serving a pair of plugs. Each hole is about 2½″ high and 5″ long and allows me to slip in a hand to get at the ignition cables and to direct the plugs into the holes when replacing them.

I normally cross-switch the tires during the same service so I change the plugs while the front wheels are removed, thus giving all sorts of room in the wheel well. The job could be done with the wheels in place, but not quite so easily.

Since the wheel well would be a rather awkward place to work with a pair of snips, I cut the holes with the air-driven panel cutter mentioned in Chapter 1. Its little 3″ wheel zipped quickly through the sheet metal, making it easy to cut out a small rectangle and then enlarge it in one or more directions as needed. Once I had the holes cut to a size that allows easy access, I put a mounted stone in an air die grinder and smoothed off all the burrs and rough edges to prevent injuries. Since the holes were large, I made four cover plates from a scrap of galvanized material and provided each with three sheet-metal screws.

Even including the time spent measuring and cutting the access holes, this plug change took me no longer than it usually does and cost me much less aggravation. On future changes it should take half the time! I surely appreciate Gib's casual comment. Modified for your particular situation, it may solve a similar problem for you.

TAPERED GAP GAGE

Speaking of spark-plug service, I recently came across a handy spark-plug gapping gage. Since new plugs require gapping to specs for the particular engine they are to be installed in, this is necessary with all plug changes. While the little wire gages or an ordinary set of feeler gages will do the job, they do take some fiddling to get the proper gap.

My gage is a stainless-steel disc about ⅛″ thick and 1½″ in diameter. The rim has been formed into an accurate taper with a scale along side it that indicates its thickness in thousandths from .020″ to .100″. It also has a small hole with a thin inside rim that serves as a convenient gapper.

All you do is slip the thin part of the rim into the plug's gap and rotate the disc until the rim fills the gap; then just take the reading at that point on the scale. This tells you exactly how many thousandths off the gap is. The gage makes the whole job of adjusting plug gaps easier than with the older type of gage. I find it speeds up my plug-gapping chores considerably.

BALL-END HEX WRENCHES

If you have a GM car or truck with ignition points instead of the newer electronic ignition, you probably appreciate being able to set the points to the proper dwell with a hex wrench while the engine is idling instead of having to remove the distributor cap, reset the points, and reinstall the cap about a half a dozen times until you hit the correct dwell. Even this operation sometimes is difficult, especially with the distributor mounted on the back of the engine in a hard-to-reach position that can make it impossible to get a straight shot at the little window with an ordinary hex wrench.

A ball-end hex wrench is a great help in this situation. Similar in operation to the pseudo universal socket extension mentioned earlier, this wrench has a screwdriver handle and has the end of the blade formed into a six-sided ball shape. While it turns the internal hex head screw, it also acts as a universal joint and works when up to about 15 degrees out of line with the screw. A big help. Mine is ⅛″ across the flats. I'm not sure if this size fits all GM distributors. (That would be too easy!)

These wrenches come in all common hex wrench sizes and are useful anywhere an internal hex head screw is difficult to get at with a normal hex wrench. Their only drawback is that, due to the necked down portion, tightening down hard with this wrench may break it. To alleviate this problem, the wrenches are also made in a conventional L shape. The long end has the ball end for ease of installation while the short end has a standard straight end for maximum torquing.

SOLDERLESS CONNECTORS, CRIMPING TOOL

One can't do much automotive work without running into some electrical wiring work. Hooking up new accessories, replacing old ones, repairing old wiring, adding new, there's always some new electrical connection to be made. A good crimping tool and a supply of solderless connectors is invaluable in this work. The connectors are available in many types and sizes. They can provide terminal ends with holes to fit anything from the tiniest screw up to a fair-sized bolt. It's much easier and usually provides a better electrical connection to slip one of these onto a screw or bolt and secure a nut down on it than it is to just wrap the wire around the shank of the screw and hope for the best when you tighten it. A solderless connector also makes subsequent disassembly and reassembly much easier.

Other available connectors make wire splicing easy, and they result in a self-insulated splice without requiring wrapping with tape or heat-shrink tubing. The crimping tool provides for a sturdy, long-lasting, solderless connection that is not subject to the corrosion and vibration failures common to soldered joints.

Auto supply houses, hardware stores, and industrial tool suppliers often have starter kits

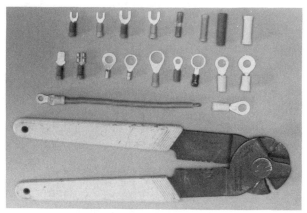

Solderless connectors and a crimping tool are invaluable in auto electric work. This one cuts wires, strips insulation, and has three different sized crimping detents. The wire sample has its left end prepared for installation and the right end shows a completed terminal. Below are a few of the many terminals available to fit almost any need.

that include a crimping tool and an assortment of connectors. Additional connectors are available either in large assortments or in small packages of individual types and sizes as needed.

STAND FOR TROUBLE LIGHT

The 15-watt fluorescent trouble lights that have recently become popular do a good job of providing glare-free light. But even with factory provided extra hooks to hang the light horizontally, it is sometimes difficult to position the light for "hands free" light on the job. Friend Bill created a new stand for his, and I followed the design for the stand shown. It has been a great help in positioning the light where needed.

The heart of the stand is a short piece of 1¾″ OD steel tubing, the inside of which just fits snugly over the handle end of the light. It was necessary to trim off a small raised circle of plastic just below the switch. A 1¼″-wide slot was hacksawed in the tube for a length of 3½″ to allow the switch boss on the light to slide down

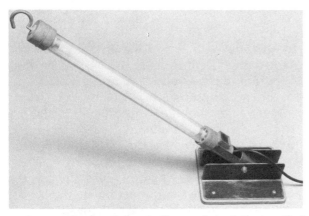

Light stand is easily made from a bit of thin-walled steel tubing, some light angle, and a plywood base. It allows the light to be positioned anywhere in a 180-degree arc.

into the tube and to provide an exit for the cord. The base of the slot was sawed on around to about two-thirds of the diameter of the tube to allow some flexibility in the sides of the tube so that it could expand slightly to a snug grip on the light. The base was made from two short pieces of light-gage 2¾" angle, fastened to a rectangular scrap of ½" plywood with four sheet-metal screws.

A ¼" hole was drilled through the lower end of the tubing and through both vertical arms of the steel angles. The holes in the tube were filed square to accommodate the heads of a pair of short ¼" carriage bolts. These allow the nuts to be tightened without requiring a wrench on the inside bolt heads. Two individual bolts were used instead of a single long through-bolt, which would tend to compress and distort the tube before the joint was tightened enough to hold any desired position. The unit was assembled with washers under the self-locking (nylon insert) nuts which were tightened just enough to hold the tube at any angle.

In use, the base can be put on the floor under the car with the tube laid back horizontally to shine directly up at the underside of the machine. It can also be placed at various spots under the hood with the tube swung over 180 degrees so that the light shines directly down. In a wheel well during a check of your brakes, it can be swung to a vertical position to illumi-

nate directly to the side. It can also be set to any angle in between as needed. Of course, any time the stand is not needed, the light can be easily pulled out and used without it.

IN-CAR TOOLBOX

Providing you have the necessary tools available, you can make a roadside repair of various minor ailments that would otherwise necessitate the calling of a tow truck. Even though you may have insurance which covers this expense, calling for help can cost you time and trouble. Often just carrying a couple of basic tools in the car can quickly get you underway.

Although it is impractical to take a selection of your workshop tools in the car on every trip, it is quite simple and relatively inexpensive to provide a small tool kit for each vehicle. Keep it under a seat or in another convenient storage area.

There are a number of small toolboxes available that are about 4" x 5" x 12" in size and which hold a surprising array of tools, if they are wisely chosen.

Some suggestions include: a four-way screwdriver whose handle has reversible segments which contain a large and small slotted blade and a large and small Phillips blade; a small set of end wrenches, fractional or metric, as appropriate; a pair of water pump pliers, regular pliers, diagonal pliers, and long-nose pliers; a small hammer, with one end of its head steel and the other end plastic, (you may have to cut an inch or so off the handle to fit the box); small rolls of wire and plastic electrician's tape; some duct tape, which can make a temporary patch on a leaking radiator hose to get you home or to a service station (leave the radiator cap in the unpressurized position and drive slowly to prevent overheating); a small container of screws, nuts, washers, and cotter pins; and spare fuses, a fuse puller, and a couple of spare brake and turn signal bulbs.

Add any other small tools or supplies that may be called for by known problems with that particular vehicle. Stuff the remaining space with small clean rags which, as well as being needed, keep the tools from rattling while en route.

I have kept a similar toolbox in each car or

truck for twenty-five years or more and have found them to be invaluable on a number of occasions. When disposing of a particular automobile, I remove the toolbox and use it, with any appropriate change of tools and supplies, for the next machine.

NYLON TIES

These do a fine job of housekeeping in the engine compartment of a car, truck, RV, powerboat, or other machine. They can lace a bundle of wires together or secure one or more wires to any convenient rod, tube, brace, or other item to keep them away from excessive heat or moving mechanical parts.

Nylon ties come in many sizes; I have some as small as 3½″ in length and others that are 22″ long. I doubt that either of these is a limit. They have a molded nylon head with a built-in ratcheting dog, usually of nylon in the smaller sizes and of metal in the large ones.

In use, the long tail of the tie is brought round the wire bundle and anything the bundle is to be tied to. The tail is then slipped into the slot in the head and pulled tight. In some models the little ratchet dog in the head engages a row of teeth molded in the nylon tail. In the larger ones with a metal dog, the dog often digs

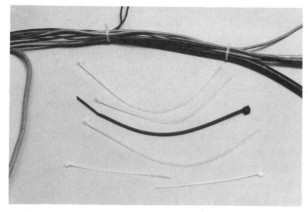

Nylon ties are a great help for any wiring job and provide a neat, well-supported installation. They are completely installed by hand, although the loose ends can be snipped off with a pair of dykes for a neater appearance.

directly into the nylon, needing no molded teeth to engage.

In either case they are irreversible and are designed as one-shot deals. Do *not* place the tongue into the head until you are sure that you have the tie encircling everything that you need to include in the bundle. Once the tail is placed in the head, it can be pulled tight but cannot be pulled back out. The circle can only be opened by cutting. The manufacturer probably considers it cheating, but you can reuse the larger sizes by cutting the tail off just inside the head. Then pull the portion of the tail that is being held in the head on through and discard it. The remainder of the tail can then be slipped into the head and pulled tight around any bundle smaller than the one previously secured. Keep this in mind the next time you receive a shipment in which the seller has bundled up a couple of bulky items with some of these ties.

HEAT-SHRINK TUBING

Used with a heat gun or other source of heat, such as a cigarette lighter or even a match, shrink tubing has many applications in automotive work. Be wary, though, of using a lighter or match around inflammable materials such as gasoline, solvent, or around a leaking carburetor.

Shrink tubing makes a neat bundle of any group of wires that have their ends available for it to be slipped over. It can also be placed onto one wire before a splice is made and then slid over the splice and shrunk in that position to protect and insulate the connection.

This material is also good for snaking a new wire through a firewall and up under a dashboard, or through other hard-to-reach areas. Just cut the terminal off the old wire, slip on a short length of the appropriate sized shrink tubing and butt the new wire up against the end of the old one. Slip the tubing over the joint, shrink it in place, and then pull the old wire through bringing the new one along after it. This method has also been used to replace worn cables, such as aircraft control cables, by pulling out the old cable and snaking the new one around pulleys, fairleads, and cable drums, in a fraction of the time that would otherwise be required.

A heat gun, samples of shrink tubing, and a shrink tubing wire splice are shown in Chapter 1.

ZIPLOCK BAGS

In disassembly work, Ziplock bags keep small parts much neater than the usual assortment of old tin cans, at least one of which usually gets knocked over and the parts scattered. This is especially true when working on a car or RV outdoors in a driveway or on bare ground. It also applies to an airplane on an open ramp or to dockside work on a boat. Here the Ziplock bag has another advantage; it floats when accidentally knocked overboard if it has been sealed and the contents are not too heavy.

The use of Ziplock bags is shown in photos in Chapter 3.

GOLF TEES

These may seem an unlikely item for automotive work, but they are invaluable for sealing off vacuum lines when an engine is to be run with one or more vacuum items disconnected. The most common use is to seal off the distributor advance vacuum line when checking the spark timing.

NONSLIP STEEL RAMPS

Many thousand pairs of lightweight pressed steel ramps have been sold to Saturday mechanics. Although they do a good job of raising one end of a car or small truck to make work underneath it easier, they have one problem. On a smooth concrete surface, they often tend to slide ahead of the wheels instead of allowing the wheels to climb up them.

The problem is the lack of friction between the smooth surface of the metal and the concrete. Cut out pieces of jute gunny sack material or strips from an old inner tube and place them under the feet of the ramps. This increases the friction between the ramp and the floor. Now the ramps will hold their position and allow the wheels to roll up onto them with no problem.

Lightweight ramps at first slid across the smooth concrete floor when an attempt was made to drive up them; but they held rock steady when placed on the four rubber rectangles.

Golf tees plug auto vacuum lines when running the engine with components disconnected. One is shown at lower center.

STORING RAMPS AND A CREEPER

Steel ramps and the creeper normally used with them are handy items, but you may not

Hanging them up on a wall provides an out-of-the-way home for the ramps and a creeper.

Short strip of old garden hose, screwed to a length of 1 x 3 fastened to the wall, prevents damage to both the car door and wall.

need them for several months until another major service comes due. You can get them out of the way in the interim by drilling a hole in the end of each ramp and either one or two holes in the creeper. The ramps can then be hung vertically on large nails driven into a wall in an out-of-the-way place. Hang the creeper either vertically or horizontally as space permits.

PROTECTING DOOR EDGES

Many garages are narrow enough that a car door strikes the wall before opening fully. If the wall is of masonry, this may chip the paint on the edge of the door. If the wall is Sheetrock, the edge of the car door will dent it.

To solve this problem, fasten a short length of a 1 x 2 or 1 x 3 board to the wall at the height of the maximum bulge in the door. Use masonry nails, mastic, or ordinary nails, as appropriate. Then fasten a length of old garden hose to the wood strip as a bumper. Secure it with small nails or screws after cutting holes in the outer side of the hose. That way the heads enter the hose and hold against the inner side of the hose instead of pulling the hose flat around them.

The length of the bumper is determined by how accurately your car is positioned. If you use a curb fastened to the floor to stop the wheels and have a two-door model, the bumper may only be a few inches long. For a four-door machine with no exact positioning device, you need a much longer bumper.

RV SEWER HOSE HELP

A self-contained RV is a wonderful gadget, but as with everything else, problems arise. One of these occurs regularly when connecting the sewer hose to the underground drain in a developed campground or RV park. For some reason, most builders of these facilities seem unaware of the fact that drain water only runs downhill. Invariably, if the sewer connection's location is not slightly higher than the parking spot, the builder has extended the connection itself above the ground for a couple of inches. Thus there is no way the flexible sewer hose can be laid out on the ground directly into the sewer connection so that the water drains freely through it.

The solutions to this problem are many, both manufactured and homemade. Many are either bulky, heavy, or both. Here is a drain setup that is light in weight and takes up little space.

Most building supply houses sell vinyl rain

Every location requires a different setup to provide the proper slope for an RV sewer-hose connection. The plastic rain gutter keeps the hose on an even down slope for good drainage, and the wood supports can be adjusted to different heights by hooking the proper link of a chain over a screw head. Plan the overall height of the supports to conform to the height of your vehicle's drain outlet.

guttering. One popular type comes in the form of a flat-bottomed U shape with angled sides. This one not only holds the normal 3″ flexible sewer hose but it also just slips into the usual 4″-square steel-tube bumper that stores the sewer hose.

The gutter, which comes in 10′ lengths, is cut off about 4″ shorter than the length of the bumper. That way it clears the connection on the end of the hose, which takes up nearly the full inside dimension of the bumper.

This hose support can be raised off the ground to an appropriate angle by means of short sections of 2 x 4, stacked to give the appropriate height and angle of drain. To avoid carrying these, a lighter and less bulky adjustable substitute can be made from ¼″ or ⅜″ plywood. Each of the two supports is made of two pieces of plywood hinged at the top, which is also cut out to the contour of the gutter. Near the bottom, a lightweight chain, made adjustable in length by nails in the edge of each

board, allows the angle between the two boards to be varied, thus adjusting the height.

Make one support high enough to just fit under the RV end of the hose, allowing for low spots in the parking area, and adjustable to a low enough position that it can get under the hose in case of a high spot under the RV's sewer connection position. The second support is made with a similar adjustment, but is slightly shorter to allow the appropriate slope.

In operation, the low support is placed close to the sewer inlet and is set to a height that allows the hose to turn nicely from the top of the gutter into the sewer connection. The high support is placed close to the sewer outlet on the RV and raised to give a down slope toward the park sewer. Since the distance between the RV connection and the park connection will vary between sites, any excess gutter is allowed to extend under the RV.

In some cases, an even longer hose run may be necessary. For this purpose, it is advisable to save the cutoff portion of the gutter if you can find a place to store it. It is about the lightest extension you will find, and lapped over the lower end of the long piece and atop the support, it extends your hose a couple of feet or so. You only need a single small block to hold its end above the sewer inlet.

When the long gutter is stowed by pushing it into the storage bumper, you may find that it is difficult to pull it out, since it has been pushed deep into the bumper to allow clearance for the sewer hose end connection. Solve this problem by drilling a ¼″ hole in one side of the gutter near the end. Make up a heavy wire tool with a short hook on one end and a bent up handle on the other. With this tool, you just reach into the bumper, engage the hook in the hole, pull, and out it comes.

FRONT-MOUNTED TRAILER HITCH

When you have a trailer and have to get it into an out-of-the-way place, you might consider a secondary trailer hitch temporarily mounted on the front bumper of your towing rig.

Fastened to the front bumper, this hitch makes easy work of pushing a trailer into difficult spots. The shop-modified wrench stored with the hitch is all that is needed. It's an old stunt, but a worn tennis ball still makes a good hitch-ball cover.

Driver's-eye view gives an idea of how much simpler it is to drive forward when pushing the trailer into its restricted storage location than it would be to back in.

If you get out into the backcountry away from organized campgrounds, there are many interesting places to camp. Often there is a short little side road leading 50 yards or so down to a dandy campground by a creek or river. The only problem is that there is often not enough space down there to turn around the trailer and its tow rig and you just can't see yourself trying to back the rig out that distance over a narrow, crooked side road.

With a front hitch the answer is simple. At the main road, stop with the trailer in position to be backed down the side road. Disconnect, turn the tow rig around, and reconnect to the front hitch. It is then a simple matter to drive forward, pushing the trailer backward down the road to the desired spot. Since you can easily see where the trailer is headed, and since you are steering it directly with the front wheels on the tow rig, the operation is a snap. Once you get in position, disconnect, and after turning the tow rig around you are all set for a straight pull out. If there is not room to turn the rig around, it is easy to back it out by itself,

turn around on the main road, and back it down to the campground.

The front hitch can be valuable at home if you happen to have a difficult parking situation. To park my trailer, I have to back it some 50 yards around a 180-degree turn and down a narrow drive alongside a rather steep drop-off. The front hitch makes this former headache a breeze.

Since the extra hitch is just for short off-highway operation, there is no need for any wiring for lights. Because I use a light trailer with my small truck, I have never felt a need for a brake connection. Accordingly, my extra hitch is a simple clamp-on device that can be installed or removed in a couple of minutes with a modified wrench that fits the two necessary sizes of nuts. The hitch and the wrench are kept in a storage space in the back of the rig.

Most every tow rig needs a different front hitch made to fit its particular bumper. If you have a welding outfit, you probably can make one up yourself. If not, any welding shop that installs trailer hitches should be able to do the job for you fairly easily. In either case, be sure that you provide a connection for your safety chain and breakaway brake cable.

LIGHTWEIGHT LEVELING RAMP

Having a trailer, camper, or motor home level during use is a necessity. Not only is it a discomfort to try to sleep when your bed is angled slaunch-ways, but most gas refrigerators work inefficiently, if at all, when they are not fairly level. There are a number of ramps sold for leveling a rig, but many of them are quite expensive as well as heavy. This one is light, inexpensive, and easily made in most any home workshop.

For my small single axle trailer, I used two 24″ lengths of 1 x 6 Douglas fir. Cutting these on a taper gave me four tapered pieces about ½″ wide on the small end and 5″ wide on the other end. Nine hole-saw slugs gave me three sets of different sized spacers; the smallest set being about 1⅛″ in diameter and the largest 2⅜″. Three ⁵⁄₁₆″ by 5½″ bolts and nuts, along with a half-dozen large "fender" washers, were used to assemble the ramp. If you can't find the proper length bolts, try threaded rod cut to length.

The four ¾″-wide strips″ plus three ¾″ spacers, make the ramp 5¼″ wide, quite adequate for most tires. On the bottom, two rows of slightly undersize holes were drilled and short lengths of ¼″ welding rod were driven in. Their rounded-off ends protrude about ¼″ and keep the ramp from sliding out from under the wheel.

Wood ramp, often needed for leveling an RV, is very light and quite inexpensive compared to many factory-made ramps.

At the campground, the ramp is placed alongside the low wheel and the trailer is pulled, or pushed up on it until it is level from side to side. It is then leveled fore and aft with the tongue jack and held steady with the four stabilizing jacks.

A tandem axle trailer requires a longer ramp. Perhaps you should cut it from a 1 x 8 or even a 1 x 10 in order to get the average of the two axles up to the required height. A camper or motor home might need two, or even three, ramps on uneven ground. In any case, the ramps are lighter and easier to handle than the equivalent amount of solid blocking.

A BETTER TOASTER

The design of stovetop camp toasters hasn't changed for over a half century except that some are made of stainless steel now. These little square truncated pyramids hold only two slices of bread and also seem to be unable to provide warm toast without burning it—it's either cold or it's burned black.

Being a lover of warm, unburned toast, I was interested when I saw a homemade toaster which did just that. I promptly made a copy. It only toasts one slice at a time but it does a good job of it. Here is how it's made.

From a scrap of steel cut a piece 5″ wide and 18″ long. I used 30-gage galvanized, but it could be somewhat heavier and would still be easy to cut and bend. Bend up a ½″ strip on each side, fold it over, and press it flat so that you have a strip 4″ x 18″ with two ½″ hems.

Form the strip into a circle, overlap the ends about ⅝″, drill holes and fasten the ends with three or four Pop rivets. Cut a circle from another scrap of the same material to serve as a flame diffuser. Make it just slightly larger than the circle of fire on your burner (mine is about 3¼″ in diameter). Drill three small holes about ¼″ in from the rim and secure it in place with three wires, bent over at the circle. Pass the long ends through three holes in the middle of the lower hem.

Center the diffuser, cut off the wires about ¼″ long, bend them flat against the hem, and solder them to it. The wire ends in the diffuser

Shop-made toaster makes warm toast without burning it. The unit is bent up from sheet metal.

A diffuser disc near the bottom of the toaster spreads the heat from the stove's gas burner.

plate are not soldered (it would melt) but are merely folded tightly.

Drill holes in the center of the top hem for a gridwork of wire to support the toast. I put three wires in one direction and two wires perpendicular to them. Again, cut the wires about ¼" long on each end, bend them flat against the hem and solder them. ¹⁄₁₆" gas welding rod works out well for all the wires, top and bottom. Try out your new toaster. Deep-six your old one.

IMPROVEMENTS FOR A 4 x 4

If you have a 4 x 4 for hunting, fishing, prospecting, ghost town exploring, or anything else that is more rugged than merely cruising the main drag on a Friday night, you can add a number of improvements that would be difficult and expensive to have done.

Here are some changes that I have made in a Blazer over a number of years. They have all been quite useful and may also give you some ideas of your own.

Plywood Jockey Box

When I ordered my Blazer, a center console or "jockey box" between the two front seats was

only available as part of a package which included a load of outside chrome strips. Since this stuff is the hallmark of the Friday night cruiser and is soon damaged or ripped off completely when traveling through off-road brush, I decided against it. Instead, I opted for such items as an auxiliary battery, heavier springs and shocks, and other utilitarian items.

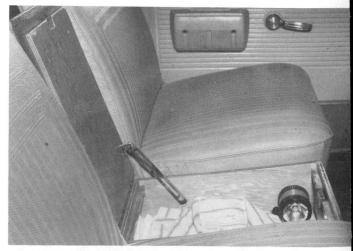

Plywood console is easy to make for RVs with bucket seats. This one fastens to the transmission hump with sheet-metal screws. Its top is covered with rubber matting and serves as a step when going into the back of the rig.

Once the rig was delivered, I quickly made a storage box from some scraps of ½″ plywood. The space between the seats was carefully measured and the box made to fit. Since there is a raised section across the floor between the front of the seats, the box has a stepped bottom at the front. Holes were drilled through the bottom of the box, the floor mat, and the steel cab floor. The box is fastened to the floor with sheet-metal screws, countersunk into the base to give the box a flat bottom. The top of the box is hinged at the back so that it is easily accessible from either seat. The top is covered with a sheet of glued-on rubber floor mat material to prevent scuffing of the plywood when the box is stepped on to get between the seats and into the back.

Once finished, the box was given three coats of gloss polyurethane varnish before final installation.

Camp Bunks and Storage Boxes

At the time I got the Blazer, I did not have a trailer. I did a lot of rough-country camping with a friend, though, and did not always want to go to the trouble of making and breaking an outdoor camp every night when moving about while prospecting or exploring ghost towns. So, I built a pair of quickly removable plywood bunks with an aisle between them and storage space beneath them. Four-inch-thick foam pads were custom cut and covered to fit the bunks. They provide a quite adequate mattress under a sleeping bag.

In addition to having storage space beneath them, the bunks are sturdy enough that all sorts of camp gear, mining equipment, and whatnot can be piled atop them.

The bunks were made one at a time from ½″ plywood. The cross bulkheads were made first, each cut to fit its particular location and fastened with small steel corner braces; one end screwed to the plywood and the other end screwed to the floor with sheet-metal screws. All were kept accessible for easy removal and replacement of the bunks. The bulkheads were made 11″ high, which places the top just above the wheel wells and allows enough height to use heavy cardboard two-piece orange crates

Plywood bunk, one of two made for my Blazer, can be removed or installed in a few minutes. The 4″ foam mattress is quite comfortable.

Front compartment comes in handy for storage. The second bunk has a solid top and an open side so that supplies can be slid in under it from the center aisle.

for storage boxes. The bulkheads were spaced to fit the boxes.

A length of 1 x 2 was let into the upper outer corners of each bulkhead but with a gap for the wheel well location. The edge of the plywood top was screwed to the 1 x 2 and several countersunk holes were drilled into the side of the 1 x 2 to secure the top of the bunk to the truck's inner side wall with sheet metal screws through large washers.

One bunk has the top fixed and the aisle side open. Boxes of food and other camp gear are stored under it by sliding them up the aisle and then sideways between the bulkheads. A small two-burner gasoline camp stove stores behind a bunk and just ahead of the tailgate. The large ice chest slides into the aisle between the two bunks.

The other bunk has a full-length wall along the aisle edge of the bulkheads and its top has a flush-mounted strip of piano hinge, allowing it to fold up against the window. This side contains loose stuff, such as tools, tire chains, tow cable, hydraulic jack, and a few essential spare parts such as V-belts, points, and a fuel pump. This bunk is normally left in the rig full time to store these items. The other bunk is slipped in only when actually needed and is stored in the rafters of the garage at other times. The sheet-metal screws are kept in a small can stored with it and it only takes a few minutes to install or remove either of the bunks.

For a couple of guys who want a comfortable bed when otherwise roughing it on a fishing, hunting, or prospecting expedition, this simple setup is hard to beat.

Heavy-Duty Bumpers

Since I intended to mount a winch on the front and a spare tire rack on the back, my next modification to the truck was adding heavy-duty bumpers front and rear.

A trip to the local junkyard provided two nice, straight pieces of 6″ channel steel. The ends of the top and bottom angle sections were cut away with a torch, cut to a curve, and the ends of the 6″ web bent around them so as to be a nice match to the width of the truck. The ends of the web were cut in a curve to match the contour of the fender area. Pieces of steel angle were bolted to the bumpers with carriage bolts

to tie the bumpers to the frame of the truck in lieu of the original brackets, although the diagonal braces were modified for the same use on the new bumper.

A coat of aluminum paint from a spray can finished up the job and allows easy touch-up of the scrapes and scratches inherent with a 4 x 4, as well as simple cover up of any modifications, of which there have been several.

Protected Tailpipe Extension

One of the first things to get damaged on a hard-working four-wheel-drive rig is the end of the exhaust tailpipe. Usually extending out below the bumper at one of the rear corners of the vehicle, it is a cinch to get knocked off, broken, or dented the first time the machine has to be turned around where there really isn't room enough.

When the bumpers just mentioned were being made, provision was made for protecting the tailpipe by cutting a hole in the curved left end of the rear bumper. A coupling for a 2″ water pipe was fitted into the hole and welded in place. A piece of flexible stainless-steel exhaust tubing with an ID to just fit the OD of the

Anyone who has ever bent or broken a tailpipe when turning around in a restricted space with a 4 x 4 will appreciate this modification—the tailpipe is protected by the heavy 6″ channel-iron bumper. Long-lasting flex exhaust tubing made from stainless steel connects exhaust to tailpipe.

tailpipe was obtained, and the tailpipe was cut off at a point where the flex tubing could be slipped over it, clamped on, and then led in an easy curve to the rear bumper. There it was fed through the coupling and cut off flush. A small bolt and nut through one wall secures it. Presto! No more problems with damaged tail pipes.

If you do this modification, be sure to make the extra effort required to find stainless steel flex exhaust tubing; it lasts for many years. The ordinary steel flex tubing commonly sold for this use rusts out in a year or two at the most. An auto supply store can special order this for you if they don't have it in stock.

Better Spare Tire Mount

When I bought the Blazer, the only spare tire mount available was a bracket which mounted it vertically inside the bed of the truck itself. While this kept the tire warm, cozy, and protected from the elements, it took up a good chunk of space in the interior of the vehicle. That was quite unacceptable in view of my plan to use the space for built-in bunks.

Later, aftermarket manufacturers offered an

Spare-tire mount not only gets the tire out from its original position inside the truck, but the tire can also be swung around and secured to the side of the truck to keep the tailgate/liftgate area clear. Shown here is the normal tire position where a through bolt, with a lock, secures the wheel to the tailgate.

exterior mount that hinged on a bracket to the rear corner of the vehicle, similar to the mount on the Ford Bronco and others. These mounts secure the spare tire to the tailgate, but every time you need to get into the tailgate, you must unfasten the bracket and swing the tire aside. You then must swing it closed again and re-secure it to the tailgate before traveling on.

Since the tailgate becomes the "front door" to your "house" when you are living in your rig in the boondocks, this rapidly becomes a major annoyance.

The spare tire bracket built for the Blazer avoids this problem. In normal use, the tire is held against the tailgate, but when you get out in the backcountry the tire and bracket are swung 270 degrees around to the side of the vehicle, where they are locked in position and left until the trip is over. In the meantime, you can get in and out of the tailgate as freely as if no rear tire bracket existed.

Although I had seen many vehicles with the spare tires permanently mounted on the side, Jeeps mostly, I checked into the legality of this before proceeding. I was told that, "Although California law requires that any object fastened to the side of a vehicle may not extend more than six inches, this requirement is NOT enforced with respect to spare tires." This apparently is legalese for, "It's not right, but it's okay."

Planning a bracket of this sort presented a problem. It would be easy enough to make a bracket that would fit up against the tailgate and mount the tire to it. But when the bracket was swung completely around to the side of the machine, the tire would then be on the inside and the bracket on the outside, making it difficult to secure to the side of the vehicle.

This was solved by hinging the wheel mount itself around a vertical tube forming the end of the tire bracket. The bracket was then designed so that in one position it would lay flat against the tailgate and would swing around to lay flat against the side of the rig.

The way it works is this: The setup is unlocked from the tailgate and swung out anywhere from 90 to 180 degrees. Then the tire and wheel is swung 180 degrees around the end of the bracket. The bracket is then swung on around against the side of the truck where the tire is once again on the outside. The whole setup is secured to a fitting on the side of the truck with the same hardware that formerly attached it to the tailgate.

Figuring out the geometry of the bracket and its hinge points was a bit of a chore. Although this probably could have been worked out on a scale drawing, it was solved in this case by a cut and try method. I bent up a mockup of the bracket from ¼″ steel welding rod and swung it back and forth. I made the necessary changes until I located the hinge points and determined the lengths of the various parts of the bracket.

Once the dimensions were determined, building the bracket was fairly easy. Since the tire and wheel weigh about 80 pounds, I used 1″ OD chrome-moly aircraft tubing (4130 steel) in order to keep the weight down while supplying adequate support. (This stuff is also very easy to weld.)

The lower hinge is a piece of 1″ steel pipe, inserted through a hole torched in the top flange of the bumper and welded to the top and bottom flanges. Since the upper hinge had to be fastened to sheet metal on the side of the truck itself, a length of the 1″ tubing was split in half and welded to a flat piece of steel. This plate was fastened to the outside wall of the machine with a handful (about 30) of Pop rivets. The hinge fitting itself was cut and bent from flat

Spare tire is locked to the side of the truck and the clearance light has been plugged in to replace the normal one, which is now covered. When I am in the boonies, I often leave the wheel in this position for several days, giving unobstructed access to the rear of the truck. The rear locking bracket can just be seen on the tailgate. It has a welded-on nut into which the through bolt is screwed and which is locked by a hasp welded onto its head. When the liftgate is raised, the white, hinged bracket can be swung out to hang a lantern over the tailgate.

Hinged bracket keeps the tire to the outside of the mount when securing it to the truck's side. When the mount is pulled away from the tailgate, the wheel swings completely around so that it is once again on the outside. Then it can be locked in position on the side of the rig.

stock and welded up. It contains a short length of 1⅛ chrome-moly tubing which just slides over and bolts to the upper fixed part of the bracket. A bolt extending across the "U" of the hinge fitting fits inside a short tube welded into the end of the swinging bracket to form the actual hinge.

Another piece of the 1⅛″ tubing was sawed in half lengthwise and the two parts used to form a hinge for the wheel to rotate around the end of the bracket. This was welded to bits and pieces of small angle iron to form a secure connection between the hinge itself and the wheel, via four bolts and lug nuts.

The entire setup is held in either position by a long bolt that goes through one of the mounting holes in the wheel. It screws into nuts welded to two formed sheet metal mounts which are Pop-riveted to the tailgate and to the side of the truck. A modified strap hinge, welded to the head of the bolt, provides both a handle for turning the bolt and provision for locking it to discourage any attempt at unauthorized removal.

When positioned on the side, the mount covers up one of the clearance lights. I got a separate light and made it part of the mount. When the tire is mounted on the side, a banana plug on the end of a short wire from this light fits into a receptacle located on the side of the truck. The receptacle is wired into the normal clearance light. Thus, both are illuminated although the normal light is hidden.

Over the years this tire mount has been sketched or photographed by a number of people who have seen it and who have expressed an intention of building a similar one. When assured that I had no intention of producing it for sale myself, one gentleman took several photos of it for an Arizona friend who manufactures RV accessories. I have since seen some of these on the road. They have been modified for production purposes and are somewhat heavier in construction, but they employ the same basic concept.

Tucked-Away Winch Mount

A front-mounted electric winch is a most useful accessory on any 4 x 4. One minor problem with them is that they usually stick out a foot or more in front of the rig. In addition to being as obvious as a sore thumb, these things are heavy and all that weight so far forward of the front axle adds to the porpoising tendency inherent in a short wheelbase machine.

When planning the construction of the heavy-duty front bumper and the installation of the

Cutting a big hole in the then-new grill allowed the winch and bumper combination to be shoved back several inches so that it did not stick out in front of the grill. Two short pieces of 2 x 4 bolted to the bumper protect the roller fairlead.

winch, which were done simultaneously, I took a hard look at the front of the then brand-new truck and saw that there were several inches of open space behind the fancy grillwork. After much measuring and considering, I worked up enough courage to saw and snip a gaping hole in this brightwork in order to slip the winch back into it. Had the truck not been equipped with air conditioning, which required a separate radiator mounted in front of the normal one, I could have moved it back a couple of inches more, where it would have been quite flush with the grill.

In addition to improving the road-handling characteristics and the appearance, setting the winch back in the grill makes it more difficult to get at the mounting and diminishes somewhat the chances of its being stolen. The usual mount is completely exposed and easily accessible.

Flexible Trail Bike Support

Motorbike carriers, similar in appearance to a pair of flattened-out basketball hoops, are readily available for carrying a trail bike on the front or rear bumper of a car or truck. Once the bike wheels are set into the hoops, there remains the problem of keeping the bike from pitching sideways (fore and aft, in relation to the truck). Bungee cords are often used for this purpose but pose a problem in keeping the two machines separated from one another to avoid scratches and dents.

The first thing that comes to mind is to connect the two with a short rigid brace that holds them apart but still secures the bike from tilting sideways. However, since the bike is sprung, it must be able to move up and down in relation to the carrier even though its wheels are held motionless.

Two strap hinges from the hardware store solve the problem. Bolt one leg of each together and modify the two outer legs, one to fasten to a fitting on the bike and another on the carrying vehicle. This creates a stand-off that prevents the bike from tilting sideways either into or away from the transporting vehicle, while still allowing it to move up and down on its suspension.

One end of the flexible strut shown fastens to a small tab permanently mounted on the front

Trail bike's wheels are held in hoops mounted on the bumper. The machine must be held upright while still able to move up and down on its springs. This bracket does the job nicely, the double strap hinges allow the bike free vertical movement while holding it away from the tailgate. Wing nuts make for quick removal. The bolt heads are brazed to the hinges and the mounting brackets remain on the truck and bike.

fork of the bike. The tab has a small bolt brazed to it and is fitted with a lock washer and a wing nut. The other end of the double-hinged strut has a small bolt brazed to it and carries its own lock washer and wing nut. This end of the strut can be fastened to either of two small fittings, one attached to the tailgate and the other to the hood of the truck.

The bike is usually carried on the rear bumper for several reasons, but if the trailer is to be towed at the same time, it becomes neces-sary to carry the bike on the front bumper. In either case, a short bungee cord is used between the bike and the truck to take up slack and prevent rattling.

If the bike is carried on the front bumper, it covers up the front turn signals; so a supplemental pair are provided. They are quickly fastened to the bumper with wing nuts and connected with spade lugs into wires that have been tied into the normal turn signal wiring.

9

THE VERSATILE DRILL PRESS

The drill press is one of the most versatile power tools available and should probably be the first power tool (other than portable tools such as an electric drill) to be considered when setting up a metalworking shop. For a strictly woodworking shop, I'd rate it a close second after either the table saw or radial-arm saw.

The drill press drives an extremely wide range of accessories so that it does many other jobs besides drilling holes. The drill press can also be modified in the small shop; often it can do some simpler versions of jobs which otherwise require a much more expensive tool.

CAUTION

Statistics show that the drill press causes the greatest number of accidents of any power tool. Fortunately, they are usually not as severe as injuries suffered on power saws.

Far and away the greatest number of drill press injuries are caused by failing to fasten down the object to be drilled, especially on thin stock such as sheet metal. The drill catches in the work, usually on breakthrough, tears it out of the worker's hand and converts it into a slashing rotating weapon, often badly lacerating the hand that was holding it.

Take time to secure your work in a drill press vise or clamp it to the table. At the minimum, *hold it securely against a bolt through the table or other stop that will prevent movement in the direction of drill rotation.*

AUXILIARY TABLES

Like jigs for the table saw, there have been many auxiliary tables described for the drill press. Again, unless you have unlimited storage space for such items, it is easy to go overboard. I'll mention a few here; most of them can be simply made from plywood to fit your press. If you need more information other than working from the basic idea, the back issues of the popular woodworking magazines in the library have detailed descriptions.

Elevated Table for Sanding Drum

Sanding drums are a handy accessory for the drill press, enabling one to sand all sorts of inside curves that would otherwise require hand sanding. Since most sanding drums are larger in diameter than the usual hole in the center of a drill press table, one cannot sand to the bottom of a vertical surface without holding it above the table. But holding it by hand makes it difficult to maintain a sanded edge that is square to the top and bottom surfaces of the work.

One answer is to clamp a piece of wood or plywood on the table alongside the sanding drum, using it to raise the work so that its full thickness contacts the sanding surface. A slightly more elaborate system is to cut a hole in this piece so that it can be clamped to the table to surround the drum, thus providing more support for the work. Either of these setups provides better support for the work than hand holding. The disadvantage is that all the work is done on the bottom part of the sanding drum. If the material you are working with is relatively thin in relation to the length of the drum, the bottom portion of your sanding drum sleeve soon wears out while the top part remains untouched. Of course, you can remove the sleeve and invert it, but in addition to being a nuisance, this may still leave the center part of the sandpaper unused.

An elevated table solves these problems. Make a plywood tabletop of a size convenient for your drill press. Cut a hole in it just slightly

bigger than the diameter of your sanding drum. (Use a hole saw, a jig saw, a sabre saw, or even a coping saw; whatever you have available.)

Elevate the table by providing two sides high enough that almost the full length of your sanding drum can be submerged into the hole without striking the bottom. Fasten on a bottom piece of thin plywood. Make it the same size as the drill press table itself to provide easy C-clamping of the auxiliary table to the main table. If you don't have a scrap piece big enough for this, a couple of narrower strips fastened to the side pieces can provide clamping lugs.

If you do not already have a sanding drum, consider purchasing one that uses clamped on strips cut from standard sandpaper sheets, rather than the ones that require factory-made sleeves. These are expensive, and replacements are not always easy to find when you need them. See the appendix or ads in the woodworking magazine for sources.

Tilt Tables for Angle Drilling

Some drill presses have a table that is adjustable to any angle, from its normal 90 degrees to the spindle to a position parallel with the spindle. Others (like mine) have only the fixed 90-degree position. Without a tilt table you have a problem with angle drilling of holes. Even if your table tilts in one plane, you still have a problem when you need to drill a hole with a two-way tilt, as for a splayed leg in a coffee table or in a chair. To solve this problem, there have been any number of tilt tables designed, varying from extremely simple (a couple of squares of plywood joined by a piano hinge) to quite elaborate setups that are complete with built-in protractors.

Before you rush down to the library to see what others have done or try to design your own tilt table for your drill press, consider this next item. You may find, as I did, that it solves most of your angle drilling needs.

Simple Angle Drilling

In almost any navigation course, one of the first things the instructor tells his students is, "If you make a 1-degree error in your compass heading, you will be off course 1 mile for every 60 miles you travel. Make a 10-degree error and

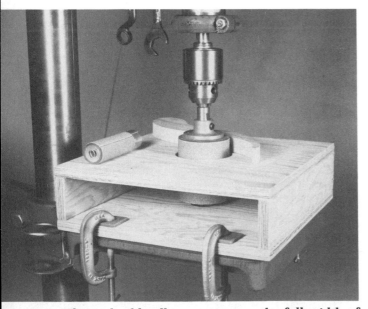

Elevated table allows you to use the full width of your sanding drum sleeve, even on thin material. Just raise or lower the spindle. This table has two working surfaces. Inverting it reveals a small hole for the little drum shown on the table.

you will be off course 10 miles for every 60 miles you travel!") It's an approximation, but it is roughly true. All too true, as most anyone who has done any navigating has eventually discovered.

Wanting a simple way to lay out angle drilling on my fixed table I recalled this old truism and decided to put it to use. First, I checked with a set of trig tables, and using the tangent function, I found that since plywood scraps come in thicknesses that are multiples of ⅛″, using ⅛″ rise for each degree desired needs a base about 7″ long. Actually the height versus base, per degree, builds slightly with the angle so that 7⅛″ is correct up to about 10 degrees, 7″ from there up to about 15 degrees and 6⅞″ at 20 degrees. After this the error rises more rapidly so that the rule rapidly loses veracity.

Within the limits of accuracy that you need for most projects, you can drill angles up to about 20 degrees quite simply just by providing a base of 7″ and heights that vary by ⅛″. (7⅛″ is 57 eighths, which ties in nicely with the rounded-off 1 mile in 60 statement.)

To use this setup, draw or scribe a line on your drill press table back 7″ from the front edge of the table. Using narrow strips of plywood, pile them up along this line to a depth of ⅛″ for every degree of tilt that you need. (A single strip of ¼″ plywood will thus give a 6 degree tilt.) Secure the plywood in position. Lay your work down so that it rests upon both

Two plywood risers, screwed to the table so that their front edge is 7″ from the front edge of the table itself, provide a 10-degree off-vertical angle. In this case, a scrap of plywood under the work bridges the distance so that the workpiece can be bored close to its edge. The two countersunk flathead machine screws in the riser blocks secure them to threaded holes in the press table.

the forward edge of the drill press table and the front edge of the plywood strip and proceed to drill your hole. If your job is too short to span this distance, use a scrap of plywood long enough to bridge the gap and secure the work to it.

Make six strips of plywood, one each of ⅛″, ¼″, ⅜″, ½″, ⅝″, and ¾″ thick plywood. Cut each 1½″ or so wide and a little longer than the width of your drill press table. When piled up in various combinations against a 7″ line on your table, these six strips allow you to drill angles from 1 to 21 degrees by 1-degree increments. If you don't have a scrap of ⅛″ material (not as common as the others) you can still drill any angle from 2 to 20 degrees, except for 19 degrees.

How do you secure the plywood risers so that they stay at the proper 7″ position while you do your drilling? There are several ways. If your work is short enough to fit between them, you can use a couple of C-clamps, one at each side of

Six strips of scrap plywood and a means of fastening them to your drill press table are all you need to drill angled holes from 1 degree to 21 degrees off vertical.

the table to secure the stack of risers. With longer work, you can drill and countersink two holes in each of the plywood strips and use flat head machine screws that screw into a pair of holes drilled and tapped into the table. Since I already had a pair of tapped holes in the rear of my table (normally used to secure a small milling table to the drill table) I use this method. But the distance of the holes from the front of the table requires that I use somewhat wider plywood strips than would otherwise be necessary in order to have their front edge at the 7″ position.

If you don't care to drill and tap into your table, just make your plywood strips a little longer, drill and countersink them a bit beyond the table's width, and use flat head machine screws, along with a pair of bent-up L-shaped clamps and wing nuts to secure the risers to the table.

With either of these methods, you will save time when using the jig if you provide two sets of machine screws of different lengths. That way you won't have to thread long screws way down through the table or twist wing nuts up an extra inch or so of threads when you are just clamping on a single ¼″ strip to drill a 2-degree angle. Flat head ¼″–20 machine screws work well. They are big enough that the heads don't pull into the wood and the threads are coarse enough that it doesn't take forever to tighten them down. Size 10–24 (³⁄₁₆″) screws work nearly as well if you happen to have some on hand.

Now you are all set up for simple angle drilling, but what do you do when a compound-angle job comes up, such as those splayed legs on a coffee table or footstool? Once again there is a simple approximation that works for most projects. Just remember that a compound angle works out to about ⁵⁄₇th of a simple angle. Thus, if you need to drill a hole that will secure a leg at a 10-degree angle when looked at from either the front or the side, just set up your jig to drill a 14-degree angle and line up your work at a 45-degree angle to your table instead of parallel to it.

Most workshoppers can come pretty close to the correct position just by eyeballing it. To get it exact so that all of your legs line up at the same angle and don't go every which way, you can work with a carpenter's square. Place your

board on the jig with a corner, instead of a side, up on the risers. Hold your square against the outside of the corner and check the reading on both legs of the square at the point where it crosses the edge of the risers. It doesn't matter what the readings are; just so they are equal. If one is a little more than the other just juggle the angle of the work around until they match. At the same time, of course, you'll have to keep the correct distance fore and aft so that your drill point intercepts the required spot (previously marked).

Suppose you want an angle of splay that doesn't readily come out at the ⁵⁄₇th ratio? Let's say you need a 12-degree compound angle. Divide 12 by 5 and multiply the result by 7. This just takes a few seconds on a pocket calculator, and the answer comes out to be 16.8. If you set your risers for 17 degrees (the ¾″, ⁵⁄₈″, ½″, and ¼″ strips will do it), the result will come out closer than you can read on all but a large and very accurate protractor.

It is a nuisance to have to stop and consider how many degrees of tilt each riser represents. Take the easy way out and mark each one with a marking pen. Mark the ⅛″ strip as "1 degree," the ¼″ strip as "2 degrees," and ending with the

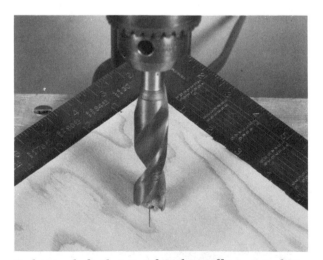

To bore a hole that is splayed equally in two directions, hold your work at 45 degrees to the table. This is easily done with a carpenter's square by aligning it so that equal measurements show on both scales at the riser block's front edge. Note that the 6″ mark on both outer scales line up on the riser block here.

¾" strip marked as "6 degrees." Then, all you need to do is add up the numbers on the strips until you get the total number of degrees you need and slip them into place.

Unequal compound angles require a double tilt setup; a second set of risers at 90 degrees to the first set, using an auxiliary table with a 7" base dimension under the new set of risers. This can get a little involved though. For most purposes, it is simpler to just juggle the angle away from 45 degrees on a scrap piece and drill a few test holes until you come up with a pair of angles that will do the job. Make a notation of the angle used as shown on your carpenter's square, such as "4¾" on the right leg and 3½" on the left leg." As you go around the base of a project drilling your holes, be sure to alternate these measurements from right to left on each corner. That way your two different parts of the compound angle each project in the desired plane.

Once you decide on a pair of reasonable measurements to use with the square, be sure to duplicate them exactly on each succeeding corner. The slightest variance changes the angles slightly and this is quite apparent when viewing the item from a position where two of the legs are lined up. Suppose you were shooting for an angle of 8 degrees in one plane. The job looks much better if all the angles are 7½ degrees rather than one at 8 degrees and another at 7¾ degrees.

V-BLOCKS

V-blocks are indispensable for accurately drilling through round stock. Machinist's V-blocks usually come in pairs along with matching clamps and are quite expensive. Fortunately, there are a number of substitutes. Simple wooden ones, preferably made from a dense hardwood, can be cut out on a power saw set at a 45-degree tilt. V-blocks can also be welded up from angle iron.

Another simple V-block substitute can be made from two short lengths of steel tubing, such as thin-wall conduit, welded or otherwise fastened together at both ends. Avoid galvanized pipe unless it is quite smooth, it's normal surface irregularities can decrease accuracy. Cutting the ends at a 45-degree angle

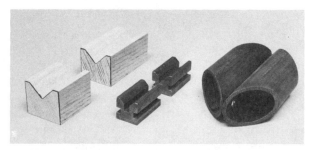

V-blocks hold round stock for drilling. Left, a pair shopmade from hardwood scraps have their edges inked to show up in the photo. Two steel machinist's V-blocks are shown in the center. These usually have a saddle clamp that hooks in the side slots. Two short lengths of plastic pipe, right, are fastened together to make a substitute V-block. Angling the ends enables them to be Pop-riveted together.

will allow the two pieces to be fastened together with Pop rivets or with shorter bolts than if the ends are cut square.

Whatever the type, a V-block of some sort is one of the first accessories you should consider for your drill press.

POINTER SIMPLIFIES CENTERING

Even though you have a V-block, all your problems in drilling round stock are not yet solved. The V-block must be very accurately centered below the spindle in order for the hole to accurately bisect the round stock and exit directly opposite to its entry point.

For accurate work, machinists use some pretty involved procedures to solve this problem. For the level of accuracy needed in most small shop work, here is an easy way to go about it. Cut off a few inches from a straight piece of ¼" gas welding rod. Put it in the drill chuck, rotate it, and using a file, cut just a slight chamfer on one end. Reverse it in the chuck, turn it at a moderately high speed, and with a file proceed to "turn" it down to a sharp concentric point.

Real machinists have some fancy ways of aligning a drill to the center of round stock. For most work this simple setup is accurate enough. The V-block, held in a drill press vise bolted to the table, has the center of its groove aligned to a pointer held in the chuck and lowered into the groove. The pointer (this one is ¼" welding rod) can have its end "turned" to a concentric point with a file while being rotated by the drill press.

With the rod still in the chuck, locate your V-block under it, and extend the quill until the point of the rod approaches the bottom of the V. Move the V-block until the center of the V is precisely under the center of the pointed rod. Rotate the rod to be sure that there is no bend in it. If the point does travel in a very slightly eccentric circle, locate the point of the V exactly below the center of this circle. On a machinist's V-block with a ¼" groove at the bottom (instead of a sharp point), reverse your rod in the chuck and extend it until you can locate the V-block so that the square tip of the ¼" rod will enter the groove.

Once the V-block is located, lock it in this position. A machinist's type can usually be held in the drill vise, as can some homemade ones. Others lend themselves to clamping directly to the table.

Remove the rod from your chuck and replace it with the desired drill. Put your work in the V-

block and as you lower the drill carefully rotate the work until the center punch mark for your hole is exactly under the tip of the drill and then proceed to drill your hole.

DRILLING ROUND SOLID STOCK WITHOUT A V-BLOCK

If you have to cross-drill a piece of solid round stock without a V-block, you can do it in your drill vise if you can spare a bit of the material for a drill bushing. Cut off about ½" of the material and then drill a concentric hole through it endwise. Use the same size drill for the pilot bushing and for cross-drilling the shaft. The accuracy of your cross bore will be determined by how accurately your pilot hole is centered in the pilot. If a lathe is available, accurately center the pilot in the chuck and use a center drill in the tailstock to get the hole started exactly concentric before finishing up the hole with the correct drill.

Place your stock to be drilled in the drill vise and put the pilot on top of it. Its center must be directly over the desired location of the hole. Tighten the vise and then position it so that the pilot hole is lined up with the drill bit and drill the hole.

This same method can be used to cross-drill pipe or tubing if you have a lathe available. You need a piece of solid scrap stock that you can turn to the exact outside diameter of the tubing and then drill a pilot hole in it.

A SIMPLE, PRACTICAL FENCE

A fence to go with the drill-press table is helpful any time you have to drill more than one hole in a straight line a given distance from one side of

Round stock can be accurately drilled without a V-block if you have a means of drilling a concentric pilot hole in a short piece of the same stock. This can be done easily if a lathe is available. Once the pilot is placed atop the work in the vise, the drill is automatically guided to the center.

the stock. It is also necessary for routing to a line, or when using a hollow chisel for mortising.

Except when mortising, which does provide a straight-edged hole, there is no need for lining up the fence precisely with the table as required with a saw. The fence can be mounted crossways on the table, fore and aft, or even slaunchways if that happens to provide more clearance for a long item.

Without any necessity for precise angular positioning, the fence can be pretty simple. The one shown is made of two pieces of ¾" stock glued and screwed together at a right angle. Either leg of this angle can be used as the fence itself, while the other leg serves as a lug for clamping it to the table. The lower fence (1⅞" high) is used when a line of holes is to be drilled with a small drill in thin material close to the edge. This allows the drill to penetrate the material before the top of the fence can interfere with the chuck jaws. The higher leg of the fence (2½") is for longer drills and thicker materials. The two fence heights also allow better positioning of a hole-spacing guide.

The fence is simply clamped to the table with

a pair of C-clamps and is located so that it is the required distance away from the point of the drill bit. Now any number of holes can be drilled in a straight line by simply moving the material along the fence between holes. A spring board helps ensure that the stock stays firmly against the fence at all times. This device can be borrowed from your table saw accessories or one can be specially made in just a few minutes to suit the smaller size of the drill press table.

HOLE SPACER

With a fence, you can now drill a row of holes in a straight line. The next thing you need is a means of spacing them evenly at a desired distance. The jig in the photo is easy to make and works well. It spaces holes in any material from thin sheet metal up to about 2" thick. Thicker stock requires a deeper fence.

The offset sole plate allows the jig to be tilted on the fence (as in the photo) so that its left edge lies flat against thin materials when the back leg of the clamp is touching the horizontal rear leg of the fence. This allows the jig to cover a wider range of stock thicknesses for a given fence height.

Make the spacer of from 16- to 20-gage galvanized steel. The sole plate is 2" wide and being 2½" long will space holes at up to 2½" from the edge of the work. The longer clamping leg is cut 1" wide and 6" long.

Bend the clamping leg 90 degrees to the sole plate. Make the front part of the clamp 2½" high, bend it back 90 degrees and then 90 degrees down, making the top just wide enough for a nice slip fit over the top of your fence. Cut off the back leg so it is ⅜" shorter than the front.

With a scrap of ¾" wood between the legs as a spacer, drill three pairs of ¼" holes spaced about ½" apart through both clamp legs. These allow the jig to be positioned at various heights on the fence as required by work thickness. Also, the holding screw can be placed close to the top of the fence to get a good grip on it. (The hole in the sole plate is to hang the jig for storage.)

The clamping screw is a ¼" by 1½" thumbscrew. Used with a wing nut it requires no

Hole-spacing jig is being used to drill a series of holes 1″ apart. A hole is drilled, the work is moved to the right until the edge of the jig exactly lines up with the edge of this hole, and the next hole is drilled. Holes are more accurately spaced by measuring edge to edge than by trying to estimate the position of their centers. Note that the drill press table fence is C-clamped to the table from the rear.

wrench or screwdriver to install or adjust. An ordinary nut threaded up all the way on the thumbscrew provides a flat bearing surface against the back leg of the clamp.

To drill a spaced row of holes, carefully measure and mark the desired distance between the first two holes at the right end of the line. Drill these holes and then lock the spindle with the drill still in the second hole to hold the work in position. Place the jig over the fence to the right of the drill; position it so that its left edge is down against the work and lines up exactly with the right edge of the first hole drilled, and clamp it securely in this position. Loosen the spindle lock and retract the drill. Move the work to the right until the right edge of the second hole lines up with the edge of the jig's sole plate. Hold the work in this position to drill the third hole. Continue this process until all the holes are drilled. In the photo, several more holes have been drilled after the first pair.

You may wonder why I use the edge of the holes as a guide rather than going from center to center. I get more accurately spaced holes if I set my jig to measure from edge to edge than I

do if I try to guess at where the exact center of each hole is located.

I also use the edge to edge method when measuring the distance between a pair of existing holes prior to laying out a new, matching workpiece. The larger the holes, the harder it is to guess at the exact location of their centers.

SUBSTITUTE SURFACE PLATE AND SURFACE GAGE

Your drill press table (which the manufacturer has machined quite flat, smooth, and perpendicular to the spindle travel) together with a 90-degree scribe held in the chuck (for safety, unplug the machine) makes a reasonably accurate substitute for a machinist's surface plate plus a surface gage or height gage. This gage marks locations that would otherwise be difficult to locate accurately, such as on a round item with varying diameters that prevent you from taking a direct measurement.

The point of the scribe can be located by measuring up from the table surface with an accurate scale. Use a scale set in a combination square and be sure that the end of the scale is flush with the end of the square. The measurement must be taken perpendicular to the table so as to avoid error. Locate the height of the scribe by using the spindle travel to set the point of the scribe at the desired exact dimension on the scale. Lock the spindle, recheck the measurement, check the table and the bottom of the work for cleanliness (no chips) and then place the work on the table in position to be scribed.

A 90-degree scribe can be made by carefully grinding a point on the short leg of a spare small Allen wrench. If you check the wrench with a square first to be sure that the angle is quite square and then do all your taper grinding on the top side (the inside) of the angle, you can also use the scribe as a height gage for odd-shaped items. Just set the item on the table and bring the bottom edge of the scribe down to where the tip just touches the top of the work.

The drill press angle vise at the rear can be set at any angle from flat up to 45 degrees. Crossed V-grooves in the front jaw allow small round work to be held accurately either horizontally or vertically. The vise at front has had its rough side machine sanded so that it can be clamped square to the table on its side. The rocking auxiliary jaw allows tapered work to be clamped. Another auxiliary jaw provides multiple V-grooves, both horizontal and vertical.

For measuring exact distances on an odd-shaped item like this cluster gear, use the drill press table as a surface plate and a scribe held in the chuck as a height gage. This scribe is a small Allen wrench ground to a point. Once accurately located, the spindle is locked, the work moved, and the distance between the table and the scriber measured with a machinist's scale. Distances from point to point on the item are determined by measuring both to the table and then subtracting one from the other.

Lock the spindle, check that the scribe still is just touching the work, remove the work, and measure from the table to the tip of the scriber for an accurate height.

VISES

Drill press vises come in several styles, sizes, and price ranges. Every drill press should have one of them as its first and most important accessory.

At a minimum, a drill press vise should have machined, well-fitting jaws that are square to a machined base surface. It should also have a pair of end slots that can be used with the table slots on your drill press to bolt the vise to the table.

Machined sides are also desirable so that the vise can be clamped to the table on its side and will be square to the table in that position. This, of course, runs the price up. If the cast sides of a vise are not too rough, and were cast with only a slight "draft" or taper, they can sometimes be squared up with the base by using a coarse metal-cutting sanding disc on a 12″ disc sander. Even though all the taper on the jaws cannot be sanded off, if the base and the lower part of the jaws can be sanded flat and square to the bottom, it will be an improvement.

Auxiliary jaws, such as a V-grooved jaw for

holding round stock both horizontally and vertically and a rocker jaw for securing tapered items, are also useful.

Angle vises, normally with a 90-degree range of adjustment, are a help when holes must be drilled at a specific angle to the face of the work. They can also come in handy for holding work pieces at various angles for filing, fitting, assembling, and other bench work. Formerly quite expensive, some much less expensive imports are now on the market. While some of them are pretty awful, others appear fairly well made and should be quite adequate for most small shop work.

CROSS SLIDE VISES AND MILLING TABLES

Cross slide vises and drill press milling tables both allow some milling to be done on a drill press with small end mills. Milling consists of such work as facing, slotting, and grooving. Examples include cutting flats or keyways on a shaft, cutting adjustment slots in flat stock, spot facing for a bolt hole in a casting, and things of that sort.

Milling with the drill press is necessarily limited to light work and fine cuts, since the drill press spindle is basically not designed to take side loads. Within limits, some quite adequate work can be done, especially in wood, plastic, aluminum, or brass. Some milling can be accomplished in mild steel, if light cuts are slowly and carefully made.

To do milling, some means must be provided to move the work under the rotating end mill. Cross slide vises and milling tables provide this capability.

A cross slide vise consists of a drill press vise mounted on slides which are movable in two directions at 90 degrees to each other by means of lead screws with a crank at the end of each one. They should have rotary scales, adjacent to the cranks, to accurately measure the distance

Drill press mill table, although limited to light work and fine cuts, can still do a lot of work in a shop that **cannot justify a vertical mill. Here an end mill cuts a slot in a short piece of aluminum angle.**

traveled in either direction. Cross slide vises, again mostly imports, are an inexpensive way to provide some limited milling capacity to a drill press.

Small milling tables made to bolt or clamp to a drill press table are another means of getting light milling capability from your drill press. Most allow more travel than a cross slide vise and are able to hold somewhat bigger work by means of T-slots in the table and various hold-downs. In addition, they usually provide a vise capable of being attached to the table for holding of small work.

A small rotary table, either attached to a mill table or directly to the drill press table, adds the ability to machine curved slots and other circular cuts. It also gives the ability to locate and space drilled holes in a circular pattern.

In years past, descriptions of attachments to a drill press to permit greater milling capability have been shown in some of the how-to-magazines. Basically, these consist of a steel clamp bolted around the drill press column to which are attached two arms. The end of each arm has a ball bearing attached, which rotates against the side of the drill chuck to take up the side load on the chuck and spindle during milling. The two arms are located so that the bearings arc about 120 degrees apart around the circumference of the chuck. They are locked in this position by means of either a fixed yoke bolted across the two arms or by a threaded crossbar that can be adjusted to the proper position.

Most of these articles did not provide much in the way of dimensions because they vary with the drill press. You can probably build one to fit your press just from the basic idea.

MORTISING ATTACHMENTS

A mortising attachment, although expensive, gives you the ability to make square holes in wood with your drill press. By making successive cuts along a fence, these can be elongated into either a through mortise or a blind mortise. Straight sided slots can be milled in wood as well.

If you haven't seen one, a mortising setup in-

Mortising attachment cuts square holes in wood. Normally used to cut an overlapping row to accept a tenon, they also cut out larger square or rectangular holes. A hollow square chisel is connected to the spindle by the yoke and is pushed into the wood as the spindle is pulled down; the auger, held in the drill chuck, is rotated and removes the material through the hollow chisel. A hold-down secured to the fence permits the chisel to be withdrawn without lifting the work.

cludes a square hollow chisel with an auger-type bit rotating inside. The bit removes most of the stock while the square chisel, with its bevels on the inside, cuts out the corners and forces the material into the rotating bit. Bit and chisel combinations often come in three sizes, 1/4", 3/8", and 1/2". The holes can be overlapped to cut larger squares or rectangles.

In addition to the hollow chisels and their bits, a mortising setup requires an attachment that fastens to the drill press quill to keep the hollow chisel from turning while permitting it to be raised and lowered along with the bit which spins inside. A hold-down is also required to prevent the work from lifting off the table when the quill is retracted. (The hollow chisel is a force fit in the work.)

If you purchase a mortising attachment, be sure to get the cone-shaped rotary stone or stones needed to resharpen the inside bevels on the chisels. Cutting out all four corners of a square hole with a single stroke requires that the chisels be kept quite sharp.

DOWEL AND PLUG CUTTERS

These are generally available in two types. One of them is strictly a plug cutter, for cutting short plugs from the face of the stock. These are then glued into countersunk holes to cover a flat head wood screw. The second type works as a plug cutter or lengthwise in the stock to cut short dowels, usually up to about 2″ long. While dowels and plugs are commonly available, one of these cutters provides the ability to make the items out of scrap wood from the project itself. This makes for more exact matching of the finish on the face of the plugs or on the ends of exposed dowels.

Dowel/plug cutters are commonly available in 1/16″ increments from 1/4″ to 3/8″ and in 1/8″ increments to 5/8″.

TABLE-MOUNTED AUXILIARY CHUCKS

For end-drilling of round stock on a drill press, a table-mounted auxiliary chuck is a great help. For small work it can be an extra drill chuck, preferably of 1/2″ capacity, or one borrowed from a portable drill for the purpose. For larger work, a small lathe chuck is sometimes useful if you happen to have one without a lathe attached to it. (If you have the lathe, work of this sort is more easily accomplished in it.)

One easy way to fasten a drill chuck to the drill table is to bolt it to a piece of steel bar. I keep an 11″ length of 1/4″ x 1″ bar hanging near the drill press. This bar has a 1/2″ hole drilled in

A spare drill chuck or one borrowed from a portable drill can be bolted to a piece of bar stock and clamped to the table, centered under the drill press chuck. This chuck holds a center drill to start a concentric hole in a piece of 1/4″ welding rod. The hole will be finished with a twist drill. Overlapping washers keep chips from falling into the chuck or its exterior gear teeth.

its center and has an extra 1/2″ chuck more or less permanently attached to it by means of a short 1/2″–20 bolt. In use, the bolt head drops into the larger center hole in the drill press table, and the bar is clamped to the table with a couple of C-clamps.

To center this chuck below the active one, a straight piece of small shafting, drill rod, or 1/4″ gas welding rod is secured with one end clamped in each chuck and with the quill extended. The table is then brought up against the bar, secured, and the bar is clamped in position. Loosen the jaws of the lower chuck slightly and then retract the quill until the shaft is clear of the lower chuck. Rotate the upper chuck and the shaft to confirm that the shaft is still concentric and that the lower chuck is exactly centered to it. Make any necessary adjustments.

When you drill a hole in the end of a piece of stock, you normally center-punch the location of the desired hole, secure the item in a vise with the punch mark centered below the drill, and proceed. Using your second chuck you have a better way that gets around the difficulty of exactly centering your punch mark and thus slightly off-centering your resulting hole.

With this setup, you will convince your drill press that it is a metal lathe and do the job as it would be done there, rotating the stock and drilling the hole with a drill held in the stationary chuck, corresponding to the tailstock chuck in a lathe.

Suppose that you have a small brass cannon that you have turned or filed to shape in the drill press chuck and need to drill its bore hole. Or perhaps you have a piece of ½″ shaft that has to have a concentric ⅜″ hole drilled in its end. Secure your stock in the upper chuck and place a machinist's center drill in the lower chuck. (More on center drills in the next section.) Turn on the drill press and bring the stock down against the center drill. Once you have a cen-

tered hole started, retract the quill, replace the center drill with a pilot drill and drill a pilot hole to the proper depth. Replace the pilot drill with the final drill and redrill the hole to size. Remove the work from the chuck and you should see that you have a hole much more exactly centered than you could ever hope to do with a center punch mark.

When using a second chuck inverted on the table in this manner, put a large-diameter washer with a ½″ center hole over the drill and atop the chuck to keep chips from dropping into the bottom chuck. With drills smaller than ½″, a second small washer with an appropriately sized hole can be put on the drill and dropped onto the larger washer. There's no point in having to clean out the chuck more frequently than absolutely necessary.

If you do not have an extra drill chuck available, there are other ways of end-drilling round stock, although it is difficult to reach the same degree of concentricity. Take a look at your drill press vise. Many of them have a vertical V-groove cut in the center of one of the jaws. This in itself will hold short stock for end-drilling. For a longer piece, check to see if the base of the vise has a slot large enough to pass your round stock. This, together with a center hole in the table, provides one solution.

Center-punch the end of the stock as accurately as possible. (You can always "move" a mark in one direction or another by restriking with the punch held at an angle toward the desired direction.) Pass the stock through the hole in the drill press table and secure it vertically in the V in the drill vise jaw, in an auxiliary V-jaw, or in a small V-block mounted on end in the vise. Center the work below the chuck, secure the vise to the table, and you are ready to drill the end of any piece of stock up to a length that reaches to the base of the press.

If your drill vise does not have a slot in the base that is big enough to pass your stock, or if your drill table does not have a center hole, you can move the table to one side and mount long work vertically off one edge of the table. One way to do this is to find a suitable small block of wood, drill it to the size of the shaft or dowel to be end drilled, and then saw it in two right across the hole. Put these pieces around the stock and clamp them onto it with a wooden-jawed cabinetmaker's clamp laid on its side.

This hole was drilled with a stationary ³⁄₁₆″ twist drill in the lower chuck. Almost perfectly centered, it checks out with a dial caliper to be no more than .002″ off center.

This clamp is, in turn, secured to the table with a couple of C-clamps.

When using this method of holding the work, you do not have a V-groove aligned square to the table to automatically line up the work parallel to the spindle of the drill press. Your drilled block, if squarely drilled, together with the square jaws of the cabinetmaker's clamp, should hold it pretty accurately in one plane, but you'll have to check and set the other one.

One way to do this is to check the column for plumbness with a good level and then align the stock with it by holding the level against the stock in the same plane. It does not matter if the drill press column is exactly plumb. Just note the exact setting of the bubble and align the work to reproduce it. If you have any doubt about the squareness of the wooden clamp and your clamp blocks, check the work against the column in this plane too. You can adjust an error here by shimming the top and bottom of the half-blocks in the wooden clamp if necessary.

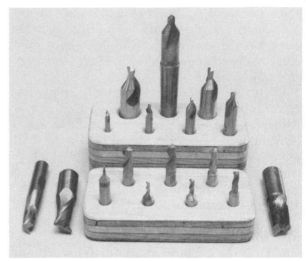

Center drills at rear are designed for a lathe, but also work on a drill press. Except for the long one with the Morse taper shank, they are all double ended which extends their useful life. In front is a selection of end mills with diameters ranging from 1/16" to 1/2". Since they cut sideways they are kept quite short to avoid bending.

CENTER DRILLS AND END MILLS

Center drills, more formally known as "Combined Drills and Countersinks," are normally used with a metal lathe to provide accurately centered holes on the ends of a shaft or other round stock. The centers are for turning the work around the head and tailstock centers. Center drills have a heavy cross section that tapers rapidly down (60-degree included angle) in the countersink section to a very short length of a smaller diameter drill. This makes them very useful accessories for a drill press. When held in its chuck, they will start a hole in an item not center-punched without wandering. They are of great help to get holes started straight and in the desired spot, especially on a curved or slightly inclined surface.

Get one of them in the largest diameter that fits your chuck, as well as one or more smaller ones for starting small holes. They are normally available in body diameters of from 1/8" to 1/2" by 16ths, plus 5/8" and 3/4", and with end drill diameters of from 3/32" to 5/16". An even smaller "Missile & Aircraft Series" has the same mini-

mum 1/8" body diameters but with end drill diameters as small as .020".

Center drills are relatively inexpensive and can be found along with end mills at a machine tool supply house or by mail order from any of a number of sources.

One or more machinist's end mills are very useful as a drill press accessory. The name is somewhat misleading since, in addition to cutting on the end, they will also cut sideways. End mills can make a flat spot (spot facing) on a curved or angular surface to simplify starting a normal drill and to provide a flat bearing surface for a bolt head or nut square to the hole itself. They can also counterbore the hole to countersink a bolt head. When the stock is moved sideways, they cut a groove (keyway) or a slot; this is similar to the action of a router bit in wood.

Small slots and keyways can even be cut without having a milling table or a cross slide vise by means of a simple jig, especially in softer materials. To cut a slot in a piece of bar stock, for example, clamp a pair of guides to the drill press table so that the stock will just slide

This ³⁄₁₆″ slot, not yet deburred, was milled in the drill press with only the cutter shown, plus two angle-iron guides clamped to the table. The work was pushed by hand between the guides and under the rotating end mill. Several passes were made, lowering the spindle slightly for each one.

between them. I used a couple of pieces of small angle iron to make the slot shown in the photo.

To diminish chattering, position these guides so that they are a very close fit to the sides of the stock and then put a little oil between the stock and the guides so that you can push it smoothly along. Mark your stock for the length of the slot, or groove, desired. Place the stock in position and hold it with one hand while carefully lowering the rotating end mill into it. Do not try to take too deep a bite in a single pass. I made about four or five passes to mill a slot completely through a piece of ⅛″ aluminum with a ³⁄₁₆″ end mill. On each pass, push the material along at a speed that cuts nicely without building up too much chatter. (You'll probably always get some chatter in any "Mickey Mouse" milling operation such as this.)

Milling a slot in this manner may be a little slow compared to the use of a vertical milling machine. But it sure is a lot faster and does a better job than drilling a bunch of holes and then trying to file the edges smooth to an accurate dimension.

End mills are useful accessories to most any drill press. One for spot facing should be of the maximum size that your chuck will hold; plus you need a few of the smaller ones. A chart of recommended end mill rpm's gives:

- For mild steel, 750 rpm with a ½″ end mill increasing speed (with decreasing size), to 3000 for a ⅛″ end mill.
- For brass, 1500 to 6000 rpm for the same sizes.
- For aluminum, plastic, or wood 4200 to 15000 rpm.

Some of these speeds will be well beyond the capacity of your drill press. Just accept the nearest you have. My drill press maximum is about 5700, for instance, but works out quite nicely in aluminum, even with a small end mill. My metal lathe has a top rpm of only *700* but still does a fair job with its milling attachment. Since the lathe has a heavier spindle and no extending quill which builds in a certain amount of "slop," it does the job with less chatter than the drill press. Of course the feed has to be pretty slow. Recommended speeds are based on maximum productivity among other things, which in the small shop is a minor consideration when compared to doing the job slowly or not at all.

WIDE RANGE OF AVAILABLE BITS

The range of bits available for a drill press is almost endless. Many of the special bits are discussed in other appropriate places in this book, but here is a quick listing for some of them.

Twist drills are the most common. Designed for cutting steel, they are also used for cutting nonferrous metals, wood, and plastic. They are not the best answer for wood and should be sharpened differently for plastic.

Twist drills are available either individually or in sets from ¹⁄₁₆″ to ½″ by 64ths. Number drills (1–80) and letter drills (A-Z) add 105 more choices in the range from less than ¹⁄₆₄″ up to ½″, although a few of them vary only a few ten-thousands from the nearest fractional drill. There should be 106 different ones, but for some reason the "E" drill is exactly the same size as a ¼″ drill. Fractional size twist drills also come in larger diameters, either with straight shanks, cut-down shanks to fit a ½″ chuck, or with a Morse taper shank.

Twist drills can also be found in metric diameters. Twist drills 12″ long, often referred to as *aircraft bits*, are available in some of the smaller fractional sizes. *Electrician's bits* are long twist drills for drilling though wood; they come in the ⅜″ to ⅝″ range and are 16″ to 18″ long. They are often used for drilling wiring holes in large lamp bases.

For woodwork, the *brad point bit* makes a cleaner cut, especially on breakthrough, and gives a more nearly flat bottom in blind holes. They are readily available from ⅛″ to ½″ by 16ths continuing to 1″ by 8ths.

Spade bits, available by 16ths from ¼″ to 1″ and then by 8ths to 1½″, are fast cutting. They make a clean hole (except on breakthrough—use a backup block) and do a good job of drilling on an angle. *Adjustable expansion bits* are available but are somewhat slow and require more power than most other large bits. For large holes, *Forstner pattern bits* do an excellent job of cutting clean, large, flat-bottomed holes. But they are quite expensive, going for as much as $50 in a 3″ size.

Hole saws for cutting relatively thin materials are available in sizes from ¾″ up to about 4″ in inexpensive carbon steel.

More expensive high-speed steel *hole saws*, available from 9⁄16″ to 6″ in size, also cut nonferrous metals and mild steel. For even harder materials, such as hardened steel, cast iron, tile, and fiberglass, *carbide-tipped hole saws* are available in a limited range of sizes and at considerably higher cost.

Different size hole saws often have different size pilot drills in their mandrels; the smaller ones have a 3⁄16″ drill while the medium sizes use a ¼″ drill. This can cause problems in some cases, as when making cutouts for wheels and you want to use a smaller hole saw to make a shallow cut indicating a tire rim. Or suppose you want to use a ¼″ axle in a small wheel cut with a saw that normally has a 3⁄16″ pilot.

Solve this problem by making a pilot from a short piece of ¼″ shaft (such as welding rod) with one end turned down to 3⁄16″. Fasten it in the smaller holesaw in place of the 3⁄16″ pilot drill. Round off the end of the ¼″ section so that it will smoothly enter a previously drilled ¼″ hole in your wheel stock. If no lathe is available, the ¼″ shaft can be secured in the drill chuck and a portion of it "turned" to 3⁄16″ with a sharp coarse file.

This setup works better and provides more concentric wheels, especially in woods of uneven density, than if the smaller pilot drill is

From left, these drills and cutters include a carbide-tipped masonry bit, a spur-tip wood bit, a twist drill, a sheet-metal drill, a hole saw, an adjustable fly-cutter, a multisize Unibit above a ¼″ paper drill, and a wood-cutting spade bit. At bottom is a long aircraft-type twist drill.

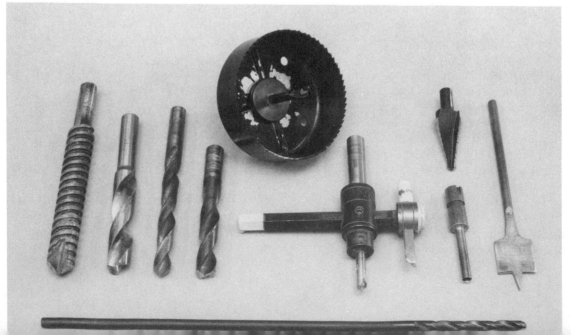

used with the small saw and later re-drilled to ¼".

Fly cutters can also cut mild steel with the high-speed steel bit usually provided. Hardened steel and other harder or more abrasive materials can also be cut by substituting a carbide-tipped lathe tool.

Painting the bit holder and the end of its rotating arm a high visibility yellow is a good safety precaution against accidentally letting your hand intrude into the circle traveled by the "flying" arm and cutter.

Unibits cut smooth holes in sheet steel, each bit being capable of cutting several different fractional sized holes.

Paper drills, available from a printer's supply, cut clean holes in paper, cardboard, rubber, and gasket material. The most common size is ¼" for drilling holes in binder paper. Most any workshop can put one of these to good use occasionally.

CUTTING OIL RETAINER

A washer, with a hole somewhat larger than the one to be drilled, makes a good well for holding oil when drilling flat stock on your drill press. Just place it on the work, surrounding your center punch mark, and fill it with a squirt or two from your oil can.

A large washer, laid on the work and centered around the drill bit, provides a well to hold oil.

SANDING

In addition to sanding with a sanding drum and an elevated table, as mentioned earlier in this chapter, the drill press also does other forms of power sanding. There are a number of contour sanders for free-form sanding with the drill press. These include many sizes and types of flap-wheel sanders, varying from 1" or so in diameter up to 6" or more. Air-inflated sanding drums are also available for free-form sanding of contoured parts.

GRINDING

The drill press can be used for different forms of grinding. Small grinding wheels mounted in the chuck grind various small items held against them to be shaped as required.

By using a small cup wheel (4" in diameter is usually considered the maximum), you can do some makeshift surface grinding jobs in the drill press. Depending on the size and shape of the job, you may be able to just slide it back and forth on the table under the wheel (oil the table and the bottom of the work), or you may be able to hold the work in your drill press vise and slide the vise on the table, again with oil. If you have a cross slide vise or a small milling table, either of these does a better job of holding the work and moving it under the wheel.

In any case, lock the spindle in a position where the wheel just touches the high points on the work and lower it a smidgen, bit by bit, as the work progresses. In any grinding operation, on the drill press or elsewhere, *be sure to wear adequate eye protection*.

WIRE BRUSHES AND BUFFING WHEELS

Both of these items can be used quite satisfactorily in the drill press; they can clean up rusted or corroded tools and buff finished work to a high polish. Rotary wire brushes come in several diameters (4" or 6" are probably the most practical) and in fine and coarse grades.

Drill press attachments also sand, grind, wire-brush, and buff. The flap-wheel sander shown in the chuck is great for smoothing odd shapes. Other smaller flap wheels are on the table along with an assortment of small grinding wheels, wire brushes, and cloth buffing wheels.

For rust removal, the coarsest available is usually best. Buffing wheels are used with various cutting and polishing compounds that come in stick form and are held against the wheel to "load" it before the wheel is used on the work to be polished.

Again, *be sure to wear eye protection*; the wires on a wire brush often break individually and are thrown off by centrifugal force like small steel needles. Buffing wheels throw off fine particles of the polishing compound.

TAPPING ATTACHMENTS

After drilling a piece of work that is to have threads tapped into it, it is often a problem to get the tap started squarely in the hole. An inexpensive piloted spindle tap wrench, made to be used in either the drill press or a lathe, helps get the job done right. The tool consists of a tap wrench with a deep centered hole in its upper end and a close fitting shaft that slides in the hole.

After the hole has been drilled in the work, and without disturbing the position of the work, the drill is removed from the chuck. The tap, tap wrench, and pilot are inserted in its place. The spindle is lowered until the tap will enter the work with the pilot positioned full depth into the tap wrench. Lock the spindle and the pilot holds the tap wrench quite square to the work. Then you turn the tap wrench han-

This tapping guide uses the drill press to get the tap started square with the work, which otherwise is quite difficult. Once the hole is centered under the spindle, the tap wrench pilot is secured in the chuck. The tap wrench turns freely and slides vertically on the pilot but remains vertical and centered over the hole. The drill's electrical plug emphasizes that this is not a powered operation.

dle to thread the tap into the stock. This is not a powered operation; the drill press only holds the tap squarely at right angles to the work to avoid an angled set of threads, an all too common occurrence when hand tapping.

If you do a great deal of tapping, you might want to investigate the power-tapping attachments that are available for a drill press. There is more than one brand available, and they are found at an industrial tool supply house or in a machine tool supply catalog. Prices begin at about $250 and up. Mostly up.

BACKUP BLOCK

We all know that using a backup block of some sort helps to get a cleaner hole with less "breakout" when drilling holes in wood, whether we use a twist drill, spade bit, or brad point bit. But many people are not aware that a hardwood backup block can prevent grabbing on breakthrough and reduce deburring when working with metal.

In addition to having a small board handy to the drill press table for backing up flat stock, you should keep a few small scraps of hardwood available in sizes that can be placed in the drill vise under any piece of material clamped in it. Try this in your drill vise and compare the results without a backup. The improvement is well worth the small effort involved.

To spotface this shaft exactly ³/₁₆″ deep, the spindle was lowered until the end mill just touched the work and then locked. A ³/₁₆″ drill bit was laid on the depth stop (upper right) and the stop nuts were run down against it and locked. Now the spindle can be unlocked and the bit removed. The spindle will stop at a depth of exactly ³/₁₆″ in the work.

PRECISE DEPTH SETTING

When setting the depth to be drilled on most jobs, it is quite adequate to place the work on the drill press table and extend the quill until the tip of the bit is alongside the work at the desired depth, either "eyeballed" or measured with a rule. The spindle is locked. Then the depth-setting nuts are run down until they meet the stop and are locked together.

Sometimes you need a more accurate depth setting than this provides. Suppose that you are about to mill a keyway in a shaft. You want the depth to be exactly ³/₃₂″. Lock your end mill in the chuck and bring down the spindle until the end mill just touches the shaft, which is se-

cured in a pair of V-blocks or in the drill press vise. Lock the spindle and then hold the shank of a ³/₃₂″ drill atop the stop block. Run down the stop nuts until they touch the drill shank. Lock the stop nuts, remove the drill, unlock the quill, and cut your keyway to exact depth.

This method works with small pieces of wood, such as a scrap of ¼″ or ½″ plywood, or with a bit of metal bar stock of the required thickness.

OFF-TABLE DRILLING

It is sometimes difficult to drill a hole in the side of a large tin can, a piece of thin pipe such

Items that are difficult to drill on the table, such as this large thin ring which might distort under pressure, can be easily handled off to one side by using a clamped-on wood block. It takes only a few seconds to rough shape the block with a rasp to fit the circle.

as stovepipe, the edge of a hoop, or a similar item without deforming it. Move the drill press table to one side and clamp a wooden strip to it, of adequate size and length to support the top surface of the work under the drill, but off the table and to one side. For large work a 2 x 4 may be needed; a smaller stick will do for smaller items. The top of this backup piece can be quickly rounded with a wood rasp to fit the inside curve of the work.

HAND CARVING

If you wish to add some "hand carved" touches to a wooden bowl or other project, lower the drill press table and swing it to one side. Secure the work to it and fasten a flexible shaft into the drill chuck. Use ¼" shank burrs of appropriate shapes in the flexible shaft chuck and carve your design into the work free-hand.

DEPTH STOP FIX

The pair of knurled round nuts for adjusting the depth stop on many drill presses often vibrate loose and change the depth setting. Try using either a rubber washer (my preference) or a lock washer between the two nuts and you should find that the adjustment then holds with finger tightening. Also, it is still easily adjustable.

Rubber washer (this one is fabric reenforced) between the two adjusting nuts on the depth stop keeps them from vibrating loose and changing the depth setting.

OTHER JOBS

If used with common sense and care not to overload the spindle with heavy pressures, the drill press will substitute for several other tools.

For gluing up light work, unplug the cord, place the work to be clamped on the table, and put a suitably sized scrap block on top of the

With a punch in its chuck, the drill press becomes a light-duty arbor press to drive a short shaft out of a bearing. Socket wrenches, which come in many diameters, are aids for supporting press work.

work to accept and distribute the pressure. Provide clamping pressure by pulling down the chuck against the block. Maintain it either with the spindle lock, or by hanging an appropriate weight from the feed handle.

The drill press also works as a light-duty arbor press to press small bearings in or out of their housings or on or off a shaft. Also, as previously noted, most drill tables provide a fairly accurate substitute for an expensive machinist's surface plate.

TWO-SPEED MOTOR

If you have a small drill press, you know that no matter how many speeds it has, there are seldom enough, especially at the low-speed end for drilling larger holes.

If you replace your present motor with a two-speed ⅓-hp motor from a discarded washing machine however, you will double the number of available speeds. Normally, other parts of a washing machine wear out long before the motor fails, and the motor from a discarded machine may have many more years of useful life.

These motors can sometimes be obtained from an appliance repair shop, a flea market, a second hand store, or from your own discarded washer. The placard on the motor tells if it is a two-speed motor, showing, "RPM 1140/1725" instead of the "1725" on a single-speed motor.

Figuring out which connections go where may be simple, mine were marked H, L, and C (High, Low, and Common) or may be more difficult if they are not marked. In this latter case, a friendly appliance repairman may be able to give you the word on it.

Once you get it doped out, wire it to a double throw, center off toggle switch in place of the original single throw switch, placard it, and away you go. (Common practice is to wire it so that the up position of the switch handle provides the high speed and the down position gives the low speed: "high is high and low is low".)

Two-speed motors are also very useful with wood or metal lathes and for many other power tools. But the drill press is normally the first candidate.

SIMPLE JACKSHAFT ADDS MORE SPEEDS

It is a common tendency, especially when drilling steel, to operate a drill press at too high a speed. Try using slower speeds with the larger drills and see if you don't find an improvement in your results. Often it also takes less time to do the job because the hole goes right on through the first time. At a slower speed, you do not have to stop and resharpen the drill because you do not burn off the cutting edge.

Unfortunately, for the larger drills, most drill

presses do not have low enough speeds available, even with the two-speed motor previously mentioned. This is particularly true when drilling holes larger than ½″ with Silver & Deming drills with a cut-down shank.

Does your drill press have a jackshaft with a third four-step pulley between the motor and the spindle pulleys? (Many of the new ones, especially the imports, do.) If not, you may be able to add one, using the column as a mount, and increase the number of speeds available, especially the lower ones.

In theory, adding the extra pulley and the second belt increases the available speeds from four to twelve. In practice, however, some of the different combinations are almost duplicates of others, and a couple of the highest speeds may be so high geared that your motor does not have the power even to turn the spindle, let alone do any useful work. With my conversion, eight useful speeds evolved (sixteen with the two-speed motor) and most of the added speeds were in the desirable lower range.

The first step in adding this conversion to your drill press is to check the top of the column to see if it is open. Look down it to be sure there are no bolts or other protrusions blocking the hollow inside part, at least for the first few inches from the top. You may find a heavy burr on the inside of the top of the column where the manufacturer cut it off with a king-sized version of a plumber's pipe cutter. In this case, you must file off the burr with a large half-round file until the inside of the column is straight and smooth.

Before you do this or any other work, be sure you can get a third pulley to match the original two. This is not always easy. In this case, the drill press manufacturer did not even sell the pulley as a spare part. In checking with a nearby industrial gear and bearing supply house, I found they carried one identical to the motor pulley, except that it had a ¾″ bore instead of a ½″ bore. However, they also carried needle bearings that were a press fit into the pulley and that would rotate freely on a ½″ shaft. Since the third pulley is strictly an idler, this was even better than if I had found an exact duplicate of the motor pulley, which would have required boring out for the installation of needle bearings or a bronze bushing.

I bought the pulley and two needle bearings

(they were short and the pulley has a fairly long shaft hole). These parts along with two new V-belts were the only items I bought for the project. Hold off on getting the belts until you have the jackshaft conversion in place and can get a better fix on the exact lengths needed.

Once you have found the necessary pulley, you can go to work. Clean out the inside of the column as mentioned above and then make a plug to fit it. The one shown fits a column that has a 2½″ inside diameter. It was glued up of plywood circles cut with a hole saw and then turned in a wood lathe to a snug, but easy turning fit inside the column. It is 5″ long, although a slightly shorter one would probably work. Note that the larger diameter of the uppermost plywood segment allows it to rest on the top of the column and hold the plug in position.

A ½″ hole for the jackshaft was drilled vertically in the plug, ⅝″ off center. When the plug is turned in the column, this allows the jackshaft, and its idler pulley, to move fore and aft so that adjustment of the motor mount can tension both belts, not just one. For a larger column, you can increase the offset to ¾″ or so. The jackshaft itself is prevented from turning in the plug by a screw coming in from the side. It bears against a flat spot on the shaft.

The twin-horn yoke on the top of the plug was

Get extra speeds on your drill press with this setup. The plywood plug fits inside the press's support column. The extra step pulley here is an idler and spins on the ½″ shaft. The "horns" on the plug allow it to be twisted to tighten or loosen the belts by moving the off-center idler shaft.

added to provide handles for easy turning of the plug to release tension on either belt when changing belt positions on the pulleys.

Put a washer on the shaft and slip on the idler pulley, its needle bearings or bronze bushing having first been pressed into place. Note that the thickness of the top segment of the plug, the yoke, and the washer must bring the pulley up to a point where it lines up with the spindle and motor pulleys (within their adjustable range).

Either the motor or the spindle pulley must be reversed from its previous orientation so that their line up of large to small grooves are now the same, with the jack shaft pulley being inverted in relation to them.

Measure for the two new belts. Their lengths should be such that when they are tightened the position of the jackshaft should be off to one side of the column at roughly a right angle to a line between the motor and spindle pulleys. This allows the maximum range of adjustment for tightening the belts.

Get the belts, install them, and give the machine a try. You should find that you have available a much lower range of speeds than before, as well as some higher ones.

Due to the configuration of the two belts and the jackshaft, some of the former mid-range speeds will be missing. Since these are some-

times needed, you can make a horseshoe-shaped collar out of a scrap of ¾" plywood that can be slipped under the idler pulley. This raises it the approximate equivalent of one groove (to get it clear of the belt) and allows you to use a single long belt direct from the motor to the spindle.

Due to the similar lineup of the motor and spindle pulleys, only one speed (1 to 1) is normally available. In order to get two speeds in this mid-range, I use an offset belt; from groove #2 on the motor pulley to groove #3 on the spindle, or vice versa. While this is somewhat unorthodox, the mid-range speeds do not normally impose a heavy load, the belt does not have to be highly tightened, and it works quite well. The two extra speeds (four with the two-speed motor) fill in the "flat spot" quite nicely.

This is an easily built attachment that will add a great deal of versatility to any drill press not factory equipped with a jackshaft. It can be made, if necessary, with no other power tools than the drill press itself.

If no lathe is available, the plywood circles can be cut with a hole saw of the nearest larger size and mounted between two nuts in a makeshift arbor (a headless bolt for instance). This assembly is placed in the drill chuck and "turned" to a slip fit in the column bore with a

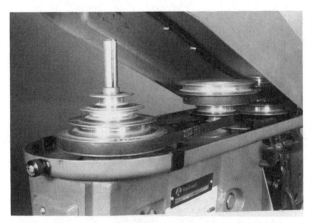

Idler in position. The plug and jackshaft have been dropped into the hollow drill press support column. When changing speeds, the eccentric movement of the jackshaft enables the belt between the jackshaft and spindle to be loosened. The original hinged motor mount tightens to tension both belts. The

motor pulley was inverted from its original position. To regain "lost" intermediate speeds, a single belt is used. A U-shaped plywood collar raises the idler pulley and the single long belt is offset to run from grooves 3 to 2, or 2 to 3, to recover two intermediate speeds. (You get four with the 2-speed motor.)

wood rasp and/or coarse sandpaper. Put the plywood circles on a rod of the same diameter as the pilot hole left by the hole saw when gluing them, in order to keep them aligned. After gluing, a bit of final sanding should give the proper fit to the column.

WOOD TURNING

In Chapter 7 I discussed how small metal turnings could be made with a drill press. You can also make small-to medium-sized wood turnings with it if no wood lathe is available.

All sorts of small items can be turned from wooden dowels, up to the maximum diameter that the drill chuck will handle, usually ½″. Use the same type of angle-iron rest and lathe tools made from old files described in Chapter 2. Some very small work can be shaped without

conventional tools by means of rasps, coarse files, or coarse-to medium sandpaper.

Larger stock can be turned with a jury-rigged version of a regular wood lathe's screw center. Depending on the size of your work, use a medium-length, large-diameter woodscrew (#10, #12, or #14) or a short lag screw. Cut the head off to a length so that when it is mounted in the drill chuck, the threads will extend just slightly into the chuck. The remainder of the unthreaded shank is in the chuck. Drill the end of the stock with a pilot hole that can be turned onto the screw reasonably easily. Place a washer on the screw so that it rides against the chuck jaws to provide a bearing surface for the end of the work. Support the tail end of the work on a makeshift tailstock secured in the vise as described for metal-turning use. Start with a low speed to avoid vibration until the work is turned concentric.

Wood turning can be done with the stock held by a large woodscrew, with its head cut off and the shank secured in the chuck. The makeshift angle-iron tool rest steadied the cutting tool while turning this hardwood tool handle.

Small faceplate, either shopmade or obtained as a wood-lathe accessory and fitted to the chuck with an adapter, allows turnings such as this small bowl to be made in the drill press. The table was swung to one side to become a tool rest.

A faceplate for small work can be made by welding or brazing a large washer to the top of the head of a bolt with its threads cut off. Drill three or four equally spaced holes in the washer near the rim and secure the work to the improvised faceplate with short roundhead screws.

For faceplate work, bring the table up next to the work and swing it to one side until one edge just lines up with the center of the work. Use the table's edge as a tool rest for cutting on the bottom end of the work (in the photo, cutting out the inside of a small bowl). Turning on the side of faceplate work is done with the improvised angle-iron tool rest.

With a little ingenuity, a little practice, and a few minutes of sanding your work while it is turning in the "lathe," you will be able to turn out quite respectable small wood projects.

The drill press is certainly no match for a lathe. But if you cannot justify either the space or the expense of a lathe for an occasional turning job, a good drill press can be reasonable substitute.

A SIMPLE PROJECT

As an example of what can be done on a drill press without a lathe or other power tool, consider the accompanying photo of a small picture framer's hammer. It was made with a square head and a bent handle for driving small nails in alongside the backing of a wooden picture frame.

The head was cut 3½" long with a hacksaw from a piece of ⅝" square steel that happened to be at hand. A 3" length of ¾" square stock might be even better. A test hole in scrap metal showed that a ¼" drill provided a wringing fit on the ¼" gas welding rod to be used as a base for the handle. Had it been sloppy, a slightly smaller letter drill (D or C) could have been used and the end of the rod "turned" in the drill press with a file or emery paper to get a proper fit. A ³⁄₃₂" hole was cross-drilled through the head for a Rollpin (also known as a spring pin or tension pin) to secure the handle to the head.

The handle segments were cut from ¾" particle board and ⅛" tempered hardboard (for con-

Drill press was the only power tool used to make this offset-handled picture framer's hammer. The handle was made up of alternate hole-saw plugs from particleboard and tempered hardboard. Tension pins lock the head to the shank and provide a stop for the front end of the handle. The shank is ¼" welding rod.

trasting stripes) using a 1" hole saw with a ¼" pilot. The wider center stripe was made with three adjacent hardboard circles.

The handle rod was cross drilled for another ³⁄₃₂" Rollpin to hold the front part of the wooden handle and its end was threaded ¼"–28 for a nut to secure the handle. The end of the rod was then drilled with a center drill.

A Rollpin was pressed into the handle and a washer placed against it, followed by the particle board and hardboard circles with a fresh coating of glue on each. Another washer followed, and the nut was then threaded on and tightened. After the glue had dried, the head end of the handle was placed in the drill chuck and the center-drilled outer end was lowered onto an improvised center. The center had been "turned" from another short piece of ¼" welding rod and was then secured in the drill press vise, centered below the chuck. Now mounted in the drill press, the handle was turned to shape with very coarse sandpaper and finished with finer grades.

After the handle was removed from the drill press, the center-drilled end of the rod was ground off, the handle was given several coats of polyurethane gloss varnish, the head was put on the handle, and the other Rollpin was pressed into place. The head was then locked in a vise and the handle was given the 15-degree bend required to keep your knuckles free of the work.

10

THE INDISPENSABLE METAL LATHE

The metal-turning lathe, sometimes referred to as the "King of Machine Tools" and "The Only Machine Tool Capable of Reproducing Itself," is the tool that has led to the development of all of today's machine tools.

Today, probably more so than ever before, there are many choices open to the small shop-owner considering the purchase of a lathe. New lathes are available in many sizes and qualities. There are inexpensive models from the Orient and more expensive (and generally more highly regarded) ones from Europe. Occasionally there is also an excellent buy in a good, used American machine; American lathes are now almost gone from the marketplace.

Lathes hold their prices quite well. If you buy a small, inexpensive lathe and later decide to upgrade, you will probably be able to recover most or all your original cost when you resell the old one.

You can actually teach yourself to operate a metal lathe with a single small book. *How To Run A Lathe* was published by the South Bend Lathe Works over several decades in dozens of editions and in literally millions of copies. If you can find or borrow a copy (many libraries have it), you can start from scratch and will

soon be doing all sorts of jobs that were previously impossible for you.

V-BELTS ON FLAT PULLEYS

If you are looking at used lathes, you will find that many of them have a flat belt between a three- or four-step pulley on the headstock spindle and another on the countershaft. Flat belting to match is still available, although you may have to hunt around a bit.

The countershaft will probably also have a large diameter flat pulley to receive a belt from a small pulley on the motor. (Metal lathes turn quite slowly compared to a wood lathe.) There is no need to hunt up a flat belt and a flat pulley for your motor. Just get a correct size V-pulley for the motor with a V-belt to fit it and of the proper length.

Align the two pulleys and let the flat bottom of the V-belt ride on the flat rim of the countershaft pulley while it drives it via the conventional V-pulley on the motor. Even though it only rides on the narrow bottom of the belt, the much larger diameter of this pulley provides a lot of area and slippage here is unlikely. I have had my little South Bend lathe set up this way for many years, and when I do overload it, the belt slips either between the countershaft and the lathe or on the small diameter V-pulley at the motor itself.

Unorthodox, but it works! A V-belt really does work well on a large-diameter flat pulley when used in conjunction with a small V-pulley. This large, flat jackshaft pulley provides so much surface area that if the jackshaft is overloaded, the V-belt slips on the motor's V-pulley.

LATHE TOOLING

If you buy a new lathe, you will probably find that even though a number of accessories may be included as standard equipment, you get little or no actual tooling.

If the lathe has a turret-type tool post, you can get started with a few tool bits, ground to shape and sharpness. If it has a rocker-type tool post, you will need some tool holders of the proper size to fit the tool post. (A straight tool holder, a left-hand tool holder, and a right-hand tool holder gets you started.) Depending on the size of your lathe, these tool holders accept different sizes of square high-speed tool bits, which you grind to shape and sharpness. The smallest lathes accept 3/16" square bits while most small lathes use 1/4" or 5/16" square bits. Larger lathes have 3/8", 1/2", and even larger bits,

Assortment of tooling for a small lathe includes: (top) a boring bar in a holder and three other boring bars; (center) straight and angled tool-bit holders, cut-off tool holders, a knurling tool, and a 60-degree threading tool; (bottom) six 1/4" square tool bits—one unground, three sharpened to various configurations, and two with cemented carbide tips.

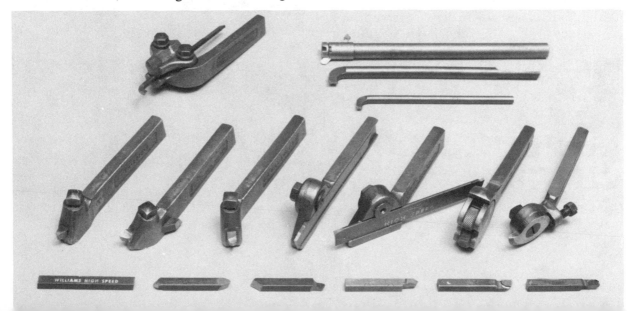

although few of these are ever seen in a home workshop.

Before you get very far, you will want a cutoff tool holder, along with its special thin bit, and a boring tool holder. A knurling tool holder soon becomes a must for the added professional touch, and practicality that knurling brings to your work. If you do much threading, you may want a special formed threading tool and holder. But threading can be done quite adequately with a normal tool bit ground to the proper shape.

Used lathes are often available and can vary from a bargain to well overpriced. Watch the classifieds under Tools and Machinery, or Miscellaneous for Sale. Magazines such as *Home Shop Machinist* usually have several used lathes offered. The current issue offers four, from 6" to 12" in swing and from $300 to $1,500 in price.

If you buy a good used lathe, you may find that, contrary to expectation, there is little if any tooling with it. This stuff seems to have a habit of getting up and walking away when a lathe sits unused for awhile. There should be no problem however, even if the lathe is no longer made. Most tooling, including tool holders, is made by outside companies and fits many different lathes of the same approximate size.

With an "orphan" lathe, do be sure though that you get all the accessories that went with it, and that they satisfy your needs. Such things as three-jaw and four-jaw chucks were usually provided by outside vendors and may be purchased to fit or can be adapted to your lathe. But other items, such as the complete set of change gears for threading, the steady and follower rests, taper attachments, and items of this nature, were probably supplied by the lathe manufacturer and may be extremely difficult to locate. Adapting others to fit or building them from scratch is not impossible but may be difficult or impractical. (The "Wanted" listings in the H.S.M. classifieds often outnumber the "For Sale" ads!)

AVOIDING TOOL CHAOS

Once you have your lathe in operation, your tooling and accessories tend to multiply. Al-

though you can keep many of the items in drawers under the lathe bench, there are a number of others that you will change back and forth regularly. If you do not have easy access to them, the lathe bench can get quite cluttered and you spend much of your valuable time searching for things that should be at hand.

Many bench-mounted lathes have space available just behind the lathe itself. Instead of

Particleboard easel keeps lathe tools handy. Allow extra space; your tool assortment will surely grow. Blocks glued to the back help hold larger items, as with the drill chuck.

piling your tools back there where it is hard to reach, make an easel-type stand to keep the stuff in order, in open view, and much more accessible. If you do not already have a stand, start by digging out your most often used lathe tools. Lay them out on a bench to determine the necessary size and shape for a stand to fit your needs.

The stand in the accompanying photo was made from ¾" particleboard, which was easy to cut, although plywood could also be used. The ½" plywood back brace is cut so that the stand leans back about 10 degrees for stability and also to keep the tools in place. Note that to adequately support some tools backing blocks were glued to the main board to increase its depth. The entire stand was given three coats of polyurethane varnish to prevent the particleboard from soaking up any oil or grease on the tools.

Occasionally an observant visitor to the shop will ask, "Of what use are the printed labels on the stand, when the tools cover up many of them so that they cannot be read?" The answer, of course, is that the labels are only there to show where tools are to be replaced. The labels are clearly readable any time the tool is not in its place.

Making big adjustments in chuck openings, especially with a four-jaw chuck where each jaw is moved individually, is a slow process with a normal chuck wrench. A shopmade speeder handle greatly accelerates the process. This one has a stepped head to fit the sockets in two different chucks.

SPEEDY CHUCK ADJUSTMENT

Making major changes in diameters on a three-jaw chuck takes a lot of twisting of the chuck key, and four times as much with the four-jaw chuck where each jaw must be adjusted separately.

A shopmade speed wrench similar to the socket wrench type does the job in a hurry. Since my two chucks need slightly different size wrenches, my wrench has a stepped head to fit both of them. This works out fine since no real pressure is put on this wrench; the normal wrench is inserted to full depth for the final tightening of either chuck.

The body of the wrench is easily bent up from ¼" gas welding rod; the business end is milled

or hand filed to shape, drilled, and brazed on. A free-spinning handle is provided (an Allen screw in the handle seats in a groove in the rod). The time required to make this tool will be repaid many times over during future chuck sizing.

SAFETY AID

When either chuck is opened to accept large-diameter work, the jaws extend well beyond the round body of the chuck and become a potential hazard. Since the job often requires that your hands be quite near the rotating chuck, this leaves you open to the possibility of a nasty bruise or cut if your hand should accidentally be struck by it.

Cut a rubber band wider than the width of the jaws from an old inner tube and slip it over the extended jaws for a safety cover. It will tend to brush away your hand rather than injure it.

Heavy rubber band made from an inner tube and slipped over extended chuck jaws can protect your hand from serious cuts should you accidentally bump into the rotating chuck.

When using a cutoff tool, slow speed, heavy feed, minimum blade extension, and cutting close to the chuck all help to make a smoother cut and avoid squeal and chatter.

CUTTING-OFF HINTS

Working with a cutoff, or parting, tool in a metalworking lathe is often an exercise in frustration. The tool may cut slowly or roughly or it may squeal, chatter, dig in, or break off the work before the cut is complete. Here are a few suggestions that should help to alleviate some of these problems, although they may not eliminate them entirely.

Speed and feed are very important. Many of the problems associated with cutting off come from too high an rpm and/or too slow a feed. A maximum speed of 500 rpm is best on plastic, soft brass, or aluminum. Use about 300 rpm for copper, bronze, or hard brass. A good number for mild steel is 250 rpm, about 175 for medium-hard steel, 100 for hard steel. (These speeds are good for work up to about 1½" or so in diameter.) On many small lathes some of the lower speeds require engaging the back gears.

One important factor in avoiding squeal and chatter is maintaining an adequate rate of feed; the trick is to start and maintain a steady chip. With the harder steels at too high an rpm, the required feed rate may be at or beyond the stall-

ing point of a small lathe. Use a slower rpm rather than a feed so slow that it will not maintain a constant chip.

If you have a rocker-type tool holder, you may be able to improve your cutoff work by substituting a solid ring under the cutoff tool holder. Turn it to a thickness that will bring the top of the blade to the center line of the lathe. Keep the extension of the tool holder beyond the ring as short as possible. Do the same with the extension of the blade from the tool holder. For cutting off anything over 1" in diameter, extend the blade only a short amount at first and increase the extension in small increments as the work progresses.

On harder materials, a bit of back rake helps avoid chatter and makes a smoother cut. Try from about 5 degrees up to as much as 10 or 15 degrees for the harder steels.

To make a complete cutoff without the small nub usually left when a square tipped cutoff tool breaks off the work, grind the end of the blade to a 15 or 20 degree angle with the point on the cutoff, or tailstock, side of the work.

Always cutoff as close to the chuck as possible. For long work that is to be cut off near the center, use a steady rest and hold the end to be cut off loosely in one hand. Never attempt to cut off a piece with its free end held by the tailstock center, although the center can be used to help avoid chatter until the work is close to being cut off.

CENTER HEIGHT GAGE

If your lathe has a rocker-type tool post, every change or adjustment of a tool bit requires that it be reset or rechecked to center height. Since the centers are not readily available to check against, a center height gage of some sort can save a lot of time.

A height gage can be as simple as a piece of cut sheet metal. Just cut it to a length that equals the distance between the flat part of the lathe bed and the point of the center. Fold it lengthways to an open angle which allows it to stand square on the lathe bed and use one of the upper edges to align your bit. This type has a disadvantage in that the tool bit tip is often not in a position where there is a straight shot from it to the lathe bed.

A height gage similar to the one shown here and dimensioned to fit your lathe, can save you time and trouble. The body was made from a

Center height gage lets you adjust height of cutting edge without having to run the carriage and tool up to the center. The long arm allows it to reach the bit regardless of the tool's position relative to the carriage. You manipulate the tool-post rocker with your right hand to position the height of the cutoff bit prior to securing it with the Allen wrench.

cutoff steel scrap that is large and heavy enough to stand firmly on the lathe bed. This one happens to be just over 1″ in diameter and 1¾″ long. The hole for the pointer was drilled into a chamfer on the end of the base. The end of the pointer can be adjusted to exact center height by twisting it slightly, after which the locknut is tightened to hold the position.

The pointer was made from our old favorite, ³⁄₁₆″ gas welding rod, with one end ground to a long tapering point and then bent about 60 degrees. The other end of the pointer, and the base, are threaded 10–32. Both the base and the shank of the pointer are knurled to prevent oily fingers from slipping.

The gage can be quickly picked up and set anywhere on the lathe bed with the pointer turned at whatever angle is required to reach the tip of the tool bit. The bit can then be quickly adjusted to exact center height or slightly above it, as desired for the work in progress.

EASY TURNING ON A BOLT ARBOR

While it would be nice to have a complete set of arbors or mandrels for a lathe, purchasing them would be too expensive for the average home shop, and to make a set would cost a great deal of valuable time.

Fortunately, for many purposes, ordinary bolts and nuts can substitute as mandrels. A long bolt can be secured head first in a chuck so long as its head is beyond the inside end of the chuck jaws. The work (a pulley, a model flywheel, etc.) is slipped over an unthreaded section of the bolt extending out from the jaws; it is secured against the jaws with a washer and nut on the bolt's threaded end.

If you do not have a bolt of the exact diameter required, use one of a smaller diameter along with a quickly made bushing or sleeve to fill the gap. Make the bushing slightly shorter than the thickness of the work so that the washer holds the workpiece, rather than the bushing, tight against the chuck jaws for turning.

If the work is so long that your longest bolt

Small flywheel is held on a simple bolt arbor for turning of its face and perimeter. A heavy washer placed between it and the chuck jaws holds it away from the chuck.

will not reach entirely through the chuck to clear the bolt head, cut off the head and secure the appropriate length in the chuck. If the work is long enough that the improvised arbor extends more than a couple of inches, center-drill the end of the bolt and engage the tailstock to give additional support.

KNURLING IN THE LATHE

Knurling is one of the fun things that really adds to the enjoyment of having a lathe. Although knurling is practical, providing for a much better grip on metal articles, it is also ornamental and gives a very "professional" appearance to otherwise simple items. A casual visitor to your shop, who may not be impressed in the slightest by some accurately machined work that you turned to a beautiful sliding fit, will often look admiringly at a simple knurled article and ask, "You did that?"

Knurls normally come in three grades, coarse, medium, and fine, and in two patterns,

diamond and straight. The diamond pattern is most common, while the straight knurl is usually cut only in narrow bands, such as on the edge of a round adjusting nut.

Knurls are normally held in a tool holder, sized to fit the tool post on your lathe. Other arrangements, such as hand-held holders, are sometimes used. Tool post knurl holders normally come in two patterns: one holds a single pair of knurls with each angled opposite to the other in order to produce the diamond pattern; and the other is a triple holder with three different pairs of knurls, any of which can be rotated into cutting position. I have a single-type tool with a pair of medium diamond knurls but would prefer a three knurl tool with medium and coarse diamond patterns, plus a medium straight knurl. A fine knurl is pretty dainty for most items.

Knurling provides a good deal of sideward thrust on the lathe, especially when working with steel. The work should be held as close to the chuck as possible and be supported with the tailstock center when feasible. Long thin work should have a steady rest.

To knurl, set your lathe to its slowest back geared speed. Flood the work with oil during the operation. Diamond knurls are normally started at the right edge of the work with the knurls overlapping the edge of the work about one-half their width. Feed the tool into the work with considerable pressure; enough to produce a definite pattern and then feed the carriage longitudinally to the left; by hand for

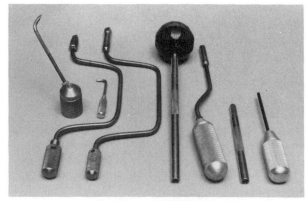

Tools that have had knurls added to them to give an attractive nonslip grip.

Knurling is fun and gives a professional look to your projects. This knurling tool has two roller bits with teeth that angle in opposite directions. Both rollers contact the work at the same time to form diamonds as they are traversed back and forth across the face of the work. Other tools have a rotating head with three pairs of rollers that form either fine, medium, or coarse knurls.

short knurls, or with power feed for longer ones. Stop the feed when about one-half the width of the knurls is off the end of the work, reverse the longitudinal feed, increase the cross feed to force the knurls deeper into the work and proceed back across the face of the work. Do not allow the knurls to become fully disengaged from the work at any time until the job is finished.

Fine knurling may be completed in a single pass. Coarser knurling and harder material will require two or three passes. Heavier pressure and fewer passes usually results in a better appearing job than more passes with light pressure.

If you have a lathe, but no knurling tool, it should be a top item on your list of "wants."

BORING

A drill held in a lathe tailstock chuck will make holes in work turned by the spindle, up to the diameter of the largest drill at hand. For larger holes and holes that have to be finished to an exact diameter for which no drill or reamer is available, the process of boring is used. Boring tools can also cut internal threads with a lathe. For any boring operation, an initial hole is needed in the work; either existing in the work or cut with a drill to the largest diameter feasible.

In order to provide rigidity and prevent chattering, the boring tool holder should be as large and as solidly built as your lathe can accommodate. The pattern illustrated is a good choice for many small lathes. The top section is reversible to hold either a small solid bar or a larger sleeve-type tool-bit holder.

Solid bars in various sizes are adequate for light work, particularly for the shallower depths, and are required for small diameter holes. But with larger bores and greater depths, a heavy sleeve-type bar is required. In any boring work, do not extend the bar any farther from the tool holder than is absolutely necessary.

Most sleeve-type boring bars hold the cutting bit (a short section of a normal lathe tool bit) in either of two positions: 90 degrees and 45 degrees to the bar. The 90-degree position is used where the bore continues all the way through the work, while the 45-degree position projects the bit so that a hole can be bored into a corner or with a flat bottom.

While boring can be done with the tool at any position on the circumference of the work, it is considered standard practice to do it with the tool on the centerline of the work. (When boring a taper this is absolutely necessary in order to have the taper produced true to the angle set.) Boring on the centerline allows a better "picture" of the effective rake and clearance of the tool, both of which can vary with off-center settings.

In any boring operation, it is essential to provide enough clearance on the tool bit so that the heel of the bit does not rub on the bore and prevent the tip from cutting. The smaller the hole, the greater the clearance angle that must be ground on the bit.

When a gear, a pulley, or other item needs its center hole rebored to accept a larger shaft, accurate centering is necessary. Since it is difficult to precisely center an existing small hole, secure a short length of shaft of the diameter of the original hole in the item. Use a dial indicator or other centering device against this shaft to accurately center the work in a four-jaw chuck.

For accurate measurements when boring, a telescoping gage is normally used. This is placed in the hole with its plungers compressed; the plungers are released to contact the sides of the hole, locked, and withdrawn. Extension of the plungers is measured with a micrometer or a dial caliper. Telescoping gages are available either individually or in sets. A set

of six covers the range of holes from 5/16" to 6" in diameter. A set of four expanding small hole gages does the same job on small holes from 1/8" to 1/2" in diameter.

For boring very small holes, the straight end of a solid boring bar can be used. The top half of the bar is ground off for 1/2" or so, leaving a half-moon shape. The end of the bar is ground at a small angle both horizontally and vertically to provide clearance. The tool is set at a slight angle to the bore before being advanced to enlarge it. This tool is known as a cannon drill.

Internal threading is done in much the same manner as other boring except that the tool bit must be properly configured to form the thread and the correct threading gears engaged.

SUBSTITUTE BORING BAR

If you do not have a boring bar of the correct size for a job at hand, try making up one from a suitably sized Allen wrench. To reduce any tendency to chatter, cut/grind the short leg to the minimum practical length before grinding its top and end to the required cutting-bit shape. A high-quality wrench should cut well in mild

Threaded pipe coupling is being bored out to make a sleeve. Keeping the boring bar's extension as short as practical minimizes chatter. A carriage stop, just above the operator's finger, assures that each cut will be made to the same depth.

An Allen wrench ground down to form a cutting bit makes a good boring bar and is available in most any size needed. Note the smooth cut inside the aluminum workpiece. The top clamp on the boring bar has been reversed, and a small V in it holds this bit. Inverted, the larger V holds a heavy bar used with inserted bits.

Telescoping gage takes internal measurements. After its plungers have been released to fit the hole, they are locked and withdrawn. The spread of the plungers is measured with a dial caliper.

steel as well as on softer materials such as brass and aluminum. (For brass, use zero rake to avoid digging in.)

Depending on its size, this bit may be mounted in either a normal tool-bit holder or in a conventional boring-bar holder. As with all boring, work with the least possible extension to avoid springing of the tool and the attendant chatter.

Duplicating a taper. The angle of the compound rest must be set so that the dial gage, which is mounted in the compound rest, does not move when traversed along the Morse taper shank. This aligns the compound rest to duplicate the taper.

MATCHING A TAPER

To match a taper, secure the original tapered part in the chuck and mount a dial indicator on the tool post. Adjust the angle of the compound rest until the dial indicator does not show any movement when run back and forth with the compound feed while it is set to the exact center line of the taper. Lock the compound rest at this setting.

Remove the original part, secure the new workpiece in the chuck, and proceed to turn an exact duplicate of the taper by using the compound feed only.

REALIGNING THE TAILSTOCK CENTER

With a lathe that does not have a taper attachment, any taper longer than that which can be made with compound-rest movement is made by offsetting the tailstock an appropriate distance and then turning the work between centers. After this has been done, the tailstock center must be returned to exact alignment or any

Indicator of any type can be held in the chuck and rotated around the tailstock center to quickly and accurately check its alignment after taper turning by tailstock offset. This dial can be read from either side. If yours cannot, use a small mirror to read it after swinging it 180 degrees.

subsequent turning will be tapered in proportion to the amount of error.

There are almost as many ways of realigning the center as there are machinists, but the one shown in the accompanying photograph is one of the easiest and most accurate. Mount a dial indicator in the chuck so that it can be set to indicate against the side of the tailstock center. Rotate the chuck back and forth by hand and adjust the tailstock until you get an identical reading from the indicator when on the horizontal centerline at both the front and rear sides of the tailstock center.

AVOIDING A MINOR INJURY

When properly center-drilled, the work in a lathe bears on the sides of the 60-degree center and the actual point of the center is an open hole. Thus there is absolutely no need for a sharp point on either the headstock or the tailstock center. Rounding off the sharp tips slightly by filing or grinding can save you a nasty scratch in case of a careless hand movement.

HANDY PIPE CENTER

Turning a piece of pipe or tubing of any length can present a problem, especially if you do not have a steady rest and if its internal diameter is too large to seat on the tailstock center.

Since any pipe too large for the tailstock center is also too large for any normal center drill, using a larger fixed tailstock center is not a satisfactory answer. The best solution is to provide a large-diameter ball-bearing center mounted on a taper to fit the tailstock. These are available but like many such items, they are expensive to purchase for occasional jobs.

If you have a ball-bearing live center for your lathe (a useful addition and relatively inexpensive), a simple shopmade bullnose attachment solves the problem at little or no expense. The one shown is 1¹³⁄₁₆″ in diameter; its size was limited by the stock it was made from, a piece

Shopmade bullnose center, slipped on the ball-bearing tailstock center, will center and support the tail of this pipe for tuning.

from a broken rear axle from a medium-sized truck.

A short piece of the material was mounted in the three-jaw chuck, the end faced off, and a hole was then drilled and carefully bored to a hand push fit over the tailstock center. The hole was made deep enough so that its face can bear against the end of the ball bearing case of the center. The taper was turned (using the compound rest) to the normal 60 degrees, although for larger diameters, a greater angle will keep it from becoming too long. Angles of 70 or 75 degrees are often used.

The taper was continued down to a diameter just slightly under that of the normal center. A finish cut was taken, and the piece was then cut off with a parting tool. There is no need to continue all the way to a point, since the normal center will take any smaller pipe without an accessory. The piece was case-hardened, although this is not absolutely necessary, and it has given good service on a number of occasions since then.

If you have a bigger piece of stock, use it. This one accepts 1½″ pipe; one 2⅛″ in diameter or larger takes 2″ pipe.

PREVENTING TAILSTOCK CENTER SLIPPAGE

Drilling large holes with an oversize Silver & Deming drill held in a chuck mounted in the tailstock or directly with a large taper shank drill may cause the taper of either the chuck or drill to slip and turn in the tailstock. In addition to being an annoyance, this can quickly score the tailstock internal taper, which is expensive to replace. This can be even more serious if the lathe is an "orphan" with no replacement parts available.

Chalking the taper with common chalk prior to insertion may help. This use of chalk is somewhat controversial among machinists. Some swear by it; others at it. If it works for you, fine.

You can prevent the chuck from turning by inserting a suitably sized rod (or even the chuck key itself) in a chuck key hole. The outer end of

Two methods of holding a large Silver & Deming drill to prevent its twisting the chuck's taper in the tailstock. For one, a lathe dog (center) is secured to the drill and is held against the top of the compound rest. Another way shown here is to put the chuck key in one of its pilot holes; this keeps the chuck from turning by pressing against the compound rest. With this large drill the lathe dog is the better bet, because with the chuck key setup the drill shank can still slip in the chuck. Either way the carriage must be advanced with the drill to keep the restraint atop it.

the rod or key should rest against the top of the cross slide. To set this up, remove the tool post and insert the chuck loosely in the tailstock. Line it up so that the key or rod bears against the top of the cross slide before tapping the chuck to secure the taper in place.

A pair of locking pliers clamped to the body of the drill and resting on the cross slide is another deterrent. A lathe dog of suitable size can also be clamped to the drill and rested atop the cross slide to prevent the drill from turning.

MEASURING TAILSTOCK DRILLING DEPTH

Measuring the depth of a hole being drilled is not always easy. Due to the bulk of the drill chuck, it is not possible to lay an ordinary scale alongside the drill or the tailstock spindle to get an accurate measurement. Some spindles are graduated, which solves the problem. If yours is not, here are some solutions.

First, make a starting mark on your spindle. To do this, insert the drill chuck firmly into the taper and then slowly retract the spindle until it just comes up against the end of the taper. Extend the spindle back out a turn or two and mark the top of the spindle, at the edge of its housing, with a sharp cornered Swiss file. This provides two benefits; it not only gives you a mark for starting spindle travel, but also provides a guide to prevent the taper from being inadvertently loosened by retracting the spindle too far.

Once you have the spindle marked, determine the number of threads per inch on the spindle actuating screw. With the spindle set at your mark, count how many turns of the tailstock handle it takes to extend the spindle exactly one inch. To measure this, use the end of a scale that is exactly 1" wide. Most combination square blades are, for instance. If you don't have a 1"-wide scale, go to another known width and make a correction. For a ¾"-wide blade, just count the turns it takes to extend the spindle the width of the blade and add ⅓ of that number to get the threads per inch.

Sixteen threads per inch is a common number. With that figure, each complete turn of the tailstock handle advances the drill 1/16″ or .0625″. A half turn advances it 1/32″, and a quarter turn advances it 1/64″. Starting with your drill's point against the work, and with the spindle mark zeroed, it is easy to drill a hole to a desired depth to the nearest 1/64″. Just count the turns as you advance the spindle. If your hole has to be a given depth at the full diameter of the drill, just start the hole and then line up the drill with the beginning of its full width at the face of the hole. Now reset your tailstock to zero the spindle mark and count your turns from there.

If your spindle has a different number of threads per inch, make up a small table that tells you how many turns (and fractions of a turn) are needed to advance the spindle a given amount. If this is inconvenient, another way of measuring tailstock advance is to cut a spare scale into short pieces that can be laid flat

By starting with the file mark flush against the housing, a thread gage can be used to measure drilling depth (7/16″) here). Counting turns on this tailstock's handle also counts 16ths of an inch.

against the spindle without the tailstock housing and the drill chuck interfering.

On my lathe, with the spindle retracted to the zero mark, a ¾″ length is the most I can get to lay flat against the spindle, and the maximum spindle travel is 1½″. Thus, two pieces cut from a scale, one ¾″ long and the other 1½″ long, measure any possible spindle extension. For deeper holes, drill to 1½″, reset the spindle to the zero mark, and continue, adding the measurement together. Brazing the two small scales to the ends of a short handle will keep them together.

The thread gage from your tap and die set also measures small tailstock extensions. Use the 8, 16, or 32 threads-per-inch blades to measure depth in eighths, sixteenths, or thirty-seconds as desired. Just count threads to get the required depth. Grind off the tips of these blades so that they start at the point of a thread, rather than at the base. This allows the measurement to be taken with one point flat against the spindle housing and has no effect on the normal use of the thread gage.

Another simple way of measuring hole depth is to set a pair of dividers to the desired dimension and then check them against tailstock travel to determine when the desired depth has been reached.

A frequently nuisance when drilling with the tailstock is caused by extending the spindle too far and disengaging the threads; they must be reengaged, of course, before the spindle can be retracted. If the drill happens to be caught tightly in the hole, it becomes necessary to loosen the tailstock on the lathe bed and push it forward while turning the handle, in order to get the threads to reengage.

To avoid this, determine the point at which the threads disengage. Reengage them and back up two turns. Use your Swiss file to make another mark on the top of the spindle alongside the spindle housing. Thereafter, when that mark shows up at the face of the housing, you know that you have only two turns left until disengagement.

FELT WASHER

If you don't have a ball-bearing tailstock center or for some reason are not using one, you know that you have to keep the dead center lubricated as the work turns on it. If you get engrossed in your project and forget to give it an occasional squirt of oil, it can easily run dry on you. By the time you hear it squeal, the damage is done and your hardened tailstock center may be badly galled.

One easy answer to this problem is to take a thick felt washer, saturate it with oil, and slip it

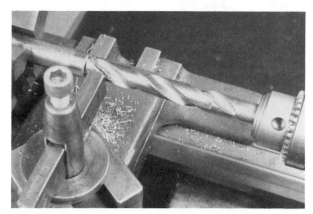

A tool holder, reversed in the tool post and advanced to bear lightly against the side of a large drill, will often keep it from chattering or jumping around when starting the hole.

If you don't have a live tailstock center, an oil-soaked felt washer slipped on the dead center keeps it lubed.

on the center before inserting the center in the end of the work. A well-soaked felt takes care of most lathe jobs; for an extensive job it may be necessary to give the washer an additional shot of oil if it appears to be drying out. Afterward, resaturate the felt and keep it in a small airtight container ready for the next time.

DRILL-STARTING GUIDE

When starting a hole with a large tailstock-mounted drill, the drill sometimes tends to chatter and jump around even though provided a pilot hole. This can often be prevented or greatly reduced by inserting one of your tool holders backward in the tool post and advancing it to press lightly against the side of the drill, just short of where it enters the hole. Once the full diameter of the drill has entered the work, the tool holder can be removed and the drill will continue to cut smoothly.

TAILSTOCK PILOT AIDS CHUCKING

Chucking an odd-shaped piece of work accurately in a four-jaw chuck for boring and facing can be tedious and time consuming.

If the work permits the drilling of a pilot hole

Fast way to chuck an offset, or odd-shaped, item in a four-jaw chuck: mount it on a pilot held in the tailstock chuck and adjust the jaws to it. This is much easier than putting the work in the chuck and moving it (and the four jaws) around till a center-punch mark lines up with the tailstock center.

at the desired center, do this in a drill press before attempting to chuck it in the lathe. Then put a short piece of rod of the same diameter, or even the drill itself, in the tailstock drill chuck. Slip the work onto this pilot and advance the tailstock and the work up to the headstock chuck.

With the work thus held in a centered position, the four jaws of the chuck can be rapidly adjusted to fit the item, while the centered position is maintained. During the final tightening of the chuck, take care to withdraw and reenter with the pilot to be sure that the work is still accurately centered.

MINIATURE TOOL POST GRINDER

As described in Chapter 2, you can make a vise mounting attachment for a small high-speed hand grinder. All it takes is a corner brace and a pair of geared hose clamps.

Welding two more steel segments of the same size to one arm of the corner brace makes it possible to mount the grinder in the lathe's tool post. The grinder still can be put in a vise when needed.

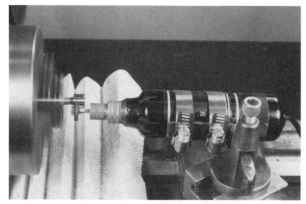

High-speed electric hand grinder, clamped to an angled bar held in the tool post, provides a tool-post grinder for light work. The accordian-folded paper towel catches grinding grit and advances and retracts with carriage movement.

This setup makes a dandy tool-post grinder for small work; the grinder can be used with any of its accessory wheels. The grinder's mount can also be held in the jaws of the lathe's milling attachment vise for even greater versatility. To get opposite rotation between the grinding wheel and the work, just run the lathe in reverse.

If you have a larger high-speed grinder, check the manual or parts list to see if a lathe mount is offered as an accessory. Mine provides an inexpensive mount which fastens directly to the compound rest in place of the tool post. It has an adjustment that allows its center height to coincide with the center of most small lathes of 8" to 12" swing. This attachment allows all sorts of grinding that is too heavy for the little model maker's grinder, but without the considerable expense of a conventional tool-post grinder.

PROTECTING THE WAYS WHEN GRINDING

Whenever you use a tool-post grinder, the lathe bed should be protected to keep thrown-off particles of abrasive grit from the ways. Once it gets on them it is difficult to remove completely and any particles that work their way between the ways and the carriage can cause wear and damage.

The usual answer is to place a rag over the ways to catch the grit. With the necessary movement of the carriage as the grinder is traversed along the work, however, it is difficult to keep the cloth in place to completely cover the ways.

A piece of heavy paper, folded into accordian-type folds, can do a better job. Placed between the headstock and the carriage, it expands and contracts as the carriage moves back and forth to keep the ways protected at all times. For a small lathe and with a short carriage travel required, a folded paper towel is enough. For a larger lathe or a longer grinding job, a larger piece of paper will be required. When the job is done, remove the paper carefully to avoid spilling the grit and undoing your efforts.

PROTECTING A THREADED SHAFT

When machining a threaded shaft between centers, the setscrew of the lathe dog can easily damage the threads when it is tightened to prevent slippage. To avoid this, find a nut that fits the threads and saw through one side of it with a hacksaw. Thread it onto the shaft into a position where it can be placed in a lathe dog. The lathe dog setscrew will squeeze the nut to the shaft rather than bearing directly on the threads itself.

The washer being turned has a hole much larger than the diameter of the bolt being used as an arbor. It was placed between the smaller washers and the bolt was lightly snugged into the nut being held in the chuck jaws. The large washer was tapped back and forth until centered. Then the bolt was tightened. By this method, the washer's perimeter can be turned concentric to its center hole.

To prevent a lathe's dog's setscrew from marring a threaded shaft, saw through one side of a nut. Then use the setscrew to tighten the nut onto the threads and against the dog.

TURNING LARGE WASHERS

To machine the edge of a large washer without a proper sized threaded mandrel, you can use a nut and bolt of a smaller size than the inside diameter of the washer.

Secure the nut in a three-jaw chuck, set slightly back from the face of the jaws. Screw in the bolt with the large washer sandwiched between two smaller washers that fit the bolt. Snug up the bolt just a bit beyond finger tight and then center the large washer by tapping it to one side or another as required. Once the washer is centered, tighten the bolt securely and proceed to turn the washer to the desired diameter and/or contour.

TURNING SMALL WOOD PARTS

A metal lathe can make a small wood turning, even when it cannot be turned between centers. Just fabricate a substitute for a wood lathe's screw center by cutting off the head of an appropriately sized woodscrew and securing its shank in the three-jaw chuck.

Drill a pilot hole in the workpiece and turn it onto the screw. Put a thin wooden disc, with a hole to slip over the screw, between the chuck and the work. That prevents the chuck jaws from marring the base of the work.

Large woodscrew with its head cut off provides a makeshift screw center for turning wood in the metal lathe. The plywood disc prevents marring of base by chuck jaws.

A LATHE CARRIAGE STOP

A carriage stop is a useful accessory any time repeated cuts are to be stopped at the same point along the work. Unless this accessory came with your lathe initially, it may be difficult or impossible to find one to fit it later. It will also probably be quite expensive if you do find one, particularly if it has a micrometer stop adjustment.

Fortunately, it is a fairly simple gadget to make and will be well worth your while. The one shown was made for my 8″ South Bend lathe and was machined with the help of a lathe milling attachment and a ¼″ end mill. (Lathe milling attachments do not necessarily have to be paired to a specific lathe, but are made in several sizes, each of which may fit a number of different lathes in its size range.) If you do not have a milling attachment, the carriage stop can be made by hand using a file, although with a little more effort.

Dimensions, of course, must be figured out to fit your lathe, but to give you some idea of size,

this one is made from a block of steel that is ⅝″ thick and approximately 1⅜″ wide and 2″ long. It must be big enough to clamp on to the bed of your lathe. It also must be big enough to provide a mounting hole for the adjustable stop bolt that is high enough to make contact with the lathe carriage on a surface that is flat and perpendicular to the ways.

Cut the block to size and lay out the slot to fit over the edge of the ways. This one was rough cut by making several hacksaw cuts to slightly short of the final line. The steel between the cuts was knocked out with a cold chisel. The block was then secured in the milling attachment and the slot finished to depth with the little end mill.

The block was then set in the milling vise jaws at a 45-degree angle and the V-cut to fit over the V-way was made with the same end mill. This is the only part that may be difficult to make by hand, but with a little care and some patience, it can be roughed out with a hacksaw and trimmed up with a file to get a nice square fit on the V-way of the lathe.

If you happen to have a lathe with flat ways rather than V-ways, such as many of the Atlas models or the Sears Craftsman-labeled Atlas's, the V-cut is eliminated.

Drill a hole through the bottom leg of the block and tap if for an Allen head setscrew. Instead of letting the hardened screw bear directly on the bottom side of the lathe way, which could chew it up, I made a little inverted cup with a flat top. It sits like a cap on top of the setscrew. Since it is less than 3/16" thick, it doesn't take up much room, but space must be allowed for it when you plan the cutout in your block.

Another hole is drilled crosswise through the block in the proper position for a bolt to contact the side of the carriage. Tap it for the bolt that you are going to use. I used a 5/16" x 24-threads-per-inch bolt that I happened to have.

This particular bolt has a 12-point head and nut rather than the usual hexagonal shape and can be turned by a normal 12-point box wrench or socket, but not by an open-end wrench. Whereas a normal 5/16" bolt needs a 1/2" wrench for its head and nut, this type needs only a 7/16" wrench for the nut and an even smaller 3/8" wrench for its head.

After the stop is secured to the lathe bed in an approximate position, the bolt is turned in the block to stop the carriage at the exact location desired and then locked in place with the nut. I went with the 12-point bolt head because turn-

Carriage stop is clamped to the lathe in an approximate position, and the final adjustment is made with the bolt, which is then secured with the locknut. The carriage then contacts the stop at the same point on each cut. Power feed is *not* used to the stop, obviously, but can be used to move away from it.

ing it one point relative to a mark on the block moves the stop about 3½ thousandths. Turning a normal hex bolt head one point moves a 24-threads-per-inch bolt about 7 thousandths. It's not exactly a micrometer adjustment, but its close enough for most longitudinal measurements.

A short 3/8" x 7/16" box wrench and a 1/8" Allen wrench are kept on the lathe tool stand so that no "hunting" for the tools is necessary when the carriage stop is required. I initially pressed a small, turned aluminum handle onto the long leg of an ordinary Allen wrench (to make it easier to pick up and handle), but found the conventional wrench awkward in this upside down position. So, I switched to a small ball-end, screwdriver-handled hex wrench which does the job more conveniently.

PLANING AND KEYWAY CUTTING

Cutting a keyway, planing a flat on a shaft, or other light milling or shaping operations can be done in a lathe without a milling attachment or other milling tool.

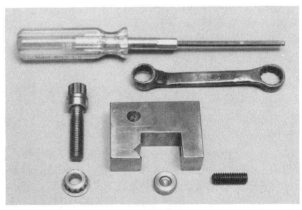

Carriage stop is a worthwhile accessory for any metal lathe. The only difficult chore in making one is hogging out the U-shaped cut and its V-cut to fit the lathe's front way. The small cup at bottom keeps the setscrew's tip from marring the lathe, and the bolt and lock nut at left provide a fine adjustment. The two tools needed are kept on the easel tool stand.

Planing a flat on a shaft is done by locking the lathe's spindle, mounting a square ended bit sideways in the tool holder, and hand traversing the carriage repeatedly across the work. Remove a very small chip with each traverse.

Appropriately shaped bit mounted in a boring bar cut this keyway by repeated hand traversing of the carriage. With an indexing attachment, external and internal splines could conceivably be made by this process, but it would require lots of patience.

In the case of a keyway or a flat along a shaft, secure the work in the chuck or between centers and lock the spindle by engaging the back gears. If working between centers, wedge the lathe dog against one side of the faceplate slot to get rid of any backlash. Shape a tool bit to do the particular job and turn it on its side in the tool holder. When bringing it up to the work, align the tool holder at such an angle that any tendency to dig in swings the bit away from the work and not deeper into it.

Move the cross feed to take a very light cut and make the cut by moving the carriage manually. Start by only advancing the cross feed a thousandth or so for each pass. If practical, increase the feed on subsequent passes until you find the comfortable maximum for the material being cut. In planing a flat, you will probably have to decrease the depth of your cut as the flat gets wider and more material is removed.

Internal keyways in a pulley or gear can also be cut in this manner by mounting the tool in a boring bar and pulling or pushing it out of or into the hole. Pulling, rather than pushing, often results in less tendency to dig in.

In the absence of a knurling tool, a substitute nonskid or decorative finish can be put on a handle with an indexing attachment (described

later) in combination with a V-shaped threading tool mounted on its side. The setup cuts a series of evenly spaced grooves longitudinally along an item. Then you use the same tool as a normal lathe tool to turn grooves around the diameter of the work, with the same spacing as the longitudinal grooves.

Hand planing or shaping in the lathe goes slowly, but without milling equipment available, it can be faster and easier than doing the job accurately with a file.

DRILL-POWERED END MILL

In some lathes, it is practical to do horizontal milling along a workpiece with a portable electric drill mounted to the cross slide. The drill has an end mill in the chuck. I don't do this myself but have seen it being done.

The lathe must be large enough that the drill can be fastened securely to the cross slide with the centerline of its chuck at the centerline of the lathe. A hardwood block brings the drill up to the proper height; the block being fastened to the cross slide as dictated by the cross slide construction, and then the drill is in turn mounted to the block. A couple of large geared-type stainless steel hose clamps should take care of the latter job.

The setup works about the same as the previously described method, except that you have a powered end mill to do the cutting instead of just scraping a fixed tool along the work. Start with a very light cut and increase as practical.

A drill with a good ball-bearing spindle does a better job with less chatter, than one with bearings that are getting a bit sloppy.

MILLING ATTACHMENT MODIFICATION

Many popular lathe milling attachments operate the vertical slide by means of a knurled handle at the top of the actuating screw. With the gibs set up closely enough to do decent work, this handle turns quite stiffly, and for most jobs, it requires a lot of turns repeated a number of times as deeper passes are made. This gets old in a hurry.

To alleviate this, I played with the idea of fastening some sort of crank to the top of the handle which would give greater leverage to ease the job. After some fiddling around, I tried a speeder handle from a socket wrench set, not for its speed, as most of the movement must be made slowly, but for its much greater leverage to ease the turning.

To connect the speeder to the normal handle, I took a large-diameter spare socket, cut off the wrench part and turned down the section around the square hole until a wide ³⁄₁₆″ flange remained at the bottom end. Three small screws pass through this flange and into holes drilled and tapped into the original handle on the milling attachment. This does not interfere with normal use of the handle, but when a long tedious job turns up, a ³⁄₈″ drive speeder handle makes it much easier.

This setup works so well that I made up a speeder handle to store with the unit so that it's always at hand. It has a 3″ throw to swing in a 6″ circle and was made from the ever-present ¼″ gas welding rod. One end is brazed into a hole

This little gadget, turned from a spare ³⁄₈″ drive socket and screwed to the top of the knurled nut on the milling attachment, allows a socket-wrench speeder handle to ease the job of turning it back and forth the many times needed by some jobs.

drilled in a cutoff ³⁄₈″ extension, and the other end is fitted with a small swivel handle.

BENT ROD ALIGNS MILLING ATTACHMENT

When setting up a milling attachment, it is imperative that it be adjusted and locked in place with the vise square to the axis of the lathe. That way, work held in the vise will be cut to a uniform depth as it is traversed back and forth across the end mill or other cutter turned by the lathe spindle.

One easy way to check this adjustment is to provide a rod bent with an offset equal to slightly less than one-half the width of the vise. Since my vise is about 2½″ wide, the bent rod (¼″ welding rod, of course) has an offset of about 1⅛″.

The rod is chucked in the lathe chuck, and the spindle is rotated back and forth by hand,

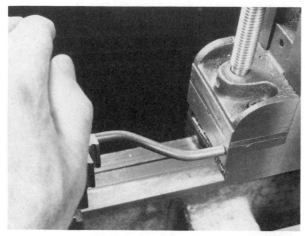

Simple bent rod, held in the lathe chuck and rotated back and forth 180 degrees, helps to align the milling attachment so that its vise is perpendicular to the lathe's axis. When the tip just touches each end of the vise, the vise is square to the chuck.

meanwhile adjusting the milling attachment until the offset rod just touches the front and back of the vise as the spindle is rotated.

INDEXING ATTACHMENT

You don't have a lathe very long before the need arises for some sort of indexing attachment. Either you want to space some longitudinal holes evenly around a circle or you need to drill them radially, as when providing holes for the spokes of a little flywheel. Of course, you can always lay them out with a protractor, but it's pretty difficult to do so with any accuracy.

If you have an older or more inexpensive lathe with change gears instead of a quick-change gearbox, you have the heart of an indexing attachment at hand. If you have the quick-change version, you need to find the gears elsewhere.

A gear, fixed to the outer end of the spindle, will divide a circle into any number of parts that will divide directly into the number of teeth on that gear. A 60-tooth gear, pretty common in change gear sets, is one of the best. It divides a circle into 2, 3, 4, 5, 6, 10, 12, 15, 20, 30,

or 60 parts. What about 8, you ask? That's a pretty common number. Right! A 56-tooth gear, also common in change gear sets, divides a circle into either the missing 8 or 7 divisions. If you need to put 9 spokes in a wheel or 11 bolt holes in a cylinder head, a 72-tooth or a 44-tooth gear will do the respective jobs.

Once you have the gears, you need two things: a way to fasten one of them to the outer end of the spindle; and some sort of dog arrangement to fit between any pair of teeth to hold the gear, and thus the spindle, in the desired angular position.

Since most lathe spindles are hollow, the easiest way to lock a gear to them is with an expanding internal mandrel. The mandrel is turned to a close fit in the spindle, an internal taper is cut in one end, and a bolt to fit the hole in the gear is provided with a matching taper on the unthreaded end.

Since my lathe has a ¾" spindle bore, I used ½" water pipe to make the mandrels.

(I made two, since some of my gears have ½" holes and others have a ⅝" bore, although I

Basic parts of a lathe-indexing attachment. The 60-tooth gear, one of several that can be used, divides a circle into eleven different divisions. The bolt at the lower left, its head cut off and turned to a taper, is slipped into the slotted mandrel which has a matching taper at its left end. The two are then inserted into the outboard end of the spindle. The gear is put on the protruding end of the bolt, followed by the placard (a convenience to avoid counting gear teeth), a washer, and a nut which locks the entire assembly together and to the spindle.

could have made just one mandrel plus a bushing for the larger bores.) The inside of the pipe was drilled out to ⅝″ and the ⅝″ bolts were polished down to a slip fit.

The compound rest was set to a 10-degree taper, and this setting was used both to bore out one end of the mandrel to a knife edge and to turn down the bolt head with a matching taper so that the larger outer end had the same diameter as the OD of the mandrel. Four equally spaced cuts were made, each 2″ long, from the tapered end of the mandrel, ending in drilled holes to discourage cracking. A slitting saw would be handy here, but these were carefully done with a fine-tooth hacksaw. One of the ⅝″ bolts just happened to be a shoulder bolt, necked down to ½″ for the threaded portion, and thus fit both the inside of the mandrel and the smaller gear bores without having to turn one end down and rethread it.

Next came the requirement to lock the gear to a solid spot on the lathe itself. This must be worked out individually for any given lathe. In my case, it happens that when the cast iron change gear cover is lifted off its hinge, it leaves a convenient ⅜″ hole in the supporting boss.

From this point it was simply a matter of building up to the gear location. First a ⅜″ rod was bent to a 90-degree angle and a washer was brazed onto it to hold it at the desired height. Another washer was brazed on the horizontal section to locate a bar at the proper point. The bar was drilled and put on the rod pointed up toward the gear. Atop the bar, a smaller strip of steel was fitted with two slots to adjust to different diameter gears. This strip is bent at a right angle and the end filed to a taper that just fits between two adjacent teeth on the gear to be used.

A spring was bent up from a piece of piano wire, (about 1/16″ in diameter and available from a hobby shop). This hooks on a Rollpin inserted in the ⅜″ rod, takes a couple of turns around the rod and then reaches out and is hooked over the bar. This holds the dog firmly between the teeth of a gear, but still permits it to be lifted out for indexing to the next position.

To avoid the tedium of counting teeth on an involved job, a couple of discs were cut from thin galvanized sheet and are scribed to indicate the locations of the gear teeth required to index to various divisions. The disc for the 60-

The dog, its end shaped to fit between gear teeth, can lock the gear and the spindle in up to 60 positions. The dog's other end has a headless bolt bent to lock into the hinge hole for the gear train cover. A wire spring around the shaft hooks over the dog to hold it between the teeth but allows it to be lifted for indexing to a new position. Two tools at bottom are all that are needed for the attachment.

tooth gear is scribed and marked (with stamped numbers) for the teeth needed to divide a workpiece into, 2, 3, 4, 5, 6, 10, or 12 parts. Divisions of 15, 20, or 30 parts still require counting; there wasn't room for them. The disc for the 56-tooth gear is marked for dividing into 4, 7, or 8 parts.

To use the indexing attachment, the proper gear is selected and is assembled on the mandrel along with the marked disc. It is inserted into the spindle with the bolt loose so that the taper is not expanded. The nut is then tightened to pull the tapered head of the bolt into the internal taper of the mandrel, expanding it against the inside of the spindle until the assembly is firmly locked together. This also locks the gear to the outer end of the mandrel. To prevent any tendency of the bolt to turn inside the spindle while tightening the nut, hold a screwdriver in the slot cut in the external threaded end of the bolt.

Once the spindle, mandrel, and gear are all locked together, the dog is inserted into a space between two teeth (the one marked 0, if a helper disc is being used) locking the spindle. Now you can drill the first hole in your workpiece, cut a spline, or whatever. When this operation is completed, the dog is lifted and the gear is turned to the next division.

With an indexing attachment available, you will soon find that you are limited in the jobs that you can do with it using just the carriage and a cutting tool. As previously mentioned, a drill fastened to the cross slide can be used if your lathe is big enough, but you'll soon want something a little more rigid, which brings us to the next item.

FLEXIBLE-SHAFT MILLING ATTACHMENT

Once again, this is an item that must be made to fit the dimensions of your particular lathe, as well as those of the available parts. So very few dimensions are given.

I wanted an attachment to be used with the compound in place, to be mounted on the normal tool post, and that would be capable of drilling or milling either longitudinally or radially in work of most any size that the lathe could handle.

A piece of ¼" steel plate was selected for the base. Several cardboard templates were cut out, placed over the tool post, and their dimensions juggled around to determine the final shape of the base. This was then laid out on the ¼" material and cut out with a hacksaw-type blade in a sabre saw; a tedious operation, but satisfactory.

The location for the shaft and bearings was determined, as well as the positions for two ⅞" holes to fit over the tool post for either longitudinal or radial work. These cover most operations with the attachment, but for occasional work with larger-diameter workpieces, an extension was provided. This is made from a piece of 2½" by ⅜" bar that was available. It bolts atop part of the normal base to extend it. To return the shaft to the correct height when this extension is used, another piece of the ¼" steel is permanently bolted to the bottom of the extended portion. Two more tool post holes are drilled through the combined pieces to

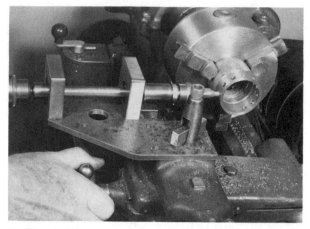

Drilling/milling attachment is needed to put the indexing equipment to work. It consists of a plate secured to the compound rest via the tool post; the plate has a pair of ball bearings mounted on it. Two shafts are used: one shown fitted with a ½"/¼" collet and the other mounting a ½" capacity drill chuck. The shaft is driven by either an electric drill or a flex shaft. Here the setup is drilling twelve equally spaced radial holes. The carriage cross-feed is used to advance the tool, a center drill.

lengthen the reach of the attachment either 2¼" or 4".

Once the base was formed, it was fastened in place over the tool post and a careful measurement taken from its surface up to the centerline of the lathe, measured at the point of the headstock's center. This became the height for the center line of the bearings that hold the attachment's spindle.

The bearing blocks were rough-sawn about 2¼" square from ⅝" steel plate and then ground square against a metal-cutting sanding disc on a 12" disc sander.

The blocks were center-punched for the required center height and secured one at a time in the four-jaw chuck, centered to the punch mark. They were drilled and bored to a press fit on the outside of the ball bearings chosen. Since the outer race of the bearings was ½" wide, a ⅛" internal flange was left on one of the blocks to avoid any tendency of working thrust to press the bearings out of the blocks.

Once bored, the bearing blocks were carefully located on the base to give the longest practical distance between them (3⅜″) to provide sturdy spindle support. The bottom of each was drilled and tapped for two ¼″ cap screws for securing them to the base from the bottom. (To assure that the bearings would line up accurately, a spindle was inserted in them and the assembly clamped to the base. Four pilot holes were drilled through the base and into the blocks. The unit was then taken apart and the holes in the blocks enlarged to tap drill size and those in the base drilled to ¼″.)

The spindle diameter, an unusual ¹⁵/₃₂″, was dictated by the size of the bearings at hand. Two spindles were turned. One has a Jacobs #33 taper to fit a drill press collet chuck which holds either ½″ or (with a sleeve) ¼″ straight shank end mills, carbide burrs, etc. The other spindle has a straight ⅝″ end with a small flat milled on it to accept a ½″ setscrew-attached chuck, borrowed from the Shopsmith.

Both spindles have an inch or so of their ends turned down to ¼″ with three flats milled on them to fasten into the ¼″ chuck on a flexible shaft. An electric drill can be used instead of the flex shaft, but the shaft drive is usually more convenient.

Once either spindle is slipped into the bearings, a collar is put on its drive end and secured with a setscrew against a flat milled on the shaft. I usually roll the Shopsmith over and use it to power the flex shaft. Its variable-speed

Attachment lines up parallel to the lathe bed to drill holes around the workpiece. The tool post is positioned in a second mounting hole which allows the attachment to be brought up to the lathe's center line in the parallel position. The carriage handwheel advances the tool. Angular drilling is done by lining up the attachment and the compound rest and advancing the bit with the compound feed. The indexing gear and locking dog show at top.

drive provides a wide range of cutting speeds and keeps my hands free for the milling/drilling job.

A small universal-type motor can be used. You can control its speed by a light dimmer switch, provided that the motor is within the wattage capability of the dimmer switch (usually 600w). Larger electronic speed controllers are expensive. As mentioned, an electric drill works but requires one hand to operate it at the desired speed (some drills have an adjustment to lock it on at any speed).

This milling attachment combined with the indexing attachment adds a great deal of flexibility to a small lathe, permitting the accurate execution of any number of jobs that would otherwise be quite difficult to accomplish. With different mountings, I use these attachments on a Shopsmith, allowing accurately indexed drilling and milling operations to be done on wood

For larger-diameter work, an extension screwed to the top of the drill/mill attachment backs it away to either of two additional positions.

as well as metal. In this case, the drive system is reversed and the metal lathe turns the flex shaft.

SCREWDRIVER POWERS CROSS FEED

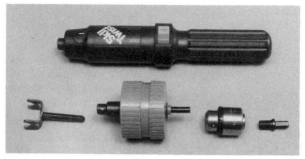

Cordless screwdriver and a speed reducer with adapters to connect them to one another and to the lathe. They combine to make a power cross-feed for a lathe not so equipped. The unit also provides power compound-feed.

While most small metal lathes have a power longitudinal feed, many of them make do with only a manual cross feed. The compound feed is almost universally manual. There may be lathes that have a power-driven compound feed, but I don't recall ever seeing one.

A manual cross feed works fine until one gets to the finish cut, when it can be quite difficult to turn the little handle slowly enough and smoothly enough to end up with a fine finished surface.

A while back, while fiddling around with one of the low-geared cordless power screwdrivers, I got to wondering if it could power a cross feed drive. Used directly, it still operates much too fast, but it works great when teamed up with one of the little planetary speed reducers designed to slow down a regular electric drill for driving screws.

My plastic-cased unit (available at most larger hardware stores) has an eleven to one reduction for driving screws and about half that reduction for removing them. Since both the screwdriver and the planetary drive are reversible, this allows the choice of two speeds in each direction, one about 24 rpm and the other about 12 rpm. The faster speed is good for most work, while the slower one is unbeatable when a really fine finish cut is wanted.

The round input shaft of the speed reducer is connected to the hex chuck on the power screwdriver. I use a ¼″ drill chuck and a ⅜″–24 to ¼″ hex adapter. Make an adapter by cutting off a threaded portion of a ⅜–24 bolt, chucking it in the lathe, drilling a ¹⁷/₆₄″ hole in it, and pressing in a piece of ¼″ Allen wrench stock. Allow ¾″ of the Allen wrench to extend to fit the screwdriver.

You can do without the drill chuck by making a direct ¼″ hex to ¼″ round adapter. Chuck a 2″ length of ½″ steel shaft in the lathe and run a ¼″

drill completely through it. Then run a ¹⁷/₆₄″ drill in 1¼″ deep. Press in a 2″ length of ¼″ Allen hex stock, leaving ¾″ protruding.

Drill and tap the other end of the adapter for a small Allen setscrew to secure it to the input shaft of the speed reducer. Its shaft should have a small flat filed in it to match the setscrew location. The output shaft of the speed reducer has a collet chuck to accept ¼″ hex screwdriver bits so another piece of ¼″ Allen wrench stock serves for the cross feed drive.

My lathe has a cross-handle drive for the cross feed; so I bent up a small steel yoke to a U-shape and provided it with a couple of open end slots which fit over the handle when pressed against it. This turns it quite positively and smoothly.

Since my compound feed is operated by a slightly smaller handle, the yoke was made to a size that would operate both of them. Thus my setup provides a lagniappe in the form of powered compound feed availability, a big help when trying to do a smooth job on a Jacobs or Morse taper without resorting to filing, which can easily vary the taper enough so that it will not grip properly.

Many current lathes have small wheels with cranks in their rims to operate the cross feed and compound. A pair of holes drilled in the face of the wheel rims could be engaged by pins on a yoke fitted to the hex drive. Or, if you don't want to drill into the wheels, you could make a circular drive unit that fits snugly over the rim and provide it with a hole to fit over the crank.

Shopmade power cross-feed faces work more smoothly than possible by hand-feed. By reversing both units, two speeds are obtained. Don't pass this up if you have a lathe without power cross feed.

Whatever your setup, it should be easy to figure out a simple drive connection.

I welded the yoke to the end of the hex drive segment. Brazing would do just as well. Soldering might work (I am not a fan of soldering anything mechanical) but if you try this, I would drill a small hole in the yoke and carefully file it out with a tiny Swiss file to a close fit onto the end of the hex. That way, you have a direct mechanical connection and the solder merely holds the two parts together; it is not required to transmit the drive strain.

If you don't already have a cordless screwdriver and want one as a power unit, you probably should get the type that looks like a fat screwdriver, rather than one of the pistol grip types. Although it does not provide as much torque as the pistol grip drivers, it is quite adequate for this job and has other things going for it. It is less expensive, and it has a thumb operated switch which runs it either forward or backward with a single movement. The others have two switches for reversing and require multiple movements, easier when done with both hands.

To use the drive, the reduction gear is secured in the screwdriver chuck, and the drive yoke is inserted into its collet. If the switch is then turned on, the whole unit operates at screwdriver speed, but provides no torque; when a

load is put on it, the yoke stops and the two halves of the reduction unit spin in opposite directions.

When you grip and hold the front half of the reduction unit however, the maximum speed reduction goes into effect and the yoke turns clockwise with unbelievable torque. If you hold the back half of the case, the direction reverses and the speed increases somewhat. The torque is decreased but is still quite adequate. Thus, you grip either half of the gear reduction to determine the speed you want, and use the switch to determine the direction of travel. In low gear the arrows on the switch indicate the direction of travel of the feed but in high gear the switch operation is reversed (a reversed reverse is a forward). If this sounds confusing, it isn't. A minute's operation will sort it all out.

If you have a lathe without a power cross feed, this gadget will become indispensable. Even if my lathe had a power cross feed, I'd put one together just to drive the compound.

IMPROVISED THREADING DIAL MOUNT

A threading dial is a great help when doing threading in the lathe. Unfortunately, being an accessory, it is not always available for some of the smaller lathes. Or if you find a good used lathe, there may not be one to go with it and that particular model lathe may be long out of production.

All is not lost, however. Any thread dial that fits a lead screw of a given diameter and number of threads per inch fits any other lathe with the same size lead screw, provided a mount is made to attach it to the carriage.

Since some mounts are part of the lathe carriage casting, this might seem to be a major problem, but does not have to be. Any bracket or weldment that can be bolted or clamped to the carriage and that fits the gear of the attachment up to the lead screw will do the job.

My dial, made for a 10" swing lathe 35 years newer than my 8" model, worked perfectly once I made a simple mount arranged so that the dial housing could be rotated around a pivot to

Threading dial from a modern 10″ lathe was fitted to my old 8″ model. The only requirement is that the unit be built for a lathe with the same lead screw pitch. A short ⅜″ shaft welded to the mounting plate allows the dial's housing to rock on it to engage or disengage the gear to the lead screw. A bit of Allen-wrench stock, brazed between a setscrew and a knurled knob, allows engagement, disengagement, or complete removal without tools.

engage or disengage the gears, as needed. Its streamlined housing looks somewhat out of place on an ancient lathe, but that's of little concern when time and effort are being saved!

A small plate was cut out of ⅛″ steel to fit up to the front of the carriage. Since the dial housing had a ⅜″ mounting hole, a short piece of ⅜″ shaft was provided. This had a shallow groove turned in it at the point of setscrew engagement so that the indicator could still be easily removed even if the setscrew chewed the shaft up a bit. This shaft was welded to the plate in the correct position to allow the gear to mesh with the leadscrew.

The dial was mounted on the shaft and the plate clamped up to the carriage at a point where the gear and leadscrew meshed nicely. Then two pilot holes in the mount were used as guides to drill into the face of the carriage itself. The carriage was tapped for the screws and the mount holes redrilled with a clearance drill.

In order that a hex wrench would not be needed every time the indicator was to be engaged or disengaged from the lead screw, a short piece of hex stock was brazed into the setscrew, and the other end was brazed into a turned knob, provided with a knurled grip. One less tool to find and engage.

PREVENTING FEED-SCREW DISENGAGEMENT

With most normal tool setups the cross-feed limit is no problem, but occasionally with an oddball setup you may run out of feed-screw travel and disengage the slide from the feed screw. This is annoying because it requires re-engaging the threads. The necessary resetting of the tool also throws off whatever measurements you were working with based on the previous setting.

An easy way to avoid this problem is to provide a warning mark as an alert that the slide is about to disengage. I used a piece of ¼″ red labeling tape. I ran the slide out to where it disengaged, cleaned the area with a bit of mineral spirits, and stuck the tape onto both the saddle and slide, right across the parting surface. After it was thoroughly pressed down, I cut it with a razor knife at the line between the fixed and movable parts. Now, when approaching disengagement, the tape shows me exactly how much more travel is available before I'm in trouble.

This arrangement also provides a quick check that the required travel is available if you

Two short lengths of ¼″ labeling tape warn that the cross-feed is nearing the end of its travel. When the tapes line up, the traveling nut disengages from the cross-feed screw.

have a questionable setup. Determine the amount of cross-feed travel required from the point where the tool engages the work and then make a quick check of the present distance between the two marks. If you need ½″ of cutting depth and the marks are ⅝″ apart, you're in Fat City. If you need ½″ of travel and the marks are only ¹⁵⁄₃₂″ apart, stop and realign your tool setup to permit enough cross-feed travel without disengagement.

ALIGNING TAPS AND DIES

Cutting threads with taps and dies, especially for a small job, is usually faster than setting up the lathe for thread cutting. Getting the tap or die started straight so that it cuts an accurate, true-running thread is not always as easy, as you have probably found out.

To get a tap started squarely, use the lathe as a helper. Center the work in the chuck, position the top wrench to start the thread, and bring up the tailstock so that its center can engage the center hole on the top of most T-handled tap wrenches.

Then, lock the headstock so that it doesn't turn. Twist the tap wrench with one hand while your other hand turns the tailstock handle to keep the tap wrench engaged and aligned as it threads into the bore. A piloted spindle tap wrench, described in the Drill Press chapter, makes the job even easier. It keeps the tap aligned without requiring the tailstock center to be constantly advanced. That leaves both hands free to turn the tap wrench.

When using a die to cut external threads, a straight start can be assured by the following method if your lathe is big enough that handles of the diestock (die holder) will clear the lathe bed as you turn the diestock to cut the threads (mine isn't). Simply find a stud or screw of the same diameter and thread pitch (the head can be cut off a bolt if necessary), and insert it in the tailstock chuck with the threaded end protruding. Run the die fully onto this thread and then bring up the tailstock until this screw touches the end of the work which is held in a headstock chuck or on the headstock center. Lock the headstock and turn the diestock. As it advances off one set of threads, it gets a straight start for the new ones.

If your lathe is too small to swing a diestock, try this method. First make the workpiece longer than required (add the thickness of the die to the length). Then turn this extra length down to where the die will just slip over it and come up against a shoulder where the actual

Seating the tailstock center in the center hole in the end of the tap wrench aligns the tap to get it started straight. This is a nonpowered operation with the headstock locked.

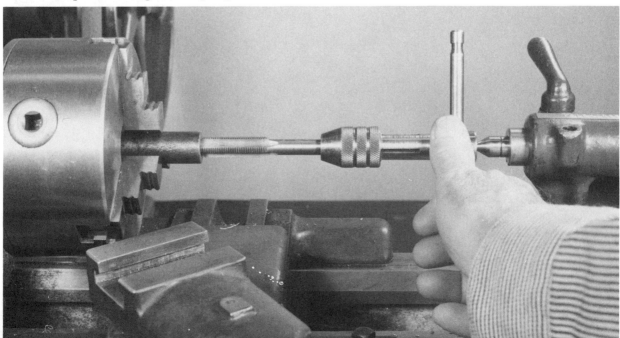

threads will start. The diestock is held against the work with one hand while the headstock is turned with the other to get the threads started squarely. Once the threads are well started, the work can be removed from the lathe and held in a vise while the job is quickly finished with room to swing the diestock.

PLYWOOD STOP STOPS PROBLEM

When turning thin-walled tubing, threaded shafts, or other items where you do not want to overly tighten the chuck jaws, turning on the end of the work often pushes the work deeper into the chuck. This can be avoided by placing a small strip of wood or metal across the face of the chuck behind the work. This piece, however, can tend to fly out of the chuck unless it is made with a shoulder protruding into the center hole in the chuck. In addition, it must be placed off center when used with a three-jaw chuck.

A small scrap of ⅛″ or ¼″ plywood, sawed into

To turn the end of thin-wall tubing without having to tighten the chuck so much that the tubing deforms, use a scrap of plywood shaped as shown. It prevents the work from being pushed back into the chuck.

the shape of a three-pointed star with rounded points, solves both these problems. For very small work, you'll need a thin-armed star so that the jaws can close well down between them, while for larger items a fatter-armed star will provide a sturdy backup.

11
FLOOR SWEEPINGS: ODDS AND ENDS OF USEFUL SHOP INFO

ELECTRIC MOTOR MOUNT

Serviceable electric motors from discarded appliances are easy enough to come by. Providing a mount for them is often a problem though. Many appliances have built-in mounts in the form of brackets or clamps that secure the motor directly to the machine. Others mount the motor by extensions of the four screws that hold the end plates and the field coil housing together. Either way, when you do find a good used motor, you usually end up with a plain round housing with a shaft extending from one end and no mount.

One easy solution is to make up a simple mount from wood and welding rod. For the base, cut two pieces of wood a little longer than the diameter of the motor. Surfaced 2 x 3 or even 1 x 3 stock works well. Measure the diameter of the motor, divide by two, and using this as a compass radius, lay out an arc in the top of the base pieces to act as a cradle for the motor. Be sure that both arcs are laid out the same distance from the bottom of the base strips. Cut them out on a bandsaw, jigsaw, or sabre saw. If the saw permits, tack or tape the strips together with their bottom surfaces aligned and cut both curves with a single cut.

Cut a 3' length of ³⁄₁₆" gas welding rod into two pieces and form each into a half circle with a diameter equal to that of the outside of the motor. I use a little circle bender, but you can get a satisfactory bend around a circular form, preferably one just slightly smaller than the de-

Two wooden blocks, curved to fit, plus two pieces of 3/16" welding rod provide a mount for this old appliance motor. Normally the nuts would be recessed, but it was not necessary here.

sired diameter because there will be some springback. The motor itself also works as a form; take up the springback here when you tighten the clamps. You should end up with two half circles, each with two straight end pieces.

Drill two clearance holes for the rods in each of the base strips. Space the holes equal to the diameter of the motor plus 3/16" and equally spaced from the ends of the arcs. Counterbore the bottom of each hole 1/2" or a little deeper, to provide space for a washer, nut, and a bit of rod overhang.

Stand the motor on end and fit each of the bases and clamps together. Pull the rods tight, mark them, and then cut both ends short enough so that when the nuts are drawn up tight, the ends of the rods will still be short of the surface to avoid interference when the mount is fastened down.

Thread the ends of the clamp rods either 10–24 or 10–32 to fit the nuts and die available. Assemble the mounts to the motor and tighten the nuts. Be sure to keep the bottom surfaces of the two mounts aligned so they'll sit flat and you're ready to go.

The mounts can be fastened to a machine or to a workbench by screws driven up into them from the bottom, or by screws or bolts driven down through the ends of the base strips outside of the clamp rods. In this case, you may

want to step down the ends to allow the use of shorter bolts/screws. Slots can be provided for belt tensioning, if needed.

CENTERING JIG

One sometimes needs to drill holes centered and parallel in the ends of dowels, metal rod, shafting, or other round items. If a metal lathe is available the job is simple, if not it is difficult to center and drill the holes accurately.

Suppose you have a piece of 1⅜" round closet pole that you wish to make into an off-feed roller for a table saw. For bearings, you intend to use 5/16" lag screws; one screwed into each end of the roller, with the unthreaded portion of their shanks turning in drilled holes in a support bracket. In order to roll smoothly, the holes must be centered and aligned with the roller.

Make a simple jig from a small block of wood. A piece of close-grained hardwood is best, but a bit of 2 x 4 will do. Set the block on the drill press table narrow side up (or use a drill guide such as a Portalign). With a 1⅜" spade bit, drill a hole about 2" deep. Retract the bit and replace it with the drill for the pilot hole for the lag screw (1/4" or maybe 17/64" should

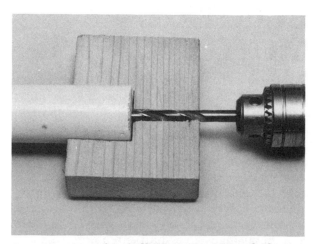

Cutaway view of a drill-centering jig made from a block of wood. The jig makes a centered parallel hole in round stock. In actual use both the stock and the drill bit are completely surrounded by the block with its concentric guide holes.

be about right; check one of your screws in a hole drilled in a piece of scrap first). Continue on through the jig with your smaller drill, the spade bit's pilot hole centering the small holes to the large one. A drill press or the drill guide will assure that both holes are parallel. If your second drill is not long enough to go completely through the jig, drill as deep as possible and then saw off enough of the block to uncover the hole.

To use the jig, insert one end of the roller into the large hole. Chuck your pilot hole bit in a portable drill and run it through the small hole from the other end of the jig and on into the end of the roller, continuing to the necessary depth.

Dowels are not always accurately sized. If yours is a little small for the hole, wrap a turn or two of tape around it to fill out the hole in the jig and to keep the dowel centered. With narrow tape use two or more widths to keep it aligned with the hole. If the dowel is a trifle large, sand it down to fit. Be careful to sand evenly around the circumference to insure that the ensuing pilot hole is centered.

If you have need for them, you can provide two, three, or more different size-centering jigs in a single block. A jig for centering holes in metal shafting or rods will be more accurate when made from a piece of steel bar stock or other scrap of metal.

CUTTING GASKETS WITH BALL BEARINGS

Old ball-bearing balls of different sizes are very helpful when making small gaskets, such as a carburetor flange gasket for your lawn mower engine.

Place a piece of the gasket material over the part that the gasket is to fit and locate a ball (one considerably larger in diameter than the hole), over one of the bolt holes and tap it with a hammer. This will cut the material between the surface of the ball and the edges of the hole. Remove the cutout and slip in a bolt or screw of the correct size to hold the gasket in position. Proceed to the next bolt hole, repeating as many times as necessary.

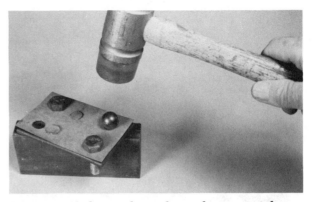

With three holes made in the gasket material, two bolts align the gasket for a fourth hole to be cut by a swat on the ball bearing. Note the crisp edge of the precisely located third hole. The block holds the work off the bench so the bolts can be inserted.

Where there is a large hole to be cut, make cross slits first to avoid stretching or deforming the gasket material. If the hole is to be larger than the capability of the largest ball available, use the ball end of a ball-peen hammer to tap around the perimeter of the hole until the cut-out is complete.

This is an old trick, dating back at least to Model T Ford days, but it is still a very useful one.

ALUMINUM SHIMS

The thin aluminum from empty beer or soft drink cans is a readily available source of metal stock that can easily be cut by a sturdy pair of scissors if metal-cutting snips are not available. The printing can be removed by soaking with lacquer thinner, if desired.

Keep some handy for any job in which a thin piece of metal is required. This material is especially good for shim stock where an exact thickness is not required. Most cans seem to run from about .005 to .007 in thickness (ordinary typing paper is about .004). You may want to cut a few donut-shaped shims to put between the various blades and cutters on a dado head

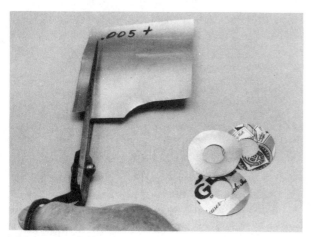

Aluminum from empty drink cans makes useful shim stock where exact thicknesses are not needed. Holes in the washer-type shims were cut with a hollow punch, exterior rounded with scissors.

Inverted drill vise secured atop round stock makes for a safer cutting operation than just holding the work by hand as it is pushed through the saw.

so as to be able to provide a dado cut of precisely the fit desired.

BANDSAWING ROUND STOCK

Wood or metal round stock can often be cut more safely on a band saw if a drill press vise is laid over it upside down, and its jaws are clamped to the stock. The stock and vise should rest flat on the table.

Scoring caused by a setscrew on a round shaft is shown at left. A flat, milled or filed on the shaft (right) solves this problem.

KEEPING A MAGNET CLEAN

A workshop magnet that has picked up steel chips or filings can be cleaned by picking off what can be easily removed and then using the sticky side of a piece of masking tape to remove the rest.

Once cleaned, cover it with a thin sheet of clear plastic kitchen wrap. Then, when you pick up chips and filings with it, you can quickly unload it by removing the magnet from the wrapping over a waste receptacle.

PROVIDE A FLAT

Any place where you use a setscrew to hold a pulley, gear, crank, or collar on a shaft, be sure that it engages a flat on the shaft. Otherwise, the score marks that the setscrew may raise on the shaft can make it difficult or impossible to remove the item later without damaging it.

If a shaft does not have a flat, file or mill one into it in the proper location. While you are at it, replace old slotted head and square head set-screws with Allen head setscrews for better holding power and greater safety. Be sure that the setscrew is of the proper length so that it does not protrude.

HANG 'EM UP

Small screw eyes or even cup hooks often provide a better seal than the normal caps on tubes of cement, glue, or sealer. They also provide a means to hang the tube on a nail or on a pegboard fitting.

EASIER RETURNS

When small parts are kept in plastic drawers, tin cans, mayonnaise or baby food jars, etc., it is easy to find the needed part by dumping the contents out on the workbench and sorting through them. Then the problem arises of how

Small parts poured out to find the needed item are a nuisance to put back in the container. Pouring them into a shoebox cover, with a corner cut out, allows quick sorting and easy repouring into their container. With bigger items, a sheet-metal "flat funnel" permits them to be scooped up with its wide end and poured back from the narrow end. A plastic bottle, cut as shown, also makes a dandy scoop. Cut the bottle with its narrow side as the base, and it becomes a rain-gutter cleaner.

to get the unused items back into the container.

One easy solution to this is to pour and sort them in a shoebox cover rather than on the bench. Cut away sides of the cover at one corner, thus making a narrow opening through which the items may be poured directly back into the container.

For bigger or heavier things, a triangular piece of sheet metal with two bent-up sides leading to an open corner can provide a sturdy answer. Or you can use a triangular-shaped piece of thin plywood or hardboard with a pair of wood strip sides. If you'd rather use the bench to sort, a flat-bottomed scoop cut from a rectangular plastic medicine "bottle" also does the job.

While you are cutting up medicine bottles, another one of the same type, but cut so that the narrow side forms the base, will just fit many flat-bottom house gutters and makes short work of cleaning out the leaves and other debris.

For either of these scoops, a short piece of large dowel, broomstick, or other round wood stock provides a handle. Fasten it to the bottle top with three ½"-long screws through the top of the cap and into the wood. The #6 pan-head sheet-metal screws are about right and their full-length threads get a good grip on the end grain in the handle.

DRILLING ANGLED HOLES

Trying to start a bit to drill a hole at an angle, rather than square to a surface, can be tricky. Twist drills tend to slip and slide off the mark.

The hole (in either wood or metal) can be started at the correct angle by making a jig with a hole of the same size that has been drilled at the necessary angle. You just clamp the jig to the workpiece and use it as a pilot to guide the drill into continuing on into the work at that angle.

How do you get the angled hole in the jig? That's easy. Just cut off the face of the jig itself at an angle perpendicular to the angle of the hole you want. This makes it possible to drill the pilot hole through it, square to the surface, either in a drill press or with an electric drill.

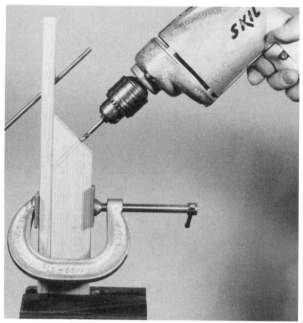

The drill then exits the jig at the angle necessary to start the hole in the work. Use a small square to mark one side of the jig to show precisely where the pilot hole exits.

With this mark, line up the jig with the hole's desired location in the work and clamp the jig to the workpiece. Insert the drill in the jig's pilot hole and drill on into the work. The jig keeps the angled drill from skidding on the face of the work and aligns it to continue into the work at the proper angle. Once the hole is well started, the jig can be removed if it hinders the drill from reaching full depth.

To drill angled holes through the strip of wood at left, a jig was made by cutting off the end of a small block at an angle perpendicular to the desired hole. From this flat face, a pilot hole was easily drilled through the jig at the angle desired for the hole through the workpiece. This jig is clamped against the work at the proper location to guide the drill into the workpiece. Just above the jig, a previously drilled ¼" hole has had a piece of ¼" rod slipped through it to illustrate the successfully angled hole. This procedure also drills angled holes in metal.

SMALL PLASTIC WHEELS

Never throw away a pair of unused refrigerator rollers, or pass up an inexpensive set at a garage sale. Depending on the model, they usually have either four or five nice little plastic wheels per axle, for a total of thirty-two to forty per pair.

They can be cut up to provide wheels in sets of four to five or eight to ten for such things as table saw infeed/outfeed rollers. Or completely. disassemble them to make wheels for toy cars, trucks, or other items.

Large-diameter arcs or circles can be quickly and accurately drawn with a chain, awl, and a pen or pencil. A 3′ chain can draw a 6′ circle.

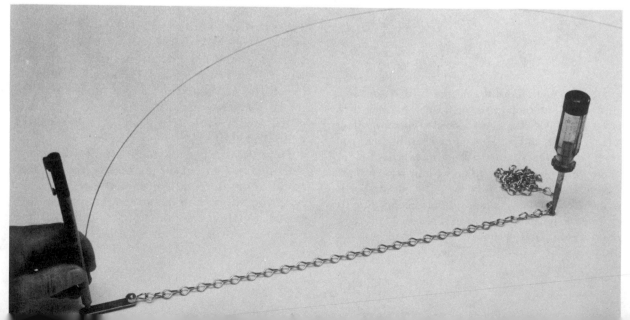

A CHAIN COMPASS

No matter how large a compass you may have, there always comes a need to draw a larger circle or arc than the compass handles. A string can be used, but it may stretch and distort the circle and it can be difficult to tie it to the exact length to get the radius desired.

A piece of very light, flat link chain makes an excellent nonstretching, large compass. Just put an awl or a nail through one link and into the center of the circle and use a pencil in the appropriate link to swing an arc.

If smaller graduations in size are needed than the size of the individual links permit, cut a scrap of metal slightly longer than one link and drill holes in it ⅛" apart. Fasten the piece to one end of the chain. Placing either the pivot or the pencil in one of these holes permits the compass to describe any circle within its overall length to graduations of ⅛"

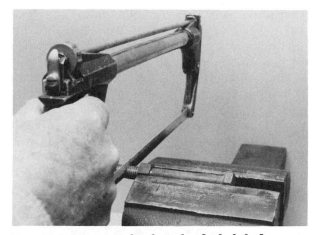

Running a nut onto the threads of a bolt before cutting it off makes good sense. After the cut, unscrewing the nut reforms the burred and distorted threads and makes reinstallation of the nut easier.

NO-FALL TOGGLE BOLTS

Winged toggle bolts are dandy items to hold heavier things to hollow walls—until the time comes that you have to take down and replace the item. When you remove the screw, the wings fall down into the wall. If you don't have a new one handy, you're faced with a trip to the hardware store.

To avoid this problem, mix up a bit of epoxy just before installing the toggle bolt. Open up the wings and smear a bit of epoxy on the inside of their tips. Once you install the bolt and pull it tight against the wall, the epoxy hardens to hold the wings in place, even if you remove the screw. Keep the epoxy on the inside of the wings and it should not rub off or smear.

DEBURRING CUT THREADS

How often have you hacksawed off some excess thread length on a bolt or screw only to find

that after deburring the cut end with a file, grinding wheel, or rotary wire brush, the nut still doesn't want to start onto it?

One solution, if you're not already using it, is to run a nut onto the threads first, then cut it off outboard of the nut, smooth up the cut, and turn off the nut. This reshapes any minor deformation at the end of the threads and the nut should now restart onto the threads with no problem.

HANDY THINNER BOTTLE

Mineral spirits (paint thinner) is a convenient item to have around a workbench to wipe up minor spills, clean a dirty tool, remove stuck-on labels and price tags, degrease an article before attacking it with a spray paint can, and half a hundred other little jobs.

Usually thinner is kept in the paint storage area, often in another area or in the garage, and once tracked down is in an unhandy gallon container from which you end up spilling as much as you use.

Save a small plastic bottle from among those

that are acquired in any household. The ideal bottle has a screw-on top with a self-sealing lift up spout, which squirts a small stream when turned over and squeezed.

Once filled, it will suffice for all sorts of minor clean-up jobs for a month or more before you have to refill it. You can do the same with glue if you buy it in a large container. In addition to the thinner bottle, I keep a small plastic bottle of both white and yellow glue on the workbench. A strip of Labelmaker tape on each keeps them identified.

PIPE CLEANERS

Pipe cleaners, for the pipe some folks smoke, are another handy item to have at your workbench. If you've never been around a pipe smoker, these things are about 6" long, ⅛" in diameter, and consist of a fuzzy material (cotton?) wrapped around a pair of tiny twisted wires.

There are two different types and both are useful around the workshop. the coarser one, which has a few stiff plastic threads interspersed among the softer stuff, cleans small holes, grooves, deep corners, and suchlike. The fuzzy ones are great for getting glue into cracks, holes, and other tight spots. Touch up paint or varnish in tiny areas with them or remove fresh varnish or paint from screw holes or other holes that have to maintain a clearance for bolts that allow them to be assembled and disassembled.

Pick up a small packet of both types the next time you go to town. You'll find dozens of uses for them.

SPEEDY ARCS AND CIRCLES

Many things you build, whether from wood, plywood, sheet metal, or other materials, need their corners rounded off to provide a nice appearance. Usually you hunt up a compass to lay out the arcs. This requires a bit of fiddling around to find the proper center points so that the arcs come out tangent to both edges.

If you have the usual assortment of wrenches

Ends of box wrenches, of various sizes, can be used to draw arcs needed for trimming off corners. Socket wrenches help draw arcs or full circles of many sizes.

available, you have a number of convenient templates at hand, not only to draw arcs and circles of many sizes, but which let you see what the particular arc will look like on the material before it is drawn.

Either end of a box wrench or the box end of a combination wrench will serve to draw arcs. Socket wrenches are used to draw either arcs or full circles. Either one is just laid on the work so that it is tangent to both edges; there is no need to find the center. The appearance can be seen and compared to larger or smaller sizes before any lines are drawn.

With a fairly complete set of wrenches, I have available literally dozens of handy templates with diameters from less than ⅜" up to 1½". Even eliminating the not-too-common ¾"-drive sockets, the others go up to about a ⅞" radius (1¾" diameter), enough for most needs.

BENDING JIG

There are all sorts of jigs available for bending small tubing, but good ones are expensive if you don't have need of them often. Every once in awhile though, a job comes up such as a new gas line from a fuel pump to a carburetor or a replacement for a damaged brake line, where tube bending must be contended with.

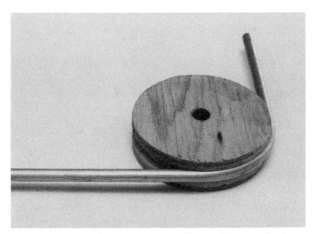

Tube-bending jig was originally a slug made by a hole saw. Mounted on a bolt mandrel, it had a groove turned in it to fit the tubing's diameter. It permits bending tubing without flattening it too much.

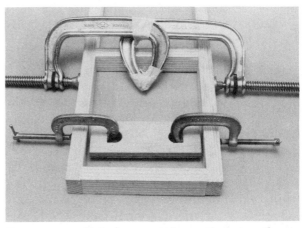

Team up two 4″ C-clamps and tape them together to do the job of an 8″ clamp. If your two largest clamps won't span the work, add a scrap of plywood with two holes, cut as shown.

If you don't have a bending device, it is much easier to kink and flatten the tube than it is to make a smooth bend in it. With ordinary woodworking equipment however, it is easy to make some simple bending jigs.

For short radius bends on small tubing turn a scrap of wood in the lathe to a slightly larger diameter than the desired bend. Then turn a groove in it of a width and shape to match the diameter of the tube and of such a size that its diameter is just a bit under the size needed on the inside of the bend. (It will usually spring back a little.)

For larger radius bends, use a bandsaw, jigsaw, or sabre saw to cut a circle of the proper radius (again just slightly smaller) from a scrap of plywood whose thickness matches, or is just a bit greater than, the diameter of the tubing. Then cut two slightly larger discs for flanges and clamp, glue, screw, or nail the three discs together.

TWO SMALL CLAMPS MAKE A BIG ONE

It is axiomatic that no one, never, ever, has had enough or large enough clamps to take care of the next job that came up. When a larger clamp is needed and if the job has an open center, as when clamping up a frame or a drawer, two C-clamps can be combined to double their individual capacity. Just put the two plain ends together and hold them in place while the two adjustable ends are tightened onto the work. Taping the two clamps together before clamping simplifies the job.

If an even larger span must be clamped, cut a strip of ¾″ plywood to an appropriate length and bore a large hole near each end for inserting the plain end of the clamps. Squaring off the outside end of the holes with a chisel gives a better seat to the clamp. Plywood is preferred since its cross grain structure is much less apt to pull apart under a heavy load.

DRILL EXTENSION

You sometimes need to drill a hole in a deep pocket where an ordinary electric drill won't fit or in a corner where the size of the drill housing prohibits it from drilling a perpendicular hole in the desired spot.

Most small hand drill (eggbeater) chucks of the twist-on type are smaller in diameter than the geared types used on electric drills. That means the chuck can fit up closer into corners, although the cramped space may not provide space for their large hand-turned gear drive.

Fortunately, some of these chucks have a standard bolt thread. One that I have fits on a 5/16"/24 bolt (S.A.E.), while another has an oddball thread which makes it useless for our purpose. There are a couple of ways to make an extension for your electric drill from a standard-thread chuck.

If your chuck has a 5/16" bore, you can turn the shank of an adapter bolt to 1/4". Make a coupling from a short length of 3/8" bolt shank and drill it to 1/4". Braze the adapter shank into one end and a length of 1/4" welding rod into the other. If you don't want to make a coupling sleeve, you can drill out the bolt itself to 3/16" and braze in a length of 3/16" welding rod, which will handle most jobs with this small chuck, although it won't be as strong as a 1/4" extension.

If your chuck has a larger bore (3/8" or more) just drill your adapter bolt to 1/4" and braze the extension directly into it.

If you don't have a lathe, you can substitute with the drill press, using metal turning methods outlined in Chapters 7 and 9. If you don't have brazing equipment, its easy to prepare the

parts and have it done or, you can make a coupling from a larger bolt (to provide a heavier wall) and tap it for a couple of setscrews to hold the parts together. Be sure to provide flats for setscrew seating.

Since most of these small chucks are only 1" in diameter, you now have an extension that drills a small hole perpendicular to the surface as close as 1/2" to a sidewall or a corner. The extension can be made any length you wish, up to the 3' length of a standard welding rod. A much shorter one is usually adequate; 12" serves most needs and 18" should take care of almost every possible requirement (except the one that will turn up immediate after you've cut your extension).

The chuck can, of course, be kept on its normal eggbeater drill shank until the extension is needed.

C-CLAMP PADS

The next time you cut up some 1/8" tempered hardboard for a project, don't throw away any small leftover pieces. Instead, cut them into squares that are about 1 1/2" on a side, give the edges a quick rounding with a piece of 100 grit sandpaper, and store them with your C-clamp supply. They make simple but effective pads for clamping any work that might otherwise be marred by the clamp itself. In addition to protecting your work, they prevent scarring of machine surfaces when clamping jigs or stops onto saw tables, fences, and the like.

HYDRAULIC PRESS MODIFICATION

Over the past few years, a number of lightweight 12-ton hydraulic presses have flooded the market for around $100. While a bit on the flimsy side, they have made a small press available to many of us who would not otherwise be able to justify the cost of a press.

The height of the worktable on the most popular of these presses is adjusted for different jobs by setting the table on a pair of heavy pins

Drill extension gets into deep spots where the drill can't go and its 1" diameter chuck allows it to drill 1/2" from a side wall. The closest that the drill alone can get to an obstruction is 1".

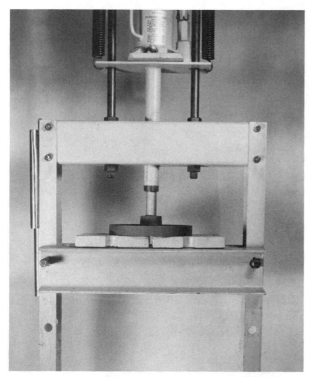

Worktable on this press previously could only be placed on top of pins inserted in various holes in the uprights. This made the distance between adjacent table positions a full 6″. Drilling four ¾″ holes, one in each end of the two channel iron crosspieces of the work table, doubles the available positions and cuts the distance between them to 3″. Providing the same range of adjustment by making more holes in the uprights would have required drilling twenty holes. Here the pins are shown inserted through the newly drilled holes in the table.

inserted through ¾″ holes in the vertical uprights of the press. Since the holes in the uprights are 6″ apart, this makes it a large jump between adjacent table heights and setting up for different jobs can require a lot of juggling. This is compounded by the fact that the available ram travel of the press is only about 5¼″.

One could solve this by drilling additional holes in the side supports halfway between the present ones, but this would involve drilling twenty ¾″ holes through the ⅛″-thick steel angles. Instead, one can effectively do the same thing by drilling four ¾″ holes through the ends of the ³⁄₁₆″ thick worktable channel irons. The worktable can also be lifted out and brought directly to the drill press, while the hydraulic press itself would have to be taken apart to bring the angle iron uprights to the drill press table.

The holes in the uprights are 6″ apart and the pins normally support the bottom of the channel irons. But now they will also support these channels by the top side of the new holes; so, the top of these holes should be 3″ from the bottom of the channels. That way you get 3″ increments instead of 6″ ones. Since the holes are ¾″ in diameter, measure up 2⅝″ from the bottom surface of the channel to centerpunch for the new holes. Make them the proper distance apart to line up with the holes in the uprights. With the added choice of table height, you are never more than 3″ away from the retracted ram without needing additional blocking.

3 x 3 WORKBENCH LEGS

For making workbench and worktable legs, 2 x 2s are usually a little too skimpy, while 4 x 4s are often overkill. A 3 x 3 would be just right but is not normally available. A short length of 6 x 6 can be cut into four 3 x 3s with most any 10″ table saw however. Since the saw reaches only slightly over halfway through the 6 x 6, a minimum of four passes must be made.

In practice, it is extremely difficult to measure to the center of a saw blade's thickness so that all the cuts end up with the exact same dimensions. Instead, make a definite small error, say ¹⁄₁₆″, so that the smaller dimension will be on the fence side of the saw. Then make your first half cut and instead of just rolling the 6 x 6 over to make the second cut, turn it end-for-end vertically instead. This keeps the same side against the fence for the second cut. You now have two 3 x 6s, one slightly thicker than the other. Run the thicker one through the saw again twice, turning it vertically between cuts so that the fence bears against the same side for both cuts. It will then be the same size as the other one.

A second cut being made in the process of sawing four 3 x 3 workbench legs out of a 6 x 6. Because the stock was turned end over end instead of being rolled over, the same side is against the fence for both cuts. That makes the cuts match exactly without any overlapping.

After the eighth cut, all made with the same fence setting, you have four identical legs, all with the same dimensions on all sides.

Then cut these two pieces into 3 x 3s, again take a second cut on the slightly larger sides. You wind up with four legs, all square and with the exact same dimensions.

Consider this the next time you are about to build a new bench or table of any sort. The intermediate size of these legs often provides an ideal solution; in appearance, strength, and economy of material.

REINFORCING WOODEN WHEELS

To discourage warping and possible splitting of large wooden wheels on lawn and deck furniture, drill two holes completely through the board before sawing the wheels to shape. Enter through one edge of the board at its midpoint in thickness and after drilling, glue in hardwood dowels. When the wheels are sawed out, the dowels provide extra strength to the otherwise weak cross-grain direction.

Use a long electricians drill bit or a power auger bit. Dowels ⅜″ to ⅝″ in diameter work well for 1½″ to 2″ thick stock.

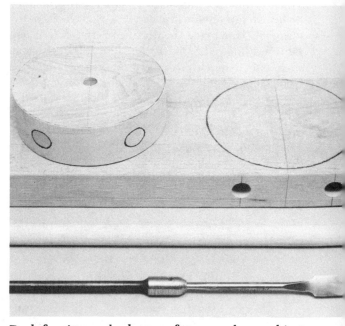

Deck furniture wheels sawn from wood are subject to splitting if inadvertently dragged sideways. Two holes (four on larger wheels) drilled across the grain and filled with glued-in dowels greatly strengthen the wheels. Glue the dowels in prior to sawing out the circle. The drill extension shown will follow a ⅝″ bit through the hole. The dowel ends on the wheel were outlined for the photo since they almost disappeared after sawing.

HANDSAW HELPER

Some situations permit only short strokes of a handsaw to be made with the very end of the saw, as when cutting a hole in just one side of a stud wall. You can make the job easier by slitting a short scrap of old garden hose or a piece of rubber tubing and slipping it onto the back of the saw. This provides an auxiliary handle that enables you to apply pressure near the end of the blade with one hand, while moving the saw with the other.

Attaching two small wood strips with a screw into end-grain would normally be an exercise in futility. By gluing in a hardwood dowel and running the screw into its side, holding ability of the screw is greatly increased. Use a long screw and a setback dowel to avoid splitting at the end.

Scrap of hose, slit and slipped onto the back of a handsaw, is a big help when short strokes must be made with only the tip of the saw.

PREVENTING SCREWDRIVER DAMAGE

While a screwdriver never seems to slip on rough work, it seldom fails to do so on finish work, leaving an unsightly gouge. To prevent this, get a small piece of tempered hardboard or thin plywood. Drill two or three holes in it that just clear the heads of the range of screws you normally use.

Start the screw into the pilot hole, slip on the

WOODSCREWS IN END GRAIN

When it is necessary to fasten a screw into end grain, especially if it will be expected to take much of a load, cross drill the piece near its end and glue in a dowel across the grain to provide a stronger anchorage for the screw(s).

A short dowel can be used in a piece of ¾" plywood near either an end or a side for the same purpose. In this case particularly, be sure to drill a large enough pilot hole for the screw in order to prevent splitting the very short dowel.

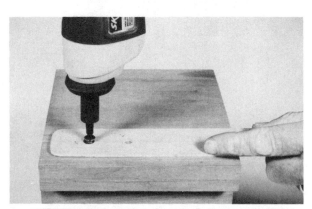

Protective strip avoids an accidental ding should the screwdriver slip out of the slot.

protective piece, and drive the screw with full protection of the finished surface. For small screws, try a punched rubber strip or one of the other aids described for "No Ding Nailing" in Chapter 4.

KEEPING DOWELS ORGANIZED

Tin cans fastened to a wall in vertical pairs can be used to keep different sized dowels, welding rods, music wire, or other similar items separated and neatly contained. Cut the bottoms out of the upper set and space vertically between the pair as required by the length of the items to be held.

TIGHT CORNER JOINTS

Corner irons are very useful for fastening and bracing corner joints; wood to wood, wood to metal, or even metal to metal. They are particularly handy for projects that may have to be disassembled from time to time, such as plywood bunks, a grub box, or other camping gear in the back of a station wagon or pickup truck.

Thin cardboard shims locate two of the four holes in each corner iron. When the shims are removed, the screws pull the joint tightly together.

To layout the joints so that they pull up tightly, place a thin cardboard or metal shim under the base leg of the corner iron while locating, drilling pilot holes for, and driving the screws on the other leg. Remove the shim and then locate, drill for, and drive the base leg screws. This pulls the joint tightly together.

When using corner irons with wood, especially thin plywood or particle board, use sheet-metal screws. They are threaded full length; while wood screws have a partially unthreaded shank. When used to fasten a thin item, such as a corner iron, most of the unthreaded shank on a wood screw extends into the wood and is useless.

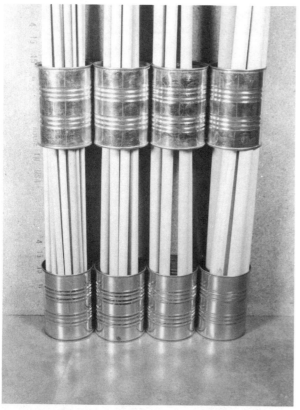

Two rows of tin cans—the upper row having their bottoms cut out—fastened to a wall avoids chaos in storing dowels, welding rods, etc.

A SAWING AID

When sawing a long cut in wood, metal, or plastic, a pair of locking pliers often works as a "third hand" on the far end of an open kerf. It holds the two sides of the cut in position and prevents binding and chattering. Use a small pair of ⅛" hardboard squares to protect the surface of the work.

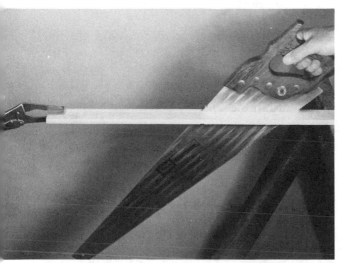

When sawing off a long, thin, narrow strip, locking pliers secured to the ends over the kerf keeps it open and prevents binding and chattering.

CHALK TALK

If you sometimes label wood parts with a pencil—"Inside Top, Bottom, Drawer #3," etc—you may have the very devil of a time removing the pencil marks by erasing or sanding prior to finishing. Instead, try doing your marking with a stick of chalk. It wipes off easily with a damp cloth.

A couple of sticks should also be kept with your files for chalking files prior to use. This helps keep them from becoming clogged with filings, producing a quicker and smoother finish. Chalk is available at most stationery stores.

A FANCY FOLD

Like most of us, you probably use a full sheet of sandpaper by folding it into quarters. You also know that after the two outside faces have been worn down, the inside faces are less effective, having been dulled by rubbing together while the first pair were being used. Avoid this by

If you cut from one side to the center when folding a full sheet of sandpaper into a quarter-size pad, you can fold it so that no two cutting faces rub together. This makes for longer life and more effective sanding when the two inside faces are finally used.

FOLDING SANDPAPER

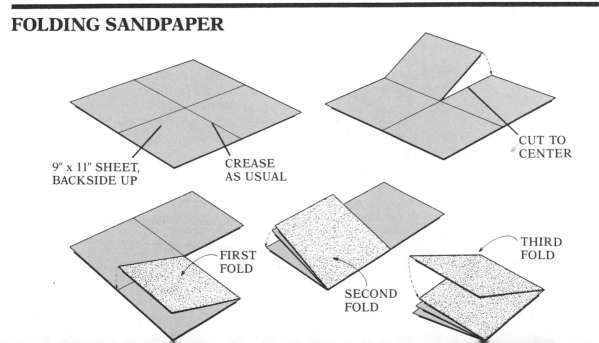

9" x 11" SHEET, BACKSIDE UP

CREASE AS USUAL

CUT TO CENTER

FIRST FOLD

SECOND FOLD

THIRD FOLD

cutting to the center of the sheet on one of the fold lines and then folding the sandpaper in such a manner that the cutting surface of each quarter faces the back side of another quarter, rather than letting two cutting faces rub together. This is more easily done than described and gives longer and more effective life to each sheet.

If unused quarter sheets and other scraps of sandpaper are kept handy (I have a manila file folder in my sandpaper container), they can save you breaking out a brand new sheet for every small job.

PAD STOCK SECURED WITH DOWELS

Pad sawing is a time-saving procedure in which a number of thin sheets of wood or plywood are fastened together and then cut with a band saw, jigsaw or sabre saw with one cut. The pad is usually held together by nailing or bound tightly together with duct tape or masking tape.

Another useful way of holding sheets for pad sawing is to temporarily clamp them together

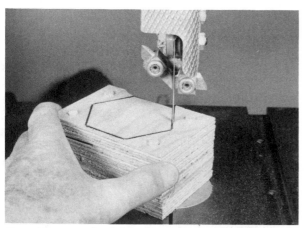

Securing a stack of thin sheets for pad sawing can be done by drilling them and tapping in dowels. This eliminates the need for nails, which may inadvertently be sawn into, or possible slippage that can occur when pads are held together with tape.

and drill several holes in the waste parts of the sheets which are then fastened together by tapping in close-fitting dowels that have been cut to a length equal to the thickness of the pad. This method avoids the possibility of slipping, as well as any danger of sawing into hidden nails while on entry or escape routes during the sawing.

SCRIBE IT STRAIGHT

It is difficult to scribe or draw a straight line along a length of shafting, pipe, or other round material using only a straight edge. If you do not have a key-seat rule available, try a straight piece of angle iron of an appropriate size. Placing the inside of the angle against the round material automatically lines it up accurately.

For best results, the angle iron should be no wider than the diameter of the round stock. Narrow angle iron will accurately line up with a round item that is considerably larger in diameter than the width of the angle iron.

EASIER TAPPING WITH LARGER DRILLS

Hand tapping can be a difficult procedure, especially in the tougher steels, and often leads to broken taps if not done carefully and slowly.

The recommended size tap drill is usually planned to give a 75% thread depth; that provides near maximum strength while still keeping the tapping operation practical. In cases where maximum thread strength is not a major factor, as when you are tapping for a screw that will only hang a wrench conveniently to the side of a machine, a somewhat larger hole (number drills are handy here) makes the tapping operation easier and faster. There is also far less chance of breaking the tap, and you get more than adequate thread strength for the job at hand.

Next time you have a thread to be tapped, consider its usage. If maximum strength is not necessary, make it easier on yourself and your tools by drilling the hole a bit larger than recommended. Comparing the diameters of the suggested drill, the one you actually plan to use, and the OD of the screw, tells you about how much you are cutting down the thread depth from the recommended 75%. Many machine tapped holes are cut with only a 50% thread depth and they obviously are still quite satisfactory.

TAP GUIDES

In previous chapters, I have discussed the problem of getting taps started straight and mentioned methods for doing this with the assistance of a drill press or a lathe. But what about bench work where it is necessary or more convenient to tap a hole without having either of these power tools available?

One simple method is to clamp on a block

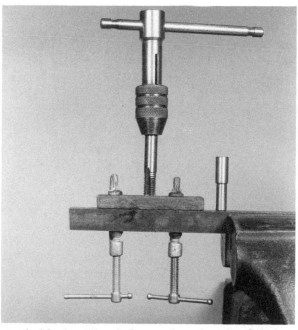

Guide block with a hole equal to the OD of the tap can be clamped to work to get a tap started straight. Block should be as thick as the diameter of the tap. A dual diameter pilot, shown at right, can be used to align the block for clamping. Or both holes can be drilled with the guide block clamped in position.

with a guide hole drilled to the outside diameter of the screw or bolt.

This block should be thick enough to cover the tapered part of the tap so that the tap's full diameter enters the top of the guide. Since the length of taper may vary greatly, even among adjacent taps in the same set, no firm rule can be given. A ½" thick block will usually suffice for a ½" tap, while a ¼" block may be adequate for the smaller machine screw threads.

It is essential that the guide block be clamped onto the work with its hole concentric to the tap drill hole. This can be accomplished in several ways. One is to clamp the pieces together, run the tap drill through both, and then drill the guide hole just through the guide block. If it is more convenient, the smaller holes can be drilled separately, the two pieces clamped together with the tap drill inserted in the two to line them up, the drill then removed and the larger hole drilled through the guide block only.

Another method which is quite useful if you have several holes of the same size to thread, or if you often cut threads of a given size, is to make up a pilot shaft containing both diameters. This will let you drill the two holes separately and still clamp them together concentrically.

Making a pilot shaft is easy. Assume you have some holes to be tapped ⅜"–16, and you intend to drill with the recommended ⁵⁄₁₆" tap drill. For a pilot, use a piece of ⅜" rod, shafting, or the shank of a ⅜" bolt. Turn part of it down to ⁵⁄₁₆". Without a lathe, this can be done in the drill press with a coarse file, although more slowly. Drill your ⁵⁄₁₆" tap drill holes in the work and a ⅜" hole in your guide block. Then, one at a time, using the pilot shaft, align the guide block concentrically with the tap drill hole, clamp it on, remove the pilot, and tap the hole.

IMPROVISED GEAR PULLER

If your tools do not include a gear puller, you can improvise one to pull a gear from its shaft. All you need is two or three bar clamps to team up with a small block of wood and a bolt that is just slightly smaller in diameter than the shaft.

Put the bolt through a hole drilled in the cen-

Two or more bar clamps, combined with a block of wood and a bolt and nut, make an improvised gear-puller. The nut, threaded onto the bolt below the block, allows the clamps to pull the gear off the shaft. Bolt must be a bit smaller than the shaft.

ter of the wood block, and run a nut onto it to take the load. With the fixed jaws of the clamps equally spaced behind the gear and the adjustable ends against the block, line up the end of the bolt with the end of the shaft. Then tighten each clamp equally in turn to pull the gear off the shaft.

The same setup can remove a V-pulley if you are careful not to apply pressure to the thin outer flange. Depending on your pulley and clamp configuration, you may have to use small scraps of plywood to apply the pulling force at a thinner section of the pulley inside the flanges.

12
POTPOURRI: SOLUTIONS TO MANY VEXING PROBLEMS

CARRYING LONG ITEMS

Have you ever gone out to buy a long piece of lumber, a 21′ length of pipe for a TV mast, or some other lengthy item that you did not want cut, and then had the very devil of a time trying to secure it to the top, or side, of your vehicle in order to get it home safely? Next time try this solution.

A few years ago I went down to a steel supply house to buy three 20′ lengths of ¾″ square steel tubing for a project. The counterman, seeing my Blazer, offered to cut them in two, saying, "You'll never be able to tie them tight enough to the top of your rig without putting a permanent bend in them, and even then they'll probably work loose."

Not wanting them cut, I demurred, saying that I'd work it out somehow. He took one end of the tubing, I took the other and we laid them

Long, limber items such as these lengths of ½″ square steel tubing are normally extremely difficult to transport. They are easily carried when slung from the front and rear axles.

out lengthwise on the ground directly in front of the truck. Then, as the man retreated to the counter and watched curiously, I drove the truck forward and over the steel. Taking a couple of short pieces of ¼″ rope from the cab, I got under the front end of the truck, lifted the tubing up and secured it tightly to the front axle. I did the same thing at the rear axle and was tying a red flag to the rear overhang when the steel man sauntered back.

"I've been here 27 years," he said, "and I've never seen that trick before. You've just shown me something that is going to save many of our customers a lot of grief. Thanks."

Before you try this dodge on your rig, look under it to be sure there is a straight shot from front to back without interference from the muffler, frame, gas tank, etc., and that there is enough clearance to allow for normal spring action while enroute. This gimmick works well with most pickups, vans, and suchlike, but may not be practical on cars that have very little ground clearance. If your cargo is particularly limber, you may want to tie it loosely to the front and rear bumpers as well. Again, consider the effect spring action will have on any rough road on the way home.

Put all or most of any overhang at the rear. If you have it at the front, someone may not see it and back into it after overshooting a stop line at an intersection. Be sure to red flag the rear overhang. Most steel suppliers and lumber yards have plastic or paper flags available if you don't already carry one.

TENSION PINS

Are you familiar with tension pins, sometimes called spring pins or Rollpins as they were originally tradenamed? They've been around for forty years or more, but are mostly used in manufacturing and industry. You may have seen them many times in everyday items (Vise Grip, for one, has them) and not known what they were or their advantages. Now that they are readily available in hardware store assortments, they're worth knowing about.

Tension pins are commonly available in diameters of from ³⁄₃₂″ up to ¼″ and in various lengths. They are made from sheets of spring steel, rolled up into a tube with an open seam. Each size is precisely made to have a diameter that is a few thousandths of an inch larger than its nominal size and each end is given a short taper. Thus, they can be easily pressed or driven into a drilled hole corresponding to the size of

Tension pins (spring pins, Rollpins) are great gadgets. This one holds the gear securely on the shaft but permits it to be easily removed if required. Examples of some of the different diameters and lengths available lie below.

the pin. This compresses them slightly and once in place, they expand against the side of the hole for a semipermanent installation. They are easily removed if required.

Tension pins can take the place of bolts and nuts, rivets, or setscrews in many applications. They are especially useful in an assembly where one part has to move in relation to another. In this case, one part is drilled to the nominal size and the other part drilled just enough oversize to provide a movable fit. (Number drills come in handy here.)

Two examples of this are movable yokes fastened to a shaft or rod and wheel assemblies on small toy cars. In the latter case, a long tension pin is pressed into one wheel, passed through a clearance hole in the body, and then the other wheel is pressed on.

Do you have a pulley or a gear that you have trouble keeping secured to a shaft because the setscrew won't stay tightened? Drill through the pulley boss, and the shaft, and insert a tension pin. One caution; although tension pins can easily be inserted into blind holes, they may be extremely difficult or impractical to remove, especially if driven flush. Thus, be wary of using them in this manner unless you are quite sure that you won't want to take the assembly apart later. If you don't want to drill the full-size hole completely through the part, it may be wise to continue on through with a smaller pilot hole. You can later enlarge it from the back side if it becomes necessary to press out the pin.

Regardless of whether you call them Rollpins, spring pins, or tension pins they're great gadgets; get a handful of different sizes and keep them in mind as you develop new projects.

FENDER WASHERS

If you have to bolt something to a piece of wood, you know that even though you use a washer you are probably going to crush the wood and indent the washer into it when you tighten the nut enough to secure it properly.

Fender washers, once more commonly known as wood washers, are the answer here. For any given bolt size, they have a much larger outside diameter than that of a normal washer. Since they cover much more area, the nut can be pulled down tighter without crushing the wood fibres. You can find them in large hardware stores.

HOLDING PAINTED OBJECTS

Spray-painting small items with two or more coats takes a long time if the bottom has to be painted as well as the sides and top. You spray the top and sides and then must wait for it to dry before turning it over to paint the bottom. In addition, the paint sometimes sticks to the newspaper or other surface on which you painted it.

Modified clothes hangers and "paint pins" are a couple of gadgets that can help with this problem. Cut a few wire coat hangers in the middle of the straight lower cross wire. Straighten the wires out and then bend the two

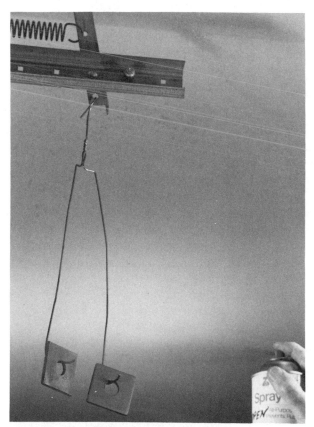

Wire coat hangers, cut, bent, and hung from above, are great for spraying small objects with holes. The hooks are bent as needed.

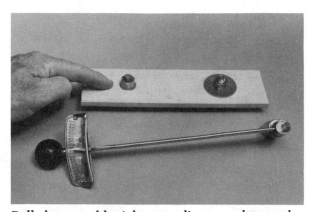

Pulled reasonably tight, an ordinary washer crushes the wood fibers and buries itself. The fender (wood) washer on the right leaves the wood undamaged even though the bolt has been equally torqued.

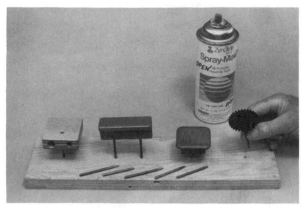

Paint pins hold up objects for spraying on the scrap block. They dry without sticking to anything.

only about 25¢ per gallon, it is more so now that the stuff sells for as much as $2.50 per gallon.

At the end of each day's work, the painter cleaned up his brushes and rollers in thinner and then, instead of throwing it away, poured the used thinner into a 5-gallon can. (For a home shop, a 1-gallon can is usually adequate.) Overnight, the paint settled to the bottom of the container, leaving fairly clear thinner on top. On succeeding days, he poured off some of the old thinner, used it for the initial brush cleaning, followed up by a final rinse in fresh thinner which was then poured into the can.

Using this process, you can keep your brushes clean and expend only about half the normal amount of thinner. The reclaimed thinner, rather than fresh material, can also be used for the initial stages of cleaning dirty, greasy, or oily tools and parts as well as for wiping up spills or cleaning a workbench top.

Over a long period of time (several years in a normal home shop) the can will gradually fill up with the settled-out semisolid goop. When it gets too deep, just pour the clear liquid off the top, discard the can in an approved location, and start a new one.

long pieces so that they extend down from the curved hook, more or less parallel. Bend appropriate hooks on the ends, and you have a place to hang up and paint most any small item that has a hole or a pair of holes in it.

The items can be sprayed while hanging from any convenient spot, or while you hold the hanger in one hand. I hang them from the rail of an overhead garage door and spray them in position, since they are in the middle of the room and away from anything that might be bothered by overspray.

For painting other items, such as a row of cabinet knobs that have screw holes in the backs of them, I use what I call "paint pins." These are nothing more than 8 penny nails with their heads cut off. The cut shank is rounded off on a grinding wheel and the pointed end ground to a long taper. I have a scrap of wood with an appropriate number of holes drilled partially through it and sized to be a loose fit on the paint pins. I put the pins in this block, pointed ends up, and set the objects to be painted, screw hole downward, on them.

SAVING THINNER

Here is a tip that a friend learned many years ago from a professional painter with whom he teamed up to build a house. Worthwhile even back then when mineral spirits (thinner) was

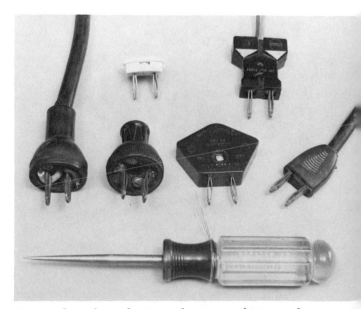

Many plugs have laminated prongs that can be spread apart by a pointed object to make better electrical contact.

BETTER ELECTRICAL CONNECTIONS

Before bending the prongs on an electric plug to improve the contact, take a good look at the prongs themselves. Some of them are of laminated construction, folded over at the outer tip. A better connection can often be made with this type of plug by spreading the halves of each prong very slightly with a small knife blade or an awl inserted just short of the tip.

SIMPLER LADDER CARRYING

To save the time spent finding the balance point every time you pick up a ladder, find it once and then mark it on one or both of the side rails with a stripe of paint, duct tape, electrical tape, or other marking.

This is especially helpful on a ladder that has had a set of adjustable stabilizing feet added or has some other modification so that it no longer balances at the obvious midpoint.

A SAFER SHORT LADDER

Although a small two-foot stepladder has many uses around the home and shop, it is not the safest thing to climb when positioned away from a wall or handgrip.

A piece of ¾" thin wall electrical conduit (½" is a little too limber) about 4½' long mounted to one rail not only provides safety when climbing and descending, but gives a handgrip for balance when working overhead with the other hand. The ¹⁵⁄₁₆" mounting holes provide a fit that is sufficiently secure but which allows the handrail to be quickly removed on the rare occasion when it would interfere with positioning the ladder.

A ¾" thin-wall conduit handle, added as shown, gives greater security when using a short ladder.

Four bolts go through the side rail and are secured with nuts. The fifth one is a screw that extends through the outer wall of the tubing, preventing it from twisting or pulling out of the block.

MORE LADDER SAFETY

If several tools must be used atop a normal height stepladder, a tin can of suitable size can be secured to a side rail near the top with a small C-clamp. A medium-sized C-clamp secured horizontally to a rail makes a handy hammer loop, or a bottomless tin can may be clamped on as shown in Chapter 1.

CARRY A TAPE

How many times have you seen a handy device, made a mental note of it, and later when you went to duplicate it, found that you had to "re-engineer" the item because you didn't have a couple of necessary measurements. Suppose another time you and your spouse were shopping, and you saw a dandy whatsis that you wanted for a certain spot. If it fit. It looked like it would, but it could possibly have been a little too big. Or too small. So you asked a clerk if he had a tape available so that you could make a note of its size. Nine times out of ten, he would look at you as if you'd just stepped out of a flying saucer!

The answer to these and other minor problems is to carry one of the little 8′ long by ¼″ wide pocket tapes at all times. Less than 2″ x 2″ in size and with an overall thickness of ⅜″, the pocket tape is small and light enough that you'll never notice it in your pocket.

I've carried one for over thirty years and have used it hundreds of times.

MEASURING LARGE DIAMETERS

Accurately measuring the diameter of a large cylindrical object, such as a water tank for which you wish to make a form-fitting curved mount, can be a problem if it has domed ends, or ends with a central protrusion of some sort. Of course, you can always wrap a tape around it to get the circumference and divide by pi, but

Two squares provide easy measurement of diameters that cannot be measured directly and that are too large for available calipers. Measured on the inside of the large square, this diameter is 12¹⁵⁄₁₆″.

that can be a nuisance if you don't have a pocket calculator with you.

Two squares, such as a carpenter's square and a try square, do this job on many items. Just place the large square against the cylinder so that the inside of its two legs are touching the sides. Then put the base of the try square against the inside of the long leg of the carpenter's square. Slide the try square along until its blade touches the side of the cylinder, 180 degrees from where the other blade of the big square is touching it. Read the diameter directly on the inside face of the long leg of the carpenter's square.

An ordinary 2′ carpenter's square combined with an 8″-blade try square (9½″ overall) will measure a round object up to 19″ in diameter while two carpenter's squares (if you have another carpenter handy) will measure up to a 28″ diameter.

STUD-LOCATION NOTEBOOK

If you build a new house or an addition, taking the time to make a notebook of stud and header locations can be very useful, not only during the latter part of the construction but for many years to come.

Years ago, I built a very small house as an

enjoyable, educational and profitable project. Knowing that after the walls were covered I would later need to find stud locations for various reasons, I took the time to fill a small notebook with stud, header, and other pertinent items, such as vent pipe locations. Taking one room at a time, such as "Living Room," I began with "North Wall," started at the left end with a long tape and, allowing ½" for the thickness of the sheetrock that would be added, marked down the distance from that wall surface to the center line of each stud, all the way to the far wall.

This is more easily done if you have a helper to hold the end of the tape and to write down the measurements as you call them off, but it can be done more slowly by yourself. Have your helper hold the end of the tape against the adjacent wall about 4' high (midwall height). As you proceed to the right, call out each dimension, after mentally subtracting ½", to the center of each stud. A sample measurement (actual) goes something like this. ½", 11½", 2' 3½", 3' 7¼", 4' 11½", 6' 3½", 7' 7½", etc. Other notes are added such as, "6" header over door," or next to a door or window where there are multiple adjacent studs, "Solid from 12' 3¼" to 12' 7¾"". Throw in any other pertinent information such as "Wall full of wires both above and below junction box, 2" plumbing vent through stud, 3' 4" high," etc.

This worked so well that some years later when my wife and I were having a house built, we took a loose leaf notebook out to the house one day shortly before the sheetrock was to go up. When the builder found out what we were up to, he said, "Oh, you don't have to do that, all the studs are 16" apart." That's true, of course, but once the walls are up, you have to guess at which end they were started from. Unless the wall just happens to be a multiple of 16" long, the last stud will be less than 16" from one end of the wall. In the case of a long wall that is intersected by two walls perpendicular to it, neither of these walls may align with the stud locations in the long wall, again throwing off the 16" rule. There are also extra studs in a wall around doors and windows and where an intersecting wall takes off on the far side of a wall for another room.

We continued with our measurements, somewhat to the amusement of the workers. Before the house was finished however, the builder and the foreman came to me on several occasions to say such things as, "Say Roy, do you have your book handy? I've got to put an exhaust vent through the wall for the clothes dryer, and I don't want to run afoul of the plumbing vent for the washing machine."

We've been in the house for over a dozen years now, and the notebook still comes in handy a couple of times a year. Even though I've got one of those great little electronic stud finders mentioned earlier, there is still lots of other useful dope in the notebook, such as where the furring strips for nailing are located in the concrete retaining wall that makes up the bottom 2½' of a shop wall on the lower side of the house. This wall drives the electrons crazy and although the gadget gives out signals, they're difficult to interpret correctly. The book also tells me where not to nail into a stud to avoid putting a nail into electrical wiring, or into a plastic plumbing drain or vent line, and so on. If you build, a similar notebook will be well worth the time it takes you to make.

FASTENING STEPS TO CONCRETE

On a sloping lot, you usually end up with one or more retaining walls, either built along with the house or added later. Once a low retaining wall is up, you often wish to have a couple of steps to negotiate it more easily. But if no provision was made for this at the time the concrete was poured, steps can be difficult to attach.

One way to solve this problem is to make up a steel frame for the steps. Simply form it to and hang it over the top of the wall. We've got two of them around the place, both formed from scrap steel bar and/or angle stock. If you've got a torch, it's easy to bend and weld up a couple of brackets with a U-shaped top that will hang onto the top of the wall.

One of our units needs only a single step and this is supported by a 90-degree welded joint in the two angle irons, the bottom flange of which supports the wooden step. This unit uses flat stock for the U-shaped parts, which are welded

An 18″ length of 2 x 12, some angle iron, and some bar stock make up this handy step. Screws through the angle iron into the wood secure the step, and a piece of strap iron welded between the bar stock on the upper side of the retaining wall ties these ends together. An assist handle (rebar) is mounted on the wall above.

to the angle irons that support the step. Three steps are necessary below the second wall, so the sides of the angle iron brackets are bolted to wooden stringers. One leg of each angle iron was cut away where they are bent over the top of the wall.

DOUBLED STEPS SAVE SPACE

You occasionally run across a situation where a short staircase is needed, but there just isn't enough horizontal room to accommodate them. So you end up either putting up with a set of stairs so steep that they are dangerous, or you make do with a ladder.

This problem can be solved by making a set of stairs with two risers for each tread width, thus doubling the number of steps that can be accommodated in a given horizontal distance but still using normal riser height. The only catch, a minor one, is that one has to start the ascent or descent with a particular foot, either

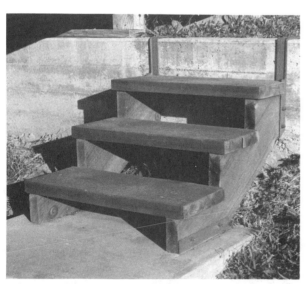

Redwood steps bolt to partially cutaway angle irons that hook over the top of the retaining wall. At bottom the stringers bolt to angle irons that are held by bolts set into the concrete.

Doubled as shown, four steps extend into the narrow storeroom only as far as two normal steps would.

left or right, depending on the construction of the stair. You don't have a choice.

As shown, the stair needs three stringers instead of two, in order to double up on the risers for each tread width. These stringers were made from 1⅛" plywood scraps but ¾" plywood will do the job with perhaps a bit of bracing needed. This particular stair is a little inefficient since each riser is a bit low at about 7⅜" each. If I were to do it over, I'd make it with three steps instead of four. Since the top of the retaining wall, which actually constitutes a fifth step, is 37" high, that would work out to 9¼" per step; better for this case.

These stairs take no more room than the two step unit (three including the wall top) that they replaced. The old unit with about 12⅜" rise per step was definitely too steep to be safe.

If you have a space problem, doubled steps can provide a reasonable answer. Check with your local building inspection department, however, before embarking on any project where steps of this type would be built in. Those shown just stand in place and are used as a safer substitute for a ladder.

NO-DUST DOOR STOPS

No-dust door stops, common in some parts of the country but not in others, save a lot of time in floor cleaning.

Most interior doors have a stop, usually about ½" x 1½", nailed onto each jamb and continuing to the floor. At floor level, this creates two little right-angle pockets into which a vacuum, broom, mop, or most any other cleaning device can not penetrate. Dirt and dust love these little corners however and quickly build up nasty little dirt crescents unless they are arduously cleaned out by hand.

The answer to this problem is to hold the door stops about 4" off the floor, thus avoiding the four little dirt catchers on each door. Cut them off at a 45-degree angle to make them look more finished and to avoid a corner that might catch a broom or mop.

The ideal time to provide these is during new construction, but they can be added, or more

Mockup of two doorstops shows how the "dust free" model on the left allows a clean sweep without the two dirt-catching corners of the normal doorstop.

correctly subtracted, when a room is being repainted.

Mark the stops straight across with a try square and cut the lower part free with a wide wood chisel. Or saw most of the way through, being careful to not cut into the jamb, and then finish up with the chisel. Sand any rough edges and fill any nail holes in the exposed part of the jamb, add a bit of primer, and you're ready to repaint.

Cutting the stops off at less than 4" above the floor requires a broom to be held at more of an angle to get into the corner between the jamb and the floor. This negates some of their usefulness, especially if a thick carpet and pad are involved.

HANDY POCKET SCREWDRIVER

How many times have you needed a screwdriver to tighten a loose screw, loosen a too-tight adjustment, or remove or replace an item and had none at hand? One can hardly go through life carrying a pocketful of tools, but most of us are already carrying several incipient screwdrivers with us.

The handles of many ordinary keys c⸌ be filed or ground to provide screwdriv⸍ pability. As ordinary house key wit⸍ handle can have its sides shaped both a large and a small blade w⸍

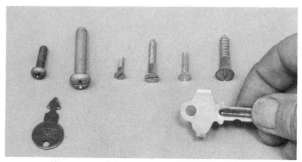

Old key, ground as shown, provides two sizes of screwdrivers for slotted screws. Another flat key has had its tip ground to turn Phillips screws.

them will fit most slotted head screws. The side of another key can be ground to a point that will turn Phillips screws. Some keys with a pointed end will fit Phillips screws with no modification. Use one cautiously though. If you bend the key, it may not serve its original purpose and leave you locked out. Better to use a key, of which most households have a supply, that no longer fits any known lock. A little touch-up with a file or grinder provides a good fit for many average-sized recessed head screws. Your screwdriver key will become a handy helper.

SAVING PERTINENT PAGES

In our earliest school days, most of us were taught to respect, revere, and care for books old or new. This was excellent advice, and most of us have heeded it throughout our lives, sometimes to the point where books take up a good part of our homes. As with all good rules, sometimes we have to make exceptions though.

Go to any used book store, flea market, or friends of the library sale, and you'll often find books or sometimes whole sets of books at giveaway prices. Many of these bargain books have items of interest to small workshoppers. At a flea market not long ago, I paused to browse through eleven books that were part of an outdated home handyman's encyclopedia set. Most of it was of little interest, but scattered throughout were a number of useful items and workable shop ideas that were new to me.

The seller saw my interest and offered, "Give me $2 for them all, I don't want to take them home and have to make room for them." I too couldn't spare the space, but bought them, took them home, and went through them in leisure moments with a small razor knife in hand. Coming to a page or an article of interest, I cut the pages out. From the set, I probably saved the equivalent of one book, but it consisted of valuable hints, tables, and other information which I placed in file folders labelled Woodwork, Metal Lathe, Drill press, Finishing, and so on, along with other shop info previously collected on these subjects. The cut-up books were then shamelessly discarded, my conscience salved by the realization that I have saved some of the information and would put it to good use.

Keep an eye open around old books. There are a lot of old machine shop books available, for instance, in which most of the information is archaic but which do contain tables of cutting speeds and much other information that is quite useful to home workshoppers.

EASY CLEANUP

For easy cleanup of greasy or gooped-up tools and other objects, give them a shot from an all-purpose household cleaner of the type that comes in a plastic spray bottle. Let it stand a moment, and wipe clean.

For cleanups that are even more difficult, such as gum and pitch on circular saw blades, try a spray-type oven cleaner. Note and observe any applicable cautions on the label of the cleaner.

TRACING WITH A CLIPBOARD

A clipboard not only holds sheets of paper while sketching plans and keeps papers handy during construction of a project, it is also great for doing tracing work.

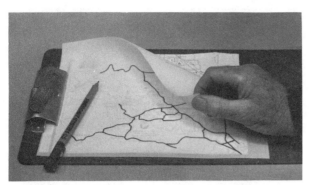

Clipboard is helpful when using tracing paper. It allows the tracing to be lifted to check the master. The paper is held securely so there is no need to reregister it when lowered back onto the master.

Clip the tracing paper atop the item to be copied. The clip allows the tracing paper to be raised as necessary to check the work being copied without the necessity of reregistering it each time. The clipboard also provides a handy portable desk or drawing table, allowing you to work anywhere that is convenient.

PLYWOOD I BEAMS

For spanning widths of up to 8', shopmade plywood I beams can provide lightweight and inexpensive substitutes for heavier beams. As little as ¼" plywood or even ⅛" can support a surprising load if cut several inches deep (most of the strength of a beam comes from depth rather than thickness) and if it is provided with top and bottom cap strips to prevent it from twisting and bending. The cap strips can have a groove dadoed into them and be glued on, or they can be made in pairs and glued and nailed to both sides of the top and bottom edges.

Beams of this type can be put to good use anywhere it is helpful to keep weight down while still maintaining adequate strength, as in a home built trailer or other RV.

DEEPENING AND STIFFENING STEEL I BEAMS

Although few readers will actually find a need for this item, it serves so well to illustrate some of the philosophy behind this book that I feel compelled to include it.

Some years ago when Americans were, if not welcomed, at least tolerated in Iran, I had some time to kill in Tehran. Armed with a local map, I left the hotel for a long walk through the city.

A couple of hours later I came upon a construction site where several workers were busy with an unusual procedure. They had a number

Glued-up I-beam sample has a web of ⅛" x 3" plywood and two ⁵⁄₁₆" x ¹⁵⁄₁₆" soft-pine cap strips.

Wooden I-beam supports 128 lbs of lead, more than 292 times its own weight, with no visible deflection.

THE I-BEAM TRICK

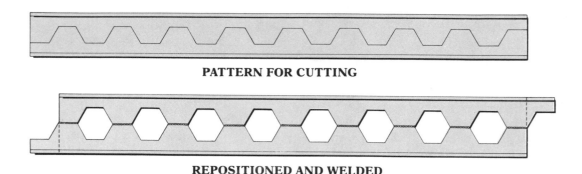

PATTERN FOR CUTTING

REPOSITIONED AND WELDED

Laid out and torch cut as shown, a steel I-beam can be repositioned and welded (on both sides) to make an I-beam about 1½ times as deep. This provides more stiffness without the added weight and expense of a larger beam.

of steel I beams which appeared to be about 8″ deep and perhaps 40 feet long. These were laid on their side and one man, using a template, marked the web off in a zig zag pattern (see drawing), with a welder's soapstone marker.

Next a workman with a cutting torch cut them along this line, separating each into two pieces, both having a toothed partial web. One section was then moved endways an amount equal to one half the distance of one tooth from another and the flat tops of the teeth were then aligned. Both halves of the beam were shimmed up to hold them carefully in this position, and a welder proceeded to arc the two halves back together, after which the beam was flipped over and the seams welded on the other side. The beam ended up a few inches shorter but was now about 12″ deep and contained a row of hexagonal lightening holes along its full length.

None of the workers spoke English but, since I showed interest, the man who seemed to be the foreman went to great length to explain it to me using sign language. First he pointed to a high-rise building under construction about a half block away where the I beams were being installed as floor beams between stories.

Then, in an elaborate pantomime, he sort of bounced up and down and indicated that the deeper modified beams were stiffer and less flexible than the originals, thus giving adequate stiffness to the building. With the use of less steel, the beams were lighter and less expensive than if deeper ones had been purchased.

Lightening holes in beams are valid from an engineering standpoint and have been used in aircraft construction for decades. They are not usually cut in steel beams though, since the weight saved is not worth the added labor cost. These people, by the ingenious design of their cutting and welding, were making deeper stiffer beams containing lightening holes, from smaller and less expensive beams.

Watching this operation provided another of life's little lessons on the advantages of resourcefulness and ingenuity. Granted, in another country with much higher labor costs, such a procedure might not be cost effective compared to just buying larger beams. But for a small workshopper, for whom costs are often more of a factor than extra time, it gives an excellent example of the value of a little productive thinking.

13
PROJECTS

If you wanted to, you could spend all your time in your shop building projects from plans and ready-made kits. There certainly are enough of them around. As enjoyable as building one of these items may be, it is not quite the same as working on something you designed and built yourself to fill a need around the house.

The projects in this chapter have been chosen to show how you can develop projects on your own. It is not hard; you just have to decide to do it and then exercise a little imagination. Once you get started, you will begin to see ideas that you can adapt to solve a particular problem or that will form the basis of a whole new project. Books, magazines, and the world around you are full of ideas, if you only learn to look for them.

In a way, this is similar to collecting, except that here you are looking for ideas and techniques. Those plans in books and magazines will tell you a lot about designing projects that are sturdy and durable. Also, while the project itself may not interest you, there may be one unusual technique involved that you could use elsewhere. This is not only true of project plans; you can get hundreds of ideas from factory-made items in hardware stores and even department stores if you only bother to keep your eyes open.

Materials are a big part of engineering your own projects; in fact, sometimes it is an interesting scrap that gives you an idea in the first place. You will find projects in this chapter made from a wide range of odds and ends that can be found around the shop or out in the desert. That great idea can come from just about anywhere. All it takes is a few odd scraps, imagination, and some know-how.

BOOKENDS FROM SCRAP

Bookends are usually seen in pairs. Pairs are necessary for holding a few books on a desk or table, but in a large bookcase single bookends are often more useful to separate different categories of books or to hold up just one end of a row that does not quite fill up a shelf. Around my house, we have bookends by the dozen. Most are shop made and most of them are singles and made from many different materials.

Bookends from Beer Cans

Scrap aluminum can be melted down and poured into a suitable mold to make bookends. I have a heavy old cast-iron miner's mortar and pestle for hand grinding ore for sampling. It has an interesting shape inside. I decided it would make a good mold for a pair of bookends and so proceeded to melt down some old aluminum beer cans.

I melted them in a cast-iron cook pot using a welding torch with a rosebud tip. This was not very efficient (an understatement). The very high temperature of the torch flame combined with the extreme thinness of the metal tended to burn it rather than melt it. Eventually, I got a pool of molten metal after which it went somewhat better, although it took several hundred

Pair of bookends made from some 300 aluminum beer cans that were melted and poured into the cast-iron mortar at left. The casting was sawn in two vertically. Self-stick felt on bottoms and sides of the bookends completed the job.

cans to get an appreciable amount of molten metal. Next time, I'll try using barbecue charcoal along with an air flow from a small blower to increase the oxygen supply.

After pouring and cooling, the casting was turned out of the mold. The top, which became the bottom of the bookends, was faced off slightly with a Vixen file, and the piece was carefully cut into two halves with a power hacksaw. This could have been done by hand, although with much more effort. The bottoms and the flat sides were faced with self-stick felt to complete the job. The result was an attractive and practical pair of bookends which many people find hard to believe came from a pile of discarded aluminum beer cans.

Bookends from Steel Pipe

I've made steel bookends from heavy pipe, either with the ends cut off at a 45-degree angle so that they lean against the books at a diagonal or with a mitered and welded joint. Both these had the base partially filled with lead to stabilize them. I have also made bookends from short cutoffs of railroad rail, pieces of rebar, and welding rod of different diameters.

Once cleaned up, steel holds up well indoors

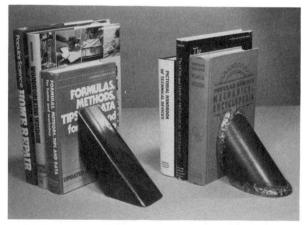

Single bookends are normally used against the end of a row of books when the other end is held by the bookcase wall. One is made from 2¼″ square steel tubing and the other from 3½″ pipe. The round one has a trim of melted-on brass rod. Both have lead poured into the tip of their base to give stability and to avoid tipping if an adjacent book is removed.

Two more steel bookends. One has a base made from a scrap of nonskid steel walkway. Its brazed-on uprights are ³⁄₁₆″ and ¼″ welding rod with their ends angled to lie flat against the book. The uprights on the other are ½″ and ¾″ rebar with their ends squared off and corners gently rounded to avoid any gouging of the book.

in a fairly dry atmosphere; if rust is a problem, there are clear protective coatings available in spray cans, or you may prefer to paint them.

Plywood Bookends

Plywood can also be used to make any number of differently shaped bookends. Their construction was described in the plywood chapter and some of them are shown here.

Plywood has an unusual quality in that if you use it in a project where the face of the material shows, such as with the top of a table, desk, or similar item, any raw plywood edge left showing looks terrible. However, if the article is built so that the visible parts all consist of edge grain with no face showing, it acquires an interesting textured appearance and looks great. Conversely, if a product shows almost all edge grain, but has a bit of face grain showing, the face grain looks out of place! Some of these bookends, cut out and glued up into Art Deco inspired shapes, show approximately equal amount of face grain and edge grain and this also seems to "work" visually.

A cube provides an attractive shape for a bookend. About 3″ to 4″ on a side is a good size. I've made them out of plywood, brazed up ⅛″ welding rod, and from a chunk of soapstone.

Welding Rod

The welding rod cube, which consists of dozens of dark steel rods going every which way and connected with contrasting brass joints, is

Edge-grain plywood bookends play with angles. One has had its parts glued together alternating vertically and horizontally. The other was glued up as a straight block, then sawn twice at 22½ degrees, and the pieces twisted around and reglued to provide two 45-degree angles. Like the other plywood pieces, these have 1½″ spade-bit holes bored in their bases that have been nearly filled with molten lead.

Plywood bookends, showing only edge grain, were made by gluing up a block and then sawing it in two diagonally.

These two, showing roughly equal amounts of face and edge-grain, are reminiscent of 1930s Art Deco architecture.

Two cubes. One was sawn from a chunk of soapstone. The other was brazed up of ⅛" welding rod, squared off on a disc sander, and then power wire-brushed to gently round off any rough edges.

a fascinating one. When someone expresses interest in it, I tell them that it is "a cube with its cover removed," and then add, "I'll bet you never realized what went on inside one of those things." This usually results in one of two reactions: a pause and then a chuckle, or a longer pause followed by a strange look!

Soapstone

Soapstone, if you happen to have a deposit nearby, cuts nicely with a band saw and can provide all sorts of interesting bookends, paper-

weights, and suchlike. One friendly caution. Move your saw and sander outside before working the stuff. I didn't and it took me a couple of days to clean up. The fine dust got into all the open shelves and cabinets, and I had to air dust several times to flush it out. Worse yet, the smooth concrete floor was as slick as a freshly waxed dance floor and had to be washed twice with mineral spirits to get rid of the powder.

One angular hunk, since given away, had two right-angled flats sawed to provide a base plus an upright for the books, and ended up having the look of a rugged but attractive mountain peak.

METAL SCULPTURE

Several years ago while sniping for gold on the Yuba River, I came across a gnarled mass of rusted metal that had obviously been tumbled by the river over miles and miles of boulders. A closer look showed two bungs which indicated that it had been a 55 gallon gasoline or oil drum, although now bashed in to a quarter of its original size.

Intent on the big nuggets that had to lie just around the next bend (they're still around some other bend), I dismissed it and traveled on. Later, home from the trip, I remembered the

Soapstone pyramid shows both sawn and broken surfaces; the steel unit was power hacksawed from railroad rail.

Hanging from a high ceiling, this metal sculpture is actually a 55-gallon oil drum, river tumbled to one-fourth its original size.

mangled drum and considered how it might become an interesting piece of "sculpture." It kept nagging at me until a couple of months later when wife Helen and I went up to the Gold Country to spend a few days in a historic hotel in one of the old mining towns.

We headed up the north fork of the Yuba one morning and after some searching found the battered drum. I had thought that it would be a simple matter to carry or roll it up the bank to the road but was surprised to find that it was full of wet sand (it weighed in at 190 lbs.).

Fortunately I had the Blazer with its winch. Helen got a quick checkout as a winch operator and some three hours of hard work later, after much rigging of a snatch block to work it around boulders the size of a house, we had it up on the road and in the back of the machine.

At home, it took a month of spare time to get all the wet sand out through the bung hole with a long handled scoop and to dry it out, sandblast, and paint it inside and out. Finally, I hung it from the high ceiling in the living room by a length of 1/16" aircraft cable. Nicknamed "The Lost Meteor" by daughter Mimi, it is a most interesting and unique piece of sculpture.

CHANDELIER IN THE SAGEBRUSH

One morning many years ago, longtime friend Al Kinney, now gone but with whom I wandered the West for over twenty years, came back to camp from a post-breakfast walk saying, "Come see what I've found in the sagebrush."

Just a short distance from camp, he showed me where a big old horse-drawn wagon lay rotting away in the sage. It had obviously been there for many years. Most of the wood frame and body were rotted away. The wheels had fallen off and the spokes and felloes were mostly gone, but three of the big wooden hubs, each surrounded by four iron bands, were still intact.

Thinking that we might do something with them, we liberated them, Al taking one and I a pair.

On arriving home and cleaning them up I found that they were so dried out that when the

Base of this chandelier, one of a pair, is a hub from an old wagon wheel that had been left in the desert for many years.

iron bands were slipped off, the hubs themselves had split into several pieces. For several years they sat in a corner of the workshop while I had a vague notion of someday making them into a pair of table lamps, but fortunately never quite got around to it.

Later, when we were planning this house, I happened to see an article in one of the house/home magazines on a Mexican-influenced kitchen that someone had done. In it they had a chandelier which consisted of a short hanging piece of 6 x 6 timber with wrought iron arms extending from all four sides, each having a light at its end. Quite attractive.

Something nudged my mind to the ancient pair of wheel hubs and to the realization that our new house would have a high beamed ceiling in the living room that was just crying for a pair of rustic chandeliers.

We had the appropriate wiring installed during construction, and when the house passed final inspection the living room ceiling had a pair of plain porcelain sockets with bare bulbs installed. Puzzling to the inspector but quite legal.

Later, after we were in and things had settled down a bit, I dug out the two old hubs and dissected them again. This time I stained the wood parts a rustic ruddy brown and when re-assembling them drilled several small holes through the hoops at strategic spots. These were sized to just fit the heads of small finishing nails driven flush with the surface of the hoops and used to tie the parts together a little more securely. Once the metal was given a coat of flat black paint, the nailheads almost disappeared.

A couple of long strips of 1⅝" wide by 16-gage (¹⁄₁₆", remember?) steel came from a junkyard and were cut into ten equal length pieces. A bending jig was made by cutting a slot in one end of a short, large diameter piece of pipe and a scroll was bent up on one end of each piece. Ten 4"-diameter "dishes" were made to fit under the lamp sockets on top of each curlicue. The other ends of each strip were cut to a point having a 72-degree included angle (360 divided by 5) and welded together to make a pair of five-armed brackets.

The chandeliers were assembled with a length of ¼" gas welding rod (what else?) that had a ring formed at the top to which a length of heavy chain, specially made for hanging large lamps, was attached. Just inside the top, the rods pass through plywood discs which keeps them centered. The bottom of the rods extend through the center of the brackets and are each held with a couple of nuts, locked together to prevent loosening.

The metal parts were all painted flat black, and the units were wired and installed. They looked good and drew favorable comment but something about them still bugged me. The ⁷⁄₁₆" nuts on a ¼" rod just looked out of place on those big hubs!

A couple of years later, once again out in the boonies, we explored an abandoned mine and mill that had had its machinery removed and scrapped. One big machine had been fastened to its concrete base with 1⅛" bolts, secured with nuts that were 2" across the flats. Two of the nuts, rusted to the bolts, had apparently resisted disassembly; so the wrecker had just bro-

ken out the cast iron base of the machinery leaving the long bolts, complete with nuts, extending into the air like a pair of industrial age flowers.

We hacksawed them off, just below the nuts. Later, not even attempting to remove the rusted-on nuts, each nut was chucked in the lathe and the bottom side of the bolt was faced off along with a light cut taken on the nut itself. This end was then drilled and tapped for a ¼"–20 thread and counterbored to fit over a ⁷⁄₁₆" nut. The second locking nut was removed from the bottom of each chandelier and after rust removal and painting, one of these salvaged bolt ends was screwed onto the end of each rod and up against the bracket, resulting in a much more realistic appearance.

DRAWER PULLS

Browsing through an antique shop in a little desert town, we found some old glass doorknobs that had turned purple from years of exposure to a brilliant sun bearing down on various front and back doors. Since they would not fit a modern door lock, they were fairly inexpensive.

Although we were not sure what we could do with them, we bought a dozen. Later experimentation showed that their internal threads fit a standard ⅜" bolt although they were originally screwed onto the threaded square shanks that operate old-fashioned mortised-in door locks.

Sun-purpled glass doorknobs have had part of their bases sawn off to make bathroom-cabinet handles.

I cut off the bosses that formerly extended into a standard door so the knobs would fit closer to a surface. Then I drilled ⅜″ holes through the doors of a bathroom vanity and bolted on six of these large doorknobs to make unusual but very attractive cabinet pulls. Four others serve as pulls for the doors on a hall cabinet.

TELETYPE ROLLS FOR SHOP SKETCHES

When several unneeded rolls of teletype paper were about to be discarded by a neighboring dumper at the county disposal area, I rescued them and brought them home. I built a small plywood box with a dowel axle for the roll and with a shop made shear attached, similar to the ones that grocers had for cutting wrapping paper.

I keep the roll at one end of my workbench. A piece of the paper can be ripped off at any convenient length to sketch out a possible solution to a problem, rough design a new project, or simply to record how an electrical item was wired or a mechanical item fitted together before disassembling them. A roll of any similar paper will last a long, long time and is well worth making a holder for.

Wider rolls of paper can be sawed into rolls of a more practical width. While this may leave the paper with a rough edge, it is of little consequence for this purpose.

NONFADING FLOWER

It's nice to have something to brighten up your workshop, especially if you occasionally have lady visitors or if you are perhaps a lady workshopper yourself.

Junk mechanical items carefully chosen and assembled can be made into an attractive, long lasting flower that requires no sun, no watering, no fertilizing, no weeding, and that doesn't fade or drop leaves.

Mine has a vase that was a defective cluster gear from an automobile transmission. It was given a coat of reddish brown primer. The stem is a length of ½″ rebar painted green. A couple of washers are tack welded onto the stem to keep it centered in the hole in the "vase." The

Teletype paper roll is held by two nails that go through holes in box.

Made from brightly painted junk, this workshop flower invariably brings forth a smile.

bright yellow petals of the flower are the cutter from a discarded lawn edger with its teeth curled forward in varying amounts. The flower's center is a 2⅛" diameter, 20-toothed, orange gear; the face of it has been struck a number of times with a rounded off center punch to give it a mottled appearance. The end of the bent stem, extending forward through the center of a larger hole in the gear, is painted a chocolate brown.

The various parts of the flower are welded or brazed together, but it stands free in the center hole in the cluster gear vase. If you don't have a torch available, the parts can be epoxied together; an item such as this is not subjected to any mechanical strains.

Most any workshop with a typical supply of mechanical odds and ends should provide the makings for one or more flowers or other sculptures to "Brighten the soul."

WHIMSY WITH A CARBIDE TIP

If you occasionally suffer from acute attacks of whimsy, an electric engraver and a masonry drill, both carbide-tipped, can assist you indulging this insidious illness.

Combine the tools with the effects of your seizure and proceed to embellish that long-dead Pet Rock or other water-rounded rocks that you find at the seashore or in the bed of a nearby creek.

If a given rock does not want to be drilled or engraved, try another of a slightly different appearance. The hardness of common rocks varies greatly; a masonry drill will zip right through one, but may need to be constantly resharpened to slowly worry its way through another.

The examples shown should provide a starting point to get any genuine whimsy enthusiast off and running.

FIREWOOD HOIST

When planning our house, we knew that transporting firewood from the downhill side of the house up to the living room would be a chore; so we prepared for the later addition of a firewood hoist from the downstairs workshop. One segment of the lower part of a combination TV, stereo, and bookcase wall was provided with two doors and a removable bottom for later use as an upstairs terminal for the hoist. The floor was framed to provide a larger opening just below this part of the cabinet.

At the time, this opening was covered over with Sheetrock along with the rest of the workshop ceiling, and it was not until after retirement several years later that I found the time and the courage to break open the shop ceiling to devise a hoist. Firewood hoists are not unusual, but this one has a different mechanical solution that might solve a similar problem for you.

Since the upper woodbox has doors that open at the front, rather than being top opening, I planned to build a frame into which the firewood would be loaded. This frame would then be lifted up till its top was level with the opening in the cabinet floor. At this point, I wanted the wood to feed upward in the frame as I took out a portion at a time. I also wanted to perform both of these separate movements using one electric motor and only one switch. After much head scratching, sketching, and model experimentation, I came up with a solution.

The wood-carrying frame was welded up from ¾" square steel tubing and provided with four rollers to climb and descend on a pair of 1"

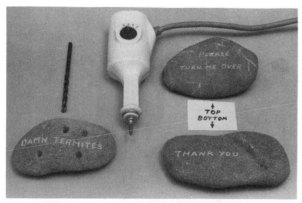

Carbide-tipped tools such as this small masonry bit and electric vibrator should not be allowed in the hands of anyone with a whimsical mind!

Firewood hoist in a corner of the workshop. Two counterweights, filled with lead, are near the top of the photo. The four tines of the "forklift" protrude from the bottom of the frame. Their extra length is needed when they rise in the tapered frame.

Top third of the firewood load shows inside the living room cabinet. After this wood is removed to the fireplace, turning on the switch at the upper right side of the cabinet hoists more of the load into the cabinet. At lower right, the top of the firewood frame shows at floor level. Three vertical bars discourage wood from spilling into the room.

pipe rails which, instead of being vertical, ascend at an angle to provide space for the "boiler room" behind the lowered woodbox. Complete, the frame weighed about 50 lbs. A pair of counterweights were made from steel tubing and filled with melted lead until they weighed about 30 lbs each. Connected to the frame with ⅛" aircraft cable over a pair of pulleys, they overbalance the frame by about 10 lbs and lift it up till halted by a pair of stops with its top at cabinet base level.

Next, a four-tined forklift arrangement was built to ride up and down on the back part of the frame, the tines extending forward. The tines were filled with lead, bringing the weight of the forklift to about 20 lbs. When lowered, it adds to the weight of the frame to overbalance

the counterweights by about 10 lbs. and the frame is held at floor level.

A reversible ⅓ hp electric motor was coupled to a 20-to-1 reduction gear box, which was V-belted to a cable drum at a 2-to-1 reduction. A single cable doubles around a pulley to halve the load and speed of operation, thus adding up to a total 80-to-1 reduction from motor speed. This brings the travel speed down to a practical rate while increasing the torque to a point that easily lifts all the firewood that can be loaded into the machine.

The hoisting cable goes around a pulley on the forklift and has no connection to the frame that surrounds the firewood. When the switch is actuated to the up position, the cable drum starts to reel in the cable, raising the forklift which lifts the firewood. If the frame were to be restrained at this point the forklift would just lift the wood out of the frame and it would spill off the top onto the shop floor. However, as the

FIREWOOD HOIST

1. Frame to hold the firewood rolls up and down on four rollers riding two angled pipe uprights. The frame weighs 50 lbs. It is connected by cables to two 30 lb counterweights. Their 60 lbs overrides the frame by 10 lbs and lifts it to the upper floor where it is stopped at cabinet floor level by two mechanical stops (not shown).

2. Forklift has been added. It has four tines and rides up and down two of the frame's five rear uprights on two pair of rollers. The forklift weighs 20 lbs; its weight added to the frame's 50 overrides the counterweight's 60 lbs by 10 and the complete unit sinks to floor level, lifting the counterweights (not shown). A cable from the forklift goes to a cable drum driven by a reversible motor through a gear reduction and V-belt (not shown). The lifting cable is connected to the forklift only; not to the frame itself.

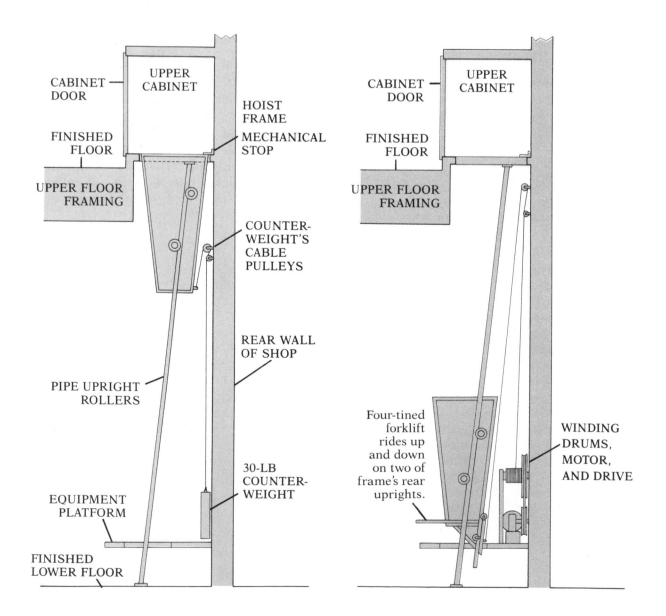

CABINET DOOR

UPPER CABINET

HOIST FRAME

FINISHED FLOOR

MECHANICAL STOP

UPPER FLOOR FRAMING

COUNTER-WEIGHT'S CABLE PULLEYS

REAR WALL OF SHOP

PIPE UPRIGHT ROLLERS

30-LB COUNTER-WEIGHT

EQUIPMENT PLATFORM

FINISHED LOWER FLOOR

CABINET DOOR

UPPER CABINET

FINISHED FLOOR

UPPER FLOOR FRAMING

Four-tined forklift rides up and down on two of frame's rear uprights.

WINDING DRUMS, MOTOR, AND DRIVE

3. When the switch is actuated to "up," the motor winds the cable around the drum to lift the forklift plus the firewood supported by it. This relieves the frame of the weight of the forklift and the firewood, so the counterweights again overbalance the frame and the entire affair rises as a single unit until the frame contacts the stops. With the frame stopped, the forklift rises on the frame and lifts the firewood up out of it into the upper cabinet from where a portion is taken to the fireplace. After it is removed, the switch is actuated again and another segment of the load raised into the cabinet; this sequence being repeated until all the wood has been removed from the forklift, now level with the cabinet floor. The switch is actuated "down," the cable drum reverses, the forklift's weight carries it to the bottom of the frame where it again overbalances the counterweights, and the entire unit descends to the lower level.

End view of the "boiler room" shows the hoisting drum and cable. The drum was turned from a glued-up plywood block.

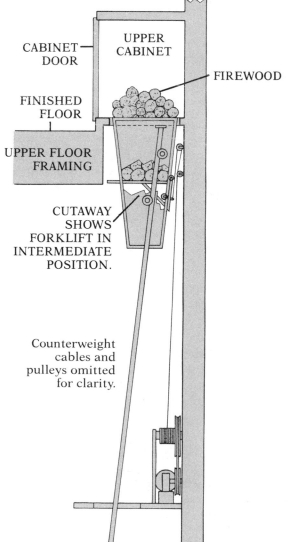

CABINET
DOOR

UPPER
CABINET

FIREWOOD

FINISHED
FLOOR

UPPER FLOOR
FRAMING

CUTAWAY
SHOWS
FORKLIFT IN
INTERMEDIATE
POSITION.

Counterweight
cables and
pulleys omitted
for clarity.

View of the mechanism with its debris-deflecting cover removed. With the frame against its upper stops, the counterweights hang just above the base. Note the "high tech" downside limit switch at right. It is actuated by a flexible rubber finger on the side of the frame.

forklift starts to move, its weight is taken off the frame, the counterweights overbalance the frame, and it moves up with the forklift as a unit, still surrounding the firewood.

When the top of the frame reaches the level of the cabinet's floor opening it is halted by the stops while the forklift continues lifting the wood up out of the frame, bringing it into the cabinet where three short vertical bars keep it from spilling out onto the floor.

When the switch is released, the forklift holds its position, and the firewood is taken out and carried to the hearth. More wood is then hoisted into the cabinet and moved to the hearth; this operation is repeated until the last of the wood is taken off the forklift tines. In practice the wood is usually lifted into the cabinet in three segments and carried to the hearth in about five armloads.

When empty, the down side of the switch is actuated and the forklift descends until it reaches the end of its travel. At that point, its added weight overbalances the counterweights, and the whole thing continues on down. Limit switches at both top and bottom function to stop the unit at the proper points.

A trap door in the floor of the cabinet is kept closed when the hoist is not in use, to avoid unwanted air movement between the levels.

After installation, which took three months of measuring, experimenting, and building, the machine worked well right from the start with no "bugs" and has provided trouble-free service for several years now.

FIRESIDE FIREWOOD HOLDER

The problem of lifting wood to the living room level being solved, I wanted to provide some storage so that the hoist would not need reloading in the middle of an evening. A container on the hearth that would hold a full hoist load could be backed up by a load waiting in the workshop to be brought up when needed. Having filled the fireside container, the hoist could be reloaded the next day to be ready again when needed.

Steel firewood holder holds a hoist load of wood. Another load is normally ready in the basement to replenish the empty holder.

It was decided that a solid bottom wraparound unit would catch most of the dust and dirt brought in with the firewood and make for easier cleanup than if it were scattered over the hearth from an open rack.

After figuring that a scrap that was roughly 2' by 5' would do the job nicely, I went to a nearby salvage yard where I bought a flat piece of 10-gage sheet steel measuring 23" by 63", almost the exact size desired. After it was derusted with a rotary wire brush, the ends were tapered, rounded, and lifting handholds were cut and bent—all done with a torch.

The only difficult part was making the two large radius bends between the bottom and the ends because the steel tended to warp and bulge. With considerable heat and a number of blows from a heavy hammer, the work was eventually shaped into the desired form.

Furnished with four short legs to hold it up off the hearth and painted a flat black, it nicely holds a full hoist load of firewood.

SOME HANDY STEP STOOLS

Reaching high storage areas is a problem, but keeping one or two step stools handy provides a safe, easy way to get at the upper shelves in kitchen cabinets, bedroom closets and a living room bookcase. You can make these step stools in your workshop and even design them to fit your particular need.

We have three shopmade step stools. One, kept in the kitchen, serves the main floor of the house. It was welded up from ½" thin wall steel electrical conduit and has two steps of ¾" plywood topped with nonskid rubber matting. It is 20" high, 13½" wide at the base, and 10½" wide at the top. These dimensions provide adequate height for the jobs at hand and allow it to be garaged underneath a butcher block in the kitchen. The feet, made from 1⅞" diameter

STEP STOOL (1)

Welded up from thin-wall conduit and fitted with plywood steps topped with rubber matting, this step stool poses at its "garage" entrance under the butcher block.

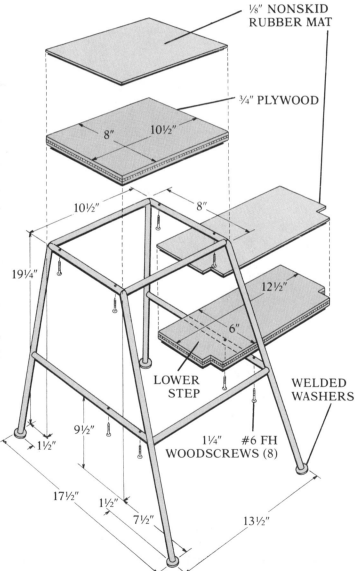

⅛" NONSKID RUBBER MAT

¾" PLYWOOD

8" 10½"

10½" 8"

19¼"

12½"

6"

LOWER STEP

WELDED WASHERS

9½"

1¼" #6 FH WOODSCREWS (8)

1½"

17½" 1½"

7½" 13½"

washers, give it stability on padded carpet in the living room and bedrooms. It is painted a flat black to match its step-top mats.

Another stool, used downstairs, is built entirely of ¾" plywood. Its top step is 15" high and the sides project about 3" above that and act as carrying handles. The sides and steps were all cut out with a band saw but could be made with a jigsaw or sabre saw. The steps are glued and nailed into dados sawed into the sides at a tilt to fit the step's slightly different lengths. Before assembly, the edges of all wood parts except the front and back of the steps were rounded off by a run across the router table using a ¼" radius quarter-round bit. This step-stool also has the nonskid rubber matting and is also painted black.

The third step stool is in my workshop. Since

These step stools were made for the office and workshop from ¾" plywood scraps. The design on the left was developed to allow a band saw to cut the handle holes at the top.

STEP STOOL (2)

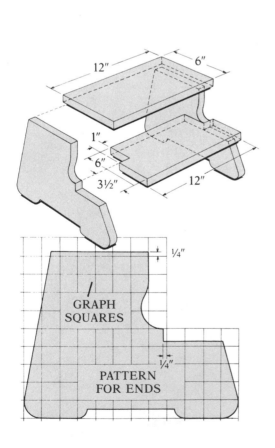

STEP STOOL (3)

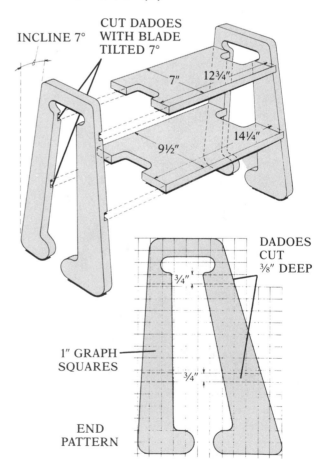

I am the only one who uses it, it does not need to be as high and so is only a bit over 10″ tall (or short!) Like the second stool, it is made from four scraps of ¾″ plywood; two sides and two steps with all edges slightly router rounded. Sprayed a tool gray, it is parked under the storage drawers of the Shopsmith. I often move it around the shop by hooking a toe on it and sliding it into position.

HIDING A CALCULATOR

Some years ago, before they became popular and the price skyrocketed, wife Helen got me a beautiful old oak rolltop desk one Christmas. Sometime later, not being a complete old fuddy-duddy, I acquired a modern electronic calculator with a printed tape readout for record keeping. Since this appeared a bit anachronistic atop an early 1900s desk, I looked for a way to hide it while still keeping it handy. The answer proved to be in an unused area in the right pedestal—a large open space behind a door below the single top drawer.

I cut a length of ¾″ oak into a strip 1″ wide

When the job is done, the plywood shelf slides in, the door is closed, and the modern calculator no longer looks out of place with the old rolltop desk.

and made a ⁷⁄₁₆″ groove ⅜″ deep in it. This was cut into two pieces and each was glued and screwed to the side walls of the opening. Next, I cut a piece of ⅜″ plywood to a width that would slide smoothly in the two grooves, and sawed an oval hole through its front end for a handle. A couple of holes cut partially through it accept the two rear feet on the calculator and hold it in position.

The machine's electric cord exits through a hole in the back of the desk to a nearby receptacle and is provided with sufficient slack that the machine can be pulled forward and out into the open.

To get at it, I just pull the door open and slide the calculator forward. It sits adjacent to my right leg where it is quite convenient for me to reach the keys with my right hand. The job done, it is slid back into the opening, the door closed, and the desk is back in 1906.

TRICYCLE-TOWED CHILD'S CHARIOT

Two children with one tricycle can lead to tears, especially if the second child is not yet big enough to operate the machine but still wants to "get into the act." A lightweight trailer, easily towed by the tricycle, can change the tears to laughter.

I made a trailer from ½″ thin wall electrical conduit by bending several pieces of it into a classic chariot shape and welding them together. The bends were made with a conduit bender. You may be able to borrow one of these; if not, have an electrician make the bends for you. The bender makes all bends to the same radius, usually about 5″.

I found the wheels at a flea market; they were originally the swiveling front wheels from a wheelchair, but you can substitute any sturdy small wheels such as those sold for replacement on a mower. I put the axle at the rear of the chariot so that there would be no tendency for the tongue to lift and disengage the hitch.

A safe but simple hitch was made by drilling a hole in a step on the tricycle and reinforcing it with a welded-on washer. A short downward-

CHARIOT

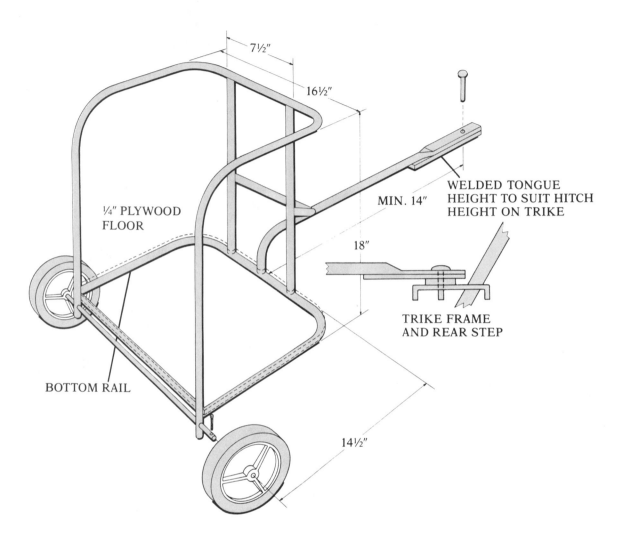

7½"

16½"

WELDED TONGUE
HEIGHT TO SUIT HITCH
HEIGHT ON TRIKE

¼" PLYWOOD
FLOOR

MIN. 14"

18"

TRIKE FRAME
AND REAR STEP

BOTTOM RAIL

14½"

facing rounded-end rod on the front of the chariot tongue drops into this hole to connect the two units. Done this way, there is no protruding hitch on the tricycle to possibly injure the child in case of a fall.

Kate and Michael double up as charioteers while sister Sarah provides the "horsepower." After several years of hard neighborhood play, the chariot needs only a fresh coat of paint to be like new.

LIGHT FIXTURE FROM REDWOOD AND PLASTIC

We had difficulty finding a suitable light fixture for our entry area. While shopping, we saw one with a design that appealed to us, but it was the wrong color and too large. Since it was unavailable in a smaller model, I made some mental notes and later built a similar one to a suitable size.

I bought an 8' length of resawn 1 x 6 redwood (one side rough sawed) and cut its edges at a 30-degree angle, arranged so that the rough side would be on the outside (to give texture). These edges were then run through the saw to make a kerf about ⅜" deep, perpendicular to the beveled edge. The board was then cut into six 15" lengths.

A pattern was made for a modified oval, one

LIGHT FIXTURE

Strip of redwood 1 x 6, a small piece of amber-colored textured plastic sheet, and some lamp parts from the hardware store make a handsome light fixture for the entry hall.

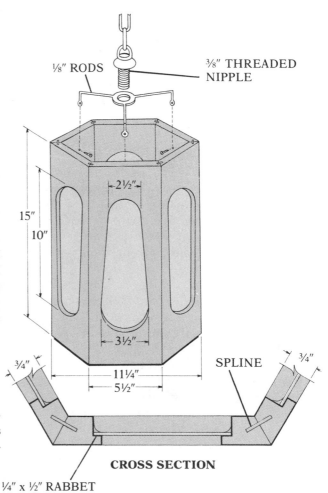

⅛" RODS

⅜" THREADED NIPPLE

2½"

15"

10"

3½"

SPLINE

¾"

¾"

11¼"

5½"

CROSS SECTION

¼" x ½" RABBET

end wider than the other, and this was marked on each piece and cut out with a sabre saw. A rabbet was cut around each hole on the inside to take an amber colored textured plastic window. These were cut to shape from a small panel obtained at a building supply store, and glued in.

The six sides were glued together with a strengthening spline spanning the saw kerfs in the edges. The pieces were arranged so that the design of the windows alternated; one had the wide side up, the next had the wide side down. I bent up eyes in three short pieces of welding rod to accept wood screws through the eyes and into the inner surface of every other side piece, near its top. I bent the rods again at a 90-degree angle and welded them (could be soldered or epoxied) to a large washer. I attached a lamp socket to the washer and connected the lamp to the ceiling mounting flange by a short section of lamp chain.

SHEAR WALL PROVIDES A WINE RACK

Looking for an idea as to how and where to build a wine rack in a cool storage area off the workshop, I happened to note that one end of an open stud foundation wall was backed by ⅜″ plywood to give it shear strength and prevent any endwise racking.

After satisfying myself that a number of relatively well spaced holes would not appreciably diminish its strength, I decided to make this wall into a wine rack. A little measuring determined that the space between the 16″-on-center studs would comfortably hold four standard 750 milliliter bottles or three of the larger champagne or 1.5 liter wine bottles.

A 1½″ hole saw was chosen to provide adequate clearance for the necks and the holes were laid out and bored. To prevent tear out on the back side, I bored the holes all approximately half depth from the front, and then went around to the rear side to complete the holes. Based on the space available, 140 holes were made for standard wine bottles plus an-

One hundred fifty-eight holes in this plywood shear wall, plus appropriately scalloped strips in front, provide cool horizontal storage for wine in the basement storeroom.

Holes were sawn halfway through from each side to avoid splintering; the matching scallops were cut with a sabre saw.

On the other side of the retaining wall, spacer strips keep boxes stored there from accidentally knocking any of the bottles out of their holes.

other 18 1¾″ diameter holes for the larger ones.

Some lengths of pine 1 x 6 were sawed in two at a 45-degree angle to make 1 x 3s with a beveled lower edge.

The top edges were scalloped with a sabre saw to line up with the holes in the plywood. The resulting strips were nailed onto the outer edge of the 2 x 6 studs at such a height that when bottles are inserted in the rack they lie at a slightly top downward angle. This keeps the corks moist to prevent their drying out and also keeps the bottles from vibrating out of the rack in case of minor earthquakes, sonic booms, and suchlike.

TABLE CENTERPIECE

Having some odd ends of 1½″, 2″, and 2½″ black (ungalvanized) pipe at hand, I decided to make something decorative out of them. The largest was cut 12″ long, and two each of the medium and smallest were cut 9″ and 6″ long respectively. I made patterns from a scrap of thin cardboard and cut four long, pointed cutouts in each piece with a cutting torch. I heated the points and bent them slightly inward, giving a sort of gothic cathedral appearance.

Bases were torch cut out of flat steel and interior cups for votive candles were sawed from appropriately sized thin wall tubing. I brazed in bottoms. The cups for the two shortest pieces sit right on the bases, the middle sized ones sit on a short pedestal, and the tallest one has a longer pedestal to bring the candle flames up to the height of the openings.

The cut edges of the gothic points had brazing rod melted onto them and intermittent patches of brass were torched onto the lower part of the pipes. The result is an attractive five-piece candlelit table centerpiece that can be arranged in various spacings, either by itself or with bits of greenery.

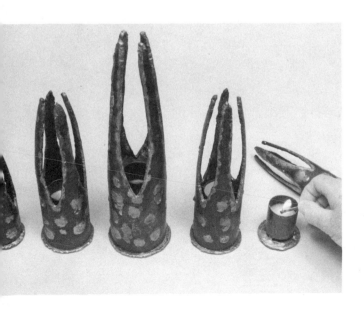

Odds and ends of black pipe and other steel scrap, plus some slopped-on brass brazing rod, make up this five-candlepower table centerpiece.

A PATIO WALL PLANTER

While visiting one of the old Spanish missions in California, my wife and I once purchased a little cast bronze replica of a mission bell. Another time, at a garden shop, I bought a small replica of St. Francis for my wife. These two items gathered dust for some time. I finally combined them with some leftover roof shakes, a scrap of redwood plywood, and a redwood board to make a deck wall planter that provides another example of how a workshop can transform a few odd items into a useful and attractive article. In this case, it not only provides a setting for the garden patron's figure, but evokes romantic memories of the early history of the area during the days of Spanish rule.

Small figure of St. Francis from a garden shop, a miniature bronze bell bought at an old Spanish mission, plus some odds and ends of redwood were combined to make this patio wall planter.

PATIO WALL PLANTER

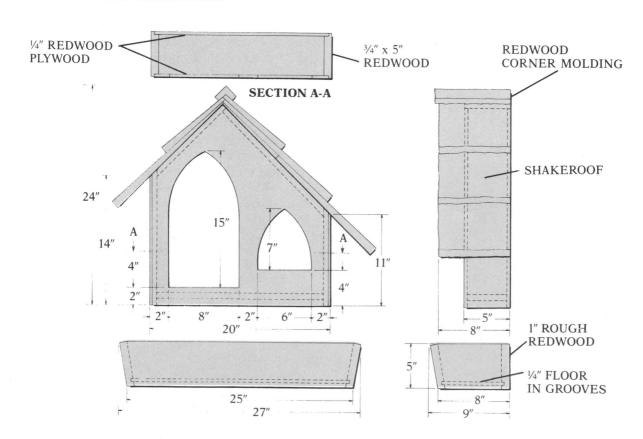

¼" REDWOOD PLYWOOD

¾" x 5" REDWOOD

REDWOOD CORNER MOLDING

SECTION A-A

SHAKEROOF

24"

15"

A

14"

7"

A

4"

11"

2"

4"

2" 8" 2" 6" 2"

20"

5"

8"

1" ROUGH REDWOOD

¼" FLOOR IN GROOVES

25"

5"

27"

8"

9"

MOTORIZED TOWBAR

Moving a small airplane in or out of a crowded hangar by oneself can be a precarious operation. It is difficult to do the work of pushing or pulling the airplane into position while still keeping an eye on the wingtips and tail for clearance to other wings, tails, fuselages, and hangar parts.

You can buy motorized tow bars that connect to the nose wheel and do the work while allowing the operator to watch for various hazards. But like everything else associated with an aircraft, they are expensive. When Bill needed one for his Cessna, he decided to build it himself. The result in my opinion is an excellent example of "Scientific Design."

For power, Bill used a ½" capacity, variable speed, reversing electric drill which is already geared down and provides a lot of torque. To increase this to the required amount and to slow the machine down to a desired safe crawl, he acquired an inexpensive 40 to 1 worm geared hand winch along with a pair of lawn mower wheels.

A welded steel tube frame connects the various parts. The drill motor is fastened at the top, its pistol grip forming half of the handlebar-type handles. A long shaft securely chucked in the drill travels down to a flexible coupling, which in turn is connected to the input shaft of

Towbar is welded up from round and square steel tubing. Spring-engaged cups that secure onto nosewheel tow lugs are released by cables from a hand grip at the top.

On a cold Nevada winter morn, Bill demonstrates his shopmade electric towbar for maneuvering his Cessna in a crowded hangar.

the geared winch. The two wheels are mounted on the ends of the winch's output shaft.

Since the wheels are mounted directly to the shaft and since the gearing is irreversible, a small pair of free-turning wheels are mounted so that the rig can be easily moved about by raising the handle until the drive wheels are free of the surface. A pair of hinged grips engage the tow connections on the nose wheel and are actuated by a cable arrangement extending up to a third handle at the top of the column.

To use the towbar, it is rolled to the airplane, attached to the nose wheel strut, and connected to an electrical outlet. The operator pushes downward on the handles to give traction to the wheels and turns on the drill motor (forward or reverse) at the desired speed. From his position in front of the airplane, the operator can easily maneuver the plane around obsta-

A worm-geared hand winch, fitted with lawnmower wheels secured to its extended shaft, forms the heart of the drive unit. Since the worm drive is irreversible, raising the drive wheels allows the unit to be rolled around on the smaller wheels.

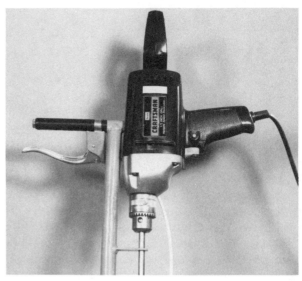

Power is supplied by a ½″, variable-speed, reversible electric drill chucked onto the drive shaft. (A screw in the side of the chuck keeps it tight.) A bolt into the drill's auxiliary handle fitting fastens it to the tow-bar handgrip.

cles as necessary, or he can stop instantly if required.

For some readers, this idea may open up other interesting possibilities. A husky ⅜″ or ½″ reversible drill can provide a simple and inexpensive power unit, with reduction gearing, reversing switch, and associated wiring already built in, for powering all sorts of home and workshop projects. For items that are used only occasionally, the drill can be de-chucked between times and be available for normal jobs.

Some examples: I probably could have built my firewood hoist more easily by using a heavy-duty ½″ drill as the power unit. It certainly would have eliminated a lot of involved wiring as well as some of the reduction gearing. One could make a power hoist for lifting heavy items in the workshop or garage. Someone in a rental unit could build an inexpensive garage-door opener to save the effort involved in lifting a heavy overhead door. A stairside power lift for an invalid or elderly person could be developed and powered this way. A small carousel or other outdoor toys could be powered with a drill. A little thought will surely show how this concept can be used to provide a helpful solution for powering one or more of your future projects.

14
TIPS FOR SHOPSMITH OWNERS

When the Shopsmith Mark V came on the market over thirty years ago as a successor to the earlier Mark II and the original model 10ER, it was the latest and most highly engineered model of the Shopsmith concept—that of combining several power tools in one unit that takes up considerably less space than individual separate tools would. It still has that advantage. The second major feature of the Shopsmith was that by using only one stand and one motor it was much less expensive than purchasing several separate tools. That premise is no longer valid.

After the Mark V came out, the formation of conglomerates became popular in American business and Shopsmith was gobbled up by one of them. Somewhere around this time, the Mark VII was brought out. Bulkier, heavier, and more expensive than the Mark V, it offered little actual advantage, didn't sell well, and was soon dropped. The conglomerate eventually spun off Shopsmith, which passed through several hands and finally went out of production for a number of years until it was picked up by the present ownership.

The new company was highly sales oriented and made relatively few engineering changes in the Mark V until fairly recently. The last few years have seen incorporation of improvements to bring it up to date.

One thing has changed though: the price relative to separate tools. Direct comparison is difficult due to inherent differences in the tools, but I think it is fair to say that today one could purchase a set of individual tools of equivalent quality and of equal or greater capacity, for about the same price.

There are a few drawbacks to the multiple tool concept. Well designed individual power tools are more convenient to operate and usually do a somewhat better job than a machine which has the necessary compromises built into it to permit it to duplicate the work of several different tools. With individual tools, time is saved since the tool does not have to be changed over from one configuration to another. Thanks to its engineering, though, changes on the Shopsmith can be made quite easily.

Due to its table saw blade being mounted on a sliding quill (necessary for the drill press function), rather than on a solid arbor, many serious woodworkers feel that the resulting "slop" in the saw blade, especially after a little wear on the machine, makes it less than satisfactory for accurate work. In an effort to alleviate this, Shopsmith added another bearing to make a two-bearing quill. It is a definite improvement but, due to the necessary sliding quill design, it is only partly effective. Some play is still evident. All units with a serial number greater than 190,000 have the two-bearing quill. A retro-fit kit for earlier models, but only those built since 1972 (serial #1001–190,000), is available.

Also because of the multitool design of the machine, the Shopsmith table saw is of the "tilt table" type, rather than the generally favored "tilting arbor" type, considered to be easier to use.

What all this amounts to is that if you are considering woodworking machinery and intend to do really fine woodworking, you may be wise to consider the alternatives. If, however, you only have minimum space available, or if your woodworking has to share space with metalworking machinery or other tools and interests, the Shopsmith may be your best answer regardless of its price and minor disadvantages.

I have owned a Shopsmith, including both the original model 10ER and the Mark V model, for well over 35 years. If I had to make the choice again, considering the type of work I do and the space available, I'd probably opt for another one.

SOME NEW DEVELOPMENTS

If you have an older Mark V, but are not on Shopsmith's current mailing list, you may not be aware of some of the other changes that have been made in the past few years. Some of these are available to upgrade older models.

One of the most useful improvements, in my opinion, is the new wider extension table; 7½" wide compared to the 4³⁄₁₆" width of the older one. This new table not only allows more leeway for moving the fence without having to move the headstock and table assemblies, but its offset mounting allows greater cutoff capability when it is mounted at the left end of the machine.

If you have a single extension table and have considered getting a second one, the added usefulness of the new larger table could be a deciding factor. If you already have two extensions, you can purchase just the new extension table top itself and use the mounting from your old extension.

Other retro-fit kits include band saw blade guides with better bearings, a quick clamp for the miter gage, and improvements in the jointer, router, and planer.

One of the major complaints about the Shopsmith over the years has been directed at the small size of the saw table itself, although this has been partially made up for by the use of an extension table or tables. In an attempt to rectify this, Shopsmith has made major changes in the table setup; so much so that they have designated the new model as the Mark V model 510 at a $300 increase in price, while continuing the former model as the Mark V model 500. In addition to the larger table on the new model (17½" x 22" instead of 14" x 18¼"), Shopsmith includes four extension tubes and two floating tables, one of which can be supported by telescoping legs.

This contraption is pretty flexible, and when the rip fence is put on an extended floating table, its accuracy of cut is questionable. This was brought out at a recent shopping mall demonstration where, after some sharp comments and questions from the audience, the salesman demonstrator admitted that the floating extension table system provided more style than substance.

The larger table and some of the other features that go with it are a definite improvement however, and the new table system is available as a retro-fit kit for a rather hefty price of around $500.

See the appendix for Shopsmith's address if you have a machine and are not on their current mailing list.

STORAGE UNDER WALL CABINET SAVES SPACE

When not in use, it is normal to roll the Shopsmith against a wall to keep it out of the way. This can be combined with a storage cabinet or a set of shelves on the wall, built with the bottom shelf just high enough so that it clears the machine. With this setup, the Shopsmith can be pushed under the shelves and against the wall. The cabinet or shelf projects forward over the machine so that items in storage are easily accessible at all times.

I store my accessories on the wall under the cabinet and park the machine so that its front, or operator's side, faces the wall. To work with the Shopsmith, I pull it out a distance commensurate with the size of the job at hand and then work between it and the wall. This way the attachments and accessories are right behind me when needed. I don't have to detour around the machine to get to them.

ACCESSORY STORAGE

Instructions that come with the Shopsmith give plans for a rack to hold attachments and accessories. One that they have shown is a piece of ½" plywood, 3' by 4'. You will probably find that you need more space. I use a piece of ¾" plywood, which provides more strength and flexibility for mounting accessories. It is just over 3' by 6½' and I could fill a full 4' by 8' sheet if space were available. Also, ¾" particle board would do as well and at a savings in cost.

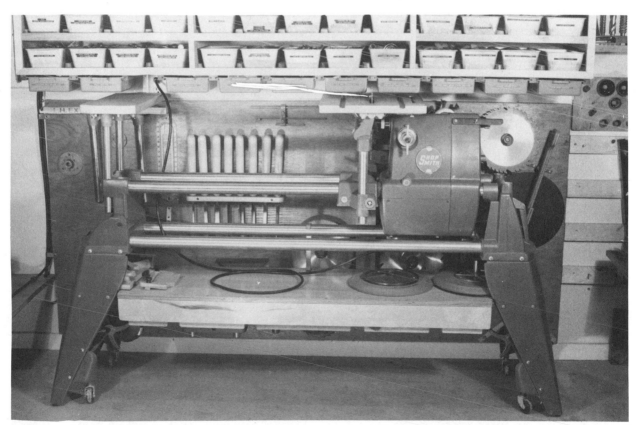

Garaging the Shopsmith under a wall cabinet allows the space above it to be put to use. Pulling it straight out positions the operator between the machine and accessories stored on the wall below the cabinet.

Twenty square feet of ¾" plywood below the cabinet keeps many accessories at hand. The open space at left is not wasted; the saw table hangs there when the lathe function of the tool is used.

STORAGE DRAWERS

The Shopsmith comes with eight prepunched holes, four in each sheet metal bench end about 8" below the level of the lower tubes, to attach a suggested wood shelf.

My shelf is 15½" wide with the ends narrowed to fit inside the bench ends and is made of ¾" plywood. Rather than attempt to fasten it with woodscrews into the end grain of the plywood edge, some ¼" gas welding rod was cut to length (about 14½", but measure first, they vary slightly) and each end threaded ¼"–20. The shelf was then lifted into position from the bottom, the four rods slipped through the holes beneath it, and nuts screwed onto the eight ends. Two clips, one at each end, slip over a rod and are screwed to the underside of the shelf to prevent end movement.

The back of the shelf is kept from sagging

Five drawers hung from the machine store smaller accessories and their associated tools. The wide center drawer holds 12" sanding discs.

SHELF AND STORAGE DRAWERS

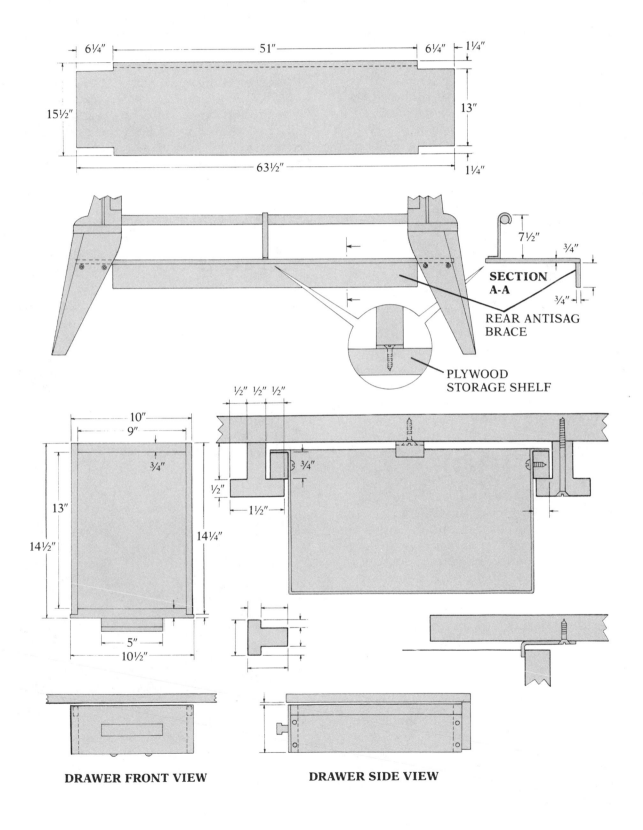

SECTION A-A

REAR ANTISAG BRACE

PLYWOOD STORAGE SHELF

DRAWER FRONT VIEW

DRAWER SIDE VIEW

under load by a 4"-deep strip of ¾" plywood glued and screwed to the shelf. The front is supported by a bracket in the center made from a piece of ⅛" by ¾" strap steel. The top of the bracket is curved and hangs on the lower tube at the front of the machine. The bottom end has a right angle bend and is fastened to the plywood shelf with two wood screws.

Five drawers hang from the plywood shelf. The number and size can be varied to suit whatever you wish to store, but having one of them about 13" wide is useful to store spare 12" sandpaper discs in their envelopes, as well as extra 10" saw blades of various types if you do not keep them mounted on their own arbors.

My four smaller drawers contain various accessories and attachments, both purchased and shop made. If your drawers seem a little empty at first, don't worry. They'll soon fill up and you may wish you had more.

I made the drawers of bent-up galvanized sheet steel, mainly because I had a new little bending brake that I wanted to try out. I gave the drawers plywood fronts and backs. A wood strip alongside each top edge of the drawer hangs from (and slides in) inverted T section wood strips screwed to the bottom of the shelf. The drawers could just as easily be built of wood and hung the same way.

SAW ARBORS

The Mark V comes with an arbor with a 1¼" hole for mounting circular saw blades. This limits you to using only Shopsmith's own series of 1¼" hole blades. For years the only way to get around this, in order to take advantage of the many 10" blades available with a standard ⅝" hole, was to purchase one or more Shopsmith ⅝" universal arbors, now referred to as molder/ dado arbors. These are pretty expensive, especially if you mount one on each of several blades so that you can change them as a unit instead of having to swap blades on the arbor every time.

Shopsmith now sells a ⅝" saw blade arbor for about two-thirds the price of the molder/dado ⅝" arbor; this makes having an arbor for each blade somewhat more practical.

If you do have more ⅝" hole blades than you have arbors, you can make the changing pro-

cess easier, safer, and quicker. Instead of hunting up and fiddling with a pair of adjustable wrenches, get a pair of wrenches that fit the arbor and keep them at the tool. Then change the blades with the arbor mounted on the machine. (Be sure to unplug the power cord any time you change blades, for safety.)

A ⅞" open end wrench plus a ¹⁵/₁₆" box wrench fit my universal arbor. Double-check to see that yours are the same size before you look for a pair of good used wrenches at next weekend's flea market. I cut off the unused end on each of these wrenches so that no time is wasted trying the wrong end on the nut.

SHOP-MADE SANDING DISCS

Many people, myself included, feel that the Shopsmith's 12" sanding disc is one of its best and most often used features. There is one problem though. Since the laws of nature work as they do, once you've got a coarse sandpaper disc mounted, the very next thing that you need to sand requires a fine grit. Mount the fine paper, and it won't be five minutes before you desperately need the coarse!

Trying to remove partly used paper discs so that they can be replaced later is frustrating, if

A ⅝" arbor lets you use saw blades other than Shopsmith's 1¼" models. The base of the wrench was ground to give a better fit on the unusual beveled nut. The molder-dado arbor on the spindle also fits ⅝" blades. Wrenches to fit, kept at the machine, save blade changing time.

Three shopmade 12″ sanding discs along with cans of spray disc-adhesive. The plywood disc at upper right is mounted on the large lathe faceplate. The other two, of particleboard, are fastened to smaller sanding discs.

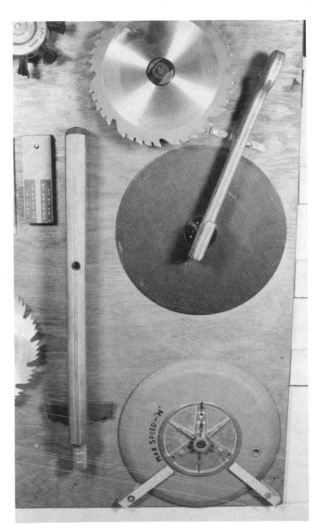

Two spring holders keep discs pressed against the board to deter loosening of sandpaper. The upper holder has a compression spring under the extension. The lower one has two sawn hardwood springs cut so that a curved pad at the outer end of the lugs presses against the disc.

not often impossible. Shopsmith has an answer for this. "An additional disc for each grade of sandpaper minimizes changeover time." True, but at the current price for each additional disc, it gets expensive. Here's an alternative. Get a good piece (no bends, warps, or voids) of ¾″ plywood and cut a circle slightly over 12″ in diameter. Center it on your large faceplate and fasten it with three short #14 roundhead screws. Mark the faceplate and the plywood so that you can always remount it at the same position. Set the machine up as a lathe and turn the plywood disc to an even 12″ diameter. Chamfer the back side of the disc, leaving not over a ¼″ rim.

Check the disc for balance as you increase the speed. The disc should run smoothly to at least "H" (about 1675 rpm) on the speed dial. If it does not, the disc can be balanced by drilling lightening holes part way through it from the back side in an arc near the rim.

Several methods can be used to determine the heavy side. If a long, straight piece of ⅝″ shafting is available, mount the disc on one end and put the shaft on a couple of short pieces of angle iron laid crosswise on a bench. Put one piece at the very front edge. Let the disc hang over the edge of the bench, and it will roll back and forth, stopping with the heavy side down. Mark it, drill a lightening hole in the back, and recheck the balance. Repeat as required.

If a ⅝″ shaft is not available, a ½″ shaft can be used as an axle, mounting the faceplate and disc on it with a plastic ⅝″ to ½″ reducer such as is used to mount a ⅝″ hole grinding wheel on a ½″ shaft. Either this shaft or the ⅝″ shaft must be long enough so that its weight keeps the disc itself from overbalancing it and tipping off the bench.

Another possibility, if only a short shaft is available, is to mount it in a couple of bearings held in a temporary mount. The disc can also be balanced by suspending it. Drill a small hole lengthwise through the exact center of a short piece of ⅝" dowel, slip a close fitting length of cord through it, and tie a knot on the back side. Fasten the dowel in the faceplate and hang the disc from an overhead support. Note and mark the heavy side. Once you find a method of balancing the disc to fit the materials at hand, it is easy to get the balance accurate enough that it will operate as smoothly or better than the stock disc.

Extra sanding discs can be made from ¾" particleboard. In spite of the material's homogeneous appearance, though, discs will often be way out of balance, requiring a surprising number of lightening holes. Once balanced, they work quite well.

I keep four different discs available: the original one, a second on the large faceplate as just described, and the third and fourth on a 6" and an 8" disc, both having a ⅝" shaft hole. These were each drilled for equally spaced screws into the back of the wood disc.

SMALLER SANDING DISCS

If you do a lot of sanding of small items, make yourself a couple of 9" discs to screw on your small faceplate and use 9" sandpaper discs, which are inexpensive and readily available from Sears and other stores.

If you have a nearby industrial tool supply house, it can be an excellent place to find both the 9" and the 12" sandpaper discs, usually in a wide range of grits and in metal cutting (aluminum oxide) as well as wood sanding (garnet) types. In addition to avoiding the long wait for mail order items, you can often get the discs at a considerable saving.

Tool supply houses also sell the 6" x 48" belts used on the belt sander (this is a standard size). Sears and other retailers also sell replacement belts of this size.

The 2" x 2" x 12" crepe rubber sandpaper cleaner mentioned earlier in this book will save you its cost many times over just for cleaning the 12" discs: it is truly "magic." If you have the belt sander or other power sanders, it is doubly useful.

SPRAY DISC ADHESIVE

If the sandpaper discs that you use do not have an adhesive backing, try a spray-type rather than the brush-on kind. It goes on quickly, evenly, and seems to hold better. You should find it at an industrial tool supply house or at an auto parts store that caters to automobile refinishers.

Regardless of the type of adhesive, mount your sanding discs on a wall hung board by a spring holder that presses the face of the discs against the board. That helps to keep the paper from pulling away from the discs while in storage.

MAKESHIFT SURFACE GRINDER

While no substitute for an industrial surface grinder, the 12" disc sander faced with aluminum oxide steel cutting paper can do a fair job of light metal grinding where no great accuracy

Coarse aluminum-oxide sanding disc makes a fair substitute for a surface grinder. Here it smooths a bookend sawn from a railroad rail. Note the sheet-metal guard to keep grit off the way tubes.

is required. I have used it for such jobs as smoothing the ends of short pieces of railroad rail cut off for bookends.

If you do any metal grinding, be sure to protect the tubular ways of the machine from the grit and grindings that would otherwise collect and score the mating surfaces of the headstock and saw table assemblies. This can be done with a sheet of metal, cardboard, or heavy paper. I use a piece of light gage sheet metal 8″ wide and 12″ long with its ends bent to match the radius of the tubes. It just fits over the tubes and has enough of an apron front and back so that falling grit is kept clear of the ways. When I'm done with a grinding job, I just lift it off and dump the debris in the waste bin.

REPAIRING TABLE DISTORTION

If you have done much heavy sanding with the disc sander, you may find that the narrow part of the left side of the table, outboard of the left saw slot, has become bowed down. In addition to affecting the angle of your sanding, this also destroys the accuracy of your sawing, as well as affecting the accuracy of other functions of the machine.

With care, this portion of the table can be bent back to its original flatness. Use a straight piece of angle iron and three C-clamps. Two of the clamps fasten the angle iron to the table parallel to the edge and just above the bent section. Since the metal will spring back slightly, it will have to be bent somewhat beyond the desired position. Allow room for this by using ¼″ spacers between the table and the angle iron at the points of clamping.

Place the third C-clamp over the angle iron and the deepest part of the bend and tighten it to force the bent part back into position. Proceed slowly, stopping to eyeball it from the end and moving the clamp back and forth on the bent section as required to get it back to its original flatness. As it approaches the correct position, check it carefully in both directions with a straightedge.

Once you again have the table quite flat and true, you can brace the thin left edge of the table to prevent, or at least discourage, distortion by making a steel insert for the saw slot. Bolt it inside the slot against the vertical lip of the table.

I use an insert made from ¼″ x ⅞″ steel bar stock. Stock 1″ thick would work as well, perhaps even better. The center section of the in-

Pulling distorted table edge back into position. Spacers between the angle iron and table permit the strip to be pulled just beyond flush so that it springs back flat. The steel brace sits on the table with four bolts that clamp it against the table's vertical lip. A cutaway in the brace allows the table to fit down over the headstock for maximum saw depth. This piece is not made until after the table edge has been pulled flush.

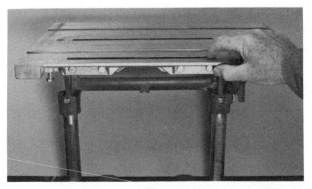

Completed table repair. Four bolts, in line with my thumb, secure the brace against the table lip. Part of the brace shows at center where its cutout is not as wide as the one in the table casting. My forefinger points to the top edge of the insert, almost flush to the table top in the auxiliary saw slot. (On newer models the distortion problem seems to have been solved by eliminating the extra saw slot.)

sert must be relieved so that it fits down over the headstock of the machine in order to get the maximum depth of saw cut. It is this thin section that causes the original weakness in the aluminum table. The steel is tough enough to reenforce the table even though it is also partially cut away.

Once the steel insert is sized and shaped, clamp it into position and drill four small pilot holes, two at each end, through the insert and the vertical lip of the table. Remove the insert and enlarge the holes in the table to ¼". Run a #3 drill through the insert holes for tapping to ¼"–28. If you don't have ¼"–28 bolts handy, use a #7 drill for ¼"–20 bolts. Either way, drill and tap the holes. Measure carefully and cut off the bolts so that they just come flush to the face of the insert but do not protrude. Assemble the unit, tighten the bolts, and you are back in business.

This repair does cut down on the width of the saw slot somewhat, leaving it about ⅜" wide. The only time that this may become a problem is if you tilt the table 45 degrees to cut a bevel using this auxiliary saw slot. This can be alleviated by filing or grinding a 45-degree chamfer along the top inside edge of the insert. You will have to take care to have the table accurately centered over the saw blade prior to lowering it, but this is a small price to pay for having a properly flat and considerably stronger table section.

TABLE SAW INFEED/OUTFEED ROLLER

Infeed/outfeed roller(s) for a normal table saw can be built to an established height since the saw table height is fixed. With the Shopsmith however, the table must be raised and lowered to determine the depth of cut. Thus, any roller used must also be adjustable in height.

A roller combined with the Workmate, described earlier in this book, is ideal here because it provides the necessary height adjustments. Without a Workmate, or if you need a second roller to provide both infeed and outfeed for long stock, you can make adjustable

One infeed/outfeed roller assembly is fitted to its sawhorse while another is folded up for storage. Slots permit positioning the roller to match the movable saw-table height even on an unlevel surface. Balls allow movement parallel to the saw even if the unit is not exactly parallel to the machine.

height rollers with a pair of sawhorses for the supports. Cut slots in the risers to provide the height adjustment and secure the setting by ¼" bolts with wing nuts over large "fender" washers. When not in use the rollers fold flat to hang on the wall and the bolts, washers, and wing nuts are left in the sides of the sawhorses.

This particular pair have movable-ball furniture casters for support of the stock, but straight rollers can be used instead. Rollers can be made from various items. Wood closet pole stock 1⅜" in diameter with carefully centered large wood screws for axles will make a satisfactory roller. A better one can be made of 1½" PVC pipe, thin wall electrical conduit, or galvanized pipe. If you use the latter, pick a good smooth section and/or file or grind down any irregularities in the galvanizing. Bearings can be made of hardwood, turned on the lathe to a press fit in the pipe and center drilled for a suitable axle, or can be a pair of ball bearings from your spare parts bin.

MITER SLOT ADAPTER FOR ROUND STOCK

Cutting round stock such as dowels, closet pole stock, or plastic pipe on either the table saw or band saw can be dangerous. If not securely held, the material has a tendency to rotate; the saw's teeth can grab and damage the stock or even throw it violently from the table.

The shop-made accessory shown is a big help for cutting round material. The traveling V-block makes it easy to hold the stock securely while traversing it across the saw blade, instead of having to hold it against its tendency to roll on the table while being pushed by the miter gage.

Only two parts are required for the sliding V-block. One is a piece of angle iron about 6¼" long. This allows it to be used with both the table saw and the band saw. Without the band saw, you can make it somewhat longer if you wish. I used 1" angle, but a somewhat wider angle would perhaps be even better for cutting larger diameter round stock.

The second piece provides a minor problem. Instead of having the generally standard ⅜" by

¾" miter gage grooves, Shopsmith uses a slightly smaller one, an apparent ploy to get you to buy their miter gage accessories such as a tenoning jig. A ⁵⁄₁₆" or ¼" by ¾" piece of bar stock can be made to fit by carefully filing one side of it until it is a nice sliding fit in the grooves. Mine is 6" long. A much shorter slide could allow some angular movement in the groove; longer would require more filing. This piece is then welded to the V-block so that the two pieces are exactly at right angles to one another.

Tack weld one side of the V-block to the slider first and then check it for square to the slider and/or the miter gage slot, adjusting as necessary. When you are quite satisfied as to its accuracy, weld the other side. Then finish welding the tacked side. Allowing the V-block to extend about 3" on one side of the slider and 2½" on the other side will permit it to be used on both the table and band saws. (If you have the new model 510 machine with the larger saw table, the 3" dimension may need changing.)

Since my slider was a scant ¼" in thickness, it tended to rock slightly in the miter groove. This was eliminated by bending both ends down very slightly until they bottom in the groove—without lifting the angle iron V-block from the table.

The holes in the slider serve no purpose other than to hang it up; they just happened to be in the scrap of bar stock I used.

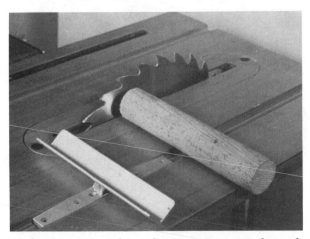

Angle-iron miter-slot adapter saws round stock more safely than with a miter gage alone because the stock has a tendency to roll it as it moves across the table. With the adapter, the stock is held firmly in the angle iron's V while the unit is slid forward to traverse the saw.

TIGHTENING THE MITER GAGE SETTING

The knob that secures the adjustment of the miter gage has a coined edge to provide a better grip, but since it is only 1" in diameter, it is still difficult to tighten it sufficiently by hand to hold the setting. There are few things more discouraging than cutting some miters and finding that the setting has slipped and the angles are in error.

If you have ever had this problem, take a close look at the adjustment knob. It has two small holes through it at right angles and, lo and behold, the long Shopsmith ⁵⁄₃₂" Allen

Cross-drilled holes, provided in the miter gage knob, permit tightening with an Allen wrench.

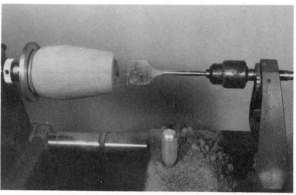

First step in hollowing this deep vase was to bore a 1½″ hole by advancing it against a bit held in the tailstock chuck. Note that the plywood spacer permitted cutting to the bottom of the work without digging into the faceplate.

wrench, used for so many adjustments on the machine, just fits. Use it as a lever to cinch the knob down more than finger tight. This *is* mentioned in the manual, but it is somewhat buried and you may have missed it. I certainly did!

PLYWOOD SPACER

When turning small diameter work on a faceplate, it is sometimes difficult to finish off the base of the item without digging into the faceplate with the tool. This can be avoided by cutting out a small circle from ¼″ (or thicker) plywood and mounting it between the faceplate and the work to provide a buffer between them.

Deep tool rest made from an old ¾″ bolt is positioned to enter the work. Its welded-on end just clears the 1½″ hole.

DEEP TOOL REST

If you make any deep small boxes or bowls using the lathe function of the tool, you will find it worthwhile to make or have made a special deep tool rest for this work. This can be made from a ¾″ diameter round steel bar bent (with heat) to shape; weld a short crossbar on it for the tool rest. Mine was made from a long ¾″

bolt with its head cut off; it still has threads on one end. Before bending the shaft, turn or file a shallow groove in the shank at the position of the setscrew so that any ridges formed by the end of the tightened screw will not prevent removal of the tool rest from its socket.

With the rest deep inside the work, a side and end-cutting tool made from an old file easily hollows out the inside contour of the vase.

Shopmade screwdriver-handled hex wrench is inserted in the tool rest setscrew. A similar factory-made tool lies on the saddle next to a hole that keeps it handy during lathe work.

Redwood vase and some accessories used to make it: a plywood faceplate shim, the deep rest, a spade bit with a short spur, a threaded chuck with its #2 Morse taper adapter and a ball-bearing tailstock center which takes the same adapter. The handle helps hold the work while it is stained and varnished. The work is reinstalled on the machine for sanding between coats.

HANDY HANDLED HEX HELPS

If you do much lathe work, you know that you continually have to change the position of the tool rest, and that the standard L-shaped hex wrench for this is somewhat unwieldy.

Instead, get a $5/32''$ straight hex wrench with a plastic screwdriver-type handle, available at a larger hardware or tool supply store. Or you can make one. Mine has a turned and knurled aluminum handle with a drilled hole of a size between the minor and major diameters of the wrench, into which the straight section of a wrench, with its "L" cut off, was pressed. Either way, you will find the modified tool much more convenient for lathe work. Once you have one, a ¼" hole drilled in the center of the tool rest saddle (table carriage) is a handy place to keep it during your lathe operation.

Shopsmith also sells T-handled hex wrenches. While not quite as easily maneuvered as the screwdriver-handled ones, they do provide more torque for such jobs as securing arbors on the spindle. These are also available locally if you don't want to make up the minimum $20 order to get one.

KEEPING FACEPLATE SCREWS

For faceplate work, get a small tin or plastic box for storing #14 roundhead screws in sets of three each of various lengths. I have a small candy tin about 3" x 4" x 1" deep with a hinged lid. It is a dandy.

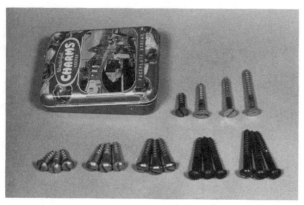

Assortment of various lengths of #14 roundhead screws, some flathead screws, and a small can or box to hold them, keeps things organized.

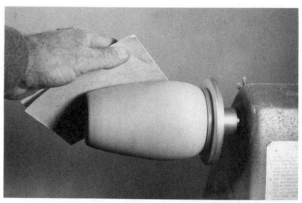

Rotation is reversed if the work is mounted on the outboard end of the headstock. Sanding in reverse provides a smoother finish during final sanding.

As for the #14 screws, they are quite large and may be hard to find. They are well worth having though. Smaller ones do not completely fill the holes in the faceplate and can allow the work to slip slightly, causing difficulty and sometimes spoiling the project. If you also have a screw center, be sure to get a few #14 flathead screws in several lengths for use with it.

REVERSE SANDING

Don't forget that a final touch of fine sandpaper on a turning being rotated in the opposite direction will result in a smoother finish. This can be done on faceplate turnings by transferring the faceplate to the outboard end of the headstock. With a spindle turning, just turn it end for end and remount it between the centers.

OTHER TAILSTOCK CENTERS

In addition to the standard tailstock "dead" center, there are a couple of others that are useful. One is a "live" center in which the center itself is attached to a ball bearing and ro-

tates with the work. This eliminates any requirement for lubricating the junction of the work and the center and avoids the tendency of the work to overheat or burn. Shopsmith sells these centers, but you can often find one locally for appreciably less. All you need to know is that it has a #2 Morse taper. If you happen to have a small metal lathe that has a live center with a #1 Morse taper, an inexpensive #1 to #2 Morse taper sleeve allows it to be used with either machine.

Shopsmith also sells a tailstock chuck arbor, an adapter with a #2 Morse taper on one end and a short ⅝" shaft, flatted for the setscrew, on the other. This allows you to mount your drill chuck on the tailstock. You can then mount any type of drill bit on the tailstock and drill or bore holes of various sizes in the center of either spindle or faceplate work.

The tailstock chuck can be coupled with another drill chuck mounted on the spindle. You can buy another ⅝" mount chuck (rather expensive) from Shopsmith for this purpose. Or, if you have another ½" drill chuck available, you can make (with access to a metal lathe) an adapter to fit it to the spindle.

Using the two chucks (one on the headstock spindle and the other on the tailstock) allows you to concentrically drill the end of dowels, small shafts, model ship cannons, and things of that sort much more accurately by rotating the work onto a fixed drill held in the tailstock chuck.

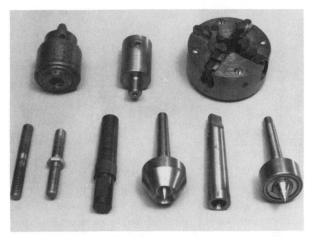

More adapters. The upper shopmade one (center top) allows either the threaded drill chuck or the four-jaw chuck to be secured to the unthreaded ⅝" spindle. Bottom row, left shows two arbors for turning gearshift knobs. With threads to match different shift levers, one end is screwed onto threads tapped into the block, and the other end put in a drill chuck mounted on the spindle. Next is Shopsmith's adapter for mounting their unthreaded drill chuck in the #2 Morse tailstock. Finally, two ball-bearing live centers, one for wood and one for metal and both having a #1 taper to fit a metal lathe. Also shown here is a #1 to #2 sleeve that allows the centers to be used on the Shopsmith.

Four-jaw chuck, mounted on its adapter and having independently adjusted jaws, holds work off center for eccentric drilling. The center drill provided an accurate start.

SMALL THREE- OR FOUR-JAW CHUCKS

If you are fortunate enough to have a small three- or four-jaw chuck, either as an accessory to a metal lathe, acquired at a flea market, or bought new for the purpose, you will find it helpful to make an adapter to mount it on your Shopsmith spindle. With it, you can mount all sorts of wood, metal, or plastic pieces for turning or drilling, without having to provide holes for a center or for faceplate screws.

The little 3" four-jaw chuck that I have fortunately has a ½"–20 thread; the same as many ½" drill chucks. Thus, I can mount it on the headstock with my shop-made adapter and use the Shopsmith drill chuck on the tailstock chuck arbor when this combination of chucks is

called for. If I need the two drill chucks, I mount a spare ½" drill chuck on the same adapter and again use the Shopsmith drill chuck on the tailstock.

When needed, I can mount the four-jaw chuck to the tailstock by using the adapter and the tailstock chuck arbor and at the same time have the Shopsmith drill chuck mounted on the headstock. A #3 Morse to ½"–20 adapter allows the chuck to fit the headstock of my metal lathe when a smaller chuck than the 6" four-jaw is called for.

One or two judiciously chosen adapters, whether purchased or shop made, can provide you with much more flexibility than you already have.

DRILL PRESS TABLE BRACE

Many of you who do metal work as well as woodwork have bought the Shopsmith planning to use its drill press function for both materials. If you've done any heavy work however, you have probably found that there are drawbacks. For one, the small thin tubes supporting the table just don't compare with the heavy metal casting on a regular drill press. Shopsmith does an okay job in the table saw mode, where the tubes are loaded in compression, but when used as a drill press they are subjected to bending which can result in out of line holes or even broken drill bits. Bending can also cause difficulty with heavy wood boring, such as when drilling square holes with a mortising bit.

One answer to this problem is to make a brace from a 9″ x 13″ piece of ½″ plywood. Place it an an angle between the table and the extension table tubes. The ends of this brace are chamfered on both sides so that at one end they will bear nicely against the joint between the tubes and their base, and at the other, against a strengthening rib cast into the table. A cutout in one end of the brace lets you tighten or loosen the extension table handgrip lock. The brace works with the table in either the 90-degree drill press position or in the horizontal position.

Horizontal drilling is a handy extra capability for Shopsmith owners. By positioning the table horizontal and at the proper height (as shown in the accompanying photo), the table provides a guide for drilling a hole or holes any required distance from the edge of the stock. Note that the rip fence holds the stock against the thrust of the drill in this

Rather than going to the trouble of upending the machine, you can do most drill press work in the horizontal position. Here the work is held in a drill press vise laid on its side and clamped to the saw fence. The table brace lies at a flatter angle with the table horizontal.

mode. (Be sure to put a piece of scrap stock between the work and the rip fence.)

This brace works most effectively when the machine itself is in the horizontal position. In the vertical position, this brace effectively eliminates adjustment of drill press table height. Thus, the headstock must be moved and this is best done before raising the machine to the upright position.

Attempting to change the height of the headstock with the machine vertical is awkward and could be unsafe, although a method of doing it is shown in the literature that comes with the machine. However, once you get accustomed to drilling in the horizontal position (Shopsmith calls this a horizontal boring machine) you will probably find it is every bit as good as drilling in the vertical position, without the bother of raising and lowering it.

SECURING DRILL PRESS VISE

Another problem with using the Shopsmith as a drill press for metal work is that the table is basically a saw table and as such is not provided with slots for fastening a drill press vise.

One "Joe McGee" solution for this is to fasten

Plywood table brace holds the table rigidly against drilling pressure. It works with the table either vertical or horizontal.

With the table vertical, a drill press vise can be bolted to a plywood strip that is then clamped to the table. An angle brace adds rigidity.

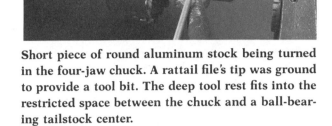

Short piece of round aluminum stock being turned in the four-jaw chuck. A rattail file's tip was ground to provide a tool bit. The deep tool rest fits into the restricted space between the chuck and a ball-bearing tailstock center.

the vise to a suitably sized piece of ½" to ¾" plywood. Depending on whether you use bolts or large flathead machine screws, the underside of the plywood is counterbored or countersunk to clear their heads.

Once the combined vise and base is placed so that the work is in the proper location relative to the drill, the plywood base can be secured to the table by a couple of C-clamps.

METAL TURNING

Metal turning can be done in a limited way on the Shopsmith by methods described in Chapter 7. There are some advantages to the Shopsmith over a drill press for this work. The job is done in the normal horizontal position and one does not get a kink in the neck from continually twisting the head sideways trying to get a "normal" view of the operation. The tailstock and tool rest are already available; no need to jury-rig them as on a drill press.

Files with their tips ground to the proper shape will work fairly well as chisels, particularly on softer metal such as aluminum or brass. If you attempt much work on mild steel, get some high speed steel lathe tool bits or carbide-tipped bits and provide a long handle for them.

Metal turning without a metal lathe is slow going, but with patience and perseverance you can get some surprisingly good results.

After rough turning of the taper, the stock was drilled using a tailstock chuck and then hand tapped. Removed from the chuck, it was reversed, threaded onto the mandrel, secured with a locknut, and chucked in the drill chuck for turning of the top and grooves. Finishing was done with emery paper.

Accurate drilling of round stock can be done by turning the work onto a fixed drill held in a second chuck mounted on the tailstock. Started with a center drill and continued with a ³⁄₁₆" drill, this hole in a ¼" rod leaves a wall that does not vary more than .002 in thickness, quite reasonable for a makeshift job.

SHOPMADE INDEXING ATTACHMENT

An indexing attachment for the lathe function of the Shopsmith is just as useful as the one described earlier for a metal lathe. It divides a circle into a desired number of divisions and locks the spindle, and thus the work, at each of these positions while a hole is drilled from a fixed position. The attachment is then moved, or indexed, to the next position and another hole is drilled into the work at a precise angular relation to the first one; the process continues until the circle has been completed. The most common use for indexing is to drill equally spaced radial spoke holes in the hubs and rims of wooden wheels.

The upper outboard spindle, being directly connected to the main spindle, provides an excellent means of attaching an indexing device to the Shopsmith. One improvised method is to fasten a wooden circle to the outer spindle and provide it with drilled holes for inserting a locking pin. The problem with this is the difficulty of getting a high degree of accuracy when laying out the holes on this master circle. Trying to divide it accurately with a protractor is quite difficult.

A gear, fastened to the outer end of the spindle via a shopmade adapter, becomes an indexing attachment when provided with a dog to engage its teeth. Almost any gear works here; the number of available divisions depends on the number of its teeth.

A better solution is to use the precisely cut teeth of a metal gear. The gear is secured to the spindle and provided with a fixed dog to engage between any two teeth and thus lock the spindle in as many different positions as the gear has teeth. The necessary gear, or gears, may be found in many places. If, like many of us, you keep a collection of all sorts of mechanical parts, you may have some odd gears in one of your "junk" drawers or boxes. If not, junkyards, flea markets, auto wreckers, yard sales, and garage sales are likely sources.

In looking for gears, consider what divisions you are likely to need. A 12-tooth gear will divide a circle into 2, 3, 4, 6, or 12 parts, but not 8, a desirable one. A 24-tooth gear will divide into 2, 3, 4, 6, 8, 12, or 24 parts. Gears with a larger number of teeth provide even more divisions. Having a threading gear set for my metal lathe, I use one of them, secured with a shop-made adapter.

If you find a gear with a ⅝″ center hole and a setscrew to fasten it directly to your outboard spindle, you're all set. A gear with a ½″ hole might be drilled out to ⅝″ if its boss will still be thick enough to hold a setscrew. Other gears with smaller or larger holes can be fitted to the spindle with an adapter turned from a bit of steel bar stock. If you don't have a metal lathe, you can get one made at a small machine shop.

If it is impractical for you to have a metal adapter turned, you might even make a hardwood adapter on the Shopsmith. Leave a very thick wall on the adapter and tap it for an extra long setscrew, which should hold adequately. The gear can be fastened to the adapter with a pin or machine screw through it, or even with a large wood screw.

If you use the outboard spindle to drive accessory tools such as the band saw, you can size the adapter to fasten onto the 1⅛″ coupling adapter that you already have on this spindle.

One way or another, you should be able to fasten most any gear securely to the outboard spindle. The adapter must provide a solid attachment of the gear to the spindle with no "slop," and the gear must be concentric with the spindle. Since the size and shape of the adapter vary according to the thickness and center hole diameter of the gear, no dimensions can be given here.

Once you have the gear and a means of securing it to the spindle, you need a dog that can be engaged between its teeth to hold it in the various positions. How you make this depends on the diameter of your gear(s). I have a 7″ piece of 1″ angle iron with one leg mostly sawed and ground away, leaving a lug which is filed to just fit snugly between a pair of gear teeth. This dog is secured to the sheet metal headstock housing with two machine screws and some spacers. The nut on one screw is left somewhat loose and the other one is provided with a wing nut. Together they allow the dog to be quickly adjusted to fit gears of slightly different diameters.

Caution! Before drilling through the sheet metal housing, remove it and check your proposed location to be sure that there is clearance for the screw heads. Some parts of the housing are a very close fit to the headstock inside.

RADIAL DRILLING ATTACHMENT

Once you have an indexing attachment for your Shopsmith, you need a means of using it. This requires a way of mounting a drill so that it can be positioned relative to the work and then moved inward to actually drill the hole. With a metal lathe, this can be done by an attachment to the carriage, allowing radial drilling or milling by advancing the cross feed and longitudinal work by carriage movement. Since the Shopsmith has neither a cross feed or a movable carriage, other means must be found.

A suitably sized hardwood guide block works quite well, and to reasonable accuracy for most woodworking operations. Drill a hole (with the drill for the job at hand) through the guide block; use the horizontal boring function of the machine so that the hole will be square to the block.

If you will be using a spade bit to bore large holes in your work, drill the guide block's pilot hole to fit the shank of the bit, rather than its full diameter. This will then require inserting the shank through the guide block before securing it into the chuck.

With your workpiece mounted on the ma-

Fairly accurate indexed drilling can be done with a simple guide block clamped to the table. It works when drilling radially, longitudinally, or even at an angle. Here twelve equally spaced holes are being drilled at a 45-degree angle. Make the guide block as wide as practical to avoid drill wobble and drill its pilot hole parallel to the table by using the machine's horizontal boring function.

chine via a faceplate or between centers, clamp the guide block to the saw table. Locate the block and adjust the table height to a position where the pilot hole is lined up to drill the desired holes radially, longitudinally, or even at an angle, as desired. Install the drill bit into your electric hand drill and proceed to drill your holes. The guide block fixes the position of the drill, and the indexing determines the distance between holes.

The guide block itself works as a depth stop if it is clamped in such a position that the chuck jaws touch it when the required depth has been reached.

If you have a metal lathe and have a radial/longitudinal attachment for it, or made one as described in the metal lathe chapter (A Flexible

Drilling/milling attachment from the metal lathe has been borrowed and fastened to a plywood base provided with a strip to slide in the Shopsmith's miter groove.

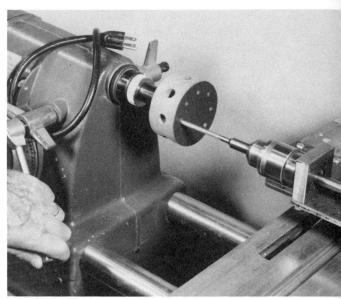

Eight radial holes have been bored by using a 56-tooth gear on the spindle. With the drill jig turned 90 degrees and clamped to the table, longitudinal holes are drilled by advancing the work onto the bit.

Shaft Milling Attachment), you can adapt it to the Shopsmith to provide somewhat greater accuracy than the pilot block method.

My adapter was made by gluing two pieces of ¾″ plywood together to make a 1½″ block. A hardwood strip was cut to a close sliding fit in the saw table's miter gage grooves and then glued and screwed to the bottom of the block. Wide shallow rabbets were cut in this adapter block to align the milling/drilling attachment in either the radial or longitudinal drilling position. Large wood screws were provided to quickly attach it to the block in either of these positions.

To provide stability, several large spade bit holes were bored nearly through the block and poured full of lead. These serve to balance the offset weight of the attachment and allow the entire unit to move smoothly and without vibration in the miter gage groove.

For radial drilling on the Shopsmith, the attachment is fastened to the block in the proper position and is powered by either an electric hand drill or a flexible shaft. The work, which can either be mounted on a faceplate or between centers, is held fixed by the indexing attachment and the drill advanced into the work

by sliding the attachment in the miter gage groove. A depth stop can be clamped to the table as needed.

For horizontal drilling, such as a series of drilled holes around the face of a wooden circle (rather than radially into the edge of it), the attachment is fastened at 90 degrees to its previous position on the plywood block. The block is then located at the proper distance and secured to the table with one or more C-clamps. In this case the miter gage slide does not move but serves only to locate the jig at a 90-degree angle to the work.

The attachment does not slide in this mode. Instead, you use the movable quill to feed the work to the fixed rotating drill. This works even though the spindle is prevented from turning by the indexing attachment. This setup is only for faceplate or screw-center mounted work; work held between centers cannot be moved this way because the tailstock center is fixed.

The quill's depth control can make holes of a uniform depth. If through holes are to be made, a backup block can be clamped behind the work. Move the block periodically as the work is indexed around the circle.

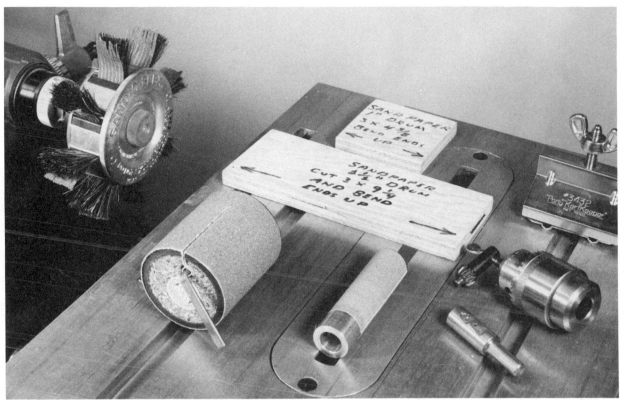

Some dandy gadgets from other makers fit the Shopsmith. The sander mounted on the spindle is great for irregular shapes. The sanding drums on the table use inexpensive shop-cut sandpaper sized by plywood jigs. A key turns a wedge to lock the paper to the drum. For freehand work, all these sanders fit a ⅜″ drill chuck by means of the shopmade adapter. The same adapter allows the Shopsmith chuck to be held in a ⅜″ drill to hold accessories with a ½″ shank. A KerfKeeper is helpful with the small saw table.

OTHER ACCESSORIES

In addition to the many accessories sold by Shopsmith, there are a number of others that are manufactured to fit the machine. Flexible sanders containing several rows of sandpaper strips that extend from a drum similar to spokes on a wheel are great for sanding odd-shaped items, especially when using the sanders that have the sandpaper ribbons slit into several narrow strips. At least one of these is made in a model to fasten directly to the Shopsmith spindle.

If you have a Shopsmith drum sander you know that while it works great, the sleeves are expensive to replace, as well as requiring mail order purchasing with the resulting $20 minimum. They are not a common size and are seldom available locally.

At least one manufacturer makes several sizes of sanding drums that use sandpaper cut from standard size sheets and cleverly attached to the drum. They provide models made to mount directly to the Shopsmith spindle.

KerfKeepers, mentioned earlier, help a lot when ripping long stock on the small Shopsmith saw table.

See the appendix for information on these items. It will also be well worth your time to occasionally check the ads in some of the woodworking magazines for other innovative tools that either fit or can be adapted to the Shopsmith.

INDEX